GENDER IN HIS

Series editors:
Pam Sharpe, Patricia Skinner and Penny Summerfield

The expansion of research into the history of women and gender since the 1970s has changed the face of history. Using the insights of feminist theory and of historians of women, gender historians have explored the configuration in the past of gender identities and relations between the sexes. They have also investigated the history of sexuality and family relations, and analysed ideas and ideals of masculinity and femininity. Yet gender history has not abandoned the original, inspirational project of women's history: to recover and reveal the lived experience of women in the past and the present.

The series Gender in History provides a forum for these developments. Its historical coverage extends from the medieval to the modern periods, and its geographical scope encompasses not only Europe and North America but all corners of the globe. The series aims to investigate the social and cultural constructions of gender in historical sources, as well as the gendering of historical discourse itself. It embraces both detailed case studies of specific regions or periods, and broader treatments of major themes. Gender in History titles are designed to meet the needs of both scholars and students working in this dynamic area of historical research.

The business of everyday life

MANCHESTER
1824

THE BUSINESS OF EVERYDAY LIFE

GENDER, PRACTICE AND SOCIAL POLITICS IN ENGLAND, *c*. 1600–1900

⊰ Beverly Lemire ⊱

Manchester University Press
Manchester and New York

distributed exclusively in the USA by Palgrave

Published by Manchester University Press
Oxford Road, Manchester M13 9NR, UK
and Room 400, 175 Fifth Avenue, New York, NY 10010, USA
www.manchesteruniversitypress.co.uk

Distributed in the United States exclusively by
Palgrave Macmillan, 175 Fifth Avenue,
New York, NY 10010, USA

Distributed in Canada exclusively by
UBC Press, University of British Columbia, 2029 West Mall,
Vancouver, BC, Canada V6T 1Z2

British Library Cataloguing-in-Publication Data is available

Library of Congress Cataloging-in-Publication Data is available

ISBN 978 0 7190 7223 9 paperback

First published by Manchester University Press in hardback 2005

This paperback edition first published 2012

Printed by Lightning Source

To Clif Beck (1922–2004)
father, adviser and friend

Contents

List of tables

List of illustrations

Figures

Every effort has been made to obtain permission to reproduce the illustrations in this book. If any proper acknowledgement has not been made, copyright-holders are invited to contact the publisher.

Acknowledgements

Years ago, as my family and I were preparing to leave for England, where I would do my doctorate, my sister asked me to write to her about the ordinary differences between life in Canada and life in 1980s England. How was milk distributed? Where were newspapers sold? How were the streets cleaned? Who walked in the park and when? The common threads of life, once viewed in their totality, reflect underlying social structures, patterns that change with time and place. My perceptions of the world, past and present, have been enriched by the observations and analyses my family shared with me: Catherine Beck, Martin CôtéBeck, Céline CôtéBeck, Clif Beck, Betty Beck, Morris Lemire, Shannon Lemire, Maurice Johnson and Matilda Johnson. I am also immensely indebted to the contributions of my colleagues in the Department of History, University of New Brunswick. The years I spent in their company were personally and professionally enriching. Gillian Thompson, Gail Campbell and Steve Turner read my work in its many drafts, offering cogent comments, suggestions and encouragement as needed over many years. They have seen this project evolve from its initial interdisciplinary exchange with those in the development field to this more historical study. Gail's particular generosity in tutoring a pretended quantifier must also be acknowledged with gratitude. Lianne McTavish brought an acuity of perception to all our exchanges which I valued immeasurably. The department ethos was always more than the sum of its parts, and my warmest thanks are extend to all the members of this department.

This project has been supported by a number of institutions. I am immeasurably grateful for the commitment shown by various levels of the University of New Brunswick, providing funding for the Women and Credit project, providing me with time as a University Research Professor. My thanks are offered in particular to President Elizabeth Parr Johnston and President John McLaughlin, Dean Peter Kent and Dean John Rowcroft and to Gillian Thompson, who, as Chair of the Department of History at a critical juncture, offered unstinted support and advice. The Social Sciences and Humanities Research Council of Canada provided research grants that were of immense assistance. In addition, receiving a Killam Research Fellowship from the Canada Council for the Arts allowed me two years for research, time that was of inestimable value. I also thank the Research School for Social Sciences, Australian National University, for the three-month fellowship in the History Programme that I held in 2001. The Textile Department at the Royal Ontario Museum provides continuing assistance with my research, for which I am most grateful. The librarians at the Bodleian Library, Oxford – and in particular Julie Ann Lambert – as well as librarians at the British Library and various archives throughout Britain have been unstintingly helpful. I also thank Alice Taylor, Heidi Coombs and Mike Reid for their assistance.

Rosemary Ommer kindly read the whole of this manuscript, a task for which I offer thanks: her interdisciplinary perspective on scholarship and the world has been an inspiration. Various chapters in various forms were read by colleagues who kindly proffered comments and suggestions; among those to whom I am indebted are Maxine Berg, Patricia Brückmann, Margaret Hunt, Sara Mendelson, Stephen Walker, Martin Hewitt, Donna Andrew, Margot Finn, Giorgio Riello, as well as several anonymous reviewers. Papers based on the research were presented at conferences and seminars such as the Economic History Society Conference, Birmingham; the Pre-industrial England Seminar, Institute of Historical Research, London; the International Economic History Association Congress, Buenos Aires; the Circulation of Second-hand Goods Conference, European University Institute; Eighteenth Century Studies Seminar, Trinity College, University of Toronto; Women and Material Culture Conference, Chawton House; Tri-campus Conference, University of Guelph; European Business History Association Conference, Barcelona. I thank the organizers of these events and the participants for their questions and observations. Earlier versions of several chapters appeared in *Continuity and Change*, Kristine Bruland and Patrick O'Brien (eds), *From Family Firms to Corporate Capitalism*, and Alexandra Palmer and Hazel Clark (eds), *Old Clothes, New Looks: Secondhand Fashion*. I appreciated the opportunity to revise and rethink these issues. Finally, to the University of Alberta my thanks for the time and resources allowed me to continue to decipher the patterns of everyday life, as these evolved across centuries.

B.L.

Introduction

Everyday practice and plebeian affairs

I N 1979, FERNAND BRAUDEL introduced his great trilogy, *Civilization and Capitalism*, with an explanation of its origins. Intending to write a single volume summarizing pre-industrial society, Braudel found to his amazement a complexity at the lower social levels which defied a unitary narrative – the tripartite form emerged as an attempt to resolve this complexity. At the top, the capitalist world of national and international trade was clear and well documented in histories of multinational banks and great East Indies trading companies; the middle world of the market economy was equally evident and recorded in growing numbers of studies. But, in addition, Braudel noted 'another, shadowy zone, often hard to see for lack of adequate historical documents, lying underneath the market economy: this is the elementary basic activity which went on everywhere and the volume of which is truly fantastic. This rich zone, like a layer covering the earth, I have called for want of a better expression *material life* or *material civilization* ... this infra-economy, [was the] the informal other half of economic activity.' What Braudel termed '*material civilization*' interacted with '*economic civilization*' in the construction of modern society. One could not exist without the other, he insisted.[1] Braudel recognized that, throughout the world, the quotidian facets of daily life were the foundation for the all other manifestations of economic, social and cultural activity, but a foundation often overlooked and too generally ignored. However, the everyday has received steadily more attention since the publication of his three-volume work. And through the writings of another generation of historians the material world of the past is being illuminated, as items from fish to homespun, beadwork souvenirs to snakeskin bags, lighting to lipstick, old clothes to washing machines are being reassessed as interpretative intermediaries to past practices and systems of life.[2] Everyday life is the sum and substance of this volume, and in the routine transactions, daily reckonings and careful expenditures of generations of common people we can see clear expressions of their expectations, limitations and convictions. England is my principal focus; but among the wealth of research findings from other parts of the world I have found many points of commonality and comparison. Similarly, the themes I address in this volume – patterns of plebeian credit and consumerism, the advent of savings culture and domestic accounting, the ubiquity and chronology of alternate currencies through the process of modernization – have a resonance which crosses international or regional boundaries, regardless of the particularities of the area examined.

As the first industrial nation, England was shaped and reshaped by powerful economic, social and political forces that defined our broad understanding of the industrial process for generations. The specific national features of English industrialization are well known.[3] I will take a less familiar trajectory, examining the day-to-day practice and social politics of non-elites, exploring patterns which paralleled better known events. Cumulatively, the shifting material habits and expectations of the labouring and middle classes represented momentous changes and the daily interactions of these men and women refashioned the environment of an increasingly urban and industrial society. This chronicle of customary and evolving patterns of borrowing, lending, saving, material culture and domestic management will bring to light rich areas of history, charting new accommodations between generations of common householders and the society in which they lived. Both were in the throes of perpetual recreation and adaptation.

In the last several decades there have been extraordinary changes in historical questions and priorities. A part of this process can be attributed to the changing composition of the academy and the theoretical perspectives which evolved in concert with these changes. Equally potent were broader societal and political movements which helped reshape the queries posed in historical research. One of the most fruitful areas of scholarship was inspired by gender analyses which fomented dynamic reappraisals, bringing new perspectives to many issues, including the formation of the first industrial nation. Among the subjects revised were, for example, the roles of working women in key industrial sectors, the interactions of gender, agriculture and proto-industrialization, women investors and those in business, as well as the place of gender in the culture of consumerism for both sexes.[4] There remain, however, lacunae in this broad historical narrative which must be explored, those elements of practice and habit which combined the private and the public, the personal and the commercial, the household and the market place. Everyday praxes expressed the hopes, beliefs and priorities of ordinary people, and these are the focus of this volume. Exploring the transformation of these norms reveals new features of society.

Before we begin, it is worth considering again the long hiatus which preceded the reappraisal of women's roles as historical actors, whether alone or in concert with men, as well as the general disregard for certain historical questions or perspectives associated with informal or domestic functions. For example, what accounts for the neglect of the household and the inattention to its pivotal functions as the clearing house of wants, needs and appropriations? Why were so many of the daily fundamentals of everyday economic life, such as the second-hand trade, so long ignored in mainstream history? In Maxine Berg's incisive study of Eileen Power, one of the most innovative economic historians of the first half of the twentieth century, Berg raises factors which speak to this question. Berg, as well as Natalie Zemon Davis, points to Power's historical sensibilities and those of others among the first generation of women economic historians. The scholarly initiatives of Power and her female contemporaries – Alice Clark, Dorothy George, Dorothy Marshall and Ivy Pinchbeck – animated the discipline in the early decades of the twentieth century, although many of the issues they raised and the perspectives they adopted were largely ignored thereafter for several generations.[5] And if in the post-war decades women struggled to achieve a place within the growing professional pantheon, it is also worth recalling the mute and invisible status of women in the theorizing of the original economic thinkers, which in itself resounded through one of the most influential disciplines of the twentieth century.

Adam Smith laid the foundation for the dominant neoclassical economic paradigms. Thereafter, most economic definitions and the institutional perspectives which they supported focused exclusively on the formal male experiences in capitalist workplaces, financial and commercial institutions.[6] As Jane Humphries observes, the discipline of economics developed with an androcentric bias at its core, employing a theoretically separate, rational and self-serving male as the analytical archetype. If emotional, social and collective bonds were missing in classical economic equations, both productive work and consumer spending were thought to involve only a lone atomistic male, unencumbered by personal obligations or life cycle influences. Similarly, as Margot Finn observes, Smith obscured the actual functioning of the market through his preoccupation with cash exchanges, a standpoint which also had significant gender ramifications.[7] Economics functioned for generations without either acknowledging or criticizing these underpinnings, and the histories written of economic growth and change often took an equally blinkered approach. Yet, over generations, the struggles to articulate a more wide-ranging historical dynamic have proved particularly fruitful, bringing important findings to the fore and tracking innovative nuances which had gone largely unnoticed.[8] The humble, ubiquitous practices that characterized plebeian lives are fertile ground for historical enquiry, mirroring in their collective daily acts the evolving expectations and aspirations of each generation.[9] You will find few heroic adventures in these accounts and few captains of commerce. Yet without a full appraisal of this history our understanding of society would be incomplete and our appreciation of its evolution would be partial.

Historical knowledge of industrializing society now includes a clearer vision of the complexities within communities and of women's, as well as men's, contributions to the societies and economies within which they lived. The process of theorizing industrial change, in both Western and non-Western nations, has become more thorough and inclusive.[10] Similarly, there have been subtle and challenging analyses of the long-accepted public/private dichotomy and a more thoroughgoing assessment of gender roles in family and community. The contributions and experiences of both sexes are now receiving a fuller evaluation.[11] Feminist scholars in economics and development economics also offer important revisions of terms such as 'work', both paid and unpaid, charting the creation of an analytical category which excluded or ignored the historic contributions of women. They challenged the assumption that women's domestic activities represented unproductive labour and insisted that the predominantly female home-based and community activities constituted real and valuable, if unpaid, labour.[12] The power of this analysis has born fruit, with some national governments, as well as the United Nations, now trying to capture the unpaid contributions within societies around the world. However, another feminist economist raises a caveat. Susan Himmelweit advises caution when using the term 'work' in descriptions of domestic activities. She observes that identifying domestic 'unpaid work' brings potential benefits, but adds that there are also significant distortions that come with that new classification. Himmelweit argues convincingly that a vital element of what she calls 'care' infuses many female-dominated activities, which account for more than a calculated exchange of labour units for wages. Narrowly defining these undertakings as 'work' actually diminishes women's contributions and equally threatens to obscure men's caring contributions to kin and community. Himmelweit argues for the importance of ascribing 'value to the personal and relational aspects of much domestic activity. By insisting that domestic contributions are valued "work", much of such caring or self-fulfilling activity is excluded and remains in the background, essential to but unrecognized by the economics of work and by a society that operates within it.'[13]

Alice Kessler-Harris remarks that 'women have not generally achieved public power for their caring roles'.[14] Studies which take into account the gender politics within households, neighbourhoods and wider communities, the complex motivations of actors, including the working of what Kessler-Harris terms the 'gendered imagination',[15] invariably uncover more intricate behaviours and subtle social patterns. The nature of work, as Himmelweit suggests, is one area where the ambiguities of gender persist. Equally complex were the changing facets of daily life which enveloped patterns of work. In the context of this volume I will assess the economic habits shaped by gender expectations, the social repercussions of state monetization, the impact of consumer desires, the social and cultural outcomes of new fiscal institutions like savings banks and the gradual but dramatic effects of applied numeric systems in domestic settings. The dynamics of small-scale credit will be the first element explored; credit practices involved various and variable motivations and uses, moulded by shifting gender norms. I look at credit from below, tracking the ubiquitous fiscal needs of working, trading people, getting by and making do. Their access to credit evolved in conjunction with societal structures and, contrary to the concepts expounded by classical economists, quotidian credit needs for production and consumption cannot easily be disentangled, blending these categories. Indeed, the ambiguities inherent in gift-giving, sharing and distributive social practices invariably tied some productive initiatives to cultural and consumptive expressions.[16] Women routinely administered this credit. However, women's pre-eminent role remained unacknowledged and unstudied until very recently, precisely because of the conundrums inherent in this kitchen commerce. Yet, for centuries, ordinary women, along with a smaller number of male cohorts, arranged material resources, including credit, to sustain themselves and their families, defining many of the features of the household/market relationship. The opening chapter in this book explores the complexities of this plebeian finance, where early modern women, along with men, borrowed and pledged, formed partnerships to trade, guaranteed loans and secured pledges in productive and consumptive endeavours. I do not suggest that the early modern era was a fiscal Golden Age for women – this study reflects the often marginal conditions in which they survived and the sometimes limited expectations within which they functioned. Over this era, patterns of lending and borrowing altered and I chart the changes and continuities. By the nineteenth century, the gradual formalization of new credit institutions paralleled an apparent masculinization of respectable borrowing and a shift in the public's response to the long-established mechanics of small-scale credit. Commerce was never gender-neutral, neither at the upper reaches of industrial capital formation, nor at the counter of the local pawnbroker.

In Chapter 3 I track new thinking on plebeian credit among seventeenth- and eighteenth-century English theorists. City dwellers from Italy to Spain, France to the Low Countries, had long relied on the low interest rates and general availability of loans from charitable lending societies, termed *mont de piété*.[17] The organizers of these initiatives, churchmen and city fathers, recognized how dependent their subjects and citizens were on small loans for petty trade, handicraft and household budgeting. Similar observations were made by English authors from at least the mid-seventeenth century, who urged the creation of comparable ventures in their country. However, the eighteenth-century Charitable Corporation was the only experiment in England to run along Continental lines, to try to bring low-cost credit to London's industrious classes. Inspired by established Continental initiatives and the evident need for small loans in England's largest city, this was part of the new discourse on credit that emphasized its social value as a disciplinary force for the working, entrepreneurial poor. Among eighteenth-century elite theorists there were new expectations of the lending and spending nexus, especially as expressed within the lower social orders. The experimental Charitable Corporation was a unique development, an innovative project tailor-made to suit London's commercial ethos. Nevertheless, the tale of the Charitable Corporation has been all but forgotten in histories of London's commercial life and gigantic frauds; yet it figured prominently in these arenas, too. The events surrounding its life and death came to shape government perceptions in the second half of the eighteenth century, determining what initiatives would or would not be supported to ease the burden on petty borrowers. Ultimately, proposals tied to personal initiative and personal responsibility received far more favourable receptions in government circles, and commercial loans or personal savings, however small, were seen as the most likely means to support most plebeian financial strategies.

Industrial growth and mercantile expansion brought an insatiable appetite for commercial and consumer credit, which was met through new financial mediums. As the formal structures of commerce and industry were set in place, expectations surrounding the use of credit also changed. Theorists and reformers, commentators and authors enjoined new forms of rational fiscal practice among the wage-earning classes and many of the old ways and old players were disdained. In the early modern era, uses of alternate currencies in the second-hand trade were an unremarkable feature of daily finance for noblemen and commoners. As I show in Chapter 4, the absence of an adequate supply of coins encouraged alternative currencies to flourish as specie substitutes, and this remained a vital element of plebeian budgeting for centuries. However, this practice was another of the manifestations of 'material civilization' overlooked by most of those who later anatomized the workings of the market. Their fixed focus recognized the output of guild workshops and mechanized factories, the cargoes carried in ships, the exchanges between financiers, ignoring the commerce that ebbed and flowed around them in their homes and along the side streets in their neighbourhoods. Alternative currencies were one of the mechanisms *enabling* routine exchanges and underpinning everyday credit.[18] As regional economies thrived, the second-hand trade also encouraged patterns of consumption where objects – apparel, decorative accoutrements and household wares – acted as stores of value to be released as needed through the market. This trade, too, reflected the particularities of class, gender and time. Consumer practices among the middle classes slowly assumed new normative features, from the seventeenth century to the nineteenth, as the old ways abated in these circles. Only among the working poor did objects continue to be purchased with a view to their possible liquidity in cash or credit, confounding Victorian middle-class perceptions of thrift and providence. Teasing out these histories brings greater colour, form and insight to the processes of change embedded in the histories of industrialization and modernization.

Throughout the period under study, a growing consumerism fired the economy, shaped the priorities of individuals and determined the allocation of resources within families, defining the wants, needs and preoccupations of non-elites, as well as elites. English society experienced a growing complexity of material culture and there were a growing number of communities in which display and distinction claimed the attention of adults and adolescents, where only the destitute forswore the practice of fashion. Fashion parallels and propels developments in trade and manufacturing wherever these occur, privileging novelty and a shifting material life. It was an ineluctable features of English life, revealing its energy and ambiguities. Dress figured as the most demotic arena where consumer politics and conflicts played out – Chapter 5 explores this history. In the past twenty years the once marginal study of the demand side, or consumer perspective, has become a mainstream facet of historical and cultural study. During this revisionist process, broad assertions have been modified and nuances added to frame a more subtle and complete portrait of the English consumer, bewigged, beribboned, buckled and shod according to personal and community priorities. Clothing purchases represented approximately a quarter of national expenditure at the end of the seventeenth century and there are few better mirrors of the strains, stresses and passions negotiated in domestic settings than popular fashions in dress.[19] The provision of a wider array of products, many at lower prices, facilitated materially richer and diverse expressions of consumer culture. The widespread engagement with fashions among England's men and women and their myriad expressions of style offer a case study of changing social dynamics. The prospect of plebeian indulgence was galling and troubling to many, who feared intemperance could lead to penury and turn working men and women on to parish poor rolls. However, the traditional responses to commoners' consumerism underwent changes in the later eighteenth century, when their cumulative purchases were recognized as being a prop to British industries, such as the cotton trade. I do not address the experience of these industries – a field very well ploughed over many generations. Rather, I explore the social politics of popular fashions and from that point address the changes in form and function which followed in train with industrial growth.

The spread of savings banks and a savings culture, the subject of Chapter 6, were interwoven with concepts of plebeian thrift, in combination with personal consumerism. The nineteenth century was a period of notable experimentation and innovation in the field of plebeian finance and, in addition to the new-style loan societies, discussed at the end of Chapter 2, savings banks sprang up across the country, introducing a new type of institution with far-reaching social and economic consequences. By the early nineteenth century, the organization of savings banks explicitly fostered what I call provident consumerism, encouraging support for routine plebeian expenditures and training participants in a new personal fiscal order. Savings banks were promoted aggressively after 1815, when economic crises loomed and social unrest flared throughout the country. These enterprises marked a qualitative departure from old practices of charity, or old plaints enjoining thrift. The seemingly modest initiatives early in the century carried great ambitions for social and material dividends. In 1816, Charles Taylor, a savings bank enthusiast, insisted that the security of the kingdom depended on 'those classes on whose industry the prosperity of the country consists, on whose comfortable well-being its internal repose depends'. To achieve these ends, Taylor promoted the London Savings Bank, garnering widespread sponsorship for this institution within ruling circles. His was one of dozens of similar ventures.

Proponents believed savings banks would ensure a regularity of fiscal behaviour among the wage-earners, 'rendering general a system of prudent economy and forethought, particularly among the industrious classes of the community'.[20] It was hoped that experiments like Taylor's, multiplied many times over, would foster national stability and industrial dynamism, at the same time as they encouraged personal independence, the rational training of children and promoted greater general comfort.[21] These institutions sparked a broad social and economic movement that ultimately engaged virtually every social class, every region, every age group and every occupational and political community over the course of the nineteenth century. The malleable tenets of saving appealed to nineteenth-century co-operatives and friendly societies, to late nineteenth-century school board trustees and trade unionists, along with Members of Parliament and radical activists. Across the nineteenth century, the practice and propaganda of disciplined saving, made palatable by sanctioned periodic expenditures, raised the expectations of generations, redefined respectable behaviour, introduced the practices of accounting into the heart of family life and revised masculine and feminine aspirations. The history and ideals of this movement add an important constituent to the cultural and economic analysis of this era.

Over the centuries studied in this volume, other far-reaching repercussions were manifest, and nowhere more than in the concept of household management. As with many parts of this tale, the impetus for the new rational, numeric administration of the family began first elsewhere in Europe, with the rising fortunes of Italy's trading citizens and the development of a new system of accounting for wealth and property, for debits and credits. However mundane accounting may appear, it marked a fundamental shift in thinking and brought radical changes in practice. Bruce Carruthers and Wendy Espeland observe that 'Rational capital accounting, in conjunction with calculable law, rational technology (mechanization), free labour, and the commercialization of economic life, is, for Weber, an element in a general process of rationalization that is both the precursor to and the consequence of modern capitalism'.[22] Along with the rise of industrial capitalism in England and the changing economics of daily life came the reorganization of family administration. The application of numerate precepts in the home, first by elite men and ultimately by plebeian women, was part of a general reconceptualization of societal norms, but one which has been overlooked to this point. Both family duties and written chronicles of domestic life altered with the application of numerate systems to tabulate homely affairs. The first proponents of this method were men, wealthy, prominent and preoccupied with great estates and ambitions. But the practice of quantification soon spread to men of lower social standing and to the other sex; the chronology and significance of this process are the subject of the final chapter of this book.

The clash between traditional duties and this new conceptual form of writing is illustrated most dramatically in the timing and application of this discipline by housewives. Wifely chores and skills in the garden, bakehouse, dairy, kitchen, parlour, parish and lying-in room were gradually reformed over many generations, among most social classes, to include quantification as a key attribute of housewifery. The talents of the housewife enumerated by the early seventeenth-century author and self-described husbandman Gervase Markham emphasized antique skills in herbals and physic, cookery, preserving, dairying, cloth and its dyes; 'the office of the brew-house, and the bake-house'. These systems of knowledge were thought the natural pursuits of domestic women, with only a passing note on the written diaries a housewife might keep.[23] However, over time, numerate record-keeping became more and more central as a tenet of careful housewifery, as a key descriptor of homely activities. And mastery of this task opened another arena for the play of gender politics.

Chapter 7 charts one of the most ephemeral but central shifts in everyday life – the numeric tabulation of the home and family. The spread of numerate thinking and its application in common domestic settings involved new priorities and new patterns of thought that were antithetical in some ways to the traditional bonds that tied together neighbours and kin and equally at odds with the expressed Victorian distaste for female entrepreneurship outside the home. In the domestic account books of men and women, and the widely published guides to housekeeping, the shift in mentalities is as evident as the changed domestic agendas. This process was part of the wider spread of numerate calculation in society, one which secured a practical and philosophical pre-eminence in the nineteenth century over all other forms of rational representation. Commercial accounts and political arithmetic were two parts of this agenda, offering a potentially profitable numeracy on the one hand and a useful philosophical numeracy on the other.[24] For property holders, bookkeeping became the most common manifestation of rational, manly attention to the details of family life. When and how did middle-class women adopt this numerate discourse? How did they interpret these new disciplines? And in what ways did class, gender and geography affect the spread of this practice? The evidence suggests a gradual piecemeal acceptance of ledger entries as the pre-eminent record of domestic affairs. Were plebeian women a particular obstacle in the spread of these practices? If this was indeed so, was it because, as John Bohstedt suggests, 'women were more involved in use than exchange, directors of reproduction as well as production, perhaps more immersed in the moral, less the market, economy'?[25] Or, perhaps, the traditional conceptualization of domestic lives could only gradually be distilled to fit bookkeepers' columns and only slowly coalesce with the pervasive utilitarian agenda for 'facts and calculations', with the 'rule, and a pair of scales, and the multiplication tables ... ready to weigh and measure'.[26] The tensions and restrictions accompanying this system of reckoning resonate in the records created by male and female scriveners; and the long chronicle of this process reveals the accommodations made over generations as family life evolved to include more analytic calculations.

For centuries, ordinary plebeian women organized the small-scale credit which sustained modest enterprises and family budgets – practices only the working poor retained in the late nineteenth century. In contrast, as numeracy spread and its applications diffused, the ideal forum where respectable women were enjoined to apply numerate skills was in the home. New disciplines and rewards were set in place, with accounting defined as one of the principal duties of Victorian wives, with the proliferation of savings institutions of every kind, with inexpensive and modish clothes and the growing comfort of common households as the reward of respectable people. Credit and consumerism, saving and domestic accounting – these epitomize the gendered economies of England, and their transformations mirror the common strategies of each age. The records of these changes chart commonplace practices which melded public and private, domestic and commercial worlds, practices which in their sum helped build the framework of daily life in the modern Industrial Age.

Notes

1 Fernand Braudel, *Civilization and Capitalism, Fifteenth–Eighteenth Century* I, *The Structures of Everyday Life*, translation from the French revised by Siân Reynolds (New York, 1985), pp. 23–4, 27–9.

2 Rosemary Ommer, 'One hundred years of fishery crises in Newfoundland', *Acadiensis* 23:2 (1994); Laurel Thatcher Ulrich, *The Age of Homespun: Objects and Stories in the Creation of an American Myth* (New York, 2001); Ruth B. Phillips, *Identities: The Souvenir in Native North American Art from the Northeast, 1700–1900* (Seattle, 1998); Cory Silverstein-Willmott, 'An Ojibway artifact unraveled: the case of the bag with the snakeskin strap', *Textile History* 34:1 (2003); Kathy Peiss, *Hope in a Jar: The Making of America's Beauty Culture* (New York, 1998); Daniel Roche, *A History of Everyday Things: The Birth of Consumption in France, 1600–1800* (Cambridge, 2000); Beverly

Lemire, *Dress, Culture and Commerce: The English Clothing Trade before the Factory* (Basingstoke, 1997), especially chapters 3–4; Karen Tranberg Hansen, *Salaula: The World of Secondhand Clothing and Zambia* (Chicago, 2000); Ann Rosalind Jones and Peter Stallybrass, *Renaissance Clothing and the Materials of Memory* (Cambridge, 2000); Joy Parr, *Domestic Goods: The Material, the Moral and the Economic in the Postwar Years* (Toronto, 1999).

3 The historiography of British industrialization has been so influential that most subsequent industrialization processes were judged against the template of the 'normal' British experience. Decades passed before European economic historians adopted a perspective sympathetic to the alternative routes to industrial growth. See, for example, John U. Nef, *Industry and Government in France and England, 1540–1640* (Ithaca NY, 1957); Phyllis Deane, *The First Industrial Revolution* (Cambridge, 1965); Peter Mathias, *The First Industrial Nation: An Economic History of Britain, 1700–1914* (London, 1969); F. Crouzet, 'French Economic Growth in the Nineteenth Century Reconsidered', *History* 59 (1974); R. Hoehl, 'French industrialization: a reconsideration', *Explorations in Economic History* 13:2 (1976); B. Ratcliffe, 'Manufacturing in the metropolis: the dynamism and dynamics of Parisian industry at the mid-nineteenth century', *Journal of European Economic History* 23:2 (1993), and, most recently, François Crouzet, Tawney Lecture, Economic History Society conference, Birmingham, 2002.

4 The particular sensitivity to gender and to women's and men's contributions is everywhere evident in the work of Joan Thirsk, including such works as 'Industries in the countryside' in F. J. Fisher (ed.), *Essays in the Economic and Social History of Tudor and Stuart England in Honour of R. H. Tawney* (Cambridge, 1961), 'The fantastical folly of fashion: the English stocking knitting industry, 1500–1700' in N. B. Harte and K. G. Ponting (eds), *Textile History and Economic History: Essays in Honour of Miss Julia de Lacy Mann* (Manchester, 1973) and *Economic Policy and Projects: The Development of a Consumer Society in Early Modern England* (Oxford, 1978). See also Leonore Davidoff and Catherine Hall, *Family Fortunes: Men and Women of the English Middle Class, 1780–1850* (Chicago, 1987); Laurel Thatcher Ulrich, 'Martha Ballard and her girls: women's work in eighteenth-century Maine' in S. Innes (ed.), *Work and Labor in Early America* (Chapel Hill NC, 1988); Peter Earle, 'The female labour market in London in the late seventeenth and early eighteenth centuries', *Economic History Review*, 2nd series 42:3 (1989); Pat Hudson, *The Industrial Revolution* (London, 1992), chapter 7; Amanda Vickery, 'Women and the world of goods: a Lancashire consumer and her possessions' in John Brewer and Roy Porter (eds), *Consumption and the World of Goods* (London, 1993); Maxine Berg, *The Age of Manufactures, 1700–1820: Industry, Innovation and Work in Britain*, 2nd edn (London, 1994); Anna Clark, *The Struggle for the Breeches: Gender and the Making of the British Working Class* (Berkeley CA, 1995); Victoria de Grazia (ed.), *The Sex of Things: Gender and Consumption in Historical Perspective* (Berkeley CA, 1996); Pamela Sharpe, *Adapting to Capitalism: Working Women in the English Economy, 1700–1850* (Basingstoke, 1996); Joy Parr, 'Gender history and historical practice' in Joy Parr and Mark Rosenfeld (eds), *Gender and History in Canada* (Toronto, 1996); David Kuchta, 'The making of the self-made man: class, clothing, and English masculinity, 1688–1832' in Victoria de Grazia (ed.), *The Sex of Things: Gender and Consumption in Historical Perspective* (Berkeley CA, 1996); Margaret R. Hunt, *The Middling Sort: Commerce, Gender and the Family in England, 1680–1780* (Berkeley CA, 1996); Lemire, *Dress, Culture and Commerce*; Christopher

Breward, *The Hidden Consumer: Masculinities, Fashion and City Life, 1860–1914* (Manchester, 1999); Katrina Honeyman, *Women, Gender and Industrialisation in England, 1700–1870* (Basingstoke, 2000); Margot Finn, 'Men's things: masculine possession in the consumer revolution', *Social History* 25:2 (2000), and *The Character of Credit: Personal Debt in English Culture, 1740–1914* (Cambridge, 2003). Generations of research into European women's lives are summarized in surveys such as Merry E. Wiesner, *Women and Gender in Early Modern Europe* (Cambridge, 1993); and Olwen Hufton, *The Prospect before Her: A History of Women in Western Europe, 1500–1800* (London, 1995).

5 Maxine Berg, *A Woman in History: Eileen Power, 1889–1940* (Cambridge, 1996), and 'The first women economic historians', *Economic History Review*, 2nd series 45:2 (1992); see also Natalie Zemon Davis, 'History's two bodies', *American Historical Review* 93 (1988). Alice Clark, *The Working Life of Women in the Seventeenth Century* (1919, repr. New York, 1968); M. Dorothy George, *London Life in the Eighteenth Century* (1925, repr. New York, 1965); Dorothy Marshall, *The English Poor in the Eighteenth Century: A Study in Social and Administrative History* (London, 1926); Ivy Pinchbeck, *Women Workers and the Industrial Revolution* (London, 1930).

6 'Women, the domestic sphere and reproductive activities are nowhere mentioned in Ricardo's *Principles of Political Economy and Taxation* ... and in Malthus's *Principles of Political Economy* ... ' Michele Pujol, *Feminism and Anti-feminism in early Economic Thought*, Aldershot, 1992, p. 23. However, in the 1980s and 1990s economists like Amartya Sen have devised alternative methods of constructing a national GNP which takes account of the time spent in tasks heretofore categorized as unproductive. Amartya Kumar Sen, *Social Exclusion: Concept, Application, and Scrutiny* (Manila, 2000) and *Development as Freedom* (New York, 1999).

7 Jane Humphries, 'Introduction' in Jane Humphries (ed.), *Gender and Economics* (Aldershot, 1995), p. xv; Finn, *The Character of Credit*, pp. 5–7.

8 An example of which is the ground-breaking Ford Lectures series, given at Oxford in 1975 and published as Thirsk, *Economic Policy and Projects*.

9 A model of this sort of historical enquiry can be found in David Levine and Keith Wrightson, *The Making of an Industrial Society: Wickham, 1560–1765* (Oxford, 1991), and, in a more modern time frame, Joy Parr, *The Gender of Breadwinners: Women, Men and Change in two Industrial Towns, 1880–1950* (Toronto, 1990).

10 A survey of the arguments and literature can be found in Honeyman, *Women, Gender and Industrialisation in England*; Berg, *The Age of Manufactures*; Jane Humphries, '"Lurking in the wings": women in the historiography of the industrial revolution', *Business and Economic History*, 2nd series 20 (1991). On the question of women and economic development see Irene Tinker (ed.), *Persistent Inequalities: Women and World Development* (Oxford, 1990), and Ester Boserup, *Women's Role in Economic Development*, 2nd edn (New York, 1986).

11 The concept of a nineteenth-century 'separate sphere' for bourgeois women, confined to the materially richer, sentimentalized household, has been critiqued by Amanda Vickery, 'Golden Age to separate spheres: a review of the categories and chronology of English women's history', *Historical Journal* 36:2 (1993). For an evaluation of this historiography of the family see Ellen Ross, 'Long live the family', *Journal of British Studies* 41:4 (2002). For other examples of recent treatments of the family and gender see Theodore Koditschek, *Class Formation and Urban Industrial Society: Bradford,*

1750–1850 (Cambridge, 1990); Hunt, *The Middling Sort*; John Tosh, *A Man's Place: Masculinity and the Middle-Class Home in Victorian England* (New Haven CT, 1999), and Karen Harvey, 'Playing with the Bee: Male Authority and the Household Economy, c. 1650–1820', unpublished paper presented at the Economic History Society conference, Birmingham, 2002. For the most important elaboration of the bourgeois capitalist Victorian household see also Davidoff and Hall, *Family Fortunes*.

12 There is a substantial literature analysing the nature of capitalist and patriarchal marriages and family life. Among the most influential of the early works is Heidi Hartmann, 'The family as the locus of gender, class, and political struggle: the example of housework', *Signs: Journal of Women in Culture and Society* 6:3 (1981). See also John Harrison, 'The political economy of housework', *Bulletin of the Conference of Socialist Economists* (winter 1973); Anne Oakley, *Housewife* (Harmondsworth, 1974); Ruth Schwartz Cowan, *More Work for Mother: The Ironies of Household Technology, from the Open Hearth to the Microwave* (London, 1983). See also the incisive analyses of international activist and feminist economic critic Marilyn Waring, *If Women Counted: A new Feminist Economics*, introduction by Gloria Steinem (San Francisco, 1988).

13 Susan Himmelweit, 'The discovery of "unpaid work": the social consequences of the expansion of "work"', *Feminist Economics* 1:2 (1995), p. 2.

14 Alice Kessler-Harris, *In Pursuit of Equity: Women, Men, and the Quest for Economic Citizenship in Twentieth-Century America* (New York, 2001), p. 13.

15 Kessler-Harris, *In Pursuit of Equity*, pp. 5–6.

16 The notions of a strict divide between production and consumption categories is criticized by development theorists, as well as some historians of early modern Europe. The varying complexities of all societies and economies require a subtlety of analysis that extends beyond the prescribed formal categories of many disciplines, as Annette Weiner has observed: *Inalienable Possessions: The Paradox of Keeping-while-Giving* (Berkeley CA, 1992), introduction. For a selected European example see Natalie Zemon David, *The Gift in Sixteenth Century France* (Madison WI, 2000). More detailed discussions of these questions can be found in the following chapter.

17 For a survey of these credit practices see Laurence Fontaine, 'Women's economic spheres and credit in pre-industrial Europe' in Lemire *et al.*, *Women and Credit*.

18 This subject was explored in depth at a conference, 'Le Circulation des objets d'occasion', European University Institute, Florence, 2002. For another example see Karen Tranberg Hansen, 'Budgeting against uncertainty: cross-class and transethnic redistribution mechanisms in urban Zambia', *African Urban Studies* 21 (spring 1985).

19 Negley Harte, 'The economics of clothing in the late seventeenth century', *Fabrics and Fashions: Studies in the Economic and Social History of Dress*, special issue of *Textile History* 22:2 (1991), and Margaret Spufford, 'The cost of apparel in seventeenth-century England and the accuracy of Gregory King', *Economic History Review*, 2nd series 53:4 (2000).

20 Charles Taylor, *A Summary Account of the London Savings Bank, including its Formation, Progress, and Present State: The Steps successively Resorted to, and their Applicability in Various Circumstances* (London, 1816), pp. 3, 1.

21 Taylor, *Summary Account*, p. 2.

22 Bruce G. Carruthers and Wendy Nelson Espeland, 'Accounting for rationality: double-entry bookkeeping and the rhetoric of economic rationality', *American Journal of Sociology* 91:1 (1991), p. 32.

23 Gervase Markham, *The English Housewife: Containing the inward and outward Virtues which ought to be in a Complete Woman; as her Skill in Physic, Cookery, Banqueting-stuff, Distillation, Perfumes, Wool, Hemp, Flax, Dairies, Brewing, Baking, and all other Things belonging to a Household*, edited by Michael Best (1615, revised edn Kingston ON, 1986), pp. vii–viii; see also Alison Sim, *The Tudor Housewife* (Montreal, 1996), pp. 29–60.

24 Mary Poovey charts the appearance and significance of double-entry accounting and the epistemological developments which led to the rise of statistics (or the modern fact) as the pre-eminent foundation for rational decision-making. *A History of the Modern Fact: Problems of Knowledge in the Sciences of Wealth and Society* (Chicago, 1998).

25 John Bohstedt, 'Gender, household and community politics: women in English riots, 1790–1810', *Past and Present* 120 (1988), p. 101.

26 Charles Dickens, *Hard Times, for these Times*, ed. Graham Law (1854, repr. London, 1996), p. 42.

2

Gender, the informal economy and the development of capitalism in England, 1650–1850; or, credit and the common people

CHANNELS OF CREDIT EXPANDED and evolved over the early modern period. In the late seventeenth century, the confluence of private lenders and government need produced more regulated structures in the form of the Bank of England; this and other more formal lending associations grew in scale and sophistication from the seventeenth century to the nineteenth.[1] However, the growing infrastructures in government, overseas trade and industry were not the only features of credit worth noting. Recent investigations attest to an unexpected gender complexity among both commercial actors and their credit transactions.[2] For example, common law restrictions on women did not preclude them from managing or organizing financial affairs, although typically women controlled small to medium-sized quantities of capital and credit. Women's invisibility to many earlier historians, as well as a predominant interest in large, celebrated ventures, meant that many subjects went unstudied.[3] Yet, on a day-to-day basis, the credit organized by women represented the majority of quotidian credit transactions, setting the tone for a fundamental feature of life throughout western Europe. The monetary structures of daily life were neither simple nor uniform, and in this chapter I explore the commercial practices found in cities and large towns in many parts of Europe,[4] where formal and informal pawnbrokers and moneylenders enabled common people to sustain their lives and enterprises.

It is widely acknowledged that credit was essential, especially to the women and men with limited and irregular incomes.[5] Seasonal work, multiple occupations and infrequent pay ensured that the wage-earners, small handicraft persons and pedlars lived with shortfalls in income. Urban residents might be especially vulnerable to income fluctuations, as cash transactions became more the norm, when juggling income with outflow presented an ever-present challenge. Thus women and men looked for short-term loans from those willing to lend. This was an imperative. And, while women's responsibilities are well known for the domestic sphere,[6] what is less well known is that women were disproportionately responsible for the management of small-scale credit for activities based in the household. In this context, reputation remained the foundation of trust and the determinant of creditworthiness; little wonder then that women guarded their own and their family's good name so carefully. Craig Muldrew suggests we think of

> reputation or credit as a currency with a linguistic, or rhetorical, system of circulation which considered wants and needs in terms of social relations of exchange and negotiation. Such linguistic evaluation, argument and description in turn had an effect on people's access to material goods, and on their judgements about what constituted wealth.[7]

The uses to which this credit was put cannot be easily categorized as either production or consumption. Indeed, those engaged in modern development work find the strict division between these economic categories unhelpful. They note that such differentiations represent an artificial distinction when discussing the complex socio-economic practices among the poor, where the two facets are so closely entwined.[8] Similarly, the credit needs of the early modern working poor and lower middle classes were directed to both productive and consumptive ends, often closely combined, with credit employed to buy consumable goods, as well as raw materials or essential services, all of which could be productively employed. Collectively, these ventures underpinned the ebb and flow of resources through generations. To more fully understand the links between the household and the market we must explore the gendered systems of quotidian credit as these evolved.

Classic analyses of the market, as devised by both liberal and Marxist theorists, ignored the often messy routine expressions of commerce, resulting in an 'impoverished theoretical framework for understanding consumer credit', in Margot Finn's words.[9] Recovering the full array of these transactions enables a more thorough theorizing of the origins of Western consumer society, of which this work is a part. In the first instance, market exchanges were rarely a homogeneous trade of cash for goods. Adaptive strategies, such as through the second-hand trade, enabled generations of women and men to balance household needs with income.[10] In this context neighbourhood pawnbrokers proliferated, offering loans on pledges at varying rates of interest. The cost of pawning and borrowing undoubtedly took a toll on many budgets.[11] One of the most frequent charges against pawnbrokers was that they levied high rates of interest; but life without credit was an unenviable option and the agency of the pawnbroker was indispensable, offering choices where there were limited alternatives. The mercantile habits of the labouring, wage-earning and trading classes created dense networks of commercial and social interaction, and, exploring these, it is possible to distinguish patterns of credit within a significant sector of the population, even if detailed accounts of the lives of working poor, at the household level, remain shrouded. In this context, women's roles were multi-faceted, combining social and economic priorities where reciprocal, cordial behaviour set many of the parameters for early modern credit relations, where married women acted as guarantors, borrowed money in their own right and acted as active agents on their own account, relying on a largely male pawnbroking–moneylending fraternity.[12] I do not offer a balance sheet on the effects of borrowing on this population. Rather, I chart the routine gender practices which underpinned small-scale credit. Running from the seventeenth century to the nineteenth, I also assess the roles played by purveyors of credit and their customers, within the context of the formalization and regulation of lending.

Community and credit

I begin in the crowded streets of south London in a district bustling with the comings and goings of travellers to the Thames-side docks, or the towns of Kent and Surrey, where hawkers trolled the streets, a place where new arrivals looked for work, food, lodgings and entertainments of all sorts. On one of the main thoroughfares a small retailer produced two ledgers which survive to this day, and through the crabbed, crossed hand of this account-ant a window is opened on the common credit culture of his time. His was a modest business in Kent Street, in the parish of St George the Martyr, a parish poorer than the neighbouring riverside parishes to the north; here John Pope citizen and haberdasher set up a trade in the vicinity of St George Church Yard, some time in the mid-seventeenth century. The neighbouring parish of St Saviour boasted inns, markets and thriving trade. St George the Martyr parish claimed more modest commerce and hosted the annual rau-cous disorders of St Bartholomew's Fair. Looming prisons and their atten-dant population were also set within its precincts, bringing a hodgepodge of people to St George's parish, where they scraped a living, scrambling to get by.[13] Yet if St George's was poorer than St Saviour's, both felt the influx of newcomers and migrants, and both parishes were touched by the river-side trades.[14] South London was a sometimes unruly quarter, with a taint of lawlessness that hung about the suburban fringes as newcomers struggled to gain a foothold among the half-million people then living in greater London. None could survive long without credit.

John Pope knew his community and understood the exigencies of daily life. The son of a Devonshire yeoman, Pope finished his eight-year apprenticeship in 1636, when he became a member of the Haberdashers' Company.[15] Some time thereafter he opened his shop, surviving the uncertainties of the politically turbulent mid-century, still in trade in the 1670s. For the most part John Pope filled his days as a haberdasher, selling essential hosiery of various sorts, as well as a few items of apparel, fabric and accessories – exactly the sorts of goods that stimulated consumer demand and sustained domestic manufacturing.[16] Two narrow day books contain records of transactions for the period 1666 to 1671, when Pope was well into middle age, an experienced retailer, with ties throughout the city and beyond. As an adjunct to his business Pope also took pawns and lent money.[17]

The men and women who walked into his shop or met him in the market place were in many ways a typical cross-section of labouring/ trading city folk who relied for their survival on the cultivation of social and economic opportunities and on the good will and financial resources of wealthier neighbours. The occupations of the borrowers reflect the opportunities in south London (see Table 2.1) and the ledgers themselves give glimpses of both long-term and ephemeral community relationships grounded in a social economy of dependence and interdependence. In total, 440 credit transactions survive in his accounts, separated physically from the remainder of the ledger which dealt with retail sales.[18] Though partial, these notes attest to an intricate system of credit and a community of reciprocal guarantors making loans available to even humble residents of this suburb. Who did Pope lend to and what were their trades? Broom makers and mop makers were most numerous, followed by cordwainers, tailors/sewers, glovers, spinners/weavers, and various construction and service trades. Plate 2.1, a dealer in brooms and old shoes, personifies features of Pope's clients – an untidy figure at the margins of the market, claiming trading status, selling recyclable detritus at the fringe of the commercial world. Yet, collectively, dealers like him were invaluable, changing new for old to suit plebeian customers. Mops and brooms were essential household tools, costing little, worn down over months and years, readily replaceable from the stocks of street sellers or market stalls. The struggle to maintain cleanliness in early modern London gave mop makers, like Audry Burton, a living which in turn ensured her creditworthiness. Audry Burton also lived in Kent Street and

Table 2.1 Occupations of borrowers in St George's Parish, Southwark, 1667–1671

Occupations	Women	Men
'Birther'/Midwife	1	–
Bricklayer	1	1
Broom maker	7	5
Butcher	–	2
Carpenter	–	1
Cooper	–	1
Cordwainer/Shoemaker/Translator	–	7
Cutler	–	1
Flaxman	–	1
Gardener	–	1
Glover	–	3
Innkeeper	–	1
Laundress	2	–
Mat maker	–	1
Mop maker	1	3
Pin maker	1	–
Putty maker	1	–
Sawyer	–	2
Sewer	1	–
Silk weaver	1	–
Surgeon	–	1
Tailor	–	3
Water seller	–	1
Wool spinner	2	–
Unknown	68	17
Total	68	52

Source: C 108/34, Public Record Office.

was doubtless well known to Pope when he lent her 10s in the spring of 1669 and she added her mark to his day book. The twelve mop and broom makers who secured loans from Pope represented one of the commonest of Southwark's crafts. Another of his clients was from the shoemaking fraternity, a 'translator', who repaired and resold old shoes. Leather trades of all sorts also flourished in south London; waste from Thames-side rope making supplied materials for mat makers; while textile and clothing along with service trades were metropolitan staples.[19] Though most of these borrowers might be ranked as poor or modestly endowed at best,

Plate 2.1 'Old Shoes for Some Brooms': a dealer in brooms and old shoes

their creditworthiness in Pope's eyes was self-evident and should not surprise modern observers, for among this heterogeneous group one finds the most vibrant, if vulnerable, commercial actors. Success cata-pulted the favoured few into a stall, then perhaps a shop; misfortune slid the hapless towards destitution. Another of the most striking features of the occupational table is the large number of women with no designated trade, though seven of these women were recorded in Pope's ledger in relation to their husbands: soldier, nailer, cordwainer, tailor, waterman, labourer and broom maker. Numbers of these women may have worked for Pope as hawkers, tramping the lanes and alleys, their fortunes reliant on his, at least for a time, selling hosiery for a small profit, borrowing and repaying in concert with the ebb and flow of their resources.[20] But, with or without formal trade designation, these women were known to Pope through routine contact at his counter – reputation was their most important credential. Women's occupational status fluctuated with life-cycle changes more dramatically than did men's; thus it is less important to know the individual crafts practised by these women than it is to recognize the functions they fulfilled within this community for their families, their friends and themselves.

The credit needs of people like Audry Burton, or the Southwark car-penter Henry Cole, had long been a reality of urban life, in spite of offi-cial disapproval. Tudor monarchs were unable to constrain credit transactions within prescribed modes, a fact noted in the preamble to a 1571 Act which noted that the earlier legislation 'had not done so much good as was hoped'. In desperation, legislators attempted to enforce common standards among pawnbrokers, such as the keeping of registers, with varying results. The 1603 Act against Brokers focused on their propensity to receive stolen goods.[21] The authors were unhappy at the proliferation of 'pawn-takers' and brokers, for 'within the memory of many yet livinge such kinde of persons tradesmen were verie few and of small number'. They decried the fact that:

> many citizens, freemen of the citie, beinge men of manual occupations and handicraftsmen ... near the citie and suburbs of the same, have lefte and given over, and daylie do leave and give over, their handie and manual occupations, and ... so set up a trade of buyinge and sellinge, and ... takinge to pawne of all kinde of worne apparell.[22]

Many, like Pope, took pledges and lent money without the formal desig-nation of broker or pawnbroker, including one who became prominent as a theatrical promoter.[23] Jeremy Boulton tracked the series of 278 pawns arranged by the south London theatrical entrepreneur Phillip Henslowe during a fourteen-month period in 1594–95, one of many Southwark property owners who offered credit to neighbours, tenants and clients, at a price, lending money as well with interest.[24] Decades later John Pope followed an analogous pattern of trade. Official dismay could not contain the commercial needs of plebeian borrowers or contain the energy of this market sector.

Pope, like Henslowe, offered several sorts of credit. Moneylending comprised just under three-quarters of his transactions, loans that were unsecured and relied most strongly on the reputation of the borrower. In contrast, pawning represented one of the most routine exchanges of everyday finance – in the Pope records pawns comprised approximately a quarter of the surviving transactions. Figure 2.1 summarizes the surviving transactions. Relationships between lender and borrowers varied, and it is impossible to discern all the nuances of these ties; Henslowe, for example, lent to his tenants in Westminster and Southwark buildings, advancing money as well to the perennially needy actors who haunted the south bank. But even his relatively well documented career is opaque on many financial dealings.[25] Fortunately, Pope's records permit a clearer reconstruction of the channels through which credit flowed and of the lives bound together through these exigencies.

Even for an informal moneylender written contracts were normal and accepted by Pope's borrowers without, apparently, any hesitation. Most loans were entered in the ledger according to a standard formula acknowledging indebtedness to John Pope, stipulating the amount and

Figure 2.1   Sex of borrowers from John Pope, south London, 1667–1671

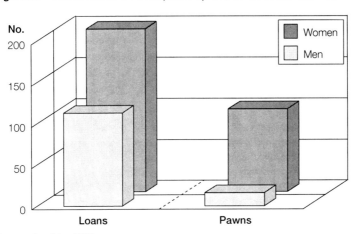

Source: C 108/34, PRO

the repayment schedule, supplemented by information on partners, guarantors or the person for whom the money was borrowed. Signatures or marks appended the contracts; sometimes these were witnessed. Lines scratched in the margin of many of these loan agreements probably recorded payments made – most agreements contained specific repayment schedules of from 6*d* to several shillings per week, the whole to be paid off over ten or twenty weeks. But for frequent borrowers it was common to find notations added to old contracts stating 'more to humphre Croswell 1–10–0' with the date.[26] Several examples of the formulaic entries follow.

4 April 1669

> henry Rose of the parish of St. georges Southwark in Maypole ally taylor do owe & am indebted unto John Pope of the same parish … the sum of three pound good and lawfull muny of England [repaid at 3*s* per week over twenty weeks].

8 June 1671

> Lent then unto Margaret James the wife of Richard James of St. Mary Overies parish in the parke in queen street labourer & Elizabeth Clark of the parish of St georges in long lane washer the sum of 20s. good muny … to be payd unto John Pope … by 12d. p weeke in 20 weekes[27]

Historians have explored the social dynamic of credit relations, plus the family and neighbourhood bonds between lender and borrower in urban as well as rural settings. In Pope's south London neighbourhood clear evidence survives of the co-operation and reciprocity among the borrowers, social dimensions which persisted in tandem with developing capitalism. Muldrew suggests we recognize the moral tenets embedded in many market activities, tenets which functioned in combination with personal ambition, or Smithian self-interest, wherein relations of obligation and dependence, between creditor and debtor, or the interdependent relations of would-be borrower, guarantor and lender, forged commercial bonds tempered by sociability.

> [The] network of credit was so extensive and intertwined that it introduced moral factors which provided strong reasons for stressing co-operation within the marketing structures of the period. Individual profit and security were important, but neither could be achieved without the direct co-operation of one's neighbours which trust entailed. As a result, buying and selling at this time, far from breaking up communities, actually created numerous bonds which held them together.[28]

John Pope stood at the hub of a circle of borrowers whose needs and interests intersected – indeed, his role was replicated in very disparate communities throughout the Mediterranean and New Worlds, with shopkeepers as key intermediaries. The most frequent borrowers, making and selling their wares, relied on him for essential resources: the mop makers Humphrey Croswell and Samuel Fellows, for example, regularly borrowed money. Croswell individually arranged fourteen loans, with the largest in February 1668 for £20, repayable to Pope on demand. The next spring, Croswell made four loan arrangements with Pope for a total of £20 10s, to be repaid over a set period. These were the largest amounts lent to any of Pope's customers and doubtless reflect Croswell's middling station and the measure of trust earned. Demand loans for amounts of about £1 were not uncommon, though demand loans of £20 were rare. There were also interesting distinctions in the gender patterns of borrowing, with proportionally more women securing loans worth less than £2 than men; 86 per cent of women borrowed less than £2, compared with just 73 per cent of men. At the upper end of the scale, over a quarter of male borrowers secured loans valued at from £2 to £20, while less than a sixth of female borrowers arranged transactions at that financial level, added evidence of women's more restricted access to resources[29] (see Figure 2.2).

All lenders had to judge the reliability of potential borrowers. Trust developed incrementally between lender and borrower and frequently

Figure 2.2 Gender pattern of borrowing from John Pope, 1667–1671

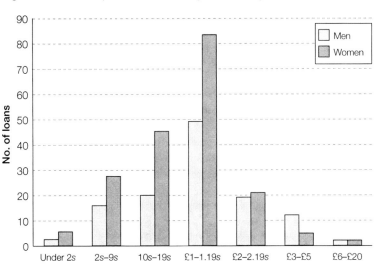

required the intervention of an intermediary known and trusted. For the newcomer this process began with introductions, affirmations and endorsements from the well established, after which the borrower developed new independent ties. Arranging and securing loans was evidently seen as an obligation by the more prominent members of the community, an obligation to their dependants and to their neighbours. Thus Jane Croswell and Humphrey Croswell both organized loans for others, an arrangement that was detailed in the written loan agreements – a loan of £1 was secured by Mr Croswell for Thomas Warde 'yer man', while Jane Croswell arranged for a £2 loan for the maid Elizabeth and another £1 for Elizabeth's mother.[30] Jane Croswell was twice as active organizing loans for others, compared with her husband, and this with less than half his total number of transactions, a significant distinction. Several of this couple's commercial interventions involved people in the same trade, possibly friends. Jane borrowed money for 'Goody Fellows' in May 1669 and in June the same year Humphrey borrowed £1 'for the use of Goodman Samuel Fellows'. Croswell and Fellows were not close neighbours, but perhaps the distance between them was bridged by their shared occupation as mop makers. These transactions suggest a modest patron/client relationship that needed some acknowledgement, for the bonds of friendship, kinship, community and business were inextricable.[31]

Loans typically came with costs attached – Philip Henslowe's interest rates averaged approximately 40 per cent per year on the recurrent small loans against pledges, a rate about double the standard rate at this time. By the late eighteenth century annual interest rates of 20 per cent were legislated for pawns and small loans under £2.[32] Unfortunately, John Pope's charges cannot be determined; no standard interest rates were entered in the ledgers, or supporting evidence from which rates can be discerned. In instances where a series of loans were noted, the total owed and interest on the loan might be rolled in together, possibly evolving into the high rates of interest found among many unregulated pawnbrokers. It is also possible that some borrowers paid no interest at all; physical evidence hints at this possibility. Beside the lending agreements, on a good proportion of the loans were marks denoting the number of shillings repaid. On a number of occasions where 10s or 20s were borrowed there are an equivalent ten or twenty lines penned in the side margin, with the whole crossed out. Pope may have held back part of the loan as interest payment, or introduced other costs with the loan, practices typical among pawnbrokers and moneylenders. But there is no evidence of this. Moreover, if Pope offered selected interest-free loans his behaviour was consistent with that of other communities in this era.[33]

Credit networks and gender

Partnerships between a novice and a borrower with an established reputation, or borrowing through the aegis of a guarantor, permitted an important measure of security to the lender and helped extend credit. Pope's ledgers contain a wealth of evidence of relationships established through the credit process. Figure 2.3 notes the numbers of female and male partnership and guarantor relationships forged between men and women; male borrowers showed an almost equivalent selection of male and female partners. Women, on the other hand, formed a disproportionately large number of alliances with other women, and over 70 per cent of women active in partnerships, or with guarantors, relied on other women to assist them. Garthine Walker noted a similar dynamic among women prosecuted for theft. Her sample from late sixteenth and early seventeenth-century Chester confirmed that the majority of women worked either singly or in confederation with other women. Research from the Netherlands paints a similar picture, and Anne McCants finds that the debts owed by poor widows were disproportionately held by other women. Similarly, my study of eighteenth-century insurance ledgers attests that gender and ethnicity effected partnerships in the

Figure 2.3 Gendered partnerships and guarantor relationships, Southwark, 1667–1671

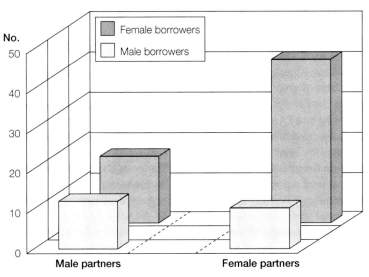

Source: C 108/34, PRO

clothing and pawning trades where women generally collaborated with other women.[34] The female sociability of street corners and kitchens, where common tasks might be shared, information exchanged and friendships forged, doubtless contributed to part of this pattern. But additionally one must recognize the complex commercial and social networks at the periphery of markets, where women were disproportionately represented. These informal bonds signal important facets of the economy and society, the 'material civilization' described by Braudel, however difficult to chart.[35] Reports on poor women eking out a living in present-day developing countries leave no doubt about the importance of women's support networks in similar circumstances at the market edge.[36]

The prevalence of women at the margins of market places is most vividly confirmed in the reams of regulations banning women's trade throughout the medieval and early modern periods. Women were physically confined to the periphery of some medieval markets and their patterns of informal, irregular trade were castigated.[37] In the sprawling, unruly suburbs of London unskilled or disabled men would also find themselves challenged to get by, joining women in the sorts of marginal trades so often the resort of those at pains to survive. William Jordan doubts that in the constrained economic activities so common to poor women there would be much evidence of credit relations. 'If we are to explore credit in female networks we will have to look elsewhere than the black and shadow markets served by forestallers', he opines.[38] The opposite is true. It was precisely within the nexus of street-corner enterprise and the informal, predominantly female trade where women actively secured small loans and short-term credit.

Women-headed families, single women and widows figured as organizers of credit in a wide diversity of circumstances. Why should we be surprised at this finding? The majority of urban women, women of the labouring and lower middling classes, were responsible for making ends meet, for matching household needs with income, stretching finite resources to meet occasionally infinite demands. The mechanisms of make-do formed their apprenticeship. Moreover, the persistent life-cycle occupational patterns for London's labouring women remained in place for centuries.[39] Records from courts of request, dealing with debts under 40s, reveal just such an instance of make-do, where exchanges of credit and services prevailed. The description of events illustrates the common sociable facets of credit through lending, pawning and the sharing of goods, all directed at keeping households afloat. Elizabeth Layton recounted how, in 1797:

When my father was pressed Mrs Russell came to my mother & she would … come & sit with her to be company. – My mother went there day after day with her childn. – We dined & supped there & went on so for 2 months – My mother paid part of the victuals Mrs Russell the rest. – Sometimes Mrs R. sometimes my mother or I fetched the victuals we eat all in common – Mrs R was then in distress. I pledged her things for her & for my mother. – Each borrowed from the other – My mother borrowed once 20s. & repaid it. – When I went for provisions sometimes my mother, sometimes Mrs Russell gave me ye money. – She [Mrs Russel] made no dem[and] – My mother supplied as much money as she … .[40]

Short-term loans, pledged apparel and shared goods can be seen as a gendered social insurance against future want, in an instance when there was no man to make a vital contribution. Untold numbers of women built their commercial niches in this environment, conducted petty trade, accepting their neighbours' pawned petticoat or waistcoat, dealing also in second-hand wares.[41] Neighbourhood women likewise employed their local knowledge to judge the creditworthy, arranging loans, or working as agents for lenders within their communities. The city fathers in late sixteenth-century Leicester made a point of suppressing just this sort of trade, characterizing the women so employed as 'evill persons'. These burgers believed that the women they termed 'Brogers or pledge women' interfered with mercantile conventions, selling old garments, offering credit and accepting goods in pawn. Because the 'pledge women' disrupted Leicester's commercial harmony, the city corporation barred them from any future transactions and appointed in their stead Richard Raynsford and William Shippon, 'and non other' – in this as in some other trades the sexes competed, as well as collaborated.[42] The trade of these townswomen was formally reassigned; however, this can not obscure either their initiative or the significance of their standing as providers of credit.

Phillip Henslowe depended on precisely this sort of female agent to identify and approve potential borrowers. Initially Henslowe's nephew worked in this capacity; but several local women ultimately became the most effective mediators – Goody Watson, Goody Nalle and Anne Nockes.[43] John Pope too relied on key female intermediaries in his affairs. Roberta Jones, a widowed laundress living in Horse Yard, off Kent Street, was the unlikely go-between arranging introductions to Pope, guaranteeing loans for her friends and neighbours. Roberta Jones was exemplary. Her occupation was undistinguished and her widowhood made her vulnerable to the grinding poverty so typical among working widows.

She had to secure a living.[44] Yet in spite of these objective disadvantages, Roberta Jones was a woman of standing in her community. Pope trusted her judgement, and men and women sought her out for assistance in their affairs. Altogether, Jones arranged more loans than any other individual, male or female, in John Pope's books. Her partners and clients came from the surrounding alleys and laneways, including two wool spinners in Long Lane, one glover in Three Tun Alley and another off Kent Street, a silk weaver in Windmill Alley, another laundress in Long Lane and a pin maker in Kent Street. Another widow, Judith Barnet, whose occupation was not specified, called on Jones to arrange a loan, perhaps hoping for a sympathetic hearing. Barnet, along with various other women whose trade and marital status are unknown, brought their cases before Jones, leaving it to her to adjudicate. Roberta Jones exercised her judgement – Pope relied on her discretion. A notation penned after one loan illustrates her standing: Roberta Jones 'douth pase her word to se it payd'.[45] What did Jones gain in return? She may have been paid a finder's fee by Pope, but, if so, no record survives. Borrowers may have given her tokens of some sort: a gift, cash or the promise of service to a woman whose good offices were invaluable. These events likely figured in the complex client/dependant relationships or kin and friendship networks that were so important, a bulwark against anonymous destitution. Throughout, Roberta Jones mediated between her neighbours' needs and those with cash to lend, exemplifying the commercial niche cultivated by numerous women in the as yet unregulated credit environments which flourished in early modern urban environs.

The initiative and enterprise exhibited by Roberta Jones were a commonplace of city life, reflecting one element of the active credit market where women were an integral part (see Figure 2.3). A broom maker, Ellen Gurnet, offers analogous examples. Like Roberta Jones, Gurnet arranged seven loans over a four-month period, and her reputation clearly carried weight with John Pope, for he accepted her personal surety for a £1 loan to Joyce Gaskin, of White Bear Alley, Newington. Beneath the contract was the declaration 'elen gurnet past her word for it'. Other evidence of female enterprise is also preserved in these ledgers. In the incident noted above, aside from the mark of the borrower, two other signatures were in evidence, those of Ellen Gurnet and Mary Shank. Mary Shank was married, one of many married women dealing with Pope. As William Jordan notes for the medieval period: the 'informality [of small-scale lending and borrowing] undermined all legalistic attempts to prevent adult women, married or otherwise, under the judicial "cover" of a male, from making contractual obligations without their husbands' or other appropriate men's consent'.[46] A similar pattern prevailed in the early modern era, whatever the legal constraints of coverture. Married women from labouring and artisan ranks secured loans, borrowed, pledged and formed alliances in credit arrangements, balancing the needs of the household, apportioning resources. The evidence uncovered from the south London community affirms these patterns, with over 84 per cent of pawns and 62 per cent of loans arranged by women.[47]

A mid-eighteenth-century witness before a parliamentary committee sketched the range of pawnbrokers' customers, summarizing the commercial channels through which this credit flowed. However, in this official description the sex of the commonest customers was nowhere mentioned and their number was implicitly disguised:

> the very poor Sort of People, such as Persons who cry Fish, Fruit, or other Wares, about the Street, and other People who may be reckoned in the lowest Class of Life, who not having any personal Credit, are obliged to have Recourse to the Pawnbrokers, and by the Money borrowed from them, are enabled to purchase the several Commodities they deal in; and by the Profits arising from thence, to support themselves and Families … .
>
> Another Class of People to whom the Business was of Service, were the middling Sort of Tradesmen … [who] are under a Necessity to employ a great Number of Journeymen; these People, by the Money borrowed of the Pawnbrokers, are enabled to pay their Journeymen's Wages …
>
> That it was likewise of great Benefit to these Journeymen, who, having nothing but their Wages to depend on, must perish when sick, or out of Employment …
>
> And lastly, To Artificers and Handycraftsmen, who, by the Money borrowed of the Pawnbrokers, were enabled to buy Materials to carry on their Businesses; and which few of them could otherwise do, by reason of their not having any personal Credit … .[48]

This catalogue illuminates facets of manufacture and trade which in many instances were indissolubly meshed with household activities, in the use of space and family labour.[49] Doubtless these patterns persisted through centuries, combining the agency of men and women, but with the particular skills of women adroitly employed in the ordering of plebeian finances.

The model housewife, whether endowed with the resources of farm and dairy, shop and servants, or a single room in lodgings, ideally expended her mental and physical assets to secure the optimum return on the labour and property arising within the family – such was her duty, her responsibility and the source of her authority within her family and community. Jan de Vries emphasized the economic significance of the household as the site of multiple interrelated activities: 'of coresidence and reproduction, of production and labor power, of consumption and distribution among its members, and of transmission across generations'.[50] Plebeian households generated productive ventures, sustained retailing and informal businesses, employing men and women, children and adults, all requiring credit. The central female roles in these undertakings have been too often hidden, due in part to the paucity of records. However, other sources survive in voluminous quantities which speak to women's established roles as borrowers and transformers of goods into cash. Historians of crime have long noted the predominance of women as receivers and pawners of stolen property and the preponderance of articles of clothing and textiles among stolen goods.[51] John Beattie first identified this phenomenon and it has been confirmed in subsequent studies.[52] These gender-determinant criminal activities mirrored equally important legal commerce. Married women were given booty to pawn not just because the penalties might be less for them than for their husbands should they be caught fencing stolen sheets or apparel. Married women pawned linens, breeches and shirts because women traditionally administered these resources, laundering, patching and pawning as needed. Their cultural and practical control of these assets meant they were theirs to control, however acquired – just as male thieves fenced lead, iron bells or shipwrights' tools. Thus the illegal transactions were part of a wider commercial confluence of legal female-dominated traffic which increased in volume over the early modern period, illuminating and confirming the long-established female duties as agents of household credit.

Lending, borrowing and the regulation of credit

Over the course of the eighteenth and nineteenth centuries legal and structural changes altered the organization of small-scale credit, changing as well the context in which women secured loans. The spread of market-directed wage-earning, the shifting patterns of employment and larger units of production gradually modified the nature of the household as work too evolved. Consumption rather than production emerged as one of the household's principal economic functions. De Vries describes the shift within the household from 'capital-forming consumption … towards the consumption of nondurables' as part of what he terms the 'industrious revolution'. With this came 'an augmentation of the decision-making centrality of the wife', women who were employed in greater numbers in the manufacture of new commodities. The proliferation of goods made for the market, the advent of the now well known consumer society in early modern England, brought new choices to households even within the labouring classes.[53] These households were 'the site of new supplies of labor, of new aspirations, and of new forms of behaviour'.[54] Credit was an indispensable element of the changed behaviour arising from this industrious revolution. However, while the organization of household loans was relegated to women, along with many of the chores associated with consumerism, the source and nature of the credit itself underwent significant changes.

Officials had always been concerned about the potential disorder and illegal behaviour centred around pawnshops. Some proposed alternatives, as will be discussed in Chapter 3, but most accepted, however reluctantly, the necessity for pawnbrokers. Similarly, prominent shopkeeping pawnbrokers disliked the competition which arose from informal competitors. Legislators and larger pawnbrokers both subscribed to the principle of regulation, and over the seventeenth and eighteenth centuries Bills were periodically tabled in the House.[55] Although few of these initiatives received parliamentary approval, their appearance on the legislative agenda denoted a continuing preoccupation with both the criminal and the commercial facets of pawnbroking. Proposals directed at restricting the circulation of stolen goods, the rates of interest charged the poor and the profit inherent in this trade ebbed and flowed in legislative circles over the eighteenth century. Ultimately, pawnbrokers won reluctant acceptance, although Parliament insisted that the trade be policed.[56] Punitive measures were proposed by large dealers as a check on informal competitors, their aim being to quash informal lenders through regulation. The scale of the trade of one of the petitioners, Richard Grainger, suggests the size of his business – on Lady Day 1745 he took in 24,328 pledges with an average value of 3s. The contrast between this trade and that of John Pope or Philip Henslowe is marked.[57] Pawnbroking was becoming a more specialized and capital-intensive venture, with women pawnbrokers directing less wealth and numbering fewer among insured pawnbrokers than their male counterparts. In 1757, 1784 and 1800, legislation was enacted dealing with the most troublesome aspects of this trade. Pawnbrokers' obligations were stipulated with regard to the keeping of pledges and records; their responsibilities were clarified on the question of receiving stolen goods; and rates of interest were fixed for loans under £10. Altogether the trade was more closely monitored, but legislative fiats were not invariably translated into community norms.[58]

Independent petty traders persisted on the margins, exercising some of the mercantile functions of their predecessors from past centuries. Evidence of their existence is sparse. However, Catherine Rogers, a labourer's wife living in Deptford, Kent, was demonstrably an unsanctioned pawnbroker. She plied a humble neighbourhood trade and would have remained invisible but for a court case in which she was a witness, in 1756. Catherine Rodgers unwittingly received a gown that was later shown to be stolen. She worked out of a front room in her family home as a pawnbroker and clothes dealer, known to customers and local (official) pawnbrokers.[59] Small dealers like Rodgers continued taking pledges but they competed with ever larger pawnbrokers whose commerce measured up in insured value to some of the largest mercantile enterprises of the day. Twenty years of insurance register entries for pawnbrokers were surveyed for the years 1777–96. Among the insured, 10 per cent more male pawnbrokers held policies for goods valued at £700 to £10,000, compared with female pawnbrokers.[60] These policy holders represent only a fraction of the total number of pawnbrokers, large and small. However, the scale of their trade and the concentration of policies for property valued at £700 to £10,000 hint at the wealth of these practitioners, over 89 per cent of whom were men. These traders benefited individually from the profits which accrued from thousands of small loans in the ports, industrial cities and county towns across the country. Suppressing the informal pledge takers was in their interest; regulation was welcomed and accepted by the new-style lender. How many informal pawnbrokers persisted in their trade? Was women's agency in lending confined, in the main, to small-scale borrowing and household budgeting? Inevitably, as further regulation ensued, irregular lending activities receded further into the shadows. However, all surviving documentation confirms that women comprised the majority of pawnbrokers' customers, a pattern of borrowing most easily accessible to ordinary women.

The trade of chandler Francis Shipley of Whitechapel, east London, confirms this pattern. Shipley, like Pope, was a multi-faceted retailer, selling groceries and chandler's wares, pawning goods and making loans to his East End customers, blending the taking of pledges with his other business dealings. He died, in 1749, with £140 of ready money in hand, including over £13 in copper coins, witness to the many small sums crossing his shop counter. Limitations in the records preclude a complete summary of his trade. Yet it is clear that Shipley conducted a long-running and vigorous traffic as a chandler, as a pawnbroker and as a moneylender. Furthermore, as with other pawnbrokers, the majority of his clients were women. Women brought in nearly 60 per cent of the pawns and owed about 53 per cent of the small loans outstanding after Shipley's death.[61]

The later records of a prominent eighteenth-century York pawnbroker, George Fettes, provide further evidence that corroborates these findings. Fettes's trade began about 1770, and in 1788 he took out an insurance policy which included coverage for £500 worth of pledged goods, with a total value of insured property of £750, placing Fettes within the middle rank of insured.[62] The surviving Fettes pledge book covers the years from 1777 to 1779, and sample periods were assessed from 1777 and 1778.[63] Over four months, all pledges were recorded, along with the name of the borrower, the goods pledged and the amount borrowed. What patterns emerge from the data? In total, 70 per cent of the pawn transactions were undertaken by the women of York and surrounding districts, less than in the Pope ledgers, where 84 per cent of pawning transactions were undertaken by women, but substantial nonetheless (see Figure 2.4). Similarly, the kinds of goods pledged were consistent across the centuries. In the sample of pledges, from 1777 and 1778, women pawned the most valuable housewares and clothing. Laundresses might pledge their irons for short periods, but typically it was the scarlet cloak or check apron that secured a loan; textiles and textile furnishings comprising over 80 per cent of transactions, the materials most directly controlled by women.[64]

As the urban population grew so, too, did the number of pawnbrokers over the late eighteenth and nineteenth centuries. Even a cursory scan of city directories reveals a growing company of pawnbrokers

Figure 2.4 Sex of borrowers from pawnbrokers, 1777–1778 and 1816. Sample size: York 2,194 transactions, Sheffield 800 transactions

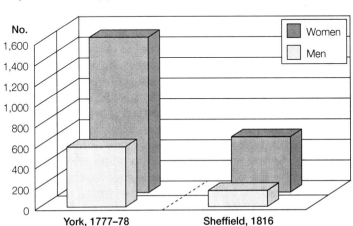

Sources: Acc. 38, York City Archives; J 90/504, PRO

respectable enough to be included with High Street merchants and retailers by directory publishers. The industrial city of Sheffield offers a case in point. The 1787 directory acknowledges only four pawnbrokers within the city precincts; a decade later, seven are listed, while in the 1834 and 1838 directories forty men and women were officially enumerated as serving a growing working-class clientele.[65] Unfortunately, only a scattering of actual pawnbrokers' records survive for this transitional period. Nonetheless, these offer vital comparative evidence of credit patterns during a time of significant economic change. The first of the nineteenth-century examples comes from Sheffield, in 1816. Men and women from the side streets, lanes and alleys of this bustling manufacturing town came to this pawnshop with goods in hand and here, too, women predominated as borrowers, with 73 per cent of the total 800 transactions initiated by members of this sex (see Figure 2.4). The categories of goods offered as pledges were also generally consistent with those presented in York and, earlier, in south London. There were variations, however; pledges of knives, forks and iron hint at the metalwares made in that district, mirroring the mutable material culture of time and place.[66] The variation in pawned goods also carried important gender meanings with implications for the organization of domestic resources. For, just as women dominated in the ordering of most housewares, with the rise of new consumer goods, new gender patterns of pawning appeared.

An increased preoccupation with time was emblematic of this era, and timepieces were prized by more numerate citizens. The fascination with watches and clocks transcended social rank as cheaper chronometers were sold new and second-hand. In this case, time was money, for watches held their value for both their decorative and functional qualities and their symbolic associations with the rational, mechanistic forces powering the new economy. Men were the principal owners and pawners of watches; likewise these timepieces were among the most important and expensive of the new consumer wares. More costly than most other personal accoutrements, they held their worth under the wear and tear under which clothing deteriorated so readily,[67] exceeding in value all the sheets, petticoats, pots and pans heretofore the principal investments of many labouring families. In the late 1770s, Fettes's York customers brought a scattering of new consumer commodities to pledge: silver spoons and buckles, thimbles and fancy buttons. Some customers also brought in watches, which made up approximately 3 per cent of all transactions; of these only one woman pledged a watch, compared with forty-nine men. However, the sums received for the watches are striking, representing among the highest returns for goods pawned, from a low of 6s to several pounds per watch.[68] The rising demand for timepieces, even among artisans and flourishing labourers, points to new gendered patterns of consumption within households and the competition for resources among household members.[69] This, in turn, affected patterns of credit. Wherever watches were commonly pawned, and wherever pawnbrokers specialized in watches, plate and jewellery, I found a sharp drop in the participation rate of women. Fifty years later, in the 1830s, watches were even more unexceptional. Pawnbrokers' ledgers, from the 1830s, are suggestive of the ties between new gender consumer patterns and the corresponding patterns of pawnbroker credit. One volume reflecting an apparent specialization in jewellery – watches, rings, brooches and the like are very numerous – had a ratio of three male customers to every female customer. In general east London trade showed a similar bond between male consumerism and watch ownership. Two databases were created from these records. The first covered two years of pledges from 1832 and 1833, with over 800 transactions sampled; the second reflects a week's entries in the autumn of 1830 with approximately eighty transactions. Watches were not very much in evidence in the first and largest sample of pledges but, where watches and their accoutrements crossed this pawnbroker's counter, 75 per cent of the transactions were handled by men. Similarly, in the smaller day-by-day sample, of the twenty-one watches pawned, nineteen were brought to the shop by men.[70] These findings are not comprehensive but they are suggestive. Invariably, the gender pattern of consumption, along with the growing plethora of consumer goods, brought unexpected repercussions to women's role as the principal organizer of small-scale credit within the family. And this factor, along with the changing institutional face of lending, reshaped gender and class norms in the organization of credit.

Women and loan societies

In the early nineteenth century, dynamic economic changes, as well as the changing political economy, spurred social and political critiques. There was particular concern about the budgeting practices of the working class, concern was articulated by liberal and utilitarian theorists which encouraged renewed support for rational and prudent domestic practices. Reliance on the poor rate was denounced by clerical and secular authors as a moral failing and the cause of a breakdown in provident behaviour; pawnbrokers, as suppliers of credit, were denounced as agents of profligacy and leeches on the poor.[71] What alternative were open to the working classes to obtain credit? For the thrifty artisan, friendly societies were a possible source of funds and had long proved their value to male and female members, as well as social theorists, not least because of the self-discipline demanded of members in well run organizations.[72] Self-help was the pervasive mantra to which small traders and even some labourers subscribed. A tract by the 'Provident Brotherhood', founded in 1789, recounted that 'many of the lower class of men joined themselves in different societies, and by subscribing such small sums as they could afford weekly or monthly, alleviated the distress of each other'.[73] Savings banks were another of the initiatives which arose at this time and will be addressed later in this book. Rotating savings and credit associations, which lent money in rotation to members who subscribed, undoubtedly flourished through friendly societies or other trade or social organizations. Called menage in Scotland, one such example from north-eastern England stipulated that officers could 'lend upon interest, such sums of money, as may be over the six weeks' payments, to any person of unquestionable stability, of whose character and circumstances the meeting are satisfied, upon security, if thought necessary'.[74] Few records survive from such initiatives, but, even where they did operate, there were limitations on the clientele served, much as earlier guild and city corporation lending was limited to members only, and this a largely male constituency. But, along with these incidental enterprises and the spread of savings banks, other experiments were under way.

Among liberal theorists and do-gooders, there was a continuing interest in alternative credit facilities for labouring, trading and manufacturing people reliant on small loans. The economic crisis which ensued after 1815 sparked the savings bank movement, as well as one of the earliest of the new generation of loan societies. Launched by a Church of England cleric, it boasted royal and noble patrons with functionaries from less exalted ranks, including genteel activists, ladies and gentlemen. They aimed to collect charitable donations, lending the money to those needy London folk who could secure a written recommendation from one of the nearly 100 subscribers. Pawns were not an option; rather, the organizers relied on the power of reputation. Resources were not directed at the poorest of the poor, but at those in need of temporary credit which could be profitably employed. 'Be it remembered, that this is a LOAN Society; not a society for giving alms',[75] reminded the author of the annual report. In their first year they disbursed about ninety loans, with over 150 given out in the second, in amounts from 5s upwards. There is no record of the sex of the recipients. However, in case studies outlined in one annual report, examples of female borrowers comprised two of the five cases detailed. Within a short time, loan societies proliferated throughout the country,[76] organized by clerics and social activists determined to promote industry and self-reliance through the careful allocation of low-interest loans.[77] In August 1835, after several decades of experimentation, an Act was passed laying out the rules and conditions for enterprises of this sort.[78] A supporter summarized the ideals of this fiscal social movement:

> To carry out the intention of the legislature in sanctioning 'loan societies' they should be conducted by the more discreet or respectable inhabitants in their respective districts. No trouble should be spared in acquiring a knowledge of the character and circumstances of every applicant. Liberality, tempered with prudence, should be their motto; and in certain cases of great worth suffering great want, they should even risk a portion of their GAIN to succour the distressed. In this way loan societies would soon become the greatest mitigators of popular discontent. They would prove to the poor man that those above him in class were mindful of his condition, and disposed to join with him in the bonds of 'friendliness and mutual help'.[79]

A scattering of printed rules and loan society forms hint at the many hundreds which sprang up around the country: some charitable, others strictly for profit (see Plates 2.2 and 2.3). Unfortunately, few operational records survive; however, where documentation is available, a very different set of gender norms appear from those found in the pawning process.[80] The first of these is the Porto Bello Loan Society, documenting both continuity and change in the patterns of borrowing. Between 1841 and 1857 the Porto Bello Loan Society lent money along much the same lines as did John Pope centuries before. A majority of borrowers were small traders of various sorts, based in the central and east London districts of Bethnal Green, Spitalfields, Whitechapel, Finsbury and Mile End, and their loans required the guarantee of another householder. Most of the loans were for relatively small sums: approximately 70 per cent of loans were for sums under £10, another 17 per cent borrowed from £10 10s to £19, and the remaining loans were for singularly large amounts.[81] Most loans were for the sort essential for the workaday baker, doll maker, sawyer, blacksmith, shoe maker, compositor, cabinetmaker or dairyman. It is no surprise to find that women borrowed smaller sums overall than did men. It is striking, however, to see the precipitous drop in the participation rate of women as borrowers and guarantors. Women still took part in both these functions, but at a greatly diminished level, holding fewer than 5 per cent of the loans sampled from the Porto Bello Loan Society, in dramatic contrast with women's traditionally high participation rates as pawners, where very different sorts of guarantees were required and different gender norms prevailed.

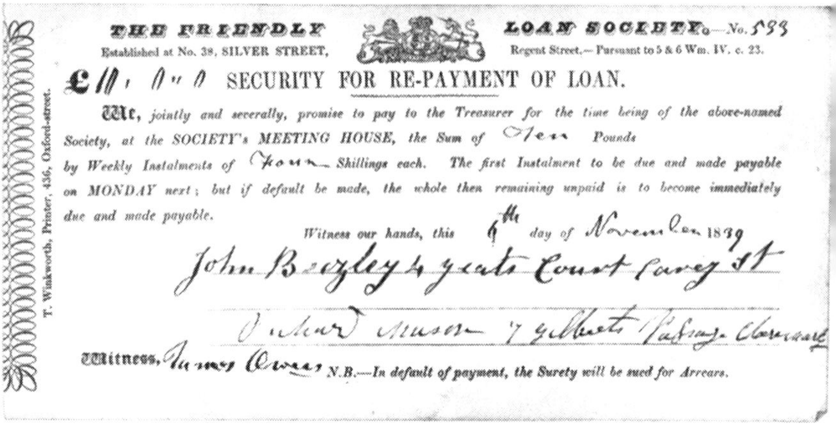

Plate 2.2   Loan form, Friendly Loan Society (London), 1839

Plate 2.3   Loan form, Independent Loan Society (London), 1839

With such a small amount of surviving documentation, I cannot claim definitively that all these organizations followed a similar tack. Aidan Hollis's research on the Irish Loan Fund shows that 'the percentage of women borrowers is roughly proportional to the ratio of single women to all men'. That is, approximately 25 per cent of the loans from the Irish Loan Fund were secured by single or widowed women and 75 per cent by men in pre-famine Ireland.[82] Only one of the surviving English loan societies approximates this gender pattern, at least for a time. Based in rural Hertfordshire, the loan society was initiated by the Rev. Edward Benbow and local gentry in December 1835. By the end of December, as the new year dawned, the Aldenham Loan Society was ready to offer its first small loans to local inhabitants.[83] In the first five years of operation, the pattern of lending closely approaches that found in Ireland, with about 22 per cent of loans secured by women and about 78 per cent by men. Little occupational information is provided about the women borrowers, except their marital status; male borrowers, on the other hand, were predominantly labourers, including as well typical village trades such as publican, postman, shoemaker, baker, wheelwright and butcher. In the early months of operation society managers did not hesitate to allow women well known in the community to organize their husband's borrowing. In fact, on several occasions wives attended the weekly office hours of the loan society and took a hand in arranging their husband's loans, following long established patterns of domestic management. But independent women borrowers were few in number and generally more anonymous. Only one woman's occupation was noted, a publican, and she was also married. The uses for the money were rarely inscribed: one widow wanted the loan to buy a pig, another wanted it to pay her rent, and both received their loans. But, in direct contrast to the patterns evident in previous centuries, men acted as guarantors for all the women for whom guarantors were listed, while only six female guarantors secured male borrowers. At the same time, the proportion of female borrowers fell with each passing year. Those women who continued to borrow were repeat customers and, by the close of 1846, when the full eleven years of business are considered, women comprised less than 14 per cent of all those receiving loans (see Figure 2.5).

The Cheltenham Loan Society opened in the 1830s, joining at least one other society formed in this West of England county. Its purpose was stipulated at the first meeting: 'to raise the character of the poorer classes by assisting them in every endeavour to support themselves and improve their condition'. The organizers, local clergy and members of the gentry, proposed that they lend from £1 to £10, from capital raised by donations, to borrowers who produced 'solvent' citizens to guarantee these loans. Recipients of poor relief were not eligible.[84] The Cheltenham initiative was launched in 1834, over a year before the one opened in Nailsworth, Gloucestershire; the former left quantifiable records for some of its history, while the latter did not. However, the Nailsworth society boasted a more prestigious intellectual backer in the chair for the first evening's meeting, David Ricardo, who later acted as a trustee.[85] His support notwithstanding, the Cheltenham society survived into the twentieth century, while the

Figure 2.5   Sex of loan society borrowers, 1836–1857

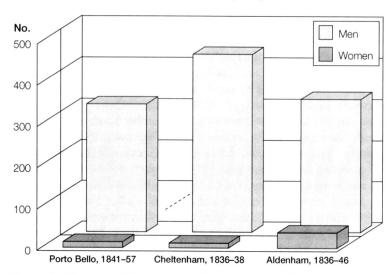

Sources: J 90/1007–09, PRO; D 2365/2/1, Gloucester Record Office; D/P3/29/14, Hertfordshire Record Office

Nailsworth initiative lasted about a decade. But both were fixed in their determination to offer the industrious cheaper credit than that supplied by the pawnbrokers in the towns and cities of Gloucestershire.[86] At the end of 1835, the officers announced they had lent the capital four times over, in small short-term loans, quickly repaid – loans were granted to 277 people. When these individuals were considered along with their family members, Cheltenham's loan managers proudly claimed, 1,257 people were affected by this initiative. News spread and in the winter and spring of 1836–37 the demands of would-be borrowers exceeded the capital available, resulting in reductions of loans, by half or more, in order to spread the money more widely.[87] The lenders were well aware of the boon they provided, since 'many of them who have received Loans have acknowledged in the warmest manner the essential service rendered to themselves and expressed a sense of the very great importance of such an auxiliary to industry.'[88]

The Cheltenham records suggest the managers were also happy to limit their clientele to men. This was an unstated preference. I found no discussion of the sex of borrowers or the marital status of potential female borrowers in either set of minutes. None was needed, apparently. Over the three extant years of the ledger, women comprised less than 3 per cent of all borrowers from the Cheltenham Loan Society, with two women making repeated loans three and four times.[89] Figure 2.5 illustrates the levels of male and female participation in the three loan societies with quantifiable records. It is difficult to argue that this level of female participation reflected women's need for credit, whether in London, Gloucestershire or Hertfordshire, since women continued to be active in various medium-sized and small businesses throughout this period and persisted in less formal hawking trades as they had for centuries.[90] At one loan society the managers insisted that women and single men provide two guarantors for each loan. In another, the necessary guarantor for a loan was to be a respectable home owner, the intimation being, a respectable male home owner. In a third instance, the form to be filled in by the sureties was printed with heading 'Mr' only.[91] In contrast to pawnbrokers, lending society managers apparently envisaged a male clientele, with men acting also as guarantors, as another manifestation of the respectable male breadwinner. In this climate women's visibility in credit markets diminished, redefining expectations and opportunities.

I cannot tell whether the surviving records from England's loan societies reflect the full picture of small-scale borrowing opportunities in all regions where these societies took root. *The Times* reported that, in 1854, over 160,000 applications were made for loans from all loan societies in England and Wales, with a total of £312,299 lent to borrowers, a comparatively modest whole, considering the millions of loans arranged through pawnbrokers annually.[92] Likewise, I cannot determine the gender proportion of loans. But surviving documentation suggests a significant gender shift among loan society borrowers when compared with pawnbrokers' customers and a shift in perspective among new institutional managers which assumed their clients would be male, limiting by implication working and trading women's alternative sources of credit both for their individual commercial concerns as well as family needs. At least one author was unsparing in his critique of the nineteenth-century lending institutional structures which channelled credit 'to only one half of the nation, the rich'. At the end of the century, loans at a 'moderate rate of interest' were still almost inaccessible to the poor, male and female; Henry Wolff believed the solution was to restructure the system of credit banks along the lines of 'people's banks', or *caisses populaire*. Wolff recognized the entrepreneurial leanings among the poor and the limited options which quashed these aspirations.

> There can be no question that the working-classes, like the employing, need credit. Their whole condition of life, their daily wants proclaim it. Loan Societies, Self-Help Societies, Friendly Societies with lending powers already actually provide for it on a very small scale, in a very

temporary, make shift, and inadequate way – just enough to indicate incontestably the existence of a want ... For the mass of the working population the pawn-shop and the petty usurer's office still constitutes the only available Credit Banks – necessary, in the opinion recently expressed by a County Court Judge, under present conditions even beneficial, but cruelly unfair, and economically unsound and ruinous.[93]

In Wolff's vision of a more democratic credit he acknowledged the wasted energies of women, including 'those poor East End working-women, who, as one of their leaders told me only the other day, are too destitute even to practise co-operative supply'. He had no doubt that the full benefits of credit had yet to reach all levels of society, particularly as the formal credit institutions relied less on reputation than monetized collateral and the poor 'have no security to offer, such as a bank would accept'.[94]

The double burden of class and gender fell most heavily on poor and working women. Borrowing opportunities for most women – through loan societies, for example – were doubtless skewed by management policies set by middle-class men imbued with hardening Victorian ideals concerning women's appropriate offices, demanding guarantees difficult or impossible for poor women to secure. The industrious women of Cheltenham and the neighbouring villages of Walkley Wood, Horseley, Nailsworth, Barton End and Forest Green faced a different response to their credit needs than did their male brethren. There is no record of credit specifically denied to women applicants as a consequence of their sex; but evidence points instead to an absence of female borrowers where in different circumstances they were so plentiful. Their absence speaks as powerfully as would minuted decisions to exclude them.

Conclusion

Throughout the nineteenth century, pawnbrokers continued to be essential conduits of credit to the working poor of cities and towns. Alternatives were more easily available to middle-class property holders; moreover, if necessity drove them to the pawnshop, their business was shrouded with the privacy they required, dispensed by high-class practitioners of the trade. The thousands of working women and men who visited pawnshops faced a very public scrutiny, in a very public exercise. A representative of London pawnbrokers estimated that, in 1866, over 28 million pledges were received by the 420 designated metropolitan dealers annually, a dependence not unique in Britain.[95] The unreliable or desperately poor likewise turned to the illegal, informal pawnbrokers who persisted in working-class districts through the nineteenth century.[96]

As anti-pawning crusaders circulated in greater numbers through working-class communities, some of these reformers questioned the honesty and economy of resorting to pawnbrokers. In a climate notable for its emphasis on working-class self-help, temperance and thrift, the credit available through the pawnshop door seemed, to middle-class observers, an easy path from temptation to folly. Reformers argued that foolhardy and incautious spending of borrowed money made a moment's indulgence the beginning of long-term penance.[97] Henry Wolff characterized credit as having two forms: the one 'demoralizing, the other educating; one dangerous … the other largely creative and purely beneficial'. Yet, as he noted, 'for the larger portion by far of our population … banking credit does not exist'.[98]

The social politics of pawning was very different by the mid-nineteenth century than in centuries past – pawning was becoming socially marginalized, its social practice largely bound up with classes whose condition often appalled and disgusted middle-class observers. Melanie Tebbutt describes the tensions surrounding the trade and its customers, the public relations campaign by the pawnbrokers and the grudging acceptance of pledging as a necessary evil by some commentators.[99] Pawning was also popularly trivialized in songs, stories and caricatures aimed at middle-class readers, in sharp contrast to the benevolent aura which surrounded other plebeian fiscal institutions, like savings banks. Authors entertained respectable audiences with tales from pawnbrokers' lairs and, viewed from afar, readers could marvel at the poor's intemperate practices. The alien settings, redolent with emotional narratives of the needy, appealed to the imagination of more comfortable readers who could shudder with a frisson of disgust as they contemplated the routine public scrutiny of personal apparel precious in sentiment, weighed and assessed for market value, in the sordid arena of the pawnbroker's shop. Indeed, the pawnshop was, as one instructive writer noted to his readers, an 'excellent … opportunity of learning the wants, the distresses, the sorrows, and the errors of the poor'.[100] The eliding of private and commercial sentiments was anathema to Victorian sensibilities. That another sector of the population accepted this as necessary bemused and intrigued the more fortunate readers.

Working people who had not yet climbed the rungs to respectability, or those struck down by injury, illness or unemployment, along with the significant number of the perpetual poor, pawned out of necessity, to meet the needs of domestic budgets, of small trades, or both. Moreover, if the routine of petty borrowing was now largely restricted to the working poor, it was the women of this class who organized most of the credit and spending. In many communities working-class women circulated to and from the pawnshop in undiminished numbers. These wives and mothers recognized that it was up to them to contrive. A chronicler of these exchanges described 'a continual fire of chaff and raillery' between the female customers and male pawnbrokers as each attempted to best the other,[101] the women's success winning whatever relative comfort the family enjoyed. As Ellen Ross asserts, controlling the mechanisms of credit afforded working-class women a source of power within the household.[102] But it was a conditional power, the context of which had shifted and narrowed since the seventeenth century, although survival in itself was a not inconsiderable accomplishment in some circumstances. One writer on the topic opined that 'Certainly the women pawn the most; but where large sums are required, men generally transact the business – but I should say they number as seven of the former to one of the latter.'[103] Whether man or woman, husband or wife, access to some form of credit provided an important flexibility for the working poor, permitting a more dynamic economic environment than would otherwise have been the case.

The formalization of lending had many implications for households, individually and collectively. Throughout the long rise of industrial capitalism, productive initiatives requiring loans were routinely arranged by women from humble households. Thereafter, as the economy and society evolved, evidence from generations of women's enterprise was obscured over time. In part, this may have come about because of the kinds of initiatives they took, many of which were temporal, transient and left little formal written evidence. Similarly, the informal plebeian partnerships forged between female and male friends or relatives came to official notice only when these contravened some injunction, when formal records were created. Within their various communities, these colloquial initiatives were well known and accepted for generations; but the informal gendered forms linking the economic and social, the domestic and the commercial, were often antithetical to conventional enterprises, more untidy, at odds with the rigid conceptualizations of later theorists. Then, within generations, the history of these age-old enterprises was first derided and then forgotten, the collective agency of generations overlooked. Thereafter, as the criteria for credit changed, so too did the concepts of womanly norms and formal credit access. Nevertheless, for centuries, the reputation for thrift and prudence which accrued to a virtuous housewife included her capacity to employ credit, whether or not such skills were acknowledged in prescriptive literature. Recognizing these economic and structural parameters offers new perspectives on the homely economy. Equally important were the generations of informal and formal pawnbrokers whose resources were employed in a panoply of ventures. In combination, this kitchen and community commerce cemented the foundations for more prominent economic structures, adding an important element to the market and generations of households. In the transformations during the rise of industrial capitalism, too little attention has been paid to the collective fiscal roles where women were so prominent and too many aspects of material life were too readily neglected. Recovering this history reveals the greater complexities of an industrializing society and enables a more complete understanding of the tangled and irregular transitions to modernity.

Notes

1 The history of national debt, credit for commerce and loans for industry defined the early histories of credit, explored with skill and ingenuity by generations of historians, including: J. H. Clapham, *The Bank of England: A History*, 2 vols (Cambridge, 1944); L. S. Pressnell, 'Public monies and the development of English banking', *Economic History Review*, 2nd series 5:3 (1953), and *Country Banking in the Industrial Revolution* (Oxford, 1956); D. M. Joslin, 'London private bankers, 1720–1785', *Economic History Review*, 2nd series 7:2 (1954); P. G. M. Dickson, *The Financial Revolution in England* (London, 1967); B. L. Anderson, 'Money and the structure of credit in the eighteenth century', *Business History* 12 (1970); François Crouzet (ed.), *Capital Formation in the Industrial Revolution* (London, 1972); Peter Mathias, 'Capital, credit and enterprise in the industrial revolution' in *The Transformation of England* (London, 1979) and *The First Industrial Nation* (2nd edn London, 1983); Jacob M. Price, *Capital and Credit in British Overseas Trade* (Cambridge MA, 1980); John Brewer, *The Sinews of Power: War, Money and the English State* (London, 1989); Julian Hoppit, 'The use and abuse of credit in eighteenth-century England' in N. McKendrick and R. B. Outhwaite (eds), *Business Life and Public Policy: Essays in Honour of D. C. Coleman* (Cambridge, 1986), *Risk and Failure in English Business* (Cambridge, 1987) and 'Attitudes to credit in Britain, 1680–1790', *Historical Journal* 33:2 (1990).

2 For example, Amy Louise Erickson, *Women and Property in Early Modern England* (London, 1993); Maxine Berg, 'Women's property and the industrial revolution', *Journal of Interdisciplinary History* 34:2 (1993); Christine Wiskin, 'Reputation, Prudence and Credit: the Businesswomen of Eighteenth-Century England', unpublished paper, twelfth International Economic History Congress, Madrid, 1998; Amy Froid, 'Surplus women with surplus money: the role of single women as creditors in early modern England', and Barbara Todd, 'London women's investments in the Age of the Financial Revolution', unpublished papers presented at the North American Conference of British Studies, Boston MA, 1999; Margaret Hunt, 'Women, credit and the seafaring community in early eighteenth-century London' in Kathleen Wilson (ed.), *A New Imperial History: Culture, Identity and Modernity in Britain and the Empire, 1660–1840* (Cambridge, 2004); Anne McCants, 'Petty debts and family networks: the credit market of widows and wives in eighteenth-century Amsterdam' in B. Lemire, R.

Pearson and G. Campbell (eds), *Women and Credit: Researching the Past, Refiguring the Future* (Oxford, 2002), and most recently Margot Finn, 'Men's things: masculine possession in the consumer revolution', *Social History* 25:2 (2000), and *The Character of Credit: Personal Debt in English Culture, 1740–1914* (Cambridge, 2003).

3 Maxine Berg explores gender politics in the evolution of twentieth-century economic history in 'The first women economic historians', *Economic History Review*, 2nd series 45 (1992), and *A Woman in History: Eileen Power, 1889–1940* (Cambridge, 1996). See also Natalie Zemon Davis, 'History's two bodies', *American Historical Review*, 93 (1988), and 'Women and the world of the *Annales*', *History Workshop* 33 (1992).

4 Craig Muldrew offers an important corrective for the study of credit in early modern England; see *Economy of Obligation: The Culture of Credit and Social Relations in Early Modern England* (New York, 1988), and '"Hard food for Midas": cash and its social value in early modern England', *Past and Present* 170 (2001). See also H. van Wijngaarden, 'Credit as a way to make ends meet: the use of credit by poor women in Zwolle, 1650–1700', and M. Bogucka, 'Women and Credit Operations in Polish Towns in the Early Modern Period', unpublished papers presented at the twelfth International Economic History Congress, Madrid, 1998.

5 For alternative credit practices remote from the needs of large commercial and government enterprises see George Hilton, *The Truck System, including a History of the British Truck Acts, 1465–1960* (Cambridge, 1960), pp. 20–3, 49; B. A. Holderness, 'Credit in English rural society before the nineteenth century', *Agricultural History Review* 24 (1984), and 'Widows in pre-industrial society: an essay upon their economic functions' in R. M. Smith (ed.), *Land, Kinship and Life Cycle* (Cambridge, 1976); W. C. Jordan, *Women and Credit in Pre-industrial and Developing Societies* (Philadelphia, 1993); M. McIntosh, 'Moneylending on the periphery of London, 1300–1600', *Albion* 20:4 (1988); Craig Muldrew, 'Interpreting the market: the ethics of credit and community relations in early modern England', *Social History* 18:2 (1993); Melanie Tebbutt, *Making Ends Meet: Pawnbroking and Working-Class Credit* (London, 1983); Richard Tittler, 'Moneylending in the West Midlands: the activities of Joyce Jefferies, 1638–1649', *Historical Journal* 67 (1994); Barbara Todd, 'Freebench and free enterprise: widows and their property in two Berkshire villages' in J. Chartres and D. Hey (eds), *English Rural Society* (Cambridge, 1990), and Finn, *The Character of Credit*.

6 Bridget Hill, *Women, Work and Sexual Politics in Eighteenth-Century England* (London, 1989), pp. 44–6; Olwen Hufton, 'Women, work and family' in Natalie Zemon Davis and Arlette Farge (eds), *A History of Women: Renaissance and Enlightenment Paradoxes* (Cambridge, 1993), pp. 15–17.

7 Muldrew, *Economy of Obligation*, p. 150. For a discussion of women's strategies to maintain and define reputation see Laura Gowing, *Domestic Dangers: Women, Words, and Sex in Early Modern London* (Oxford, 1996).

8 For example, Jayshree Vyas, the manager of a Self-employed Women's Association bank in Ahmedabad, India, notes that 'Like savings, "consumption" loans are also badly needed by poor women. SEWA Bank has never distinguished between consumption loan or productive loan. Actually, consumption loans lead to work security, in the case of the poor and the poorest, in particular. Like savings, they provide security by reducing vulnerability and contributing to their income. Living at such a precarious level, the poor are constantly vulnerable to a multiplicity of disasters … . Consumption loans can assist the poor in coping with these needs without their

having to reduce what few assets they have to raise cash, or risking the traditional moneylenders' crippling rates of interest.' Vyas, 'Banking with poor self-employed women' in Lemire *et al.*, *Women and Credit*, pp. 153–4. Ellen Ross makes a similar observation in her study of poor women's fiscal practices in late nineteenth and early twentieth-century London. 'Survival networks: women's neighbourhood sharing in London before World War I', *History Workshop Journal* 15 (1983).

9 Finn, *The Character of Credit*, p. 7.

10 Beverly Lemire, 'Consumerism in preindustrial and early industrial England: the trade in second-hand clothes', *Journal of British Studies* 27:1 (1988), and 'Peddling fashion: salesmen, pawnbrokers, taylors, thieves and the second-hand clothes trade in England', *Textile History* 22:1 (1991). This pattern of exchanging old clothes for new goods and of using clothing as a type of cash equivalent was practised widely in commercially dynamic societies. For the history of the second-hand clothes trade in Africa see Karen Tranberg Hansen, *Salaula: The World of Second-hand Clothing and Zambia* (Chicago, 2000).

11 The cost was determined not only by the interest charged but also by the number of times goods were pawned over a year. Paul Johnson notes that, once interest rates were regulated by law, an item left in pawn for a year and then redeemed 'would have a nominal interest rate of 20 per cent. A loan of 2s 6d on a good pawned and redeemed week by week throughout the year would cost … 260 per cent p.a.' Paul Johnson, *Saving and Spending: The Working-Class Economy in Britain, 1870–1939* (Oxford, 1985), p. 166.

12 Merry E. Wiesner, 'Women's work in the changing city economy, 1500–1650' in Marilyn J. Boxer and Jean H. Quartaert (eds), *Connecting Spheres: Women in the Western World, 1500 to the Present* (New York, 1987); Jordan, *Women and Credit*.

13 Jeremy Boulton, *Neighbourhood and Society: A London Suburb in the Seventeenth Century* (Cambridge, 1987), pp. 21–3, 62–92.

14 Boulton, *Neighbourhood and Society*, pp. 3, 9–11, 64–7, 220–1.

15 Ms 15857/1, Ms 15836/5, Guildhall Library, London.

16 The origins of early consumerism are elegantly described in Joan Thirsk, *Economic Policy and Projects: The Development of a Consumer Society in Early Modern England* (Oxford, 1978), especially chapter 5.

17 C 108/34, Public Record Office, London (hereafter PRO).

18 The physical organization of the volumes suggests that this was a separate section of his business affairs, clearly differentiated from his trade in hosiery and other goods. However, on a number of occasions, Pope takes goods in pawn to secure purchases or debts arising from his trade as a haberdasher.

19 See Boulton, *Neighbourhood and Society*, pp. 65–77, for a description of the trades of St Saviour's; for London trades see Peter Earle, *The Making of the English Middle Class: Business, Society and Family Life in London, 1660–1730* (London, 1989), and 'The female labour market in London in the late seventeenth and early eighteenth centuries', *Economic History Review*, 2nd series 42:3 (1989); W. Page (ed.), *Victoria County History, Sussex* II (London, 1907), p. 238. The current work of the Grameen Bank in Bangladesh, Shorebank Corporation in the United States and the Calmeadow Foundation in North and Central America illustrates the possibilities for economic development which come with micro-credit lending programmes. These organizations recognized the centrality of small-scale credit, providing access to small loans at

commercial interest, such as were available in England during the early modern period only from Pope and others of his ilk.

20 Margaret Spufford, *The Great Reclothing of Rural England* (London,1984), pp. 14–17.

21 A. Hardaker, *A Brief History of Pawnbroking* (London, 1892), p. 16; Tebbutt, *Making Ends Meet*, p. 70.

22 W. A. H. Hows, *A History of Pawnbroking, Past and Present* (London, 1847), pp. 37–8.

23 Jordan, *Women and Credit*, pp. 18–20, 32–6; Natasha Korda, 'Household property/stage property: Henslowe as pawnbroker', *Theatre Journal* 48 (1996).

24 Boulton, *Neighbourhood and Society*, pp. 88–9; Korda, 'Henslowe', p. 188.

25 Korda, 'Henslowe', pp. 192–5.

26 C 108/34, PRO.

27 C 108/34, PRO.

28 Muldrew, 'Interpreting the market', p. 169. Both Amanda Vickery and Margo Finn have traced the very long-lived tradition of sociability and commerce that continued through the eighteenth century. Amanda Vickery, *A Gentleman's Daughter: Women's Lives in Georgian England* (London, 1998), pp. 208; Finn, 'Men's things', pp. 143–7. Very similar findings are noted in North American communities, where shopkeepers played sometimes critical roles in sustaining social and economic cohesion; they also recorded some of the critical informal economic contributions of family members. See, for example, Laurel Thatcher Ulrich, 'Martha Ballard and her girls: women's work in eighteenth-century Maine' in Stephen Innes (ed.), *Work and Labor in early America* (Chapel Hill NC, 1988), pp. 83–6; Elizabeth Mancke, 'At the counter of the general store: women and the economy in eighteenth-century Horton, Nova Scotia' in Margaret Conrad (ed.), *Intimate Relations: Family and Community in Planter Nova Scotia, 1759–1800* (Fredericton NB, 1995), pp. 167–81; and Andrea Lluch, 'Financing the Agrarian Expansion: Stores as a Source of Credit, Argentina, 1900–1930', unpublished paper presented at session 71, 'Financing the everyday', thirteenth International Economic History Association Congress, Buenos Aires, 2002.

29 This finding is typical of studies into the resources available to women. See, for example, Béatrice Craig, 'Women and credit in nineteenth-century northern France' in Lemire *et al.*, *Women and Credit*, and Beverly Lemire, *Dress, Culture and Commerce: The English Clothing Trade before the Factory* (Basingstoke,1997), especially chapter 4.

30 On at least one occasion a loan of 30s was collected 'by the hands of his mayd Elizabeth'. She was obviously a trusted household member. Laurence Fontaine discusses the many social factors surrounding credit in 'Antonio and Shylock: credit and trust in France, c. 1680–1780', *Economic History Review*, 2nd series 54:1 (2001).

31 Tittler, 'Moneylending in the West Midlands', pp. 256–60.

32 Korda, 'Henslowe', p. 192. The rates of interest charged by pawnbrokers preoccupied legislators over the centuries. Between 1800 and 1872 pawnbrokers were restricted to an official rate of 20 per cent interest per annum; however, Melanie Tebbutt shows that interest rates for small repeated loans on pledges were essentially unlimited.

33 N. Jones, *God and the Moneylenders: Usury and Law in Early Modern England* (Oxford, 1989), pp. 70–1; Holderness, 'Widows in pre-industrial society', pp. 436–42; Tebbutt, *Making Ends Meet*, pp. 8–9, 74–5.

34 Garthine Walker, 'Women, theft and the world of stolen goods', in Jenny Kermode and Garthine Walker (eds), *Women, Crime and the Courts in Early Modern England*

(London, 1994), pp. 84–5; McCants, 'Petty debts and family networks'; Lemire, *Dress, Culture and Commerce*, pp. 86–7.

35 A misogynistic tract, from the mid-eighteenth century, attacked what it described as 'Women's Clubs in and about the City and Suburbs of London'. While it gave no credible information about any actual organizations, it is clear from its targets that there were informal occupational collectives of women in London and its suburbs. Some of those identified include 'Fish Womens Club by Cow-Cross', 'Quilters Club in Long-Acre' and 'Basket-Women's Club in St. Giles's'. *The New Art and Mystery of GOSSIPING. Being a genuine Account of all Women's Clubs in and about the City and Suburbs of London, with the manner of their Club Order* (London, 1760?).

36 See, for example, Abdoulaye Kane, 'Financial arrangements across borders: women's predominant participation in popular finance, from Thilogne and Dakar to Paris: a Senegalese case study', and Grietjie Verhoef, 'Stokvels and economic empowerment: the case of African women in South Africa, *c.* 1930–98' in Lemire *et al.*, *Women and Credit*. See also Marjorie K. McIntosh, 'The diversity of social capital in English communities, 1300–1640 (with a glance at modern Nigeria)', *Journal of Interdisciplinary History* 29:3 (1999).

37 Jordan, *Women and Credit*, pp. 26–8. See also Sara Mendelson and Patricia Crawford, *Women in Early Modern England* (Oxford, 1998), chapter 5.

38 Jordan, *Women and Credit*, p. 28.

39 Earle, 'Female labour market'; Patricia Crawford and Sara Mendelson, *Women in Early Modern England* (Oxford, 1998), especially chapters 4 and 5.

40 PALA 9/1/1, PRO. These dynamic systems of reciprocity persisted among poor women to this day as a type of collective insurance. See, for example, Ross, 'Survival networks', and Susan Porter Benson, 'Living on the margin: working-class marriages and family survival strategies in the United States, 1919–1941' in Victoria de Grazia (ed.), *The Sex of Things: Gender and Consumption in Historical Perspective* (Berkeley CA, 1996).

41 Lemire, *Dress, Culture and Commerce*, chapters 3 and 4. For an example of similar women-led neighbourly strategies in twentieth-century America see also Carol Stack, *All our Kin: Strategies for Survival in a Black Community* (New York, 1974). My thanks to Margaret Hunt for this reference.

42 Mary Bateson (ed.), *Records of the Borough of Leicester, 1509–1603* (Cambridge, 1905), p. 147.

43 Korda, 'Henslowe', pp. 191–3; Boulton, *Neighbourhood and Society*, pp. 88–90; A. Foakes and R. T. Rickert, *Henslowe's Diary* (Cambridge, 1961), pp. 109, 111–12, 146–8, 151–62, 254–60.

44 For observations on the vulnerability of single and widowed women see Mendelson and Crawford, *Women in Early Modern England*, pp. 174–84, 262–3.

45 C 108/34, PRO.

46 Jordan, *Women and Credit*, p. 24.

47 Margaret Hunt's findings with regard to women executrices and solicitrices in seafaring communities show similar levels of initiative, with little apparent regard for the common law restraints on married women. A similar predominance of women in credit arrangements has been found in contemporary Senegalese society, with patterns that persist as well among immigrant communities in Paris. Margaret Hunt, 'Women and the fiscal-imperial state', *A New Imperial History*; Kane, 'Predominant participation of women'.

48 *Journals of the House of Commons* (hereafter *J.H.C.*), vol. 25, p. 46.
49 Merry E. Wiesner, *Women and Gender in Early Modern Europe* (Cambridge, 1993), pp. 93–7.
50 Jan de Vries, 'The industrial revolution and the industrious revolution', *Journal of Economic History* 54:2 (1994), p. 256.
51 J. M. Beattie, 'The criminality of women in eighteenth-century England', *Journal of Social History* 8 (1975), and John M. Beattie, *Crime and the Courts in England, 1660–1800* (Princeton NJ, 1986), p. 187; Walker, 'Women, theft and the world of stolen goods', pp. 87–8.
52 Beattie, 'The criminality of women', p. 82; Patricia Crawford and Laura Gowing (eds), *Women's Worlds in Seventeenth-Century England: A Sourcebook* (London, 2000), pp. 107–8, 123.
53 Thirsk, *Economic Policy and Projects*, pp. 169–80.
54 De Vries, 'The industrial revolution', pp. 261–2.
55 *J.H.C.*, vol. 8, p. 300.
56 Kenneth Hudson, *Pawnbroking: An Aspect of Social History* (London, 1982), pp. 33, 35–41; Tebbutt, *Making Ends Meet*, pp. 70–4; Hardaker, *A Brief History*, pp. 24–36.
57 Earle, *The Making of the English Middle Class*, p. 107.
58 Lemire, *Dress, Culture and Commerce*, p. 107; Tebbutt, *Making Ends Meet*, pp. 73–5, 112–13.
59 Q/SB 29 December 1756, Kent Archives. Mary Minton of Greenwich, a widow, was recognized as a broker when she appeared before a magistrate in 1788. Q/SB January 1788. In a case in Ludlow, Herefordshire, in 1702, a widow, Mary Jones, appeared to carry on some sort of brokering business, agreeing to take in textiles and clothing from a young woman unknown to her. When the young woman returned for the goods later Jones informed her that the items were, in her opinion, stolen and she refused to turn the goods over as asked until threatened, beaten and abused by the young woman. 356/242, Examinations, Ludlow Borough Quarter Sessions, Shropshire Record Office.
60 Lemire, *Dress, Culture and Commerce*, pp. 106–7.
61 PROB 3, 48/30, PRO.
62 Ms 7253, No. 107557, Guildhall Library, London.
63 Acc. 38, York City Archives.
64 The importance of clothing as an alternative currency is discussed in Chapter 4.
65 *A Directory of Sheffield; Including the Manufacturers of the Adjacent Villages* (London, 1787, reprinted New York, 1969); John Robinson, *A Directory of Sheffield, including the Manufacturers of the Adjacent Villages …* (Sheffield, 1797); James Pigot, *Pigot & Co.'s National and Commercial Directory … in the counties of Chester, Cumberland, Durham, Lancashire, Northumberland, Westmorland and York …* (London, 1834); William White, *History, Gazetteer and Directory of the West-Riding of Yorkshire …* I (Sheffield, 1838).
66 J90/504, PRO.
67 Charles Dickens reported the practice of a compositor who spent £5 on a watch that he regularly used for short-term loans, noted in Tebbutt, *Making Ends Meet*, p. 17. For discussions of the impact of time culture see Lewis Mumford, *Technics and Civilization* (1934, repr. New York, 1963); Carlo M. Cipolla, *Clocks and Culture, 1300–1700* (London, 1967); E. P. Thompson, 'Time, work-discipline and industrial capitalism' in *Customs in Common: Studies in Traditional Popular Culture* (New York, 1993);

Margaret Hunt, *The Middling Sort: Commerce, Gender and the Family in England, 1680–1780* (Berkeley CA, 1996), pp. 53–6.

68 Acc. 38, York City Archives.

69 Giorgio Riello notes the importance of assessing consumerism within the family, taking into account the pressures inside the family which lay behind many consumer impulses. Considering consumerism purely from the vantage point of the unencumbered individual cannot possible yield a full appreciation of the varied aspects of consumerism. 'The Boot and Shoe Trades in London and Paris in the Long Eighteenth Century', unpublished PhD thesis, University College London, 2002, especially chapter 3.

70 C 110/134, PRO.

71 The Rev. Thomas Malthus is still the best known of the reforming clerics, following the publication of his *Essay on the Principle of Population as it affects the Future Improvement of Society* (London, 1798). He was not alone among the clergy in his preoccupation with this subject. See, for example, Rev. W. Otter, *A Sermon upon the Influence of the Clergy in improving the Condition of the Poor … To which is Added an Appendix: Containing the Plan of a Provident Society for a Country Village* (Shrewsbury, 1818). The clergy also actively promoted savings banks of various kinds.

72 Margaret D. Fuller, *West Country Friendly Societies* (Lingfield, 1964), pp. 1, 3, 6–8.

73 *Laws and Articles for the Government of all Members of the Provident Brotherhood, first founded by William Hill, John Gill … and William Cook, September the 7th 1789. Held at the House of Samuel Richardson … Kingston-upon-Hull* (Hull, 1789), p. iv.

74 *Articles, Rules etc. of a Friendly Society, held at W. Doxford's Wheat Sheaf Inn, West Bolden* (Newcastle, 1820), p. 13. The St James's Joint Stock Company, or Savings and Loan Bank, was established in June 1831. Its explicit purpose was not only to act as a savings bank but also to provide loans to its members. John Johnson Collection, Banking 4. Bodleian Library. Another mid-nineteenth-century example of a rotating savings and credit association (ROSCA) was described in *Rules of the Good Samaritan Teetotal Mutual Loan Society. Established May 25th, 1860. Held at the St John's Temperance Hall … Clerkenwell …* (London, 1860). Its aims were 'to raise by equal contributions from each member a fund, for the purpose of lending the same in sums of not less than Ten Shillings, nor more than Fifteen Pounds, to the industrious classes, and taking payment for the same by instalments, with interest thereon' (p. 3). See also *Laws of the Friends of Labour (Improved) Loan Society, held at … 'Sidney Arms', Sidney Street, Mile End …* (London, 1865), and Johnson, *Saving and Spending*, p. 152. For examples of comparative modern examples of ROSCAs see Shirley Ardener and Sandra Burman, *Money-go-rounds: The Importance of Rotating Savings and Credit Associations for Women* (Oxford, 1995).

75 *The Second Annual Report of the Loan Society, with a List of its Officers and Subscribers, Rules and Privileges …* (London, 1817), p. 8.

76 One of the longest-lived and most effective of these loan societies was based in Ireland. See Aidan Hollis and Arthur Sweetman, 'Microcredit: what can we learn from the past?' *World Development* 26:10 (1998).

77 The involvement of clerics in organizing loan societies was an extension of their activities in a field where they were traditionally very active as providers of loans. B. A. Holderness, 'The clergy as moneylenders in England, 1550–1700' in Rosemary O'Day and Felicity Heal (eds), *Princes and Paupers in the English Church, 1500–1800* (Leices-

ter, 1981); Finn, 'Men's things', p. 137. This initiative also owed much to similar charitable sentiments which inspired the foundation of the Charitable Corporation.

78 5 and 6 William IV, cap. 23.

79 *Hughes on Loan Societies*, quoted on the title page in W. Strange, *A Guide to the Loan Societies of London* (London, 1841).

80 Forms from these loan societies were included in the records of the Porto Bello Loan Society (J 90/1007, PRO). The rules of operation allowed considerable latitude in the charges assigned the borrower, from the cost of the application form, charges for application, to the 'Enquiry Fee' charged to cover the expenses of confirming the guarantor(s) of the loan. Interest rates were supposed to be low. However, by the mid-nineteenth century there was a considerable outcry against the excessive charges levied by some loan societies. *Times*, 23 December 1840, 5 August 1841, 1, 3, 4, 10 November 1843, 20 August 1844, 31 October 1849; Edward White, *Loan Societies: Their Uses and Abuses considered, and a Plan suggested …* (London, 1858). I am grateful to Aidan Hollis for his generosity in passing along the *Times* materials.

81 J 90/1007, PRO.

82 Aidan Hollis, 'Women and microcredit in history: gender in the Irish loan funds' in Lemire *et al.*, *Women and Credit*.

83 D/P3/ 29/14, Hertfordshire Record Office.

84 D2465/2/2, Gloucestershire Record Office.

85 At the founding meeting of the Nailsworth Loan Society those in attendance supported the proposal to 'Establish a Loan Society for the purpose of lending small sums of money to Industrious poor people living in the parishes of Avening, Horsley and Minchinhampton upon the principles of the Act of Parliament passed for this purpose during the last Session of Parliament'. D2219/6/10 Nailsworth Loan Society, Gloucestershire Record Office.

86 Pawnbrokers in business in Gloucester include those listed in *The Gloucestershire Directory, containing the Names and Residences of Professional Gentlemen, Merchants, Manufacturers and Tradesmen* (Gloucester, 1820), pp. 105, 148, 174, 193, 211–15, 227.

87 D2465/2/1, Gloucestershire Record Office.

88 D2465/2/2, Gloucestershire Record Office.

89 D2465/2/1, Gloucestershire Record Office.

90 See Alison Parkinson, 'Small Business and the Sphere Switchers: Work-life Choices and the Redundant Woman in Nineteenth Century London', paper presented at the International Economic History Association Conference, Buenos Aires, 2002. Henry Mayhew's investigation into the street sellers of London noted a wide range of female sellers, along with male ones. *London Labour and the London Poor*, 2 vols (New York, 1968).

91 J 90/1007, PRO. Surviving printed application forms from the Porto Bello Loan Society and the Tradesman's Economical Loan Company made these stipulations. John Johnson Collection, Banking. Bodleian Library, Oxford. In the John Johnson collection of banking ephemera several loan forms survive from loan societies, such as 'The Old Welsh Harp Loan Society, Established at the Old Welsh Harp, Carnaby Street, Golden Square', which shows a loan taken out in 1839 of £8 10s, the two sureties being reputable men of the district. Similarly, the form printed by the St Marylebone Discount & Loan Association (n.d.) established a further normative standard which, from its outline, excluded women. The St Pancras Joint Stock Loan Society, from 1840,

shows a similar layout of its form, with 'Mr.' identified as appropriate guarantors. Only in the St James Imperial Joint Stock Loan Society, of Lincoln's Inn Fields, was the borrower a woman, a greengrocer by trade, and she listed two men as guarantors of this loan.

92 *Times*, 24 May 1855. See below for number of pawns taken in 1866 in London.

93 Henry W. Wolff, *Co-operative Credit Banks: A Help alike Economic and Educational for the Labouring and Cultivating Classes* (London, 1898), p. 8.

94 Wolff, *Co-operative Credit Banks*, p. 7.

95 *A Few Words on Pawnbrokers, etc.* (London, 1866), p. 5. Judith Coffin describes a similar reliance on pawning among the nineteenth-century Parisian working class. *The Politics of Women's Work: The Paris Garment Trades, 1750–1914* (Princeton NJ, 1996).

96 Mrs Layton described her brief childhood employment, in 1865, in a small shop in Bethnal Green which took clothing and housewares in pawn for food. 'The practice was illegal', she recounts, 'so all articles had to be brought in when no one was about, and I was trained to help to smuggle things in.' Mrs Layton, 'Memoirs of seventy years' in M. Llewelyn Davies (ed.), *Life as We have Known it: by Co-operative Working Women* (1931, repr. New York, 1975), p. 21.

97 For insights into the interaction of urban reformers and working-class communities see Judith Walkowitz, *City of Dreadful Delight: Narratives of Sexual Danger in Late Victorian London* (London, 1994), pp. 52–68.

98 Wolff, *Co-operative Credit Banks*, pp. 5, 7.

99 Tebbutt, *Making Ends Meet*, p. 116.

100 E. Carpenter, *The Diary of a Pawnbroker* (London, 1865), p. 3. In 1851, Dickens focused at least one of his episodes of *Household Words* on the pawnshop, entertaining his readers while offering a sympathetic perspective on the trade. Tebbutt, *Making Ends Meet*, p. 116. See also Walkowitz, *City of Dreadful Delight*, chapter 1.

101 Olive Malvery, quoted in Melanie Tebbutt, *Women's Talk? A Social History of 'Gossip' in Working-Class Neighbourhoods, 1880–1960* (Aldershot, 1995), p. 68.

102 Ellen Ross, *Love and Toil: Motherhood in Outcast London, 1870–1918* (Oxford, 1993), pp. 81–3; Tebbutt, *Making Ends Meet*, pp. 72, 107–8.

103 Truths from a pawnbroker' in Viscount Ingestre (ed.), *Meloria: or, Better Times to Come* (London, 1852) p. 285.

3

Credit for the poor and the failed experiment of the Charitable Corporation, c. 1700–1750

THE HISTORY OF THE CHARITABLE CORPORATION has lingered, largely overlooked, in the footnotes of eighteenth-century financial history. Its collapse embodied all the elements of the classic bubble: the over-promotion of stock, a profitable sell-off by insiders, rumours of embezzlement, a subsequent free-fall in stock values, followed by long and acrimonious inquiries into the origins of the debacle. Interesting in itself, the rise and collapse of the Charitable Corporation has a resonance far beyond a simple swindle, one of the too frequent financial scandals in this early era of stockjobbing and financial markets. In fact, the organization at the centre of these events also stands as a milestone in new concepts of social discipline tied to the charity of lending. As the industrial capitalist system evolved, order and discipline among the working poor became a major preoccupation. Of equal concern was the capacity of the industrious classes to engage in self-sustaining ventures, to find the credit or modest sources of capital to fund wages, purchase raw materials and cover the cost of business. Access to small-scale credit was identified as a key element in a successful enterprise and a commitment to accessible credit for the poor, at reasonable interest rates, inspired the creation of the Charitable Corporation. This initiative had numerous antecedents elsewhere in Europe, as well as many and diverse descendants. However, few if any of those ventures produced such dramatic results.

Credit is discussed as much at the turn of the twentieth-first century as it was three centuries previously. Over the last several decades, small-scale loans to the deserving poor, or what is termed 'micro-credit', has receive intensive examination as one of the vital tools for economic development. Ensuring access to small loans, providing credit for the enterprising poor, is now acknowledged to be invaluable for developing nations, as well as for sectors of developed societies. Micro-credit is not a gift, it is not charity, but typically involves the provision of essential credit at high commercial rates of interest, secured in most cases through the guarantees of circles of neighbours with intimate knowledge of the reputation of the borrowers. Non-governmental organizations and charities, in addition to governments and some banks, now recognize that small-scale credit enables the working poor and struggling would-be entrepreneur to build modest concerns which can lift adults and children from poverty or provide a supplement to other incomes.[2] Micro-credit is very much a contemporary development tool. However, the rediscovery of micro-credit by Muhammad Yunus and his establishment of the Grameen Bank in Bangladesh in 1983 represents a modern manifestation of a phenomenon with a long and complex history.[3] In Western nations this goes back for centuries, the study of which not only sheds light on changing social and economic priorities, but also reveals shifting philosophical ideas about the quotidian needs of the commercial and labouring classes.[4] This singular initiative sought to lower the cost of borrowing through pawns, pawning being the most ubiquitous and important mechanism for plebeian borrowing. The proposal to introduce low-cost credit represented an important innovation, arising at a time when the subject of credit itself inspired on-going public debates about the inadequate institutional frameworks supporting this ingredient essential to plebeian industry.[5]

The practice and culture of credit evolved over the seventeenth and eighteenth centuries with, as Craig Muldrew observes, 'a reordering of notions of community relations towards a highly mobile and circulating language of judgement – what I have chosen to term the "currency of reputation" – about the creditworthiness of households both to cooperate and compete within communities increasingly permeated by market relations'.[6] In early modern England there was growing recognition, long at work in continental Europe, that credit offered at modest interest rates engendered industry and discipline among the working poor. This perspective marked a significant conceptual shift, presaging the growing dominance of liberal and capitalist priorities in English social policy and in English society more generally.[7]

The history of the Charitable Corporation opens a window on evolving mores and expectations with regard to plebeian credit and, despite the paucity of surviving records from the organization itself, the impact of this corporation is apparent. The very lack of documentation perhaps explains the reason the corporation remains so nebulous, so long overlooked, though hundreds of thousands of pounds were lost, families were ruined, political machinations infused the imbroglio and the resultant scandals reverberated through political and financial corridors for decades, doubtless changing the trajectory of later credit initiatives for the poor. Printed and written sources survive in abundance, though the business records of the corporation have proved elusive. Inevitably, given the nature of the sources to hand, questions remain unanswered and unanswerable. Nonetheless, the importance of the Charitable Corporation is incontestable as a means to assess attitudes towards plebeian credit during this transitional era. The language of charity and the language of commerce formed parallel recurring refrains over the life of this institution, ultimately intersecting, each sustaining the impetus behind the corporation. There are as well two interlocking strands in the history of the Charitable Corporation: the first is a narrative of corporate rise and fall; the second is the broader debate on the social value of low-interest credit directed at plebeian borrowers as a facet of public policy. The latter sentiment inspired the creation of the corporation and contributed to the wider European credit initiatives. Charitable and commercial impulses were counterpoints resonating throughout this study, revealing the evolving ideals of a society in the throes of commercial and industrial transformation. The circumstances surrounding the collapse of this organization speak to the other facets of risk inherent in capitalist society. In sum, the corporation's failure redefined the organization of credit available to London's working and trading classes for generations to come, while the political taint accompanying the crash destroyed for a considerable period of time the possibility of low-cost credit for the common people.

'Relieving ... these miserable people'

Credit underpinned the daily lives of labouring, trading and retailing peoples at every level of society in the early modern and modern eras. Nevertheless, for many centuries over the medieval and early modern period the question of interest on loans remained fraught, with Lombard and Jewish lenders taking the lead as providers of credit for many Europeans. The broader issue of plebeian credit was addressed first in Catholic nations,[8] when, in the fifteenth century, the Observant Franciscans intervened in the affairs of Italian city states, establishing a series of local charitable lending societies – because these arose from a Christian charitable impulse they were named *monti de pieta*, or *monts de piété*, mounts of charity. The pawn was accepted as the archetype of lending and securing credit, in recognition of the centrality of this practice in daily budgeting. Since pawning was the pre-eminent model, the

Church-run initiatives adopted the pawnshop as the most reliable means of arranging cheap, accessible credit. In this way, charity and commerce were bound together in institutions throughout the Catholic states of western Europe. The charity of lending, at lower interest rates than at ordinary pawnshops, afforded a service to hard-pressed city folk.[9] The general demand for small-scale credit was similarly evident in early modern England,[10] a fact recognized by advocates of charitable loan societies. One of those sympathetic to the sometimes usurious cost of credit looked with pity on 'poor People, who commonly pawn their best Cloaths every Monday Morning (to buy Goods to sell by Retail to get a Livelihood for themselves and their Families)'.[11] Their industry designated them deserving, and diligence at their trade might indeed preserve them, but not without the infusion of regular loans.

The proliferation of pawnbrokers distressed commentators, who, from the sixteenth century onwards, observed the steady increase of these dealers with grave reservations.[12] In 1583, Phillip Stubbes referred to 'This dunghill trade of brokerie newly spring up and coined in the devil's minting house'.[13] John Stow characterized the pawnbrokers clustered along London's Houndsditch as 'Monsters in the Shape of Men', writing that they 'profess to live by Lending, and will lend nothing but upon Pawns; neither to any, but unto the poor People only'. Stow was unequivocal: 'let me not here be mistaken, that I condemn such as live by honest Buying and Selling … No truly, I mean only the Judas Broker, that lives by the Bag, and, except God be more merciful to him, will follow him that did bear the Bag.'[14] The religiously inspired distaste for those who charged interest on loans persisted throughout the early modern era, even as these services became more imperative. Charitable endowments attempted to address a portion of the need for credit among small manufacturers and traders in London and most large provincial cities. Indeed, wealthy guild members bequeathed funds specifically to meet the need of young members beginning trade, as well as those with other credit needs. But these limited loan funds could not satisfy the needs of those outside the guilds, the growing colonies of men and women making and trading goods in London's swelling suburbs.[15] As Stow observed, speculators and traders were ready to offer what was so badly wanted, at a price.

The language employed to describe the pawnbroker's trade suggests the deep suspicion that prevailed in some government and elite circles. Most pawnbrokers mucked in with the humblest, taking in 'all kinde of worne apparell, whether it be olde or little the worse for wearinge, household stuffe, and goods of what kinde soever' – some goods certainly stolen.[16] The probable legal and olfactory character of these wares made them equally offensive to legislators. Nevertheless, these were the items most commonly owned by ordinary folk and these mutable goods secured essential credit. Those South Londoners who pawned and borrowed money from John Pope brought exactly those sorts of things to his door: 'linen things', 'curtains, valances and hat', 'bugle purse', 'man's coat', 'watch', 'chamber pots', 'brass scales', 'sheets' and 'petticoats'.[17] Although Pope's interest rates cannot be determined, it was widely conceded that short-term pawning was one of the most expensive forms of credit. In the last decades of the seventeenth century the suburbs of London were crowded with new immigrants to the city, and the metropolis was alive with the sound, sight and smell of manufacture and exchange. The need for credit evinced by men and women scrambling for a living fed the profits of a growing generation of pawnbrokers and also revived the interest in alternative means to meet this demand.

Charitable or municipal pawn offices were well established in various parts of continental Europe by the seventeenth century; in all cases, they lent on pawns and charged low commercial rates of interest. There were over eighty charitable loan banks in Italy by 1509 and the institutional model spread to France, Spain and the Netherlands, especially after their formation was advocated, in 1565, by the Pope's legate at the Council of Milan. Perhaps the Catholicism of these institutions deterred emulation in England,[18] although municipal pawnshops operated in the Netherlands and the utility of these lending houses was beyond dispute. So renowned did these institutions become that they inspired repeated proposals throughout the late Elizabethan and Stuart periods, when advocates urged the creation of similar structures in England. In 1576, Stephen Parrot proposed a type of charitable bank, without success.[19] However, the dynamic mid-seventeenth century saw a flurry of propositions for similar institutions, with one enthusiast suggesting 'to lend poore people small summes of money upon security without paying any interest'. The authors of these proposals were particularly irate that pawnbrokers charged rates that were plainly usurious: 'the brokers now take at least 40, 50, yea in some cases 100 in 100 [per cent].'[20] This preoccupation with interest rates was shared by those paying the pawnbrokers' charges and feeling the pinch from the repayments. In 1678, a petition was presented to the government from 'divers poor artificers and handcraftsmen' begging that the small loans on which they depended be fixed at a rate of $\frac{3}{4}d$ in the £ per week.[21] The request fell on deaf ears, although at this time there was an intense preoccupation with trade and credit, spawning floods of publications on the necessity to create banks for great and modest borrowers. In this context, authors recognized that the value of *mont de piété* went beyond simple charity, since flows of credit strength-ened trade and the nation.[22] They were convinced that charity and com-merce could be jointly reinforcing, one commentator writing in 1680 that such ventures could transform English society for the better, improving commerce and reducing the number of thieves. In his view, English jails were 'stored with such a number of both Sexes, as at Sessions time are seen within his Majesties Dominions, because Brokers do (against Status) exercise their extortion on all needy persons, who must take their recourse ... by poor folk turning thieves'. His solution: 'erect Banks of Loans' to serve great merchants, 'Tradesmen and Countrymen' as well 'as the poor people (that live from hand to mouth)'.[23]

At every stage, as the loan banks spread throughout Europe, clerics debated the legitimacy of charging interest on charitable loans.[24] The question of interest was hotly contested. However, pragmatic concern about the survival of lending charities combined with arguments favour-ing legal interest to win the day. Another anonymous English author was in no doubt that these institutions 'could not intrench on Usury, much less Extortion: But contrariwise ... the Banks aforesaid (in regard of the Pious and Charitable effects of them) have been universally called, *Mounts of Piety*.'[25] Practical, down-to-earth, useful charity was recognized by a growing company as more efficacious than alms, an aid to industry sustained through legal interest charges – a self-sustaining charity. Doctrines of charity were increasingly fused with commercial precepts. In 1692, the Dean of St Paul's Cathedral, William Sherlock, delivered a sermon before the Lord Mayor of London and eminent merchants of the City in which he elaborated on these proposals, confident his audience would be sympathetic to his views. Sherlock chose the topic of *The Charity of Lending without Usury*. Given his congregation, one would not expect a tirade against lending at interest; and, indeed, Sherlock offered no such insult to his listeners. Noting that Christ required lending as charity, Sherlock insisted that payment for the use of another's money was not forbidden in the scriptures. He next avowed that it was 'Trade, to which we owe all the Riches and Greatness of our Nation' and trade which was founded on lending with interest.[26] Having settled this question, his peroration climaxed with the observation that if commercial credit was sanctioned by Church scholars, providing credit for the poor was a sacred obligation: duty combined with effective social policy. This claim by Sherlock represented perhaps the most important development in the conceptualization of charitable credit in England, for in this address he insisted that lending to the poor was preferable to giving alms.

Now if we compare Giving and Lending together, Lending has much the advantage of Giving, as to the true End and Purposes of Charity.

To Lend is a greater Obligation to Industry than to give, and there cannot be a greater Kindness done to the Poor, next to keeping them from starving, than to teach them Industry. I need not tell you that there are many Poor, who will never work, while they can meet with charitable People to give; nay, who chuse to be sick … to be blind, to move Charity, rather than work to supply their Wants; but when Men have nothing to live on, but the Improvement of lent Money, which they know, they must repay … this must make them industrious; for it both encourages their Industry, and keeps the Rod over them … .

Thus what we give does but one single Act of Charity, for we can give it but once, but what we lend may circulate, as the Blood does in our Veins … that is, what we lend, may be lent again, and do a great many successive Charities … .[27]

Sherlock exhorted his listeners to open their wallets, not to give but to lend. He appealed to them in the language of commerce, a syntax they understood and approved, speaking at a time when the intellectual milieu of England was abuzz with debates and discourses surrounding the fiscal restructuring of England. Sherlock pursued the subject further by recommending that 'to make this Charity of Lending more effectual … a Publick Bank of Charity raised out of such free Loans [from patrons of the bank] will have many Advantages above any Private Acts of this Nature'. Sherlock enticed his congregation with the prospect that 'were such a Bank of Charity once settled, there would be very little need of giving'.[28] The charity of lending with interest was neatly tied to the philosophy of commercial rectitude and personal discipline; Sherlock's Sunday audience, and subsequent readers of his thesis, now had a clear agenda for both charitable and social initiatives. The combined credos of disciplining/charitable commerce offered a powerful revised version of ancient charity, in keeping with the growing liberal, rational doctrines of the nascent Industrial Age.[29]

The proposal for a London-based loan bank received serious, if erratic, consideration at the turn of the century. However, others followed Sherlock's lead, linking the creation of the Bank of England with more equitable means of providing credit for the poor, supposing that this could be an adjunct to the fiscal innovations already in train.[30] What did they hope from these reforms? In most instances, advocates of loan banks envisaged a more orderly population of petty dealers and artisans, bound to constant industry through the discipline of credit. This represents a different type of charity from the prevailing preoccupation with workhouses, focusing not on the destitute or disorderly, but on produc-tive petty makers and dealers.[31] Finally, as the century ended, a further proposal to create a loan bank was presented around 1699. The name given this body was the Charitable Corporation and it aimed to address the woes of poor borrowers, too often distressed by the high interest rates and shady practices of moneylenders and pawnbrokers. A petition for a charter was put forward in 1704 and approved in 1707 by Queen Anne, its full title being *The Charitable Corporation for Relief of Industrious Poor, by assisting them with small Sums upon Pledges at Legal Interest.*[32]

To lend to the poor one must first gather from the rich, or at least col-lect sufficient sums from the comfortably prosperous that can then be lent out. The original Continental charitable lending banks solicited gifts from wealthy congregants, sometimes at regular intervals, and employed the interest earned to sustain the enterprise. But, in the era of burgeoning joint-stock companies, it was decided that the London-based Charitable Corporation would be different, promising dividends from investments in this new charitable venture – that, at least, was the plan. At the heart of the undertaking lay faith in the power of commerce, in the generative force of invested funds dispersed in thousands of tiny interest-bearing loans. To this end, the promoters of the Charitable Corporation struc-tured a joint-stock company, raising money on the sale of shares to stockholders promised a handsome dividend from the loans to plebeian borrowers. Given the scale of day-to-day borrowing in London, there seemed a tremendous potential for profit from this charity.[33] The original capitalization was approximately £30,000 and with this the corporation set up business in Duke Street, Westminster, long a centre of the pawn-brokers' trade.[34] Promoters were determined to make their venture a financial success, as well as a charitable benefit, and they announced their opening in a four-page pamphlet, promoting the virtue and utility of their undertaking. Simultaneously shares were sold whose value depended on the interest collected from the legions of London's industri-ous citizens.

The Charitable Corporation championed the morality of its policies, along with its potential profitability. No interest would be charged on loans of 6*d* or less and the cost of borrowing under 10*s* was a mere 5 per cent per annum; borrowing more than 10*s* raised the interest rate to 6 per cent. No sooner was it launched, however, than it was fighting off rivals who also sought to assist the poor with loans. Styling themselves the Charitable Fund, these newcomers chastised their competitor in benevo-lence, announcing that the Charitable Fund 'gives or lends gratis to the necessitous Poor'. They alleged that the interest rates charged by their rivals applied for the two-month duration of the loan, even if 'the Borrower wants the Money but for a Week, or less; so that in such case, he must pay Interest at least 8 times over for the same Sum'. The Charitable Fund followed a much less onerous practice, aligning itself with the norms of Church-sponsored institutions 'in several other Cities of Italy and Flanders'.[35] But its ambitions ultimately came to nothing. Perhaps it was unable to collect the requisite donations to launch and maintain the project; it may also have suffered in comparison with its competitor, for if the corporation was less generous in its lending terms than the proposed Charitable Fund, it appealed to affluent supporters on two other equally important points. The rates charged by the Charitable Corporation were less than those levied by common pawnbrokers, while strict lending terms were imposed on borrowers. Furthermore, the spread of credit discipline was one of the key social goals of supporters of this project; adherents believed that this form of charitable endeavour would be more effective than the discipline of the workhouse, since the restrictions that came with borrowed money were self-imposed.[36] Assisting the enterprising poor also brought potential profit and stockholders were enticed to receive the rewards of charity on earth. Who could resist the opportunity for self-serving generosity? Hundreds of small and large investors were pleased to contribute their capital for a worthy cause, promising a healthy return. A full index of investors is not available for the early period of trade; however, evidence from the 1730s shows the range of male and female investors who combined worthy aims with the prospect of fiscal rewards.[37] Of 288 creditors, 109 (37.8 per cent) were women and 179 (62.2 per cent) men.[38]

Charity, credit and corruption

The Charitable Corporation faced a daunting commercial commitment from the outset, driven by the ever-present need to reward investors. To sustain itself, while seeking customers, it turned for a time to selling fire insurance.[39] But credit was its business, and it was one that evidently brought success. A look at the data from some of the few surviving pawnbrokers' ledgers for this century suggests the Charitable Corporation would have received a daily influx of apparel, tools, jewellery and decorative personal items, along with trade stock and household textiles. Evidently the corporation established itself as a reputable source of loans for the assorted Londoners who travelled to Duke Street.[40] To keep its name before the public, a further rationale was published in 1719, extolling the benefits of lending small sums at legal interest rates, reiterating the care and attention given the business. Pledged goods were kept in warehouses and always available to the owner should she or he wish to sell them. The warehouse keeper was not only responsible for the safe running of the storehouse, but also determined the creditworthiness of clients, to ensure that goods were legitimately offered and not stolen, to which end the incumbent placed a security deposit with the management. At the same time, the warehouse keeper's assistant double-checked the goods in store and gave daily accounts, matching book value to the actual items. The warehouse keeper's signature affirmed the parity between the goods held as security, the value assigned them and the credit granted the borrower. The bookkeeper then made careful records of these transactions, while the cashier checked the whole. Each month the auditor checked all transactions and the entire affair was overseen by the management committee.[41] The author confidently asserted that 'there is no Danger, that the Fund of the Corporation will ever be embezled, or sunk by Mismanagement: And also ... Care is taken, that the poor Borrower may have the Benefit of Redeeming his Pledge, as soon as he can Raise Money'.[42] In time, however, the amalgam of charity and commerce produced a conflicting agenda and the lure of profits outweighed the claims of altruism.

In 1721, the corporation petitioned to raise more capital, citing the need of 'distressed traders and manufacturers of the kingdom' – perhaps a reference to the disastrous commercial climate which followed the South Sea Bubble in 1720.[43] The request was approved and a share subscription of £70,000 was offered to the public. This was the era of stock-jobbing and speculative investment, and, although the South Sea Bubble dented investor enthusiasm for a time, the potential windfall earnings from lending appealed to a growing roster of investors from the genteel, trading and professional classes. Speculators may have felt reassured by the parallels between the Charitable Corporation and Bank of England stock, which also based its value on the profits of loans. But any parallel between the two ventures was illusory. Unfortunately, the corporation attracted company directors who saw that their returns could be far more lucrative than those available to mere stockholders or to those involved in other more closely supervised ventures. By the 1720s the composition and structure of management reflected a speculative, self-interested outlook, and, rather than continue governance through the General Court of principal stockholders, a seven-member committee of like-minded representatives was struck to oversee business dealings. The vast sums that could be raised through the sale of stock preoccupied this committee, which boasted several prominent Members of Parliament. They lobbied effectively on behalf of the corporation and their own portfolios, and determined that large subscriptions should be raised in the market, insisting that the capital vested in the corporation was still inadequate, although by now few industrious Londoners could get loans. A single example of a lending agreement survives from this era, and the document reflects some of the peculiar practices, now all too common, at the Charitable Corporation. In this instance, the firm of Woolley & Warren borrowed £500 on the stated surety of 'Sundry Woollen & Shalloons' said to be left in the corporation's warehouse (see Plate 3.1). Rather than lend £2, £5 or £10 to many thousands of necessitous dealers or craftspeople, vast sums were being lent on slight security, and many were made to company officers and friends on no security whatever. Nevertheless, in 1728, Parliament approved new shares to raise a total capital of £300,000; by 1730, the corporation was permitted to sell further shares to the combined total of £600,000.[44] Prominent new members of the corporation like Sir Robert Sutton, MP, former ambassador to Paris, and Sir Archibald Grant, MP, saw the Charitable Corporation as a gold mine they could promote publicly while draining its resources to feed their private dealings.[45] By now it was only the infusion of new monies that allowed the continued payment of healthy dividends. Meanwhile, behind the public promotion

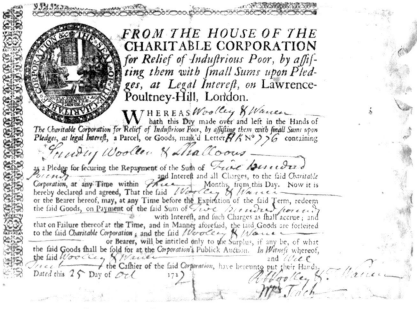

Plate 3.1   Loan form, Charitable Corporation (London), 1727

of the shares and the promise of continuing returns of 10 per cent, one of the largest embezzlements and commercial frauds in England's financial history was taking place.[46] In the top left-hand corner of the lending contract is the corporate seal, depicting Queen Anne, with the corporation's charter in hand, seated before a group of the necessitous men and women of London. The humble tradesman at the front has beside him the usual bundle of goods left as collateral; the tradeswoman at his shoulder carries a similar parcel – both quintessential examples of the most common credit practices (see Plate 3.2). The corporate motto summarizing the aims of this body – 'Loans provided with good will and sureties carefully managed'[47] – offers no foreshadowing of its ultimate fate. In this instance, fidelity, probity and charity fell victim to negligence, greed and fraud, to the great detriment of its intended clients.

In September 1726, the auditor overseeing the warehouse was fired and no other hired to take his place, leaving the warehouse keeper, John Thomson, free to seize the two keys formerly held by the cashier and the accountant. Audits, scheduled to take place weekly for the satisfaction of the 'Committee of Account', were missed. The management committee tolerated John Thomson's shortcomings as long as he did not enquire into their peculations. Large loans for considerable sums were made for valuable goods that never appeared at the warehouse and so money was given for no surety at all – the company of Woolley & Warren quickly

Plate 3.2   Detail of the Charitable Corporation loan form

became notorious for such practices. So the surviving loan form is more than just a random artefact of standard business practice; rather, it depicts some of the worst forms of embezzlement which ultimately brought about the collapse of the corporation. A conspiracy ensued in which Thomson, the warehouse keeper, George Robinson, the cashier, and various prominent committee members channelled money among the co-conspirators inside and outside the company. As a critic later described it, 'The Committee suffer'd … [Thomson] to certify for himself; there is now nobody to inspect the Warehouse, and so John Thomson certifies for John Thomson, that he has left such a Pledge in the Warehouse, i.e. with himself, worth so much, and this was allowed to the amount of Thousands at a Time.'[48] In the spring of 1731, Parliament acted on the petitions and the testimony of various witnesses which accused the Charitable Corporation of applying excessive rates of interest, in contravention of its mandate. A Bill was prepared to rein in this usurious conduct, while suspicions grew; investors, as well as borrowers, became increasingly mistrustful and pushed for greater accountability. In October 1731, as bankruptcy proceedings loomed, John Thomson and George Robinson fled the country.[49] Their confederates, company officials and legions of investors were left to sort out the convoluted schemes which combined frauds large and small. It soon became evident that vast sums were missing, to a combined total of approximately £500,000.[50] The South Sea Company debacle, a decade earlier, was the obvious point of comparison. However, at least one writer felt the betrayal by these directors was far worse. 'In a Word, the South-Sea Directors, though they exceeded the Plunderers of the Charitable Corporation in the Weight of their Offences, yet they fell short of them in Measure; for the former left the Capital behind them, but the latter destroy'd the Root, leaving only a few Branches to be divided among those who would be satisfied with the Leaves.'[51]

Containing corruption, preserving commerce

This fraud not only injured those with investments, not only former borrowers from the corporation, but public trust and commercial security were also assailed. The hazards of eighteenth-century business were sufficiently onerous in themselves. Swindles on this scale, from a body intended to help the industrious, unleashed all the latent fears of bankruptcy and failure which haunted manufacturers, traders and investors, large and small. The comparative measure of this financial collapse can be judged using the bankruptcy scale developed by Julian Hoppit, who describes business bankruptcies of more than £100,000 as 'giant'. As well, the collapse of metropolitan sources of credit, like the Charitable Corporation, wreaked havoc within the trading community, as the ripples of this crash spread from one creditor to the next. Julian Hoppit suggests that a crisis of this scale would not necessarily have generated a significant number of related bankruptcies;[52] but there is no doubt about the amount of related suffering that ensued and the discredit that now attached to the concept of charitable loan banks.[53] It also raised troubling issues about the morality of a corporate philosophy which exemplified Bernard Mandeville's much debated concepts in *The Fable of the Bees*. Mandeville claimed that private vices like avarice, vanity or consumer desires could lead to public benefits through the stimulation of trade, enabling a trading nation like England to flourish. The Charitable Corporation epitomized the view that a charitable investment for profit could yield public and private benefits, an argument bruited on a number of occasions when there were handsome profits to be made.[54] The challenge for society as a whole was to weather the storms of untrammelled greed and sharp dealing, even as they subscribed to the underlying tenets of capitalism. Meanwhile, the government was urged to help the injured and defend commerce and finance while holding the fraudulent to account.[55]

To those not immediately affected, there was a lovely irony in the conversion of a charitable impulse into such disorder, and, for a time, this latest bubble became the stuff of comedic jibes. In 1732, a character 'Stocks' described the Charitable Corporation to London audiences as 'a method invented by some very wise men, by which the rich may be charitable to the poor and be money in pocket for it'. In a similar vein, an article entitled 'Of Charity' concluded that in the case of the Charitable Corporation 'Charity begins at Home, is a Proverb which has been verified by Experience. … The Charitable Corporation for the Relief of the Industrious Poor, have been twitted with an Observation, that a Poor Tradesman must be very industrious to have any Transactions with them and not be undone.'[56] In the end very few were enriched – those needful of small loans had been neglected for a number of years, while many hundreds of investors came away much poorer. Of the investors and creditors, just under 300 people were approved by Parliament as worthy objects of charity, with outstanding debts from £2 15s for unpaid plasterer's work and £10 owed to the spinster Sarah Brion for a single share to nearly £9,000 in now worthless shares held by the gentleman Walter Molesworth and over £7,000 in worthless notes and bonds lying in the hands of Charlotte Whetstone, spinster.[57] However, the majority of the debts reflect the predominantly modest investment profiles of middle-class stockholders, who, like the necessitous Londoners, were undone by this fraud. The scale of public outrage on their behalf concerned Sir Robert Walpole and his government, as allegations of corrupt practices by Members of Parliament allied to Walpole brought an uncomfortable problem closer to home. The immediate aim was to contain the scandal, identify the instigators and attempt a seeming resolution.[58] Committees were duly struck, investigators unleashed and the history of graft and mismanagement opened to the light of day. Investigators pointed with growing assurance to the active connivance of John Thomson and George Robinson, plus the self-serving acquiescence of the committee of management and directors, like Sir Robert Sutton and Sir Archibald Grant.[59] However, Thomson, along with George Robinson, having fled to the Continent with 'Money, Notes, Jewels, and other Effects belonging to the Charitable Corporation', attracted the greatest notice. Parliament forbade other central players from leaving its jurisdiction, or from moving any assets.[60] These efforts, too little and too late, offer a unique perspective on the way in which the corporation was ultimately viewed.

From the time John Thomson absconded, diplomats attempted to track his movements and sent news to Westminster which was increasingly troubling. As Walpole's political enemies charged his allies with venality and fraud, others in the government began to hint at more sinister political intrigues, tying Thomson to the Jacobites.[61] The scandal of London's Charitable Corporation swept through Europe's commercial and court circles, and speculation intensified when Jacobite links were discerned and Thomson's loyalty was impugned.[62] Rumours swirled through Europe's capitals and the pages of the press, scandalizing readers with news of Thomson's arrest in Rome at the Pretender's behest and his quick release.[63] One informant insisted that:

> the Design of some People in the Charitable Corporation was to permit the Jacobits [sic] to subscribe for large sums [as stockholders]; which was to be Imploy'd by them towards the Carreying on of what they had or, might project, in favour of the pretender; who upon his Establishment, was to repair and Indemnify the loss the said Company (and Proprietors might have sustained) this I am assured to be, the Rail [real] Ground work of the Corporation Affaire.[64]

Shortly after Thomson's discharge from prison, a public missive arrived in London from the Pretender's agent in Rome, in which he let it be known that 'People, in these Parts' were concerned about the great suffering caused by the collapse of the Charitable Corporation and tantalized his readers with descriptions of the papers found in Thomson's possession, including the 'Minutes of his most secret Affairs'. All of these, claimed this correspondent, would be returned to the proper authorities, but not until they 'should agree and consent to certain Articles'.[65] The attempted negotiation outraged parliamentarians, who ordered Belloni's letter to be burned by the public hangman, but not before many copies had been printed, adding to the mass of pamphlets spawned by this scandal.[66] The almost daily revelations of malfeasance and political collusion fed a different type of speculation 'with which this Metropolis and the City of Westminster abound, from a Shoemaker in a Garret to the Drabs at Billingsgate, the Cynder-Wenches in a Dust-cart, and the Mumpers in a Geneva-Shop, who think they have as much right to box Politicks as a Pedant to chop Logick'.[67] The political tumult fired editorialists, Whig and Tory, who filled the pages of competing broadsheets with charges and counter-charges, as the official inquiry ground on, gathered evidence and distrained the principles.[68] Thomson depended for a time on the Jacobite community for his protection and began his own negotiation, demanding £2,500 'out of his own Effects' and permission to give the money to his aged father. Jacobites and informants offered claims and counter-claims, promising more if money were provided. In the cat-and-mouse game which followed, the distress of the creditors took second place to the political manoeuvring and the need to apportion blame as far from the seat of prime ministerial power as possible. In the spring of 1733, Thomson negotiated his return to England and testimony before the House on his contribution to this debacle.[69]

Conclusion

If John Thomson was ruined through the retribution of British agents and if his fellow conspirators were shamed and imprisoned, however briefly, theirs were minor penalties compared with the broader repercussions of the collapse. A continuing stream of petitions and reports poured out from impoverished stockholders, at the same time as corporation supporters lobbied to carry on what they saw as an essential business. The first and foremost concern of those injured was to secure some sort of compensation; a sympathetic Parliament authorized that a lottery be held, but only 15 per cent of the losses were recovered by this means, leaving many plaintiffs no better off.[70] Equally important was the fraud which enveloped the Charitable Corporation, stigmatizing the premiss of the organization as long as the memory of these events survived. However, even amid the fracas, some defended the concept which had inspired the organization.[71] John Asgill had written imaginative tracts on money and banking[72] and he now championed charitable lending, differentiating the purpose and original function of the corporation from the scandal which ensued. He argued in favour of the productive power of loans and more particularly the value of lending to the enterprising poor, men and women. Asgill's logic was simple and telling, reminiscent of the sermon by William Sherlock: 'Charity is distributed either by Loan or Gift. The Loan is for Prevention of Poverty. The Gift is Relief under it. Therefore the Loan is the greatest Charity. As it is the greater Skill in Physick to prevent Disease than to cure it.' In closing he demanded: 'Must therefore good Actions or good Intentions be condemned, because accidental Evils may arise from them?'[73] But witty disparagements circulated more widely than did thoughtful support for accessible, inexpensive credit.[74]

Nevertheless, the question of credit continued to be debated. As I noted previously, the1745 inquiry into pawnbroking led to extensive testimony before the House of Commons, where wealthy exemplars of the trade pointed to the dealers who also traded in gin or cheap goods as the source of most problems in this sector. Their testimony evidently swayed the House, and restrictions were placed on the exchange of pawns for liquor, though no further legislation was forthcoming until the next decade. From the testimony brought before the House, legislators could also see how essential this lending was to a large and diverse sector of society. Would Parliament then support pawnbrokers as the primary providers of loans for the common people? Or would the institutional structure of charitable loan banks play a further role in sustaining the economy? In 1745, supporters of the Charitable Corporation launched another public campaign, drawing a clear distinction between the criminal bent of a few and the broad needs of the many, differentiating the legitimate workings of the corporation and the all too common petty frauds which bedevilled patrons of pawnbrokers. One pamphlet noted that: 'during the whole Course of the Dealings of the Charitable Corporation with Borrowers, never any one made a just Complaint of a Fraud in his Pledge; whereas, out of more than one thousand Pawnbrokers dispersed over the Cities of London, Westminster, and Southwark (it is apprehended) so much cannot truly be said of any single one of them'.[75] The petitioners requested permission to raise 'a small moderate Capital' and accepted any restrictions proposed by Parliament to limit further capital increases in order that 'the Corporation may once more become an Asylum for needy and industrious Persons'. The request was refused; but the issue was not yet dead. In 1749, a lengthy exposition assessed the very real tensions between pawnbrokers and the advocates of the Charitable Corporation, emphasizing the international heritage of loan banks and the 'great Service to the Necessitous' other similar institutions provided. The central matter was the rate of interest charged by pawnbrokers, the more generous conditions previously provided by the Charitable Corporation and the essential service it could offer the labouring and industrious classes.[76]

Proponents of accessible, inexpensive credit employed every rhetorical device they could muster, highlighting the charity of lending at lower interest rates and the invaluable support they provided to the classes served. But neither the power of these arguments nor the needs of the many were sufficient to sway the legislature. The Charitable Corporation was not revived, neither were any alternative loan banks attempted in England for the next fifty years. Although there was a growing need for small-scale credit, no fiscal innovations would address that issue until the nineteenth century, when a new generation of charitable innovators addressed the question of cheaper credit for the labouring classes. None of the loan societies established in England in that era adopted the use of pawns. This in itself restricted the number and kinds of people deemed acceptable as borrowers, dramatically limiting the number of women borrowers. At the end of the next century, a critic of the banking system could justifiably claim that banking services, particularly with regard to credit, were still wholly inadequate for the working poor.[77] Thus the corruption of the Charitable Corporation and the neglect of its clientele left a vulnerable but dynamic sector of society to pay whatever interest the formal or informal pawnbrokers chose to apply; it also left them more economically at risk and less well served.[78] Ultimately, the field of small-scale credit remained dependent on entrepreneurial initiatives of individual pawnbrokers, whose interests were very much at odds with their clients'. Pawning at high and sometimes usurious rates continued to be the principal avenue open to the mass of petty dealers, hawkers, artisans and housewives until the early nineteenth century, and then, as I show elsewhere, women were very poorly served by the new institutional structures devised. Among the unanswerable questions which arise from this history is to what extent the absence of cheaper credit impeded the economic health and social mobility of individuals and families. Throughout this long period of modernization, credit remained an essential requisite of domestic and business management, however modest, though this came with attendant tolls and recurrent dangers for borrowers. Neither worldly goods nor bodily integrity were exempt from legal and market incursions, as Margot Finn eloquently observes in her study of the rise of a national system of courts for the recovery of small debts. 'The proliferation of petty credit contracts at the lower levels of society contributed significantly to this reformation of law and contract by commercial culture', notes Finn. However, in returning 'labourers, artisans and petty producers to the embrace of civil process, eighteenth-century courts of conscience also distanced the small debtor emphatically from the much-vaunted protections of the rule of law'. Risks and costs continued in distinctively English forms throughout this period of modernization and those dependent upon such credit paid the price.[79]

In spite of its egregious failure, the Charitable Corporation represented an important conceptual innovation in the English-speaking world. The experiment brought charity and lending together and expressed in material form the view that entrepreneurial assistance was the key to individual well-being – a fundamental liberal tenet. Debates surrounding the best way to apply this new commercial and social policy resulted in a distinctive profit-making charity, which may have stimulated economic initiatives within the metropolis, at least for a time. However, the political taint of the Corporation fraudsters and the ensuing embezzlement dissuaded Parliament from further support for this initiative; thereafter, the concept was eschewed as an element of public policy outside of Catholic and continental Europe. The association with Jacobite intrigues, coming within years of the last foray by the Pretender, in 1745, was a further fatal contamination not readily ignored by English government circles. However, within the wider economic and social context the Charitable Corporation came at a timely moment, as the foundations of industrial capitalism were being set in place. In the debates surrounding the venture, the discipline of credit was identified as a means of satisfying the 'Wants of the Industrious Poor'. William Sherlock's argument that 'lent Money ... encourages ... Industry' among the poor was matched by his equally powerful assertion that credit 'keeps the Rod over' their backs.[80] These claims would take material form in the hands of the next generation of social theorists, as well as among late twentieth-century advocates of micro-credit. Ultimately, these conceptual assertions were as important as the failed experiment itself. For even with the failure of the most advantageous plebeian credit institution, the new theories and practices of everyday fiscal management inexorably developed as central policy tenets of the Capitalist Age.

Notes

1 There is an extensive bibliography surrounding the disciplining of the labouring classes, beginning with the work of E. P. Thompson in the 1960s. More recently, historians have pointed out the discipline enforced within the aspiring middle ranks.

Examples of the former include E. P. Thompson, *The Making of the English Working Class* (London, 1963) and 'Time, work-discipline, and industrial capitalism', *Past and Present* 38 (1967); Nicholas Rogers, 'Popular protest in early Hanoverian London', *Past and Present* 79 (1978); John Brewer and John Styles (eds), *An Ungovernable People: The English and their Law in the Seventeenth and Eighteenth Centuries* (London, 1980); Paul Slack (ed.), *Rebellion, Popular Protest and the Social Order in Early Modern England* (Cambridge, 1984); Lee Davidson, Tim Hitchcock, Tim Keirn and Robert B. Shoemaker (eds), *Stilling the Grumbling Hive: The Response to Social and Economic Problems in England, 1689–1750* (New York, 1992); also Margaret Hunt, *The Middling Sort: Commerce, Gender, and the Family in England, 1680–1780* (Berkeley CA, 1996), especially chapter 2.

2 There is a vast literature arising from the contemporary studies of traditional credit practice, as well as assessments of micro-credit programmes. For examples of the former see Shirley Ardener and Sandra Burman (eds), *Money-go-rounds: The Importance of Rotating Savings and Credit Associations for Women* (Oxford, 1995), and Karen Tranberg Hansen, 'Budgeting against uncertainty: cross-class and transethnic redistribution mechanisms in urban Zambia', *African Urban Studies* 21 (spring 1985). Contemporary micro-credit initiatives include Ruth Pearson and Erika Watson, 'Giving women the credit: the Norwich Full Circle Project', *Gender and Development* 5:3 (1997); Ben Rogaly, 'Micro-finance evangelism, "destitute women" and the hard selling of a new anti-poverty formula', *Development in Practice* 6:2 (1996); Susan Johnson and Ben Rogaly, *Microfinance and Poverty Reduction* (Oxford, 1997). For a broad assessment of gender and development issues see Irene Tinker, 'The making of a field: advocates, practitioners, and scholars' in *Persistent Inequalities: Women and World Development* (New York, 1990).

3 For a short summary of the Grameen Bank story see Muhammad Yunus, 'The Grameen Bank', *Scientific American*, November 1999. For a more detailed account see Shahidur R. Khandker, *Fighting Poverty with Microcredit: Experience in Bangladesh* (Oxford, 1998).

4 See, for example, Aidan Hollis and Arthur Sweetman, 'Microcredit: What can we learn from the past?' *World Development* 26:2 (1998).

5 Margot Finn, *The Character of Credit: Personal Debt in English Culture, 1740–1914* (Cambridge, 2003), pp. 4–11, 197–207.

6 Craig Muldrew, *The Economy of Obligation: The Culture of Credit and Social Relations in Early Modern England* (Basingstoke, 1998), pp. 2–3.

7 Finn's exploration of the creation of a new court system dedicated to the recovery of small debts from this social segment illustrates the development of new thinking and practice.

8 Raymond de Roover, *Money, Banking and Credit in Mediaeval Bruges: Italian Merchant Bankers, Lombards and Money Changers. A Study in the Origins of Banking* (Cambridge MA, 1948), pp. 113–21; Brian Pullan, *Rich and Poor in Renaissance Venice: The Social Institutions of a Catholic State to 1620* (Cambridge MA, 1971), pp. 450–70.

9 See also Sandra Cavallo, *Charity and Power in Early Modern Italy: Benefactors and their Motives in Turin, 1541–1789* (Cambridge, 1996), pp. 110–11; Cissie C. Fairchilds, *Poverty and Charity in Aix-en-Provence, 1640–1789* (Baltimore MD, 1976), pp. 19, 27, 54, 58; Montserrat Carbonell-Esteller, 'Second-hand Markets and Microcredit Institutions in Barcelona, Eighteenth to Nineteenth Centuries', paper presented at the conference 'Les Circulations des objets d'occasion', European University Institute, Florence, 2002.

10 At least one 'mount of piety' was successfully established in Ireland. See M. Barrington, *An Address to the Inhabitants of Limerick, on the Opening of the Mont de Piété, or Charitable Pawn Office* ... (Dublin, 1836).

11 *Proposals for Establishing a Charitable Fund in the City of London by Voluntary Gifts and Loans of Money* ... , 2nd edn (London, 1706).

12 For example, in 1548, Felix Verhoven, a merchant from Antwerp, applied for permission to begin a trade as a pawnbroker, stipulating that his terms would be fair and modest, in comparison to others working in this trade. Those assessing his proposal found it to be 'a more charitable way ... and having an especial eye to the supportation and aid of the poor who some time be constrained to borrow but small sums of money and knoweth not whither to go for the same'. C. H. Williams (ed.), *English Historical Documents* V (London, 1967), p. 1012.

13 Phillip Stubbes, *The Anatomie of Abuses* (London, 1583), no pagination.

14 John Stow, *Survey of the Cities of London and Westminster ... Corrected, Improved ... in the Year 1720 by John Strype* ... , 6th edn (London, 1745), pp. 366–7.

15 Francis Godwin James noted that many funds designed to meet the need for small loans came to be used largely by wealthier traders and merchants as a source of cheap short-term credit. Francis Godwin James, 'Charity endowments as sources of local credit in seventeenth- and eighteenth-century England', *Journal of Economic History* 8 (1948), pp. 158–161. For an example of a charitable loan fund in York see *English Historical Documents* V, p. 1013.

16 1 James I, cap. 21, quoted in W. A. H. Hows, *A History of Pawnbroking, Past and Present* (London, 1847), p. 37.

17 C 108/34, Public Record Office.

18 James, 'Charity endowments', p. 156; Barrington, *Address to the Inhabitants of Limerick*, pp. 9–11.

19 *S.P. Dom.*, *Eliz.*, 110, No. 51, quoted in Richards, *Early History of Banking*, p. 93. Craig Muldrew notes the surge in litigation in the Elizabethan era over debts of less than 4s, reflecting the growth in transactions at that level and the pressures brought to bear on the court system. Muldrew, *Economy of Obligation*, pp. 221, 205.

20 J. Cooke, *Unum Necessarium* (London, 1648), and Balthazar Gerbier, *Some Considerations on the two great Staple Commodities of England* (London, 1651), quoted in Richards, *Early History of Banking*, pp. 95–6. Another author who advocated a 'Bank or Mount of Charity' to 'lend poore people upon pawnes' was H. Robinson, *England's Safety in Trades Encrease* (London, 1641), pp. 43–4.

21 The petitioners were asking for a commercial rate of over 16 per cent per annum, which, as it was lower than regular pawnbrokers' rates, suggests the latter's rates of interest. W. R. Scott, *The Constitution and Finance of English, Scottish and Irish Joint Stock Companies to 1720* I (1912, repr. Gloucester MA, 1968), p. 364.

22 Samuel Lambe, *Seasonable Observations Humbly offered to his Highness the Lord Protector* (London, 1657), see especially p. 16. *Reasons for the Passing of the Bill concerning Settlement of Debts and Loans upon Pawns to prevent the great Extortion of Brokers, and for the Easie Relief of Necessitated Persons* (London, 1680); Richards, *Early History of Banking*, pp. 99–105.

23 *Reasons for the Passing of the Bill*.

24 James, 'Charity endowments', p. 156; Barrington, *Address to the Inhabitants of Limerick*, pp. 8–9; Pullan, *Rich and Poor*, pp. 450–5, 465–6.

25 *Reasons for the Passing of the Bill concerning Settlement of Debts ...* .
26 William Sherlock, *The Charity of Lending without Usury ... in a Sermon preach'd before the Right Honourable the Lord Mayor ... on Tuesday in Easter-Week ...* (London, 1692), p. 9. He noted that the returns on interest also sustained widows and orphans.
27 Sherlock, *The Charity of Lending,* pp. 22–3.
28 Sherlock, *The Charity of Lending,* pp. 24–5.
29 For a full elaboration of the theorizing surrounding the issue of charity see Donna T. Andrew, *Philanthropy and Police: London Charity in the Eighteenth Century* (Princeton NJ, 1989), especially chapter 1.
30 *Now is the Time: or, The Proposal of the Loan-bank Seasonable* (London, 1694?).
31 Donna Andrew notes that 'Despite all attempts to find new solutions and employments, most of the proposed schemes turned out to be variations of the workhouse.' Andrew, *Philanthropy and Police,* p. 28. The use of charity as a means to stimulate plebeian industry was a novel exception.
32 Stowe Mss 164, f. 105, British Library; J. M. Bulloch, 'The Charitable Corporation', *Notes and Queries,* 4 April 1931, p. 237. Legal rates of interest were periodically examined and set by Parliament, beginning in the Tudor period.
33 This corporate focus was perhaps one of the most unusual at a time when a host of similar enterprises adopted a joint-stock framework. See Scott, *English ... Joint-Stock Companies* I; Charles Wilson, *England's Apprenticeship, 1603–1763,* 2nd edn (London, 1984), pp. 172–6; M. J. Daunton, *Progress and Poverty: An Economic and Social History of Britain, 1700–1850* (Oxford, 1995), pp. 343–51.
34 Scott, *English ... Joint-Stock Companies* III, p. 380; Bulloch, *Notes and Queries,* p. 237.
35 *Advertisement From the* CHARITABLE FUND *intended to be establish'd in London, by voluntary Gifts and Loans of Money, to Relieve and Support poor Seamens Families, and other Necessitous Persons ...* (London, 1708).
36 Peter Earle, Margaret Hunt and John Smail note the power of the disciplined commercial precepts within the middle class, guiding their behaviour and directing their energies. Those who routinely borrowed from pawnbrokers, who might come to rely on the Charitable Corporation, certainly included members of the middle and lower middle classes, as well as large numbers of labouring poor. Encouraging more disciplined behaviour within this latter group was certainly one of the aims of this and other social movements at the opening of the eighteenth century. Peter Earle, *The Making of the English Middle Class: Business, Society and Family Life in London, 1660–1730* (London, 1989); Margaret Hunt, *The Middling Sort: Commerce, Gender, and the Family in England, 1680–1780* (Berkeley CA, 1996); and John Smail, *The Origins of Middle-Class Culture: Halifax, Yorkshire, 1660–1780* (Ithaca NY, 1994).
37 For further insight into patterns of female investment see Barbara Todd, 'London Women's Investments in the Age of the Financial Revolution', and Amy M. Froide, 'The Role of Single Women as Creditors in Early Modern England', unpublished papers presented at the North American Conference on British Studies, Boston MA, November 1999.
38 *Report of the Commissioners appointed to Examine, State and Report, who of the Sufferers in the Charitable Corporation are Objects of Compassion* (London, 1733).
39 This was an interesting choice of sideline, since this service was also becoming essential for more London traders. Bulloch, 'The Charitable Corporation', p. 237.
40 Later testimony before the House of Commons illustrates exactly which groups were

most in need of the services provided by pawnbrokers and the Charitable Corporation. *Journal of the House of Commons* (hereafter *J.H.C.*), vol. 25, 46.

41 *Mons Pietatis Londinensis: A Narrative or Account of the Charitable Corporation ... In a Letter to ****** (London, 1719), pp. 3–6. *A Short History of the Charitable Corporation. From the Date of their Charter, to their late Petition ...* (London, 1732), p. 11. Security bonds were also required on the Secretary (£1,000), the Cashier (£5,000), the Accountant (£3,000), as well as the Warehouse Keeper (£10,000).

42 *Mons Pietatis Londinensis*, p. 6.

43 Stowe Mss 164, f. 103, British Library.

44 Scott, *English Joint-Stock Companies* III, p. 380; Bulloch, 'The Charitable Corporation', p. 238.

45 I. J. Simpson, 'Sir Archibald Grant and the Charitable Corporation', *Scottish Historical Review* 44 (1965). The cashier appointed was one George Robinson, who was also a stockbroker with an office in Lombard Street and allegedly encouraged directors like Sir Archibald Grant in their disastrous investments in schemes like the York Buildings Company (another fraudulent venture). Grant used embezzled funds to speculate on stock in the York Buildings Company, funnelling money through his broker, George Robinson. For a fuller elaboration of the York Buildings Company see A. J. G. Cummings, 'The York Buildings Company: A Case Study in Eighteenth-Century Corporation Mismanagement', unpublished PhD thesis, University of Strathclyde, 1980.

46 *J.H.C.*, vol. 22, pp. 670–1.

47 My thanks to Professor Michael Mills, Classics Department, University of New Brunswick, for his translation of this phrase.

48 *A Letter from a Member of Parliament to his Correspondent at Rome* (London, 1732), pp. 14–16.

49 *J.H.C.*, vol. 21, p. 711; *The Report of the Gentlemen appointed by the General Court of the Charitable Corporation, held the 19th of October, the 18th of November, and the 21st of December last; to inspect the State of their Affairs, etc. As the Same was given into the General Court of January 12, 1731/32. by Dr Mowbray, Chairman* (London, 1732), pp. 6–7.

50 *J.H.C.*, vol. 21, pp. 788, 797; *Report of the Commissioners appointed to Examine, State, and Report, who of the Sufferers in the Charitable Corporation are Objects of Compassion*, p. 4; *The Case of the Charitable Corporation and the Relief they Humbly Pray* (London, 1732?), p. 1.

51 *Letter from a Member of Parliament ...* , p. 31.

52 Julian Hoppit, 'Financial crises in eighteenth-century England', *Economic History Review*, 2nd series 39:1 (1986), pp. 44–6; Julian Hoppit, *Risk and Failure in English Business, 1700–1800* (Cambridge, 1987), pp. 63, 70–1, 142–3. Hoppit notes that 'The instability of credit, growth and the business environment cannot be ignored. ... Even if most businesses managed to avoid bankruptcy and failure, it is worth remembering that all firms made their decisions within this more erratic and unpredictable environment' (pp. 179–80).

53 A later author painted a dire picture of the repercussions arising from the collapse of the Charitable Corporation. This depiction may well have been overdrawn; however, there is little doubt about the scale of the genuine losses. 'The distress occasioned by this bankruptcy was appalling, pervading nearly every class of society. Large sums had

been borrowed at high interest. The small capitalist was entirely ruined; and there was scarcely a class in English life which had not its representative and its sufferers. The poor were unable to get their food; the rich were robbed of their jewels; families accustomed to affluence were starving ... the writer believes there is no parallel in commercial history.' John Francis, *Chronicles and Characters of the Stock Exchange* (London, 1855), p. 55.

54 For the views and impact of Mandeville and his critics see E. G. Hundert, *The Enlightenment's Fable: Bernard Mandeville and the Discovery of Society* (Cambridge, 1994), and Bernard Mandeville, *The Fable of the Bees: or, Private Vices, Publick Benefits. With a Commentary Critical, Historical, and Explanatory by F. B. Kaye* ... (Oxford, 1924). For a study of the creation of the new financial system in England see P. G. M. Dickson, *The Financial Revolution in England: A Study in the Development of Public Credit, 1688–1756* (London, 1967).

55 The significance of this financial crisis was clear to one author, who saw it as a threat to the material and philosophical foundations of English society. 'The two Hinges of Society, on which all Government of what Form soever turn are Property, and the Punishment of the Guilty by Property, I understand the Right every Member in Society has to the Things which he possesses: And from this arises the Duty of the governing Power in every Society, to punish those who injure or infringe the Property of Others, for without doing this, Property the Basis of Society could not be preserved.' *A Short History of the Charitable Corporation*, pp. 27–8.

56 Henry Fielding, *The Lottery* (London, 1732), quoted in Bulloch, 'The Charitable Corporation', p. 240; *The Gentleman's Magazine* II (1732), pp. 572–3. For a study of a later financial crisis see H. V. Bowen, '"The pests of human society": stockbrokers, jobbers and speculators in mid-eighteenth-century Britain', *History* 78:1 (1993).

57 What is noteworthy in the list of sufferers is the number of small and medium shareholders – men and women – with capital vested in this enterprise. Of those owed money from stocks, notes, bonds or other debts, over 55 per cent of the women were owed under £200, while 72 per cent of men were owed under £500. *Report of the Commissioners appointed to Examine, State and Report, who of the Sufferers in the Charitable Corporation are Objects of Compassion*, appendices A–F. Some commentators considered that single women were particularly deserving of recompense by the government, since they would be least fitted to earn money from other ventures. *The Gentleman's Magazine* II (1732), p. 649.

58 See, for example, the Bill quickly drawn up to prevent many of the other principals in the corporation from leaving the country. 5 Geo. II, Public Acts, cap. 32. Also Andrew Arthur Hanham, 'Whig Opposition to Sir Robert Walpole in the House of Commons, 1727–1734', unpublished PhD thesis, University of Leicester, 1992.

59 Simpson, 'Sir Archibald Grant', pp. 54–9; 5 Geo. II, Public Acts, cap. 32. They also suffered the public humiliation of having the penalties for their crimes of omission and commission debated in the House. W.S. Esq., 'A Speech for Relieving the Unhappy Sufferers in the Charitable Corporation: As it was spoken in the House of Commons, May 8, 1732' in *Five Speeches: As they were spoken in the House of Commons* (London, n.d.).

60 *Letter from a Member of Parliament* ... , p. 26; *J.H.C.*, vol. 22, p. 150.

61 Simpson, 'Sir Archibald Grant', p. 54.

62 The Paris-based ambassador, Earl Waldegrave, corresponded regularly with the Secretary of State, Thomas Pelham-Holles, Duke of Newcastle, who also travelled on

occasion to Paris. For a brief summary of the growing importance of diplomatic missions and a short sketch of Earl Waldegrave see J. R. Jones, *Britain and the World, 1649–1815* (London, 1980), pp. 42–3.

63 Add. Mss 32,777, f. 30, British Library.

64 Add. Mss 32,777, ff. 23, 24, British Library.

65 *A Letter from John Angelo Belloni, to the Gentlemen of the Committee of the Parliament of England, appointed to inspect the Affairs of the Charitable Corporation* (London, 1732).

66 Add. Mss 32,777, f. 90. The Belloni letter offered an opportunity for a full-fledged rant against the Pretender and his Tory acolytes. 'Pray, Gentlemen, give my Service to the *Chevalier* of the *Gingerbread Countenance*, and tell him, that the insolent and audacious Letter, which by the unanimous Concurrence of both Houses of Parliament, was burned by the Hands of the Common Hangman, has made many Proselytes than he imagines; and I advise him not to send another from the same Mint.' *Letter from a Member of Parliament …* , pp. 4–5.

67 *Letter from a Member of Parliament …* , p. 9.

68 *The Gentleman's Magazine* reprinted a range of editorial positions on the Charitable Corporation scandal. For 1732, for example, see vol. II, pp. 772, 782, 785, 801–2, 808, 837, 1078.

69 *The Gentleman's Magazine* II (1732), p. 1078; III (1733), pp. 99, 153.

70 Bulloch, 'The Charitable Corporation', p. 240. Those plaintiffs worth more than £5,000 did not benefit from the money raised by the lottery. Add. Mss 35,876, f. 198; Simpson, 'Sir Archibald Grant', pp. 56–8.

71 *Proposals for the Regulation, or An entire Suppression of Pawnbrokers … to which are Added some Considerations on the present Calamities of the Sufferers by the Charitable Corporation* (London, 1732). This author listed the abusive practices of some pawnbrokers and concluded that, in spite of the frauds committed by the Charitable Corporation, it met the credit needs in an essential way, much as did other loan banks in the Netherlands.

72 Among John Asgill's publications are, for example, *Remarks … for establishing of a Land-bank* (London, 1696); *Several Assertions proved in order to Create another Species of Money than Gold and Silver* (London, 1696).

73 John Asgill, *An Essay upon Charity, occasioned by the Calumnies raised against the Charitable Corporation, created by Letters Patent by Queen Anne …* (London, 1731), pp. 9–10, 15.

74 Many comments of this sort were printed and reprinted in various journals and magazines. It would be hard for an editor to resist such materials, since they provided such scope for political, moral and comedic observations. One commentary published in *The Craftsman* was later reprinted in *The Gentleman's Magazine*. The author observed that 'a Poor Tradesman must be very industrious to have any Transactions with them [the Charitable Corporation] and not be undone; and turbulent People have Nick nam'd the Managers, Gentlemen of the Industry, offering to prove that they have disposed of several thousand Pounds, by way of Alms, upon Themselves, their Relations and Creatures.' *The Gentleman's Magazine* II (1732), p. 573. See also *The Tricks of the Town, or Ways and Means of getting Money, wherein the various Lures, Wiles and Artifices practised by the Designing and Crafty upon the Unwary are fully exposed. Recommended to the Serious Perusal of all Adventurers and Sharers in Bubble*

Undertakings, the Pursuers of Pennyworths and Bargain Buyers. Chiefly collected from some Papers of the ingenious Mr John Thomson, scattered between Laurence Pountney Hill [where one of the Corporation warehouses was situated, the other being in Fenchurch Street] *and Dover* [from which he sailed to France] (London, 1732).

75 *The Case of the Charitable Corporation, As well in Regard to their Dealings in Contra-distinction to the Pawnbrokers, as to their present Incapacity to carry on Trade for Want of a Sufficient Fund* (London, 1745?).

76 *Reasons for Reviving the Charitable Corporation, in a Letter to a Member of Parliament* (London, 1749), pp. 4–8, 19.

77 Henry W. Wolff, *Co-operative Credit Banks: A Help alike Economic and Educational for the Labouring and Cultivating Classes* (London, 1898), p. 6.

78 It is perhaps little wonder that some of the many friendly societies also offered small loans to their membership, given the continuing and pressing need for small amounts of capital.

79 Finn, *Character of Credit*, p. 202. See also pp. 17–22, 197–235.

80 Sherlock, *Charity of Lending*, p. 23.

4

Shifting currency: the practice and economy of the second-hand trade, c. 1600–1850

O VER THE COURSE OF OUR LIVES we are swathed by blankets, draped by garments, our thirst quenched by drinks from glass, earthenware or metal vessels, our passage through life eased or pained by fine or ill-fitting shoes, our bodies rested on four-legged chairs, two-footed benches or stools. How these and other goods were acquired, discarded, replaced or sold in past centuries has recently become the focus of intensive study. The choices made were shaped by the priorities of time and place, rank and income, needs and desires given material shape. The possessions used, reused and amassed in greater or lesser quantities represent objective worth as well as more qualitative values within their social milieu.[1] The second-hand trade was a ubiquitous and essential trade, critical for plebeian consumer practice, essential for domestic budgeting. Through the patterns and dynamics of this trade we can appraise great societal transformations, seen from the perspective of the everyday practices of common people, where the nuances of gender and social rank found clear expression.[2] The intricate material lives of our predecessors are a means of illuminating material life where, as Fernand Braudel observed, 'there is at work a complex order, in which the assumptions, tendencies and unconscious pressures of economies, societies and civilizations all contribute'.[3] The apparently trivial exchange of new for old, payments in goods or the pledging of items to obtain credit were among the commonest and longest-lived economic strategies[4] (see Plates 4.1–4.3).

I will consider the second-hand trade first as a socially defined tool enabling consumption. The trade itself enabled complex intersecting needs for generations of plebeian and more affluent men and women. Financial, monetary and economic histories have charted the formalization of currencies, the growth of financial institutions and national economic histories, measuring the advance of regional or imperial economies,

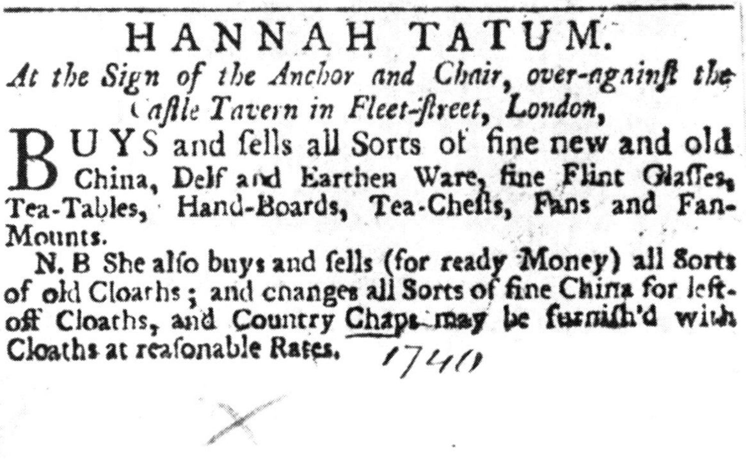

HANNAH TATUM.

At the Sign of the Anchor and Chair, over-againſt the Caſtle Tavern in Fleet-ſtreet, London,

B U Y S and ſells all Sorts of fine new and old China, Delf and Earthen Ware, fine Flint Glaſſes, Tea-Tables, Hand-Boards, Tea-Cheſts, Fans and Fan-Mounts.

N. B She alſo buys and ſells (for ready Money) all Sorts of old Cloaths ; and changes all Sorts of fine China for left-off Cloaths, and Country Chaps may be furniſh'd with Cloaths at reaſonable Rates. *1740*

Plate 4.1   Trade card, Hannah Tatum (London), 1740

the appearance and regulation of coherent systems of sanctioned coinage, banknotes and other fiscal instruments. This is a record of progress, charting movements from primitive to more advanced economies.[5] But beyond these formal parameters was a world of intricate interactions. There was also an irregular, multi-directional traffic, set within a society still dependent to a significant degree on non-currency mediums. These commercial and social expressions represent an important complexity and demand that we revise a simple unitary paradigm of commercial advancement. For even as shops grew in number and sophistication, even as imports and domestic products grew in volume and diversity, there remained persistent patterns of exchange which swirled past glass-fronted emporiums and behind formal market squares. Monetization made slow, irregular and uneven progress, and, even in the nineteenth century, cash transactions as payments for wages or goods were not everywhere the norm. Thus, across many centuries, routine patterns of barter, the translation of goods from one commodity to another and from material form to credit or cash, were a significant feature of the economy. Long-standing practices persisted in the midst of societal change, and these common praxes framed many plebeian interchanges; the longevity of these alternate economic practices requires a cogent re-examination, where the stuff of culture, class and social interaction are recognized for their organic links with the economic.

My focus will be the commonest and most widely owned commodities – clothing and accessories – goods which held the sorts of malleable

All Sorts of Earthen ware. Plates three ha'pence
a piece. Wash hands Bason two pence a piece
A white Stone Mug or a Tea pot

Toute forte de Potterie a un sol et demi par
afiette, des Basins a deux fols piece
des cruches de grais ou des pots a Thé

Plate 4.2 'All Sorts of Earthen ware. Plates three ha'pence a piece. Wash hands
Basons two pence a piece. A white Stone Mug or a Tea pot …'

characteristics including utility and status marking. They were also suitable as alternative currencies, circulating over the long period of time
when there was a scarcity of coinage, during the gradual formalization
of fiscal mediums, acting as adaptable instruments which released

Plate 4.3   Trade card, J. Rutland's Sale-Warehouse (London)

consumptive and productive impulses for centuries. Fashion likewise determined value and demands full consideration. In total, this re-examination will shed new light on the significance of the second-hand trade from the early modern to modern era.

Everyday, second-hand

The value of commodities is to some degree determined by their scarcity. And for much of human history the cost and scarceness of material goods ensured their frugal preservation. Use and reuse defined the everyday for all but a tiny minority, with the careful reassignment of worn or used commodities into new types of service. This circuit – swords into ploughshares, drippings into candles – was more than a metaphorical passage, but comprised the substance of prudent husbandry or thrifty housewifery. However, dramatic and progressive changes in trade and manufacturing stimulated regional economies, and through the sixteenth century scarcity very gradually fell away before rising abundance.[6] The second-hand trade fits within the dynamic of this process as a stimulus to exchange, as an essential prop to routine commerce that grew in scale and significance over the course of this era. At weekly markets, or within habitual retail interactions, women and men invested in material goods that fitted their immediate needs and expressed their relative position within family and community hierarchies. Beyond the buying of bread and beer, or cheese and onions, were a rising number of routine purchases of hosiery, coats, shoes and ribbons that, as Joan Thirsk notes of seventeenth-century England, compel us 'to think deeply about the economic significance of quality and variety in consumer goods, and the influence which different classes of customers exerted upon producers'.[7] The usefulness and novelty of many new commodities, or newly affordable commodities, combined with social, religious and gender expressions whether through the wearing of a white linen handkerchief or the sporting of petticoat-breeches (see Plate 4.4). Classically, much of the focus on material goods has been defined by production and consumption processes, consumption itself being 'the sole end and purpose of all production', according to Adam Smith.[8] But this assertion presents only part of the complexities vested in the goods themselves, which represented many things to their owners, including savings, assets which retained value which in turn could be released. The market itself ensured the liquidity of these items. Consumption was a multifarious process, rarely the final act in the social and economic retail interplay, a fact that was recognized by contemporaries who bought goods to enjoy, but also to ensure their future. Adam Smith was well aware of the inherent mutability of commodities, describing the typical scenario of a poor man in receipt of old clothes. These, Smith theorized, 'he exchanges for other old cloaths which suit him better, or for lodging, or for food, or for money, with which he can buy either food, cloaths or lodging, as he has occasion'.[9] What Smith terms the 'trucking disposition' stood at the root of the second-hand trade, where material goods retained many of the functional features of money, as mediums of exchange and repositories of practical value. 'Barter remained the general rule over enormous areas between the fifteenth and eighteenth centuries,' remarked Braudel. 'But whenever the occasion demanded, it was eked out, as a sort of first step towards money, by the circulation of primitive or 'imperfect' currencies ... . Under the thin surface of the monetary economies, primitive activities continued and blended into the others, in the regular meetings at town markets, or in the more concentrated atmosphere of trade fairs.'[10] What I prefer to term alternative currencies, rather than 'primitive' or 'imperfect currencies', enabled essential plebeian commercial practices: the purchase of goods, the payment of debts or the granting of credit. Without the options afforded by these exchanges many individuals and families would have been at a standstill when trying to arrange their budgets.

Currency was a fraught issue over the long early modern era, when the inadequate production of small coins bedevilled all those who needed

Old Satten Old Taffety or Velvet
Qui a des vieux Taffetas a ... tre

Plate 4.4   'Old Satten Old Taffety or Velvet', from a late seventeenth-century series of street scenes

them for transactions, especially city dwellers, who routinely employed small sums. The rise of formal currencies over the medieval period was marked by a significant imbalance in the coins available in small denomination; little wonder, as the profit for minting tens of thousands of farthings or pennies was negligible. In Europe, coins with little or no silver, called *monnaie noire*, black money, were struck by sanctioned mints, as well as entrepreneurial nobles, all circulating in the markets and all too often in short supply. Inevitably, with few authentic low-value coins available, many *ad hoc* tokens were produced to fill the void – the need was great for tokens with an agreed upon value, however small. In sixteenth-century London, lead tokens, valued at a fraction of a penny, were widely accepted in the absence of alternative legitimate coinage. It is also worth remarking that, in the sixteenth and seventeenth centuries, few people handled anything but copper or base metal coins on a regular basis, or they will have transacted their business without the benefit of any sanctioned currency.[11] In England, these deficiencies persisted through the seventeenth century, and only after the Restoration did the Royal Mint begin to supply more of the needed plebeian specie. John Evelyn's characterization of typical practices in the metropolis paints a scene of creative innovation when 'every tavern and tippling house (in the days of late anarchy and confusion among us) presumed to stamp and utter for immediate exchange [tokens], as they were passable through the neighbourhood ... seldom reaching further than the next street or two'.[12]

Although the Royal Mint made an initial attempt to meet the need for small coins, token production persisted unabated and the many surviving examples stand as material mementoes of a plebeian commerce as vibrant as it was under-served by government. Decades later, the flourish of token production in provincial centres late in the eighteenth century reflected the continuing deficit in currency for wages, as well as the persistent ingenuity of citizens, devising solutions to facilitate exchange. Peter Mathias concludes that 'informal currency ... deserves wider recognition historically'.[13] His focus was the persistence of trade tokens throughout the eighteenth century; however, his point is equally apt for a trade which left less material evidence of its vitality, but was equally essential in the working of the plebeian economy – the second-hand trade in apparel.

The second-hand trade depended on the existence of a modest surplus of goods in the general population, beyond bare necessity, the capacity of labouring and middle-ranking people to buy items filtered through other hands, some from other social ranks. Calamity could bring waves of items on to the market. But, for the second-hand trade to thrive, common people had to have more than single garments to cover their nakedness; there had to be at least the small occasions of surplus, as well as the desire for extra, the means to enhance comfort and reflect some material complexities in their lives and on their persons. The purchases of common folk were the subject of contemporary comment in England, especially where social hierarchies were challenged, as pins, buckles, laces, ribbons and hosiery trickled, then poured through retail channels and into work-roughened hands.[14] Joan Thirsk's ground-breaking study *Economic Policy and Projects* outlines the intersecting pressures of population growth, innovations in agriculture and the sometimes haphazard experiments in new consumer industries. The multitude of ventures which sprang up in late sixteenth and seventeenth-century England employed more and more of the many hands willing to work – knitting stockings, hooking lace, making buttons, growing dyestuffs – earning essential wage supplements.[15] England was not alone in Europe in having labouring and middling ranks who could budget for these niceties, but in north-western Europe it was among the earliest to express these trends in such a dynamic form.[16] This capacity to consume also showed itself in the market for clothing, a fact that Margaret Spufford confirms for seventeenth-century England, where 'people below the level of gentry were relatively well-clad; indeed, almost all of them had some new clothes'.[17] This is a critical discovery, confirming the observations made by Gregory King over three centuries ago that, in his country, clothing purchases represented a quarter of total national expenditure in 1688.[18] These garments, many ready-made, combined with the cast-offs flowing between mistresses and servants to swell the tide of second-hand wares.

The material economy took many forms, including payment for work, in the form of either a perquisite or truck. Wage payments in kind represented a significant category of merchandise flow, a steady tide of goods which coursed through formal and informal channels. The monetization of wages was a fraught question, with employers and employees jockeying for advantage; one segment of employers preferring cash, another insisting on partial or full payment in kind. London footmen were clear on their preference, rioting when it was rumoured that traditional practices were to be altered. Perquisites were a constant source of tension between domestic servants and employers. Thomas Alcock observed that 'anything ... convertible or transferable' might be claimed by servants, including 'torn-up damask clothes and broken silver, to rugs ... and metal of every description'.[19] There were both vigorous efforts to monetize all payments and pressure to continue truck and perquisites, with employers and workers taking various positions. The innumerable local regulations and prosecutions over the centuries suggest the constancy of a practice which put goods into the hands of working men and women and left it to them to decide how to turn these commodities to best advantage, feeding an alternate currency system that buoyed the economy. Without these options, individuals and families would have been hard pressed to manage their affairs.

The second-hand trade was well established in London by the sixteenth century.[20] The convergence of dealers was noted by John Stow, with Houndsditch buildings harbouring 'brokers, sellers of old apparel, and such like'; Thieving Lane in Westminster was another street thick with second-hand dealers by the close of Elizabeth's reign.[21] Each decade saw the progressive expansion of a trade which defied the prescribed models of market exchange, frustrating those who wished for a simple, regulated, one-way system of commerce from producer to seller, then buyer; and dismaying others who wished working people were hedged off from the new range of goods pouring into the market. Inevitably, the second-hand trade ensured a more malleable and complex commerce in used items, parallel to an elaborate pawning network which secured loans or credit through the pledging of goods.[22] In both instances, the hat, ring, shift, waistcoat or cloak could be both a thing to wear and display or a sort of alternative currency, linking the seller or borrower to the market arena. This traffic fuelled day-to-day transactions.

In recent years there has been growing interest in currency substitutes, what some call 'non-money', alternative currencies which facilitate exchanges. Even in modern developed societies there are a range of alternative currencies, from trading stamps to the reward 'miles' offered by airlines. Other systems can be found in developing regions, or in countries rocked by financial crises, as a way to get by. The system described as a 'social currency', devised during the financial crisis that rocked Argentina in the early twenty-first century, exemplifies the latter.[23] Operating 'parallel to the national currency to perform as a medium of exchange', these possess many of the characteristics of money – 'unit of account, medium of exchange and store of value'[24] – without being authorized by the state. The persistence of these currency substitutes into the twenty-first century suggests their significant utility and compels historians to rethink the practices common in the early modern economy, the habitual commutations which persisted across centuries. In turn, these point to the importance of species of goods which were generally available, had a value commonly agreed upon within a wide market and whose mutability ensured a ready translation into other commodities, cash or credit. There were a number of such categories of goods in early modern England.

Margaret Hunt has uncovered a complex trade in seamen's tickets, which moved freely within the seafaring neighbourhoods of London as a pecuniary token accepted among the shopkeepers, pedlars and denizens of the East End, one of several specific commodities spawned in this neighbourhood whose value was understood and whose exchange was assured within this locale.[25] In some respects, these circulated like bills of exchange whose ultimate worth was guaranteed by government payment. In similar dockside neighbourhoods Peter Linebaugh identified the circulation of chips, pieces of wood less than 3 ft in length, ostensibly scrap from the shipbuilding processes, as one of the important traditional perquisites of shipyard workers.[26] During the long reign of chips, shipyard workers could survive while they waited months for their cash wages, using the chips to settle debts or purchase goods in the interim, their value accepted by local residents and the chips becoming part of local housing.[27] Both these mediums of exchange were commonplace in their particular precincts, but their use in a wider community was problematic, since knowledge of their value could not always be assumed nor their acceptance guaranteed. Precious metals and jewels were uniquely placed as mediums of exchange. With those exceptions, at this time, the other most transmutable goods were clothing and textiles – these were the most important of the alternative currencies, the most ubiquitous, the most readily translated in the market, goods whose valuation was assured, a fact known to thieves, common folk and honest dealers. Clothing was transposed into cash at the shopkeeper's counter, at the tavern rail, at the kitchen door, or could also secure short-term credit from official and unofficial pawnbrokers – functions essential for a significant portion of the population from at least the sixteenth century through the nineteenth.[28] A functionary at the Royal Mint commented, in 1757, that the 'Copper coins with us are properly no money, but a kind of *token* … useful in small home trade.'[29] Like tokens and black money, the stuff of the second-hand trade was also 'useful in … home trade', though the flow of this commerce was vast.

Why were clothes and fabrics so commonly used as alternative currencies? What made them acceptable to pedlars and shopkeepers? First, a shirt, headcloth or breeches could be readily evaluated. A basic knowledge of textiles and their qualities was common within the wider public, especially among women, who were trained in the housewifery skills of textile care or production from an early age, but also among a significant number of men.[30] As their value was known, so their price could be determined, ensuring the ready circulation of clothing in formal and informal second-hand markets, through regional, national and international

chains of exchange. Thus, with little effort, Philip Henslowe, the Elizabethan theatrical entrepreneur and pawnbroker, lent 6s to the owner of 'A
dublet & A payer of breches for a chylld'. Henslowe's accounts capture the
dynamism of the second-hand market in Elizabethan London, where, as
elsewhere in Europe, hats and boots, stockings and coats fuelled local
economies and individual accounts (see Tables 4.1–2). Ann Rosalind
Jones and Peter Stallybrass term Henslowe's late sixteenth-century venture 'a banking system in clothes', with Henslowe relying on teams of
women to order and organize the trade.[31] This style of enterprise was
replicated over generations by thousands of similar dealers and pawnbrokers, salesmen and saleswoman, backed by the casual acceptance of
used garments in payment for wares by legions of pedlars and shopkeepers. This mutability is illustrated in the dispersal of a bequest of linen

Table 4.1   Categories of goods pawned, London, 1593–1596

Pawns	% of pawns
Clothing and textiles	62.0
Clothing and other goods	13.0
Household furnishings	12.2
Jewellery and plate	11.5

Source: Ann Rosalind Jones and Peter Stallybrass, Renaissance Clothing and the Materials of Memory (Cambridge, 2000), p. 30.

Table 4.2   Categories of goods pawned, south London, 1667–1671

Categories of pawns	No.	%
Clothing	88	71.54
Soft furnishings	10	8.13
Plate	10	8.13
Clothing, plate and household utensils	7	5.69
'Goods' (unknown)	3	2.44
Clothing and jewellery	2	1.63
Tools	2	1.63
Watches	1	0.81

Note: Total transactions: 123.
Source: C 108/34, Public Record Office, London.

given Elizabeth Busby in the mid-seventeenth century. 'One christening sheet ... she pawned to goodwife Clark of Sandford, one waistcoat ... she did sell to the wife of Thomas Hitchman, one facecloth whereof she made an apron, one tablecloth [with] which she made smocks, and two ruffs, part whereof she cut for herself, and part whereof she sold to the said Hitchman's wife'.[32]

England's cities, towns and villages held growing stocks of used garments and textiles of every quality.[33] And poor women could easily gain a foothold in this trade, where the needs of neighbours and the ease of resale were guaranteed, where their knowledge of cloth and stitchery could be an asset in either legitimate and illicit commerce. These female networks speak to another facet of the traffic: plebeian women organized and secured credit for household ventures, whether these were domestic or commercial in orientation. Trading new for old, or swapping goods, was another part of this practice rooted in antiquity, still followed through the seventeenth, eighteenth and even nineteenth centuries. However, records of such transactions are necessarily sparse, surviving only in ancillary documents, like the eighteenth-century print depicting the hawker of old shoes for brooms (Plate 2.1) and the 1740 advertisement by Hannah Tatum, of Fleet Street, announcing that she 'changes all Sorts of fine China for left-off Cloaths'. Such strategies were not rare, however alien they may seem from a twenty-first-century perspective. Genteel consumers and plebeian bargain hunters followed similar customs for generations; indeed, the practice of trading old clothes for china was so common that Joseph Addison satirized the plight of husbands whose wives metamorphosed favourite breeches 'into a Punch Bowl' or 'Tea Pot' to feed their love of china.[34] Pawning was more readily documented over several centuries, and garments or domestic textiles made up the vast majority of things brought to pawnbrokers, usually conveyed by women organizing individual and household needs. The second-hand trade in apparel was gendered and, although not totally woman-controlled, at every turn and in every corner women were actively engaged securing cash or credit through the manipulation of these items. Investment in apparel became the sum and substance of plebeian budgeting, the source of liquidity for affluent and plebeian patrons throughout Europe; England was no different in this respect.[35]

Trade in used goods was common among tradesmen, from grocers to tailors, chandlers to shoemakers. Typically, in businesses which included retail sales, some selected used goods were accepted in payment or part payment for new wares. Some retailers noted this in their trade designations, for example, but for many others it was so common a part of trade as to be unworthy of note. In my previous study of the clothing trades I surveyed many thousand insurance entries in company ledgers across the eighteenth century, selecting all of those involved in the ready-made and second-hand clothing trades, as well as pawnbrokers. Of this group, many simply listed their line of work, such as clothes dealer and wig maker, or pawnbroker and clothes dealer; but there were also those who listed interesting specializations. The sometimes extraordinary conjunction of occupations suggests how dependent many retailers were on second-hand goods: for example, the stay maker and dealer in old clothes; the alehouse keeper, dealer in bacon and old clothes; the turner and dealer in old and new clothes; and the mat maker and old clothes seller and the dealer in malt, flour and old clothes.[36] The entries in insurance ledgers are often the only surviving remnants of these traders, hinting at the hidden circulation of used goods through retail networks unremarked by most official sources. Evidence gleaned from other surviving records illustrates the most prominent and visible of the second-hand dealers: pawnbrokers. Tables 4.1–5 summarize the items circulating through five businesses, between the late sixteenth and mid-nineteenth centuries in England. I have already shown how the pattern of Philip Henslowe's south London trade matched that of a less famous successor, John Pope, a haberdasher, pawnbroker and moneylender also based in south London, later in the seventeenth century – for both men, 60–70 per cent of their pledged goods comprised wearing apparel. Similarly, probate inventories of ordinary pawnbrokers confirm that, in most cases, clothing was the most voluminous of the second-hand wares, if not the most individually

Table 4.3   Categories of goods pawned, York, 1777–1778

Pawns	No.	%
Clothing and textiles	1,831	81.0
Jewellery and watches	143	6.3
Cutlery and household utensils	77	3.4
Tools and equipment	76	3.3
Hats and wigs	51	2.2
Footwear	34	1.5
Furniture	32	1.4
Books	13	0.6
Spectacles	8	0.3

Note: Sample size: 2,265 transactions.
Source: Acc. 38, York City Archives.

valuable.[37] One hundred years following the records created by John Pope, a business ledger from York illuminates the trade in an even wider array of goods owned by ordinary women and men in this cathedral city; basic apparel was there in volume, along with some fashionable ware like the pair of Bristol stone buttons, woman's new shoes, and silver buckles.

Table 4.4 Categories of goods pawned, Sheffield, 1816

Pawns	No.	%
Clothing	660	83.0
Footwear	41	5.0
Household furnishings	34	4.0
Hats	22	2.8
Clothing and other goods	16	2.0
Cutlery and household utensils	10	1.3
Tools	9	1.0
Spectacles	3	0.4
Pictures	2	0.2
Umbrellas	2	0.2
Books	1	0.1

Note: Sample size: 800 transactions.
Source: J 90/504, Public Record Office, London.

Table 4.5 Categories of goods pawned, east London, 1832–1833

Pawns	No.	%
Clothing and textiles	548	67.0
Footwear	92	11.0
Unknown	38	5.0
Tools	36	4.4
Cutlery, tea equipment, utensils	35	4.2
Jewellery and watches	33	4.0
Furnishings	18	2.2
Hats	8	1.0
Miscellaneous	5	0.6
Umbrellas	4	0.5
Books	1	0.1

Note: Sample size: 818 transactions.
Source: C 110/134, Public Record Office, London.

The sample from Sheffield, in 1816, reflected a similarly vibrant exchange of goods for cash or credit, with over 80 per cent of pledges plebeian clothing. The 1830s sample taken from a London-based pawnbroker shows a slightly lower rate of apparel pawned; but for the women and men of east London's Lime Street, Leadenhall Street, Hackney Road and Whitechapel the garments and personal accoutrements in their possession continued to represent the easiest route to financial liquidity. Despite the variations in time and place, the ratio of apparel to other goods is very clear, with continuing evidence of the use of clothing and accoutrements as savings and currency mechanisms, with value easily realized through pawning and the second-hand markets.[38]

Initially, rich and poor alike availed themselves of the services of pawnbrokers and clothes dealers – in the Henslowe records relatively large sums were lent on quite sumptuous garments. For example, Mrs Rysse pledged her damask gown 'layd with a lace of sylke and gowld' for £5 and Lord Burte received a similar sum for his cloak.[39] These gentlefolk were apparently both comfortable using their garments to get a necessary loan. But over centuries of commercial and fiscal transformations, the elite and middle classes gradually devised more formal financial mechanisms through which to borrow and, at the same time, the traffic with pawnbrokers gradually assumed a more discreditable taint. As pawning became less the norm among the respectable classes, it became seen as the practice of the desperate, the indigent or the profligate. Nonetheless, for at least three centuries, a clothing currency circulated in neighbourhood pawnshops and in the barrows, baskets and shop shelves of second-hand dealers (see Plates 4.5–4.6).

Pawned items typically secured cash for short-term needs, with interest charged for the privilege.[40] But articles were not always reclaimed, or were sold off in bulk at the end of a life of business, flowing into the vast confluence of used stock. The networks of second-hand trade encompassed more than just urban communities, including as well regions and industries distant from the metropolis, wherever the truck system was employed. George Hilton's detailed analysis of the truck system is worthy of attention as a further indicator of the persistent use of alternative payment systems through the nineteenth century, and, wherever the truck system prevailed, there was a further circuit of goods through commercial channels as workers sought to turn these items to good account. Indeed, Hilton observes that 'a considerable part of the business of local retailers in the vicinity of the Ebbw Vale Company's works was buying and re-selling goods from the truck shops'. Some Staffordshire coal and iron masters refused to stock clothing and apparel

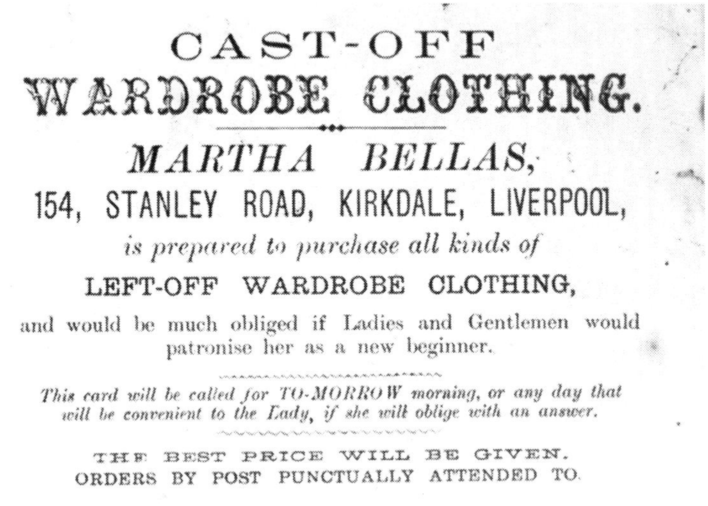

CAST-OFF
WARDROBE CLOTHING.

MARTHA BELLAS,
154, STANLEY ROAD, KIRKDALE, LIVERPOOL,

is prepared to purchase all kinds of

LEFT-OFF WARDROBE CLOTHING,

and would be much obliged if Ladies and Gentlemen would
patronise her as a new beginner.

*This card will be called for TO-MORROW morning, or any day that
will be convenient to the Lady, if she will oblige with an answer.*

THE BEST PRICE WILL BE GIVEN.
ORDERS BY POST PUNCTUALLY ATTENDED TO.

Plate 4.5   Trade card, 'Cast-off Wardrobe Clothing', Martha Bellas (Liverpool)

as truck precisely because it was so easily transposed into cash or other
goods, making the local workers specialists in tobacco resale instead.[41]
Nonetheless, the overwhelming prominence of apparel as the primary
article of exchange is worthy of comment, even as new consumer wares
came more readily to the hands of ordinary men and women, from
spectacles to furnishings, umbrellas to salt cellars. The continuing and
unique prominence of clothing in the second-hand market is only par-
tially explained by the growing volume of dresswares and the inherent
mutability of these goods. Fashion also played a role: a role in the value
assigned goods and in the animation of the second-hand market.

Fashion, value and the consumer market

Money serves as a medium of exchange and as a store of value.[42] As the
history I describe makes clear, apparel was uniquely placed to circulate
widely as an alternative exchange commodity, storing and releasing value
as required. Much of the value in garments was founded on the fabrics
of which they were made and determined by the weight, weave, pattern
and stability of the cloth and the presence or absence of braid, lace, buttons or accessories. The return on a pledged item was assured by these
physical aspects. Less tangible, but equally noteworthy, were elements of
style – cut, colour, pattern, form and texture – which added cachet to

MR. NOBLES,
GENERAL DEALER
LONDON.
DEALER IN MARINE STORES,
Cast off Wearing Apparel, &c.

Mr. N. with most respectful feeling
Beg to inform you what he deals in,
I have not come your purse to try,
Yourself will sell, and I will buy.

So please look up that useless lumber,
That long you have left to slumber,
I buy old boots, shoes, and stockings,
Jackets, trousers, and bed tickings.

Towels, cloths, and cast off linen
Cords, cashmeres & worn out woolens,
Old gowns, caps, bonnets torn to tatters,
If fine or course it never matters.

Smock frockings, fustians, velveteens,
Stuffs, worsted cords and bombazines,
Old worn handkerchiefs or shawls
Umbrellas, or parasols.

Sheep netting, canvas or carpeting,
Whatever else you have pray bring,
Of the weight I'l soon convince you,
And pay in cash the utmost value.

I purchase floor cloths, dusty rags,
Old roping, old sacking, and old bones,
Both cow and horse hair, broken glass,
Old grease, old pewter and old brass.

Old stew pans, boilers & copper kettles
Pewter spoons and other metals,
Old coins, or silver, ancient buttons,
Old copper, lead, or doctors bottles.

Skins worn by hare or rabbit,
However small your stock I'll have it.
I buy old rags, how ever rotten,
If made of woolen, hemp or cotton

I buy old iron cast or wrought,
And pay the chink when it is bought,
If you have any bones to sell,
Their value in a trice I'll tell.

So over your dwelling give a glance,
You'll never have a better chance,
My price is good, my weight is just,
And mind I never ask for trust,
So please look up what you can,
And you will find me just the man,

Mr. Nobles will call for this Bill in two Hours, and will
bring his Horse and Cart and purchase any Rags or Bones
OR ANY OLD CLOTHING
You may have got ready, and he will give
☞ The Best Price for every
Article Mentioned above.

Plate 4.6   Trade card, Mr Nobles, General Dealer (London)

commodities sold in certain markets, with certain buyers, within a finite time frame.

From the time of its genesis, fashion's force in the market was ephemeral but very real; moreover, the strength of the fashion system worked to liven the market. A general concern with the aesthetics of fashion grew in force over the early modern period, even as the expression of different styles varied from region to region, group to group. Gilles Lipovetsky contends that 'with the birth of fashion, inconstancy in matters of form and ornamentation was no longer the exception but the lasting rule'.[43] Inconstancy in the market place generated a premium for goods perceived to hold a stylish essence; whatever the quality of the items themselves, they represented traits that attracted or repelled, defining and refining the fashion circles in which the goods circulated. Mary Douglas reminds students of fashion and the consumer process to be as sensitive to expressions of dislike as to paeans of approbation. She notes that 'hated garments … [also] signal cultural affiliation'.[44] Each manifests the boundaries of groups distinguished by age, sex, social rank or affiliation, religious persuasion or political allegiance, suggesting a compelling complexity within the market place. 'As for your gold stuff, I am wondered at by everyone who sees them for buying them,' wrote a disgusted seventeenth-century Edinburgh merchant to his supplier.[45] The varied and various manifestations of 'style' refute the exclusively top-down perspective, one which subscribes to the trickle-down theory of fashion; it asks that we think again about the elements of style created by different age groups, religious communities, social networks and the genesis of competing fashions – subjects discussed at greater length in the following chapter. From the early modern period to the modern, these pervasive cultural constituents enlivened English society and infused this dynamic market.

The shifting currency of fashion is noteworthy for several reasons. First and foremost, elements of style interacted with the inherent value of a garment to determined its relative value. That clothing circulated as a ubiquitous alternative currency is not in dispute, but the store of value contained in each item was determined by several factors in addition to its functional attributes. Aesthetic attraction for at least a segment of the market was key to the recovery of investment. This last ingredient distinguished second-hand clothing from more objective mediums of exchange, since the capacity to recoup a full measure of worth for a given garment depended on matching merchandise with likely consumers. The capacity and flexibility within the second-hand market worked to bring saleable goods to the right consumers; the movement of wigs from one market to another was a case in point. By the early decades of the nineteenth century the wearing of wigs was associated in England solely with elderly men, for whom respectability was defined by those distinctive hairpieces. Wigs pawned and sold, accumulated from years gone by, risked losing all worth if peddled in English markets, where no young man would be caught dead in such a geriatric rig. In the mid-nineteenth century, Henry Mayhew's explorations of the workaday quarters of out-cast London included several studies of second-hand clothes markets, revealing many of the long-established traits of this commerce, including the careful channelling of apparel to the most suitable outlets where prof-its were assured. In the case of wigs, these were collected and shipped to Ireland, where buyers continued to be found, most likely in the rural parts of the country. More than fifty years earlier corduroy breeches had usurped buckskin among all ranks of men in England, except grooms and gentlemen who hunted; similarly left-off buckskin breeches were shipped to Ireland and other markets where corduroy was not yet in vogue. The nineteenth-century trade bill of Mrs and Miss Bridgeman favoured a sim-ilar redistribution of good to foreign markets (see Plate 4.7). For genera-tions, overseas markets along the North American coast of the Atlantic received regular consignments of clothing suited to the particular priori-ties of that community, whether fishing port, slave plantation or regional centre. In this tradition, sales of imported second-hand clothing were announced in a local newspaper in St John, New Brunswick, in British North America, part of the supplies of clothing to arrive regularly from Britain in this region.[46] Selecting the right market was clearly important,

Late of WIMBLEDON. ☞ Please note New Address!!!

Mrs. & Miss Bridgeman,
Private Wardrobe Purchasers,
112, HORSEFERRY ROAD,
LONDON, S.W.

WANTED for Export only, every description of Ladies'Gentlemens' and Childrens' cast-off Clothing, Officers Regimentals, Old Plate, Carpets, Furniture, and every description of Miscellaneous Effects. ARTIFICIAL TEETH BOUGHT.

Having a large commission to export for the Colonies, you can rely upon receiving the extreme value for anything that may be for disposal. Terms—Cash. Mrs. or Miss B. will call to-morrow, prepared to purchase any quantity you may have. If not convenient or engaged when this card is called for and letters are sent to the above address, they will be punctually attended to. Parcels or Boxes received, remittance forwarded same day, subject to approval. Mrs. & Miss B. have on connection with any persons assuming our Name.

When forwarding goods, please enclose Name and Address of Senders in order to facilitate a prompt reply.

Plate 4.7 Trade card, Mrs & Miss Bridgeman, Private Wardrobe Purchasers (London)

but the remodelling of goods was also an integral factor of this commerce. In just this way, waistcoats were remade for English clerks and caps remade from worn waistcoats. In the mid-nineteenth century, frock coats were especially valued, much in demand by England's 'working people … often working people's wives or mothers … They're capital judges as to what'll fit their men.'[47]

Style mattered. It was a key if ephemeral element of value, a fact of which all clothes dealers were well aware, and none more so than those dealing in second-hand wares. Monmouth Street was favoured by Charles Dickens for one of his urban sketches: mixing speculation and observation, he mused on the passage of garments through this kerbside emporium: 'great-coats with wooden buttons have usurped the place of the ponderous laced coats with full skirts; embroidered waistcoats with large flaps have yielded to double-breasted checks with roll collars; and three-cornered hats of quaint appearance have given place to the low crowns and broad brims of the coachman school'. Perhaps it was the waxing and waning of styles that caused Dickens to name Monmouth Street 'the

Plate 4.8   George Delamotte, 'The Pithay', 1829

burial place of ... fashions'.[48] It could equally be claimed that second-hand shops, like those in Bristol's Pithay district, were sites of transfiguration where utility and fashion found new expressions and new markets, where value was released and recycled through a recognized medium, well known and long employed (Plate 4.8).

Conclusion

Material culture intersects with social and economic patterns, altering with time and place. By the nineteenth century, the use of alternative currencies was in flux, less frequently called upon by the respectable and voluble middle class, and gradually less readily understood. In 1593, William Lord Vaux pawned his parliamentary robes without a qualm to facilitate an immediate loan.[49] James Boswell's passions were similarly fed through the aegis of the second-hand trade. Writing in the winter of 1762, he recounted, 'This day I cast my eye on my old laced hat, which I saw would raise me a small supply [of money]. No sooner thought than done. Off it went with my sharp penknife. I carried it to a jeweller's in Piccadilly and sold it for 6s. 6d., which was a great cause of joy to me.'[50] The extensive resale, barter and pawning networks of this era cannot be equated with contemporary second-hand exchanges in developed countries, where monetized systems are so highly developed and credit facilities so sophisticated. Rather, these practices flourished in the absence of other alternatives, at a time when, as Joan Thirsk first identified, there was heightened consumer activity even in the lower social ranks.[51] Equally there was a pent-up need for mediums of exchange to enable the individual and the market to interact. An extensive and generalized knowledge of cloth and clothing, combined with credit needs, permitted the growth of this phenomenon. This model remained in force until such times as other options presented themselves.

The nineteenth-century second-hand trade was most active in the courts and street corners of cities like Sheffield, Liverpool, London and Bradford, as well as in the vicinity of working communities where the truck system still persisted. Yet a smaller, discrete, high-end trade continued to serve the genteel woman or professional man facing temporary or terminal financial embarrassment. The Attenborough family offered such a service to elite clients, with establishments in many flourishing parts of London.[52] The forms I found in the surviving receipt book of George Attenborough of Fleet Street were printed in elegant script, suggesting the delicacy with which he conducted his business, soothing the distrait sensibilities of his clients. Attenborough's was a select trade, dealing almost

exclusively in costly jewellery, watches, clocks, silver plate, books and furnishings. For example, in 1849 a maid acting on behalf of Miss Georgina
Maxwell, of Surrey, approved the contract to pawn a pair of bracelets, a
gold enamelled watch, two small Indian paintings and several smaller
items for a loan of £24. Only small and fashionable articles of apparel
found their way to Attenborough's counter; in the main he dealt in the
costly accoutrements of personal, professional and domestic decor, confident in their resale value through 'Messrs Debenham', to whom he routinely channelled unclaimed items.[53] In this way Attenborough and his ilk
avoided the disdain heaped on the mass of exchanges by the lower social
classes that persisted amid the hurly-burly of working precincts.

Among the growing middle class, the receipt of wages, salaries and
interest on investments meant that they no longer saw an outlay on material goods as a prophylactic against future want. Ideally, this stratagem
was altogether unnecessary. In the suburban, residential districts where
the middle class lived the trade in discarded goods continued, but from
kitchen doors, and some of this trade was the perquisite of cooks and
maidservants, a supplement to their lean wages. Trade cards from the
period suggest the struggle for respectability (see Plates 4.5–4.7).
Respectable folk saw straitened finances as a sign of moral failing and
dreaded equally the prospect of failure and public revelation of their
need.[54] Hence the desire for discretion when they resorted to the second-
hand market and the general abhorrence of a trade which signalled their
greatest fear. The middle class, which described and defined mainstream
Victorian culture, came to regard the ancient alternative currencies as dis-
tasteful, even reprehensible. Transformations in commerce and industry
offered more secure sources of credit and more precise financial tools for
respectable citizens – indeed, for many, the very timeworn antiquity of
the second-hand trade bespoke its debased character.

Yet among the working poor the twofold functions of commodities
remained important – use value and potential in exchange – and the
swapping of goods and loans from pawns remained essential budgetary
strategies. In the mid-nineteenth century, Mayhew's chronicles of the
working and fiscal habits of London's poor reveal the vast conduits of
second-hand commerce and the persistent traffic in material goods to
meet needs and wants. Street sellers and swag-shop owners exchanged
worn for new goods, and the long-established barter of pottery for wearing apparel still flourished in London's suburbs and working districts,
allowing teacups and pottery figurines to decorate the shelves of working
households. 'A good tea-service … for a left-off suit of clothes, hat, and
boots.'[55] At the same time loans from pawns remained essential elements

of a working family's budget, even as the practice seemed increasingly bizarre to respectable observers. No stranger to London's seamy side, Charles Dickens nevertheless professed wonder at the behaviour of men and women working in seasonal trades, or self-employed, like fishwomen and costermongers, who invested in 'great squab brooches as convenient pledges, and the latter massive silver rings'.[56] There was evidently planning in their purchases of such ostentatious goods, planning which took into account the vagaries of life in their communities and the seasonal vicissitudes of their trades. These hawkers appreciated the risks with which they lived and the value of an item that would draw appreciative glances from their neighbours, and produce the required sums if pledged or sold. The ebb and flow of personal possessions was a feature of life among these poor which arose not from improvidence, but as a defence *against* penury. This pattern of consumerism was antithetical to a middle class which sought to create a permanent material world in their homes and in their dress, saving and spending in more structured, monetized forms outside the purview of street sellers. The working poor continued along a different path with different practices that only gradually intersected and melded with fully monetized structures of exchange.

Of course, affluent women and men could always afford to buy more of what they wanted than could the poor. But the repercussions of this discrepancy were mirrored not simply in the different world of goods, but also in the different world of meanings assigned to the artefacts of daily life. This asymmetry continued into the modern period, with each transaction, each purchase, each decision to consume for the labourer or petty dealer imbued with complexities distinct from those of wealthier citizens. Similar issues arise in contemporary developing societies, where intricate networks of reciprocity and a vibrant second-hand trade enable ordinary people to cope with uncertainty amid limited options.[57] The pelisse and gown brought by Mary Hinderson from her back-street room to one of Sheffield's forty pawnbrokers got her a 10s loan, perhaps because of the stylishness of the clothes; Mary Cloewith's umbrella was an even more inimitable article in working-class districts, only recently adopted as an accessory in a rain-soaked landscape.[58]

Thus the fishmonger's brooch and the costermonger's ring, bought, displayed, pawned and redeemed, epitomized a range of aspirations and interventions: investment and insurance; badges of style and social affiliation; an alternative currency fit for their lives and their neighbourhood. Victorian commentators often shook their heads when witnessing unaccountable purchases among the working poor – a coat with silver buttons, a fine bonnet or a silver watch. These may well have seemed like signs of profligacy to observers steeped in the dogma of monetized thrift. But the purchase of stylish notions also represented rational investments for these engaged in a different type of economic practice. Looking back across the complexities of modernization and the steps in this process taken by generations, I am compelled to think again about the efficient and inventive mediums employed to give life to economic desires – the alternative currencies that ensured survival and travelled from hand to hand through generations of the second-hand trade.[59]

Notes

1   See, for example, the work of Mary Douglas and Baron Isherwood, *The World of Goods* (New York, 1979); Mary Douglas, *Thought Styles: Critical Essays on Good Taste* (London, 1996); Gilles Lipovetsky, *The Empire of Fashion: Dressing Modern Democracy* (Princeton NJ, 1994); Grant McCracken, *Culture and Consumption* (Bloomington IN, 1987).

2   For example, Beverly Lemire, 'Consumerism in preindustrial and early industrial England: the trade in second-hand clothes', *Journal of British Studies* 27:1 (1988); 'The theft of clothing and popular consumerism in eighteenth-century England', *Journal of Social History* 24:2 (1990); 'The nature of the second-hand clothes trade, the role of fashion and popular demand in England, 1680–1880', *Quederno dell' Archivio* (Milan, 1990); *Dress, Culture and Commerce: The English Clothing Trade before the Factory, 1660–1800* (London, 1997).

3   Fernand Braudel, *The Structures of Everyday Life* I, *Civilization and Capitalism, Fifteenth to Eighteenth Century*, translated by Siân Reynolds (New York, 1981), p. 333.

4   Hannah Tatum's trade card illustrates that type of trade in the early eighteenth century and this was evidently a preferred way of securing new wares. Henry Mayhew comments on the popularity of this pattern of exchange in the mid-nineteenth century. Beverly Lemire, 'Peddling fashion: salesmen, pawnbrokers, taylors, thieves and the second-hand clothes trade in England, c. 1700–1800', *Textile History* 22:1 (1991), pp. 76–7; Elizabeth Sanderson, *Women and Work in Eighteenth-Century Edinburgh* (Basingstoke, 1996), pp. 108–14; Henry Mayhew, *London Labour and the London Poor* II (1851, repr. London, 1967), p. 27.

5   T. S. Ashton, *Iron and Steel in the Industrial Revolution* (Manchester, 1924); P. G. M. Dickson, *The Financial Revolution in England: A Study in the Development of Public Credit, 1688–1756* (London, 1967); Peter Earle, *The Making of the English Middle Class: Business, Society and Family Life in London, 1660–1730* (London, 1989), especially chapters 4–6; E. A. Wrigley, *Continuity, Chance and Change: The Character of the Industrial Revolution* (Cambridge, 1988); M. J. Daunton, *Progress and Poverty: An Economic and Social History of Britain, 1700–1850* (Oxford, 1995).

6   More detailed studies of these changes include Joan Thirsk, *Economic Policy and Projects: The Development of a Consumer Society in Early Modern England* (Oxford, 1978); Kenneth R. Andrews, *Trade, Plunder and Settlement: Maritime Enterprise and the Genesis of the British Empire, 1480–1630* (Cambridge, 1984); Jan de Vries, *European Urbanization, 1500–1800* (London, 1984); James D. Tracy, *The Rise of Merchant Empires: Long-distance Trade in the Early Modern World* (Cambridge, 1990); and, for a French

perspective, Daniel Roche, *A History of Everyday Things: The Birth of Consumption in France, 1600–1800* (Cambridge, 2000).

7 Thirsk, *Economic Policy and Projects*, p. 107.

8 Adam Smith, *An Inquiry into the Nature and Causes of the Wealth of Nations*, ed. W. B. Todd (1776, repr. Indianapolis IN, 1976) II, p. 660.

9 Smith, *Wealth of Nations* I, p. 27.

10 Braudel, *Civilization and Capitalism* I, pp. 439, 444–5.

11 Peter Spufford, *Money and its Use in Medieval Europe* (Cambridge, 1988), pp. 329–38.

12 John Evelyn, *Numismata* (1697), quoted in Peter Mathias, 'The people's money in the eighteenth century: the Royal Mint, trade tokens and the economy' in *The Transformation of England: Essays in the Economic and Social History of England in the Eighteenth Century* (London, 1979), p. 190.

13 Mathias, 'People's money', p. 191. For a discussion of the copper coinage produced in response to this crisis see Christine Wiskin, 'The "People's Money" Reconsidered: The Copper Coinage of the 1790s', unpublished paper presented at the Association of Business Historians conference, Portsmouth, June 2001.

14 The content of sumptuary legislation in sixteenth-century England reflects the greater array of items owned and worn by men and women below the gentry in spite of prohibitions. For example, legislation from 1533 barred 'servants, yeomen and all persons with incomes of less than 40s a year' from wearing hose from fabric costing less than 2s per yard, barred silk ribbons outright from this group, as well as 'shirts, coiffes, bonnets, hats … embroidered or trimmed with silk, gold or silver'. The recurrence of similar legal bars confirms the ineffectiveness of these measures. Francis E. Baldwin, *Sumptuary Legislation and Personal Regulation in England* (Baltimore MD, 1926), pp. 157–9; Joan Thirsk, 'The fantastical folly of fashion; the English stocking knitting industry, 1500–1700' in N. B. Harte and K. G. Ponting (eds), *Textile History and Economic History: Essays in Honour of Miss Julia de Lacy Mann* (Manchester, 1973), pp. 53–64.

15 Thirsk, *Economic Policy and Projects*, pp. 158–80.

16 This was particularly true of southern England. Thirsk, 'Fantastical folly'; Thirsk, *Economic Policy*; Roche, *Everyday Things*.

17 Margaret Spufford, 'The cost of apparel in seventeenth-century England', *Economic History Review*, 2nd series 53:4 (2000).

18 Negley Harte, 'The economics of clothing in the late seventeenth century' in N. B. Harte (ed.), *Fabrics and Fashions: Studies in the Economic and Social History of Dress*, special issue of *Textile History* 22:1 (1991), p. 278.

19 Quoted in Bridget Hill, *Servants: English Domestics in the Eighteenth Century* (Oxford, 1996), pp. 72–3.

20 Maria Bogucka, 'Women and Credit Operations in Polish Towns in the Early Modern Period'; Montserrat Carbonell, '"Pledges", Transmissions and Credit Networks: Eighteenth-Century Barcelona'; Hilde van Wijngaarden, 'Credit as a Way to make Ends Meet: The Use of Credit by Poor Women in Zwolle, 1650–1700', unpublished papers presented at session C59, 'Women and Credit in European Societies, Sixteenth to Nineteenth Centuries', twelfth International Economic History Congress, Madrid, 1998.

21 John Stow, *The Survey of London*, edited by H. B. Wheatley (London, 1987), p. 117; Natasha Korda, 'Household property/stage property: Henslowe as pawnbroker', *Theatre Journal* 48 (1996), p. 191.

22 Elizabeth Sanderson has documented a similarly vigorous trade in eighteenth-century Edinburgh. 'Nearly new: the second-hand clothing trade in eighteenth-century Edinburgh', *Costume* 31 (1997).

23 Olaf Egeberg, *Non-money: That 'Other Money' you didn't Know you Had* (Washington DC, 1995); Stephen DeMeulenaere, 'Reinventing the market: alternative currencies and community development in Argentina', *International Journal of Community Currency Research* 4 (2000); P. Liesch and D. Birch, 'Community-based LETSystems in Australia: localised barter in a sophisticated Western economy', *International Journal of Community Currency Research* 4 (2000); Jorim Schraven, 'The economics of local exchange and trading systems: a theoretical perspective', *International Journal of Community Currency Research* 4 (2000), www.geog.le.ac.uk/ijccr/, accessed February 2002. See also Ruth Pearson, 'Argentina's Barter Network: New Currency for New Times?', paper presented at the conference 'Les Circulations des objets d'occasion', European University Institute, Florence, 2002.

24 Schraven, 'Economics of local exchange and trading systems'.

25 Margaret Hunt, 'Women and the fiscal-imperial state in the late seventeenth and early eighteenth centuries' in Kathleen Wilson (ed.), *A New Imperial History: Culture, Identity and Modernity in Britain and the Empire, 1660–1840* (Cambridge, 2004).

26 Quoted in Peter Linebaugh, *The London Hanged: Crime and Civil Society in the Eighteenth Century* (Harmondsworth, 1991), pp. 378–9.

27 Linebaugh, *The London Hanged*, p. 379.

28 W. A. H. Hows, *A History of Pawnbroking, Past and Present* (London, 1847); A. Hardaker, *A Brief History of Pawnbroking* (London, 1892); Melanie Tebbutt, *Making Ends Meet: Pawnbroking and Working Class Credit* (London, 1983); Lemire, *Dress, Culture and Commerce*, especially chapters 3–5.

29 J. Harris, *Money and Coins* (1757), quoted in Mathias, 'People's money', p. 194.

30 Aside from hands-on training in these skills, published works were more generally available in the late seventeenth century to enable the further dissemination of information. See, for example, J. F., *The Merchant's Ware-house laid open: or, The Plain Dealing Linnen-draper ...* (London, 1696). J. F. offered to show his readers 'How to Buy all sorts of Linnen and Indian Goods: Wherein is perfect and plain Instructions, for all sorts of Persons, that they may not be deceived in any sort of Linnen they want'.

31 Ann Rosalind Jones and Peter Stallybrass, *Renaissance Clothing and the Materials of Memory* (Cambridge, 2000), p. 31; Korda, 'Henslowe', pp. 191–3; Peter Earle, 'The female labour market in London in the late seventeenth and early eighteenth centuries', *Economic History Review*, 2nd series 42:3 (1989); Merry E. Wiesner, *Women and Gender in Early Modern Europe* (Cambridge, 1993), especially chapter 3. Pawning garments was so ubiquitous that it was employed as a plot device in Ben Jonson's 1599 play *Every Man out of his Humour*, where a character pawns his silk stockings to pay for a warrant.

32 Quoted in Sara Mendelson and Patricia Crawford, *Women in Early Modern England* (Oxford, 1998), p. 222.

33 356/242, Examinations, Ludlow Borough Quarter Sessions, 1700–39; Petty Session, Oxford, 05–11, 1668–69, ff. 108, 110, 111; Lemire, *Dress, Culture and Commerce*, p. 100; Garthine Walker, 'Women, theft and the world of stolen goods' in Jenny Kermode and Garthine Walker (eds), *Women, Crime and the Courts in Early Modern England* (London, 1994); Patricia Crawford and Laura Gowing (eds), *Women's Worlds in Seventeenth-Century England: A Source Book* (London, 2000), pp. 107–8, 123.

34 Joseph Addison, *The Lover*, 18 March 1714, p. 1.

35 See Bogucka, 'Polish Towns'; Carbonell, 'Barcelona'; and van Wijngaarden, 'Zwolle', above. Also Patricia Allerston, 'Reconstructing the second-hand clothes trade in sixteenth- and seventeenth-century Venice', *Costume* 33 (1999); Sanderson, *Women and Work in Eighteenth Century Edinburgh*; Laurence Fontaine, 'Women's economic spheres and credit in pre-industrial Europe' in B. Lemire, R. Pearson and G. Campbell (eds), *Women and Credit: Researching the Past, Refiguring the Future* (Oxford, 2002), pp. 24–5, and for northern England see Miles Lambert, '"Cast-off wearing apparell": the consumption and distribution of second-hand clothing in northern England during the long eighteenth century', *Textile History* 35:1 (2004); for the Low Countries see Harald Deceulaer, 'Urban artisans and their countryside customers' in B. Blondé, E. Vanhaute and M. Galand (eds), *Labour and Labour Markets between Town and Countryside, Middle Ages–Nineteenth Century* (Turnhout, 2001), and 'Second-hand Dealers in the Early Modern Low Countries: Institutions, Markets and Practices', paper presented at the conference 'Les Circulations des objets d'occasion', European University Institute, Florence, 2002.

36 Ms 11936, 11937, Ms 7253, Guildhall Library; see also Lemire, *Dress, Culture and Commerce*, chapters 3–4.

37 For example, Orphans Inventory, 885, Daniel Garnett, October 1673, CLRO; Orphans Inventory, 1049, Ann Deacon, July 1674, CLRO; PROB 5/1804, George Thayne, January 1702, PRO; PROB 3/29/213, Probate Inventory of William Mackvity, July 1730, PRO.

38 Tebbutt, *Making Ends Meet*, p. 16.

39 Korda, 'Henslowe', p. 189.

40 The rates of interest charged by pawnbrokers preoccupied legislators over the centuries. Between 1800 and 1872 pawnbrokers were restricted to an official interest rate of 20 per cent per annum; however, Melanie Tebbutt clearly shows that interest rates for small repeated loans on pledges were essentially unlimited, since 'the smaller the loan the higher the interest, the heaviest rate falling on the very people who were the least able to bear it'. Tebbutt, *Making Ends Meet*, pp. 8–9.

41 George Hilton, *The Truck System, including a History of the British Truck Acts, 1465–1960* (Cambridge, 1960), pp. 29–30. The truck system likewise flourished in colonial settings where cash was scarce, eliciting a range of criticisms. See, for example, Joseph A. Ernst, '"The labourers have been the greatest sufferers": the truck system in early eighteenth-century Massachusetts' in Rosemary E. Ommer (ed.), *Merchant Credit and Labour Strategies in Historical Perspective* (Fredericton NB, 1990).

42 Jan Hogendorn, 'Slaves as money in the Sokoto Caliphate' in Endre Stiansen and Jane I. Guyer (eds), *Credit, Currencies and Culture: African Financial Institutions in Historical Perspective* (Stockholm, 1999), p. 56.

43 Lipovetsky, *The Empire of Fashion*, p. 15.

44 Mary Douglas, 'On not being seen dead: shopping as protest' in *Thought Styles: Critical Essays on Good Taste* (London, 1996), p. 82.

45 Quoted in Sanderson, *Women and Work*, p. 33.

46 The intriguing history of wigs is treated by Negley Harte, 'Shaving-off for Showing-off: The Rise and Fall of Wigs, c. 1650–1830', unpublished paper presented at the conference 'Making an Appearance: Fashion, Dress and Consumption', University of Queensland, 2003. *New Brunswick Courier*, 26 May, 2 June 1832, 23 August 1834. I thank Cynthia Wallace Casey for this reference. See also Lemire, 'Consumerism', p. 5 n. 7.

47 Mayhew, *London Labour*, pp. 27–8, 41.

48 Charles Dickens, *Sketches by Boz: Illustrative of Every-day Life and Every-day People* (1836, repr. 1881), p. 35.

49 Jones and Stallybrass, *Renaissance Clothing*, p. 29.

50 James Boswell, *London Journal, 1762–1763*, edited by Frederick A. Pottle (New York, 1950), p. 109. This was one of several recorded transactions of this sort.

51 Thirsk, *Economic Policy and Projects*; see also Margaret Spufford, *The Great Reclothing of Rural England: Petty Chapmen and their Wares in the Seventeenth Century* (London, 1984), and Wrightson, *Earthly Necessities*, especially chapters 4 and 7.

52 W. Kelly & Co., *The Small Edition of the Post Office London Directory, 1847* (London, 1847).

53 Ms 20,678/2, No. 2, No. 688,1055, 1001, Guildhall Library, London.

54 Theodore Koditschek, *Class Formation and Urban-Industrial Society: Bradford, 1750–1850* (Cambridge, 1990), pp. 187–9.

55 Henry Mayhew, *London Labour and the London Poor* I (1861–62, repr. New York, 1968), pp. 325, 334–6, 367.

56 Quoted in Tebbutt, *Making Ends Meet*, p. 17.

57 Karen Tranberg Hansen, 'Budgeting against uncertainty: cross-class and transethnic redistribution mechanisms in urban Zambia', *African Urban Studies* 21 (1985).

58 J 90/504, Public Record Office, London. There were forty pawnbrokers listed in two of the published directories to the trades of Sheffield. Typically these listings did not include the smallest businesses, or those trading informally. James Pigot, *Pigot & Co.'s National and Commercial Directory ... in the Counties of Chester, Cumberland, Durham, Lancashire, Northumberland, Westmorland and York ...* (London, 1834), pp. 949–50; William White, *History, Gazetteer and Directory of the West-Riding of Yorkshire ...* I (Sheffield, 1838).

59 Orphans Inventory, 1049, July 1674, CLRO; C 108/30, Taylor's Letter Book, London, 12 July 1756, PRO; J 90/504, Pawnbroker's Ledger, Sheffield, 1816, PRO; C 110/134, Pawnbrokers' Ledgers, London, November 1830 and 1832–33.

5

Refashioning society: expressions of popular consumerism and dress, c. 1660–1820

ASHION HAS BECOME a respectable subject of historical enquiry in recent years, a topic of debate as theorists and scholars of various stripes struggle to explain the choices and motivations of generations of consumers. The recurrent fads and mutable stylistic forms of dress and material culture among English men and women open a window on the consumer process. Their social and cultural priorities reshaped past societies.[1] Material choices mattered, for it was the everyday decisions of common folk, their desires and capacity to choose and to reject, that redirected patterns of trade, patterns of industry and patterns of society. In the early modern era, commoners' appetite for niceties was met almost immediately with legislation designed to curb sartorial desires – sumptuary legislation aimed to restrict luxuries to designated groups.[2] The inessentials which distinguished those of noble blood were forbidden to lesser beings; however, the aspirations which inspired change permeated the middling and even the labouring ranks.[3] In England, as in other societies undergoing dynamic changes, material desires were much in evidence and dress most clearly enunciated this phenomenon. In this chapter I examine the competing forces at work as the dress of the common people evolved over the long eighteenth century. Although sumptuary legislation came to an end in England in 1604, governments and moralists claimed the right to restrain material expression within the lower ranks. Tensions persisted between advocates of traditional forms for the lower orders and those among the non-elites who aspired to less deferential styles. Princely and aristocratic sensibilities might animate court styles, such as the craze for red-heeled shoes launched by Louis XIV;[4] however, material expressions among less august people also added an important complexity to fashions as a whole. Expenditure on clothing represented one of the most important social and economic forces at work stimulating the consumer process and, as I show in the previous chapter, the market for apparel was characterized by a distinctive depth and complexity. Clothes worn and revised day by day represented one of the most constant and malleable forms of consumer investment – charting the changing social politics and material culture of this most intimate and visible commodity is the focus of this chapter.[5]

Claiming fashion: the plebeian challenge

A celebration of novelty was at the heart of elite fashions, and the intent of early fashion adherents was to demarcate themselves from others, making fashion a cultural avocation exclusive to lords and ladies. However, these innovations in material life were more profound and far-reaching, representing, as Gilles Lipovetsky notes, 'a historical discontinuity, a major break ... with the form of socialization that had prevailed from time immemorial: the immutable logic of tradition'.[6] Shifting plays of colour, shape and form gained adherents with each decade, gaining as well a chorus of critics, passionate foes of the new vogues. In spite of loud cavils, the idea of fashion and the proliferation of new components of dress propelled change across a broad social spectrum. Novelty blossomed, offering a medium for individual originality or group expressions and, like a drop of oil on an expanse of water, fashion radiated far beyond its original domain. A culture of novelty and a visual aesthetics helped create a climate which sanctioned change, even as more conservative elements urged resistance to innovation. 'Here is the paradox of fashion', writes Lipovetsky: 'its flashy displays of the emblems of hierarchy played a role in the movement towards the equalization of appearances.'[7]

Tradition demanded that all acquiesce to the dictates of hierarchy and accept its manifestations in tangible form. However, unruly desires and a proliferation of choices confounded the *status quo*. There was no single, unitary set of motivations driving the consumer dynamic in dress, and to think so presupposes a slavish and uncritical interpretation of high fashion by non-elites. In reality, the inspiration for changes in dress and material display (termed fashion or style) arose from a host of intersecting factors rooted in personal, local and regional influences. As society gradually moved from an economy of scarcity to one of growing abundance, more common folk found the wherewithal to engage with a more complex material world and to express themselves through self-selected modes.[8] In this context, London apprentices could and did construct appearances defined as fashionable within their milieu. Inevitably, this switch from a more static traditional garb attracted the notice of the censorious. Novel articles, when worn by plebeians, challenged entrenched norms in personal presentation, fashion being antithetical to comfortable tradition. Joan Thirsk chronicled the rise of the English knitted hosiery trade, noting the loud official complaints in the late sixteenth century when young men 'from the courtier to the carter' were swept up in the fad for 'new fangle' hose, the legs of London's youth sheathed in the startling offending hose as they strolled the London streets. A proclivity for small indulgences could not be quenched by legislation or official proclamations, and neither spies nor enforcers could root out this contagion. Stockings patterned with clocks, multi-coloured jersey or silk 'netherstocks' signalled a commitment to new forms of dress and new social relations.[9] Over the last third of the sixteenth century, old habits were broken and new created in the midst of a remarkable series of commercial, social and economic changes.[10] Commentators correctly dated these transformations, even if they routinely overstated the purported expenditure of the newly fashion-conscious. Simply put, the material expressions of non-elites shocked observers; in response, they exaggerated and denounced the visible innovations found on the backs of urban servants, apprentices and middling folk. The number and nature of these comments are as important as their accuracy, for they noted real and profound alterations in mentalities, illustrated in the changing social politics of dress.

Fashion's power can be measured not by the spread of court styles but by the broad engagement with new forms of self-presentation, with the decline of traditional habits and the rise of new priorities of consumption among middle-ranked and labouring peoples.[11] These changes that were visible, and, in some cases, even measurable, reflecting new perceptions of the individual's place in society, as well as new relations within society as a whole.[12] More men and women rejected traditional apparel rooted in hierarchy – choosing fashion. In some cases popular fashions were modelled on aristocratic trends, as Cissie Fairchilds observes.[13] But the cultural, social and national context, as much as the individual or local aesthetic, determined the how and what of dress. Indeed, the evolution and expression of tastes in material form were moulded by a host of factors, including the age, sex, region, occupation and religion of those creating and adapting styles. Choice was key: whether a religiously inspired plainness or a fancy for floral motifs, each signalled priorities and allegiances; the concept of hierarchical emulation is too crude an analytical a tool to address this range of variations.[14] As more ordinary women and men indulged in a new culture of appearance, the elements decorating their persons became more complex and variable, with pedlars feeding these desires, carrying novelties from town to town.

gloves, pins, combs, glasses unspotted,
Pamades, hooks, and laces knotted;
Brooches, rings, and all manner of beads;
laces round the flat for women's heads;
needles, thread, thimble, shears and all such knacks,
Where lovers be, no such things lack;
Sipers, swathbanks, ribbons, and sleeve laces,
Girdles, knives, purses and pincases.[15]

The small cost of these trinkets invited the humble to indulge, although cost was always a consideration in the selection. However, there were more important variables displayed through consumer behaviour that could not be neatly twinned with the hierarchical social structure. Lorna Weatherill states that:

> The consumption hierarchy was not the same as the social hierarchy, although it is not completely different … The commercial and dealing trades were at the top [of the consumption hierarchy], with the gentry and professional people below them, although their social status was much higher … The idea of such a hierarchy suggests ways of looking at the social order and of the influence of social position on the ownership of goods'.[16]

Artisans and skilled labourers, servants and apprentices have left fewer records of their shifting patterns of consumption than have those in higher social ranks. But, even within these more anonymous classes, visible changes were evident in the proliferation of pedlars, in the lists of their wares, in the long-running luxury debates and in the surge of new industries springing up throughout England.[17] With each generation, more and more non-elite men and women exercised their powers of material self-definition reflecting their personal and evolving aesthetic sensibilities as an idiom of daily life.

There has been extensive debate about the timing of new consumer demands. If historians of the nineteenth and twentieth centuries observe waves of development in manufacturing and retailing,[18] historians of the seventeenth and eighteenth centuries have traced a swelling tide of changes in consumption and production pre-dating the classic period of the industrial revolution. The 'industrious era', as Jan de Vries terms it, gave rise to flourishing home-based production and dramatic changes in retailing which laid the groundwork for a later full-blown consumer society.[19] This process also made working people more prosperous, enabling them to change their stockings, beribbon their hats, buckle their shoes and indulge, in a small way, their collective appetite for decorative touches.[20] Phillip Stubbes remarked on this in his 1583 volume *The Anatomie of Abuses*, denouncing the resources wasted on frivolous inessentials and bemoaning the choices of Englishmen. He longed for a fixed ancient order, insisting that 'most of our novel Inventions and new fangled fashions, rather deform us than adorn us: disguise us, than become us … it appears that no People in the World is so curious in new fangles, as they of [England] … be'.[21] Stubbes's objections to the spread of fashion outside the nobility would be echoed over and again. One of the most important of these claims was that, when the visual signals of hierarchy were blurred, precedence could not be assured.

> [I]t is very hard to know, who is noble, who is worshipful, who is a gentleman, who is not: for you shall have those, which are neither of the nobility gentility, nor yeomanry, no not yet any Magistrate or Office in the commonwealth, go daily in silks, velvets, satins, damasks, taffetas, and such like notwithstanding that they be both base by birth, mean by estate and servile by calling. This is a great confusion and general disorder.[22]

The uproar over apprentices' stockings and tradesmen's silks rose in volume with evidence of these accumulated indulgences.[23]

Clothing was adaptable, a responsive element that could be amended with little outlay; accessories were mercurial and their change reflected the shifting priorities of a growing number of working people.[24] Practical haberdashery and decorative haberdashery were available for pennies.[25] And, aside from the proliferation of accessories, the fabric selected, as much as the cut or decoration of garments, advertised a discernible fashion-consciousness. The 'individual initiative and taste in trimmings and little extras'[26] that inspired those of gentle birth also transfigured the hard-wearing traditional garb of common folk.

Linens, cottons and colours

Ubiquitous heavy wools in dark browns, greens, blues and blacks, leather breeches, stuff petticoats and duffle cloaks were long-lasting, sturdy garments and could be bequeathed across the generations. Heavy woollen fabrics, in many forms, were a clothing staple as well as a major prop of the economy. Then, in the seventeenth century, the alterations in clothing fabrics brought inexorable changes for men and women; and these changes, while more protracted at the lower social levels, were as dramatic for the commoner as for the genteel. Lighter wool fabrics, termed New Draperies, began the disruption of the traditional woollen industry in the 1600s; however, I will look here at linens and cottons, which compounded the changes already under way. Throughout Europe, linens were being produced in greater quantities and in a wider range of qualities than ever before.[27] Moreover, these linens declined in price over the long eighteenth century, long before the first industrial mills went into action.[28] White shirts, white shifts, white caps and hoods, white handkerchiefs knotted round the neck became tokens of respectability for the shop assistant as well as the maidservant, for the prosperous blacksmith as well as the middling housewife. The quality of the linen varied from rank to rank. But the collars, cuffs and hems of linen undergarments signalled a common fascination with cleanliness and display. Plate 4.4, from a late seventeenth-century series depicting street sellers, may not reflect a typical hawker; but her apron, cap and sleeves mirrored this trend, even if the buckled shoes and white hose bespeak a particular stylishness. Fashions among the upper classes included white linen at the throat or cuff or covering the head, a feature as important as the richness of the main garment. White linen manifested a new social imperative, a bodily cleanliness exemplified in fresh linens. George Vigarello opined that 'collar and cuffs came to objectify the intimate. When bodily cleanliness was evoked, it was through them it was expressed.'[29] Contemporary treatises on manners advised readers to think first of their linen; if linen was white, no other element in dress was required for reputability.[30] For the Dutch, the struggle for cleanliness became an unending crusade, with constant travails to overcome dirt – white linen symbolized the transient attainment of a purer state.[31] Daniel Roche termed this project 'the invention of linen'[32] as body linen was embraced by highborn and low. Among the former, a scion of the Verney family wrote his mother requesting additions to his wardrobe in 1688. 'I hope you will consider to buy me some good shirts or else some sort of wastecoat [sic], for it is not fashionable for any gentleman to go buttoned up either winter or summer.'[33] Glimpses of white garments evoked a special thrill. Thus shirts, caps, coifs, bands, sleeves, shifts, collars and aprons assumed greater importance, sold by shopkeepers and pedlars in varieties from the finest 'Holland' to 'Manchester Coarse Linin'.[34]

Records from John Pope's south London community illustrate the developing place of linen among humble consumers. As a haberdasher Pope sold apparel, fabric and accessories, and as a pawnbroker Pope accepted his neighbours' goods as security for loans. Clothing predominated as pledges, and Pope's customers favoured utilitarian wear.[35] However, even here new standards were evident. Table 5.1 provides an analysis of the pawned clothing entered in the ledgers from 1667 to 1671 and linen makes up a clear majority, with woollen the next most common. Aprons, handkerchiefs, bodices, checked caps and pieces of fine linen lawn were pledged, along with four fashionable linen hoods. These last items were a source of considerable irritation to the authorities, since modish garments made of foreign fabrics disrupted local industry as well as social norms. The new-found fad for linens brought higher imports of French textiles and complaints aplenty that 'the laudable English fashions of former times began to alter in favour of France … The women's hats were turned into hoods whereby every maidservant in England became a standing revenue to the French king of half her wages.'[36] The garments pawned with Pope suggest the ubiquity of linen among ordinary Londoners, and even they were not without choices, for one of Pope's customers deposited modest stocks of silk and a fabric described as 'calico' as security for loans.

The appearance of East Indian textiles heralded even more dramatic changes than the spread of linens. Painted and printed Asian fabrics trickled and then poured into England in the seventeenth century, causing a frenzy among consumers, rich and poor. Men, as well as women, took to cotton clothing, with over a million pieces landed at English ports in 1684.[37] The peacock colours, striking botanic design and distinctive look of these fabrics soon caused a furore.[38] The colours themselves were an affront to custom, a visible disjuncture with dark, heavy woollens, especially when cheaper calicoes were marketed at lower prices; in contrast, powerful political and economic interests sought to maintain the *status quo*. Tradition was exemplified by the fleece. The hierarchical structure of the kingdom was founded on landed estates well stocked with sheep, producing a staple wealth for landowner and merchant, the fleece, spun and woven by many hands, covering the backs of the populace. By the 1690s the security of the woollen trade was eroding in the face of a

Table 5.1   Fabric composition of pawns, south London, 1667–1671

Fabrics	Times pawned	% of known fabrics
Linen	36	50.7
Wool	28	39.4
Linen and wool	3	4.2
Silk	2	2.8
Calico	2	2.8

Note: Number of transactions: 440.
Source: C 108/34, Public Record Office, London.

seemingly unquenchable demand for light, vividly tinted floral novel-ties.[39] Moralists accused consumers of economic treason for their betrayal of the wool trade. Some proposed a new law mandating the wearing of wool, demanding 'a total stop put to the Cotton Commodities of India'.[40] Those with a vested interest in the woollen trade painted a gloomy pic-ture, with one pamphleteer, in 1719, exclaiming that:

> all the mean People, the Maid Servant, and the indifferently poor Persons, who would otherwise cloath themselves ... in Cantaloons and Crapes, etc. are now cloathed in Callicoe, or printed Linen; moved to it as well for the Cheapness, as the lightness of the Cloth, and the Gaiety of the Colours. ... The Children universally ... appear now in printed Callicoe, or printed Linen; let any but cast their Eyes among the meaner Sort playing in the Street, or of the better Sort at Boarding School.[41]

The charges of fostering pernicious luxury were framed within a par-ticularly gendered context, where luxury was equated with the feminine and calicoes with a corruption of the social fabric. As the legal and polit-ical campaign against calico took to the streets, women became targets of polemics and physical attacks. Women's preference for washable, floral exotics was clearly evident to their critics, not least because of the breadth of their skirts and the shape of their garments, which set off the full sweep of flowered textiles. Gentlemen sported vibrant painted calico dressing gowns in private domestic settings, or wore calico shirts beneath their jackets; women wore printed goods openly, publicly. From court to court-yard women's consumer volition sparked charges of disorder, of defiance of traditional discipline. One author argued for a return to wool as 'an inducement to Virtue and Good Manners, and Servants will not think themselves above their proper Imployment'. Woollens, he insisted, 'will ... guide all other Habits of the Body'. He hinted in a concluding verse that 'Thresher John' could take a hand to instil order where needed.[42]

Women's bodies became a battleground. Campaigners swore that selfish female indulgence would be curbed, their obedience compelled if it could not be enjoined. Between 1719 and 1720 the social politics of the calico campaign reached its peak. With the apparent complicity of the authorities, women were threatened, assailed and harassed into compli-ance. In 1719, as Parliament debated the merits of protecting wool, a personal preference for calico was discouraged through the simple mech-anism of mobbing the wearer and tearing her clothes off. Vigilantes were easily assembled; one weavers' agent boasted that he had at his disposal 'Five or Six Guineas' from an undeclared source to buy drink for sup-porters. For days at a time, women who wore East Indian gowns did so at

LIVERPOOL JOHN MOORES UNIVERSITY
LEARNING SERVICES

their peril. While looking for lodgings in London a labouring woman, Elizabeth Price, recounted the terror of an attack when 'some People … took up her [woollen] Riding Hood, and seeing her Gown, cry'd out Callicoe, Callicoe; Weavers, Weavers. Whereupon a great Number came down and tore her Gown off all but the Sleeves, her Pocket, the head of her Riding Hood, and abus'd her very much'.[43] Price's wardrobe combined traditional elements, like the riding hood, with a newly stylish cotton gown, a complex amalgam of material allegiances; but even wearing a riding hood did not preserve her from a frightening assault. Attacks such as this were replicated in London and Norwich.[44] The press's sympathy was all for the weavers and the emotional travails they suffered, the 'poor Men being too much moved for their small Stocks of Patience to govern'.[45]

The attacks which accompanied the campaign against calicoes were surely unique in fashion discourse. They illustrate, as perhaps nothing else could, the gendered terrain of fashion wherein women's bodies became public political turf over which battles were waged and on which discipline was enforced by those vested in the *status quo*. Enormous public volatility was unleashed when non-elite women defied traditions in apparel. Their dress was the site of self-expression, as these women had few other venues of public presentment, as Alan Hunt notes. 'Given the denial of access to other forms of self-expression, clothing, ornamentation and grooming have provided generations of women with the means of identity, self-presentation and access to valued social status.'[46] However, in early modern England, as in other societies, upholders of patriarchal tradition believed women's appearance (and their bodies) should be controlled. 'Self-presentation' was still a hazardous exercise for women, even if some argued that the vaunted English liberties included women's choice in dress.[47] In this instance, the broader movement by middling and labouring women towards an 'equalization of appearance' met violent resistance. Nevertheless, the general equilibrium in popular dress was irretrievably altered by the early eighteenth century. Neither acts of Parliament nor mob violence could restore the ancient norms or ensure the abject compliance of women. Long after the riots ended and the ban was in place, women quietly took out their calicoes, wearing them when they could, looking for equivalent substitutes as these became available.

If linen shirts and printed gowns were commonplace by the early 1700s, by the third quarter of the century, in spite of protests and prohibitions, these same goods were plentiful even in the most humble communities. But now they were manufactured by the flourishing British cotton and linen industries. The purchase and use of linens and cottons, along with regular laundering, became normal facets of life among all but the destitute. These ordinary consumers might routinely employ the second-hand market, yet there was still a discernible commitment to dress appropriate to their age, situation and yearnings.[48] The radical artisan, Samuel Bamford, recounted in his autobiography a recollection of his mother, painting the image of a frugal artisan's wife in the late eighteenth century, her figure lightened by the bright linen and cotton she wore in cap, handkerchief and apron, housewifely order figured in her dress.

> My mother – and I have her image distinctly before me – was a person of very womanly and motherly presence. Tall, upright, active, and cleanly to an excess: her cheeks were fair and ruddy as apples; her dark hair was combed over a roll before and behind, and confined by a mob cap as white as bleached linen could be made; her neck was covered by a handkerchief, over which she wore a bed-gown; and a clean checked apron, with black hose and shoes completed her daily attire.[49]

By the 1770s, everyday textiles and clothing had changed considerably from those pawned in south London nearly a century previously, confirming the changing composition of plebeian wardrobes. The entries in a York pawnbroker's ledger were sampled for December 1777 and June 1778. Of these data, about half of the textiles pawned were unidentified by fabric, but where fabric was mentioned, cotton, linen and silk textiles made up over well over half. Of the total of pawned garments these fabrics still comprised a substantial 38 per cent in December and about 30 per cent in June[50] (see Tables 5.2–3). The customers who carried clothing to a Sheffield pawnbroker in 1816 reflected the continuing evolution of popular styles, with a greater percentage of stylish shawls brought to the counter, as well as the occasional umbrella.[51] In both communities fashion clearly mattered.

Table 5.2   Fabric composition of clothing pawned, York, 1777

Fabric	No. of pawns	%
Cotton and check	124	22
Wool	68	12
Silk	54	10
Linen	32	6
Fabric unknown	274	50

Note: Sample: 552 entries.
Source: Acc. 38, York City Archives.

Table 5.3   Fabric composition of clothing pawned, York, 1778

Fabric	No. of pawns	%
Cotton and check	77	16
Wool	61	13
Silk	41	9
Linen	23	5
Fabric unknown	265	57

Note: Sample: 541 entries.
Source: Acc. 38, York City Archives.

Britain's textile industries flourished supplying medium and low-priced fabrics and knitted goods to customers with an insatiable appetite for new decencies and modest luxuries. New shirts, shifts, gowns, aprons and handkerchiefs were easily washed and could be kept clean; the description of Bamford's mother signalled her adherence to these paradigms. White garments and accessories and floral gowns attested to the world at large the wearers' commitment to concepts of cleanliness, their membership in a common community of respectable citizenry. As with Mrs Bamford, a sense of well-being was enhanced through this display. These material aspirations were a cumulatively powerful force, supported through the complex agencies of second-hand markets, credit and consumerism, even though these fashionable impulses were challenged, resisted and ridiculed.

Contested coats and disputed gowns

What social mechanisms encouraged this growing allegiance to fashion? For many decades, the answers offered to that question relied heavily on Thorstein Veblen's theory of conspicuous consumption, viewing the evolving cycles of high fashion as simply another aspect of waste among the elites, a signal of their prestige through exquisite, transitory expenditures. Subsequent interpretations of the spread of fashion through other classes suggest envy and emulation as the driving forces. Doyens of fashion persistently examined this phenomenon from a single elevated vantage point. Too often they concluded that men and women of other social, cultural or religious conditions were trying, but failing, to measure up to a single standard of taste. These explanations are inadequate and the perspective itself is flawed.[52] Fashion has been viewed from an elite vantage point far too often, obscuring the distribution and meanings of goods among non-elites and the characteristics of plebeian styles. Alan Hunt observes that 'The dominant class may be gripped ... by an inability to grasp the possibility of aesthetic and self-expressive motives in others. ... There is an interesting story to be told about the process of adaptation and innovation that occurs alongside imitative processes in the history of fashion seen as an active manifestation of class and gender struggles.'[53] Gilles Lipovetsky provides a further elaboration of the theory of fashion and its origins. For Lipovetsky, explaining fashion as a measure of class differentiation or conspicuous consumption ignores important elements of this phenomenon. The genesis of fashion in the early modern period could not be explained with reference to simple conspicuous excess among the nobility; nor can the proliferation of fashions be explained by simple class competition. Lipovetsky's explanation plumbs the transformation of mentalities, the emerging understanding of the individual's relationship with society, a new concept of individualism.

> In order for the surge of frivolous changes to come about, a revolution was required in the *representation* of individual human beings and in their sense of self, upsetting traditional mentalities and values; we had to wait for the exaltation of human uniqueness and its complement, the social promotion of signs of personal difference ... The new ideas helped unsettle the immobility of tradition; they allowed individual difference to become a sign of social excellence ... Fashion was able to become the permanent theatre of ephemeral metamorphoses because the individualization of appearance had won a new status of social legitimacy.[54]

Lipovetsky insists that we recognize the link between the creation of fashions and the development of an individual aesthetic, using aristocratic forms as an example and tying the timing of this movement with the standard chronology of European evolution. Yet new styles were also popularized and democratized among the commonality over the seventeenth and eighteenth centuries. And, while trend-setters played some part in authorizing new vogues, elite tastes did not inspire a shoemaker to wear an 'India dimity waistcoat', a coal heaver to own two cotton shirts and one linen shirt, a milkwoman's servant to treasure a cotton gown, or another servant to bemoan the loss of her 'dark Purple [cotton gown], with white Strawberries in large Diamonds'.[55] Lipovetsky applies his theoretical concepts too narrowly when he reflects only on the noble and mercantile elites of France, with wardrobes constructed by Parisian couturier, or when he posits a narrowly Western expression of these material changes. Lipovetsky asserts that 'changes and trends would allow private individuals at least a minimal margin of freedom, choice, and autonomy in matters of taste'.[56] This observation applies equally to members of the middling and labouring ranks, who selected garments or accessories which enabled them to construct a relatively stylish figure, to engage in aesthetic display, to signal common purpose or distinctive tastes among their peers.[57]

Expressions of fashions among commoners continued as a source of friction. As the eighteenth century opened, concepts of taste were routinely discussed in the pages of the *Tatler* and the *Spectator*. From 1709 to 1711, and from 1711 to 1714, these two publications became the most widely read sources on all forms of polite expression, remaining arbiters of good taste for the remaining decades of the century.[58] Erin Mackie discovered what she calls an anti-fashion commentary which appeared regularly in these periodicals, condemning excesses, particularly in women's apparel, acclaiming instead a superior, unchanging moral hierarchy.[59] The order they sought to preserve was a stable hegemonic social structure, which equated moral authority with that of gentle birth. Novelty challenged the established order. And, even as commerce and industry flourished in the service of novelty, clashes persisted between the representatives of tradition and those pleased to dabble in fashionable pursuits, however modest.[60] It was the possibility of misidentification which most distressed commentators and moralists, fretting about the habits of the *hoi polloi*. Mutability of apparel suggested mutability in rank, a particularly troubling concept for upholders of the *status quo*. 'Pride in Dress is one of the epidemick Evils of the present Age', wrote a contributor to *The Gentleman's Magazine* in 1734. 'This Vice has inverted all Order, and destroy'd Distinction; and you shall hardly step into any Shop, but you shall see a starched, powder'd Youth, that, but for his Station behind the Counter, your Father would have address'd … as the Son of a Man of Condition.'[61] Nonetheless, the calls for a return to sumptuary laws, with stiff fines, fell on deaf ears. But, aside from Acts to protect British manufactures, there was no legislative momentum to reinstate the sorts of sumptuary laws that were still on the books throughout much of continental Europe.

In this way, ambiguity in dress persisted. On the one hand were a growing number of middling men and even skilled artisans who considered a wig, hat, buckled shoes and white hose imperative for their public persona.[62] Simultaneously, generational differences between noble fathers and sons led the latter to create a new look very different from that of their forebears. Since the time of the Glorious Revolution, political authority in England was increasingly associated with elegant simplicity, juxtaposed against the rococo excesses of the French court and its absolute monarch.[63] True Englishmen wore simple coats, reflecting their authentic political status – exquisite luxury in dress was seen as foreign, unEnglish and unmasculine. But patrician fathers shuddered to see the lengths to which their sons took this trend. Once again, in 1739, disputes over clothing were given voice in *The Gentleman's Magazine*. In this instance, scions of ancient families were accused of breaking faith with their ancestors by masking their noble lineage.

> There is at present a reigning Ambition among our young Gentlemen, of degrading themselves in their Apparel to the Class of the Servants they keep. It may at first seem very extraordinary that these Sparks should act thus to gain Admiration: But from what other Cause can it be that my Lord Jehu wears a Plush Frock [coat], a little narrow-edg'd Lac'd Hat, a colour'd Handkerchief, and in this Habit drives a motley Sett of Horses and a Coach of his own, built by his own Direction, in humble Imitation of those which carry Passengers on the Road … . I have lately observed a great Number of smart Young Fellows, dress'd in the manner of my Lord; a narrow-edg'd Hat flapp'd down, a plain Shirt, Buckskin-Breeches, and an India [cotton] Handkerchief round the Neck, seem to constitute the Character of a pretty Fellow.[64]

The author rebuked young gentlemen for 'the Oddity of their Appearance', for their willingness 'to imitate the inferior Class of Mankind'. These young men emulated the physical accomplishments of coachmen or jockeys while masquerading in clothing more comfortable in structure and more ambiguous in form than their fathers'. The pleasures of these poses were enhanced by their social transience. These youthful escapades marked the growing permeability of clothing styles, a trend which ultimately saw trousers accepted as respectable wear by the end of the century, a contribution from the working classes carried by young nobles playing at coaching and riding, in the guise of commoners. The figure in Plate 5.1 exemplifies this casual fashion, displaying youthful nonchalance in his slouching stance, hand in pocket, from the unpowdered curls of his hair to his spurred boots.[65]

Spirited young noblemen defied tradition and rejected the formal sartorial trappings of their birth, on some occasions. Labouring people had fewer choices – yet they, too, were acutely aware of the symbolic content of clothing. And, increasingly, working men shunned the wearing of livery, which carried a particular taint of subservience. Livery was an interesting example of the luxurious apparel of servants that raised no hue or cry.[66] In a very real sense, the servant's coat was not his, but rather an advertisement of his master's privilege. Employers recognized that

A BUCK of 1781.

Plate 5.1 'A Buck of 1781'

servants preferred their own clothes, even if these were less elaborate. One Londoner's advice to a rural friend, in search of a servant, spoke directly to this point.

> To Abel Dottin Jun. Esq. At English near Nettlebed
> Oxfordshire July 27 1756.
>
> Sir
> Vyse tells me he can send you a Man who will undertake to Dress Hair and look after Horses, but you must not expect him to Dress Hair very well, for no Serv't which can, will wear a Livery, much less look after Horses.[67]

Servants promised promotion, to keep them with a master, were on occasion also promised they could leave off livery if they stayed, and some servants were very explicit in their objections to livery during the course of such negotiations. As one mistress reported, 'William Foley gave me to understand that being in livery was unbecoming his future hope of being raised in the World.'[68] This reaction to livery confirms Lipovetsky's claim that fashion appealed because it allowed 'individual difference'.[69]

There is no doubt that some domestic servants accepted the anonymity and referred honour that came with livery. But, over the eighteenth century, more and more labouring men resented the subservient taint of livery, wanting instead a neckcloth and coat buttons of their choice, a coat of the colour, fabric and cut they could afford, new or second-hand, for coats signalled dependence or independence in very real ways. Badges and uniforms of various sorts were commonplace in that society. Almshouse residents were routinely required to dress in 'sad colours' in keeping with the ancient religious heritage of those institutions and the standing of the inhabitants. Workhouse inmates, charity school children, poorhouse paupers, institutional pensioners and the like traded a greater measure of security for public stigmatization – the best known surviving example being the Chelsea Pensioners.[70] Many who contributed to charities insisted that recipients of their largesse be publicly marked, sometimes with red initials stitched into the sleeve of the upper garments. The poor resisted these stigmas. In one case, a bequest made in 1712 was formally amended a century later by the Charity Commissioners, who wrote that 'the coats which the founder had directed should have his initials "P.W. in red cloth upon the left arm" were discontinued on account of the objection [of the poor] to wearing the letters, and instead thereof 7s. used to be given to each of the poor persons towards furnishing a coat'.[71]

Symbolic emblems of poverty, servitude and dependence were well known, the status of the wearer discerned in the garments. However, sensitivities were heightened surrounding the wearing of these uniforms and the issue itself elicited strong views. A mid-eighteenth-century newspaper recorded one instance where comments on a coat had explosive consequences. According to the report, two liveried servants riding through a village on a spring day encountered a man and two young women playing a game of stool ball. At this point one of the servants called out to the young man, 'What does such a Black Dog do playing with such pretty Girls?' The youth retorted in kind, 'I am not so much like a Dog as you, for I wear my own Coat, and you wear your Master's.' The liveried servant was enraged at the jibe – he was wearing livery and the livery bespoke his servile status. The exchange was followed by a flurry of blows as the servant whipped the unlucky wit, who fled into a neighbouring house. Even at that the servant's rage was not assuaged and he followed his prey, drawing a pistol and shooting him fatally.[72] This melodramatic tale appealed to the publishers of the *Bristol Weekly Intelligencer*, not only for the drama of the events, but also for the instant recognition among readers of the point at issue. 'I wear my own Coat, and you wear your Master's' – the statement constituted a stinging insult, calling into question the manliness of the servant, his social standing and autonomy, as compared with the man clad in his own coat. Little wonder that liveries could not be sold in second-hand markets where they were known as such. Self-respect increasingly demanded a coat devoid of the stigma of servitude, however plain the garment. It was not simply a love of luxury which compelled more working men to reject livery, it was their growing belief that individually selected attire was more important than the comfort of clothing which displayed the traditional symbols of mastery.

By the second half of the eighteenth century, both labouring and middling men could easily find inexpensive garments ready-to-wear, if they shrank from second-hand or could not afford made-to-measure.[73] In his autobiography the radical artisan Francis Place (1771–1854) vividly recalled the clothing styles favoured by boys of his rank, such as the first hat he chose. 'Round hats were coming into fashion, and when I was quite a child I wore one, with a gold band and tassel. My father said none but thieves and persons who were ashamed to shew their faces wore them.'[74] London adolescents defined their own style, distinguishing their generation from the next, reflecting the generational tensions surrounding appropriate clothing, a phenomenon played out in city streets in the eighteenth century long before the alleged birth of youth culture. Place likewise recalled how the sons of tradesmen and artisans, whose family could afford the cost, were fitted yearly with new clothes at the ready-made and second-hand shops prior to Easter. Place's contemporaries showed a distinct flare for dress and hair that marked their age group in the crowded metropolis.[75]

> Boys up to fifteen or sixteen years of age and many 'til eighteen or twenty years of age wore their hair long and curled on their shoulders, this was the general custom, but they who aimed at being thought knowing had fashions of their own ... had the hair on the sides of their faces rolled upon pieces of window lead about four inches long, they usually had three and sometimes four of these leads one above another the lowest receding the most. Neither pantaloons nor trousers had then come into fashion, every one wore breeches stockings and shoes, some had strings to their breeches knees .... A bunch of st[r]ings at the knees and about a dozen of buttons close together with white cotton or silk stocking shewed a lad who was especially knowing. The stockings were usually white with broad stripes ... bright red or blue ... .[76]

Christopher Breward challenges the theorists who claim the 1940s to 1960s as the origins of the first proletarian male subculture, 'followers and decoders of fashion' with 'new male consumers and male-oriented boutiques'. What Dick Hebdige observed in mid-twentieth-century London and Breward discovered in the metropolis in the late nineteenth century doubtless had it roots in earlier urban expressions of masculine culture. How otherwise can we understand the new meanings assigned by young men with curls and hats, boots and shoes laced, striped stockings and cotton neckerchiefs? These practices were surely consistent with Hebdige's observation that:

> commodities can be symbolically 'repossessed' in everyday life, and endowed with implicitly oppositional meanings ... The symbiosis in which ideology and social order, production and reproduction, are linked is then neither fixed nor guaranteed. It can be prised open. The consensus can be fractured, challenged, overruled and resistance to the groups in dominance cannot always be lightly dismissed or automatically incorporated.[77]

Male consumers of many ages and ranks were enmeshed in consumer rituals as deeply as were women, but in ways that expressed the diverse aspects of masculinity in their historical and social settings.

Hostility to and the rejection of certain styles is as important in this exercise as simply exploring communities of common taste.[78] Rejections define the boundaries of self-selected groups, and Giorgio Riello's exploration of consumerism and footwear in this period illustrates the point. For example, boots were worn by genteel Englishmen in the mid-eighteenth century for riding only; when weather conditions encouraged foreign visitors to don high boots they were frowned out of the practice, as shoes were generally preferred. Yet, at the same time, particularly stylish metropolitan youths liked the casual look of boots and affected them at public events, perhaps precisely because of the response they would elicit: the head-shaking and finger-wagging. Shoelaces were another case in point. Buckles had been adopted with enthusiasm in the seventeenth century throughout western Europe as a decorative shoe fastening and assumed various shapes for fashion-conscious men and women through the eighteenth century. In the 1780s, Parisian police officials opined that shoelaces were the self-selected signal worn by pederasts, and when the fashion was introduced in London in the next decade, some denounced shoelaces as effeminate.[79] Groups set themselves apart through the definition and redefinition of borders, and even the most apparently trivial elements of dress, whether displayed with a flourish or discreetly borne, added to the material and cultural complexity of society. In one of many responses to fashion, this rhymer observed:

> Yes, yes, my Friends, disguise it as we will,
> To Right or Wrong 'tis Fashion guides us still:
> A Few perhaps rise singularly good,
> Defy, and stem the Fool-o'erwhelming Flood;
> The Rest to wander from their Brethren fear,
> As social Herring in large Shoals appear.[80]

Singly or in shoals, these 'social Herring' defined themselves through their various markings and manifestations.

Rural men were not exempt from these forces, as Christina Fowler reveals in her study of working men on the Hackwood estate, outside Basing, Hampshire. This group were patrons of a local tailor who sold ready-made wear as well as making bespoke garments for his clientele. The tailor's records show a lengthy series of purchases from 1811 to 1815, and Fowler compared these purchases with the men's cash wages from the estate, finding very suggestive results (see Table 5.4). There was wide variation in the expenditure of these working men. At the highest level, a member of the livery staff spent 40 per cent of his cash salary on clothing, some of it made to order. We cannot be sure that the wages listed in the estate ledgers reflect the total incomes of the men, since gratuities and perquisites of various sorts remained a significant supplement to servants' earnings. But the data suggest the investment in apparel made by these men, such as the coachman who spent 12 per cent of his salary on his wardrobe and the farmhand who spent 24 per cent of his income on coats, waistcoats and breeches. The variation in expenditure among

Table 5.4   Units of apparel purchased by rural men, Hampshire, 1811–1815

Occupation	No. of units purchased	% of wages
Livery staff	6	40.0
Farmhand	7	24.4
Under-gardener	9	23.5
Postillion	1	21.4
Coachman	11	12.9
Groom	12	12.5
Under-butler	5	10.3
Carpenter	11	8.5
Labourer	6	4.5
Groom	2	3.5

Source: Christina Fowler, 'Robert Mansbridge: a rural tailor and his customers, 1811–1815', Textile History 28:1 (1997), p. 37.

this small group indicates differing personal and family priorities, as well as the aesthetic interests which drove the men. What is fully evident from this study is the attention the men paid to their wardrobe, far from the metropolis and what were assumed to be the traditional catalysts of consumption.[81]

Thus fashion assumed a multiplicity of shapes and forms among men and women from a range of social backgrounds and geographic settings. Naturally, there was a diverse span of opinions on what constituted fitting apparel. Could a lady of a certain age wear informal undress? Could a gentleman be in fashion without breeches? Were wigs essential for common men? Clothing styles were routinely modified to fit the relative wealth, age, experience, rank and habit of the wearer and, most important, to suit their sensibilities. Amanda Vickery notes the intense interest in metropolitan styles among women diarists and correspondents living in rural Lancashire. Their desire for information did not, however, translate into unthinking replication of London vogues inappropriate to their position. These genteel women selected only the elements which suited their taste and sense of propriety, displaying what Vickery called an 'equivocal relationship with high fashion'.[82]

Garments can also manifest these varied multiple meanings. In the Royal Ontario Museum, Toronto, there is a simple striped cotton jacket known generally as a *pet en l'air*,[83] popularly worn by middling and labouring women, the name suggesting its plebeian pedigree. Jackets of this sort first debuted in the mid-century as a variant of the short jackets worn with petticoats, creating an informal look. It was a dress particularly favoured in the mid-century and celebrated in *The Connoisseur* with the claim that 'nothing is so ravishing as an easy deshabille'.[84] The informality of the *pet en l'air* added to the alternatives available for those who separated their wardrobe between formal and informal wear and chose the most suitable for each settings. However, strict rules of dress affected only the residents of polite society; for the rest, informality was the norm. And, as with male fashions, women's wear included a growing range of casual garments which furthered the visual conflation of high and low style. The *pet en l'air* was an exciting new addition in 1750, yet, by 1754, a correspondent for *The Connoisseur* sneered at the number of 'red-armed Belles that appear in the Park every Sunday; hence it is that Sacks and Petenlairs may be seen at Moor-fields and Whitechapel'.[85] Red work-roughened hands and arms marked such women, and these signs assumed heightened importance as more democratic clothing styles blurred hierarchical divides. Their jackets were more ubiquitous, no longer stunningly new, confirming the wearers' less than genteel origins outside self-defined polite milieus. Visual differentiation highlighted not just clothes but physical features. But, among the Moorfield belles, the *pet en l'air*, such as survives in the ROM collection, gave pleasure and a measure of status within that community – some distance from the cultivated West End another facet of popular fashion was being defined. Among these communities, tradition's hold had broken down and the motivation to define oneself through dress drew individuals from every rank.

Conclusion

Well below the comfortable middle of society there was a widespread pre-occupation with fashion, with men and women engaged in the consumer agenda.[86] The diversity of material expressions reflects this broad consumer process: some styles replicated middle-class norms and others were particular to groups or regions. For example, the handkerchief, a common linen or cotton accessory, took many forms and was frequently the medium for political prints and social satires. Examples survive which hark back to the 1760s political campaigns supporting the popular radical John Wilkes. His image on a handkerchief appealed to a certain set of shoppers and allowed that accessory to serve political or aesthetic purposes.[87] Indeed, the prosperity of the cotton industry was founded on the generalized demand of the widest range of consumers.[88] Some members of the higher classes, like Viscount Torrington, lamented the erosion of ancient habits of dress. In a 1781 entry he damned the building of turnpikes that carried fashions more quickly to country women[89] and derided the pretensions of his new tenant farmer, very unlike his predecessor:

> who wore the same coloured course cloth all the year round, and tied his shoes with thongs: his son … when I call'd upon him, in the morning, about 9 years ago, order'd the maid servant to bring a bottle of wine … and pouring out a glass, said, 'There Colonel, perhaps theres as good a glass of claret as you ever drank at St. James's.'[90]

Ridicule followed sermonizing as the favoured method of defining elite norms. Caricaturists and satirists appealed to their patrons, mocking the stylish servant, the bewigged farmer, the well dressed sailor, the respectable shopkeeper. As Douglas explains, 'hated garments … signal cultural affiliation. Because some would choose, others must reject.'[91] The authors of these lampoons invited their readers into a common community of the authentically fashionable, to ridicule the pretensions and reduce the threat of the growing cohort of unruly fashion-conscious commoners.

The flourishing market for cartoons and caricatures soothed the sensibilities of readers defensive about the presumption of the lower ranks. A pair of caricatures epitomize these tensions: one features Farmer Giles's daughter playing the piano before genteel visitors and the other shows a city butcher's daughter back from school, charming her family with a song (see Plates 5.2–5.3). In the former the artist provides every evidence of the Gileses' inauthentic ancestry; the parents may own their estate, but the denizens of 'Cheese Hall' cannot claim an ancient pedigree and their servants unwittingly reveal the fraud. The lad with the serving tray carries an egg basket on one arm, the produce tumbling out, while the wine glasses teeter perilously towards the visitor. This is no well trained retainer, but a stable boy, as false in his pretensions as his employers. The stiff young gent sits bolt upright on the stylish upholstered chair, matrons gossip or doze in front of the stiffly stitched tribute to Cheese Hall; social dissonance overwhelms the musicale.[92] In the second of these caricatures, the butcher's daughter, back from school, flaunts her genteel figure and musical accomplishments, to the evident delight of her red-cheeked plebeian mother. Accoutrements of gentility jostle on the mantlepiece, while meat is being carved in the shop front adjoining; base commerce blends with false civility, a juxtaposition intended to amuse, or revolt, the viewer. The daughter's marketability is presumed to rest in a spurious fashionable veneer; the artist suggests her real value is more corporeal. Over the fireplace, instead of a portrait of a revered ancestor there hangs a picture

Plate 5.2 'Farmer Giles & his Wife shewing off their daughter Betty to their Neighbours on her return from School', drawn by an amateur, etched by J. Gillray

of an ox – her family's claim to social standing resides in their forebear 'Deputy Marrowfat', whose image overlooks the shop. If the targets of caricature were meant to shrink from the assaults, they did not. Shifting styles were 'banners in [a] cultural contest'.[93] Farmer Giles contrived a respectable comfort, while the Giles women contributed to the vibrant sitting-room culture of music and visiting that was integral to nineteenth-century middle-class life. The modes they embraced were unaffected by such derision.[94] Butchers' daughters wore pearls and fine cotton gowns; buckles, shawls and modish clothes continued to be worn by 'red-armed Belles' sustaining communities of taste.

In 1783, the *London Magazine* grumbled that 'every servant girl, has her cotton gowns, and her cotton stockings, whilst honest … wool … more becoming to their stations, lies to mildew in our mercers' shops'. The author called for a higher price for cottons, so clearly 'an article of luxury'.[95] But wishing could not make it so. Factory girls wanted printed cotton gowns and bought them at the earliest opportunity; labouring and middling men wanted velveteen or corduroy breeches, white shirts and neckcloths and bought these goods in great numbers. Fustian suits – corduroy, moleskin, velveret – became the wear of new generations of artisans who saw in their hard-earned, comfortably stylish garments an

Plate 5.3   Thomas Rowlandson, 'The Hopes of the Fammily, or Miss Marrowfat at home for the Holidays'

authentic reflection of their deserving political status. The fustian suit became a class signature as well as a conscious political emblem and, in 1842, the popular radical Feargus O'Connor appeared before a mass meeting of Chartist supporters in Manchester dressed in a corduroy suit, eliciting raucous applause. This outfit embodied working men's common aspirations, a common political brotherhood.[96] For the men who worked in the mills and, indeed, for working people as a whole, O'Connor's suiting symbolized an authority earned through sweat and diligent labour, plain and unpretentious, the hallmark of respectable working men. These garments were bought from any of the thousands of clothes dealers scattered through the urban landscape, patronized by men and women hunting for garments to suit their budget and their dreams. Below the comfortable middle rank, in working communities throughout the country, these careful purchases were routinely bundled up to the pawnshops each Monday and retrieved on Saturday. By 1800 the bundles contained prized watches, embossed buttons of silver or brass, shoe buckles and laced aprons, flowered cotton gowns and fine lawn handkerchiefs.[97] These wardrobes represented modest indulgencies, to be sure, unremarkable as high fashion. Yet the collective impetus of butchers' daughters and farmhands represented real and profound change, a momentum towards personal display, the creation of a complex aesthetic that defied ancient hierarchies and marked the modern era. In the nap of fustian jackets, in the sparkle of buckles and the flourish of floral gowns, we can see the demise of traditional garb and traditional mentalities, signifying new social, cultural and economic relations.

Notes

1   The literature on consumerism, fashion and material culture has blossomed in the 1980s and 1990s, beginning with the work of Joan Thirsk, *Economic Policy and Projects: The Development of a Consumer Society in Early Modern England* (Oxford, 1978); Neil McKendrick, John Brewer and J. H. Plumb, *The Birth of a Consumer Society: The Commercialization of Eighteenth Century England* (London, 1983); Carole Shammas, *The Pre-industrial Consumer in England and America* (Oxford, 1990); Ruth Barnes and Joanne B. Eicher (eds), *Dress and Gender: Making and Meaning* (Oxford, 1992); Beverly Lemire, *Fashion's Favourite: The Cotton Trade and the Consumer in Britain, 1660–1800* (Oxford, 1991); Christopher Breward, *The Culture of Fashion: A New History of Fashionable Dress* (Manchester, 1995); Victoria de Grazia (ed.), *The Sex of Things: Gender and Consumption in Historical Perspective* (Berkeley CA, 1996); Maxine Berg and Helen Clifford, *Consumers and Luxury: Consumer Culture in Europe, 1650–1850* (Manchester, 1999); Sarah Richards, *Eighteenth-Century Ceramics: Products for a Civilized Society* (Manchester, 1999); Daniel Roche, *The Culture of Clothing: Dress and Fashion in the Ancien Régime* (Cambridge, 1989) and *A History of Everyday Things: The Birth of Consumption in France, 1600–1800* (Cambridge, 2000); Katrina Honeyman, *Well Suited: A History of the Leeds Clothing Industry, 1850–1990* (Oxford, 2000); Ann Rosalind Jones and Peter Stallybrass, *Renaissance Clothing and the Materials of Memory* (Cambridge, 2000); Alexandra Palmer, *Couture and Commerce: The Transatlantic Fashion Trade in the 1950s* (Vancouver, 2001); Linda Baumgarten, *What Clothes Reveal: The Language of Clothing in Colonial and Federal America* (New Haven CT, 2002); Lou Taylor, *Establishing Dress History* (New York, 2002); David Kuchta, *The Three-piece Suit and Modern Masculinity* (Berkeley CA, 2002); Michael Zakim, *Ready-made Democracy: A History of Men's Dress in the American Republic, 1760–1860* (Chicago, 2003). The journal *Fashion Theory* was launched in 1997 and other journals also focus on this topic in thematic issues: *Textile History* 22:2 (1991), 24:1 (1993), 28:1 (1997), 33:1 (2002); *Continuity and Change* 15:3 (2000); and *Gender and History* 14:3 (2002).

2   For a survey of sumptuary legislation in England see N. B. Harte, 'State control of dress and social change in pre-industrial England' in D. C. Coleman and A. H. John (eds), *Trade, Government and Economy in Pre-industrial England* (London, 1976).

3   Alan Hunt, 'Moralizing luxury: the discourses of the governance of consumption', *Journal of Historical Sociology* 8:4 (1995).

4   Giorgio Riello discusses the various styles of footwear and the spread of styles between different social groups and national markets. Riello, *Foot in the Past: Consumers, Production and Footwear in the Long Eighteenth Century* (Oxford, 2006).

5   Access to ready-made and second-hand clothing stocks did vary with geographic loca-

tion. For an examination of issues surrounding dress in northern England see John Styles, 'Clothing the north: the supply of non-elite clothing in the eighteenth-century north of England', *Textile History* 25 (1994), and Miles Lambert, '"Cast-off wearing apparell": the consumption and distribution of second-hand clothing in northern England during the long eighteenth century', *Textile History* 35:1 (2004).

6 Gilles Lipovetsky, *The Empire of Fashion: Dressing Modern Democracy* (Princeton NJ, 1994), p. 23.

7 Lipovetsky, *Empire of Fashion*, p. 31.

8 Historians have tracked this process from a variety of perspectives. See, for example, the classic account, Charles Wilson, *England's Apprenticeship, 1603–1763* (London, 1965). A more recent account is Maxine Berg's *The Age of Manufactures: Industry, Innovation and Work in Britain, 1700–1820*, 2nd edn (London, 1994), and for an important perspective on domestic trade see Margaret Spufford, *The Great Reclothing of Rural England: Petty Chapmen and their Wares in the Seventeenth Century* (London, 1984).

9 Joan Thirsk, 'The fantastical folly of fashion: the English stocking knitting industry, 1500–1700' in N. B. Harte and K. G. Ponting (eds), *Textile History and Economic History: Essays in Honour of Miss Julia de Lacy Mann* (Manchester, 1973).

10 Joan Thirsk dates the expansion of consumer industries from this period. *Luxury Trades and the Consumer in* Ancien Régime *Paris* (Aldershot, 1997), pp. 257–62.

11 Barbara Burman and Carole Turbin discuss the changing scholarly focus on dress history and fashion over the last twenty years in 'Material strategies engendered', introduction to the special issue *Dress and Gender* of *Gender and History* 14:3 (2002).

12 See, for example, Margaret Spufford, 'The cost of apparel in seventeenth-century England and the accuracy of Gregory King', *Economic History Review*, 2nd series 53:4 (2000).

13 Cissie Fairchilds refers to 'populuxe' goods as 'cheap copies of aristocratic luxury items'. 'The production and marketing of populuxe goods in eighteenth-century Paris' in John Brewer and Roy Porter (eds), *Consumption and the World of Goods* (London, 1993), p. 228. However, it is evident that material goods varied in their importance within different communities. Lorna Weatherill noted the higher percentage of earthenware owned by decedents in the dealing trades, as compared with those from the gentry – there was a 10 per cent difference in ownership rates. Similarly, 18 per cent more gentry families possessed silverwear. Lorna Weatherill, *Consumer Behaviour and Material Culture in Britain, 1660–1760* (London, 1988), p. 184.

14 Public dress, as well as religious vestments, were hotly debated by assorted constituencies from the sixteenth century onwards. Around 1700, in Alsace, for example, conflicts within the radical Protestant Mennonite community led to the rise of the Amish, with debates over theological interpretations distilled around issues of appearance. The Amish insisted on simplicity in all things, forswearing worldly fashions, with one particular prerequisite focused on fastenings. Buttons became a sticking point, leading the Amish to prescribe only garments closed with hooks and eyes. John A Hostetler, *Amish Society*, 3rd edn (Baltimore MD, 1980), pp. 37–9; Cissie Fairchilds, 'Fashion and freedom in the French revolution', *Continuity and Change* 15:3 (2000), p. 420; Roger Lockyer, *Tudor and Stuart Britain, 1471–1714*, 2nd edn (London, 1985), pp. 165–6.

15 John Heywood, *The Four PP*, quoted in Thirsk, *Economic Policies and Projects*, p. 123.

16 Weatherill, *Consumer Behaviour*, p. 185.

17 Spufford, *Great Reclothing*; Hunt, 'Moralizing luxury'; Maxine Berg and Helen Clifford, 'Introduction', and Maxine Berg, 'New commodities, luxuries and their consumers in eighteenth-century England' in Maxine Berg and Helen Clifford (eds), *Consumers and Luxury: Consumer Culture in Europe, 1650–1850* (Manchester, 1999); Joan Thirsk, 'Industries in the countryside' in F. J. Fisher (ed.), *Essays in Economic and Social History in Tudor and Stuart England* (Cambridge, 1961). I do not suggest that this was an exclusively English phenomenon – there is an extensive literature outlining the shifting material culture of other parts of north-western Europe, including the Low Countries and the Netherlands. See, for example, Jan de Vries, 'Peasant demand patterns and economic development: Friesland, 1550–1750' in William N. Parker and Eric L. Jones (eds), *European Peasants and their Markets: Essays in Agrarian Economic History* (Princeton NJ, 1975) and 'The population and economy of the preindustrial Netherlands', *Journal of Interdisciplinary History* 25 (1985); M. Baulant, A. J. Schuurman and P. Servais (eds), *Inventaires après-decès et ventes de meubles : apports à une histoire de la vie économique et quotidienne, XIVe–XIXe siècle* (Louvain-la-Neuve, 1988); Bruno Blondé, 'Tableware and changing consumer patterns: dynamics of material culture in Antwerp, seventeenth to eighteenth centuries' in J. Veeckman (ed.), *Majolica and Glass from Italy to Antwerp and beyond: The Transfer of Technology in the Sixteenth and early Seventeenth Century* (Antwerp, 2002).

18 De Grazia, *Sex of Things*. There is an extensive literature on nineteenth- and twentieth-century consumer society, for example W. Hamish Fraser, *The Coming of the Mass Market, 1850–1914* (London, 1981); Michael Miller, *The Bon Marché: Bourgeois Culture and the Department Store, 1869–1920* (Princeton NJ, 1981); Rosalind Williams, *Dream Worlds: Mass Consumption in Late Nineteenth-Century France* (Berkeley CA, 1982); Richard W. Fox and T. J. Jackson Lears (eds), *The Culture of Consumption: Critical Essays in American History, 1880–1980* (New York, 1983); Daniel Horowitz, *The Morality of Spending: Attitudes toward the Consumer Society in America, 1875–1940* (Baltimore MD, 1985); Thomas Richards, *The Commodity Culture of Victorian England* (Stanford CA, 1990); Lori Loeb, *Consuming Angels: Advertising and Victorian Women* (New York, 1994); Erika Rappaport, *Shopping for Pleasure: Women in the Making of London's West End* (Princeton NJ, 2000).

19 Jan de Vries, 'Between purchasing power and the world of goods: understanding the household economy in early modern Europe' in Pamela Sharpe (ed.), *Women's Work: The English Experience, 1650–1914* (London, 1998), p. 214. See also Nancy Cox, *The Complete Tradesman: A Study of Retailing, 1550–1820* (Aldershot, 2000), and Claire Walsh, 'The newness of the department store: a view from the eighteenth century' in Geoffrey Crossick and Serge Jaumain (eds), *Cathedrals of Consumption: The European Department Store, 1850–1939* (Aldershot, 1999).

20 Thirsk, *Economic Policies and Projects*, especially chapter 5. See also Margaret Spufford, 'Fabric for seventeenth-century children and adolescents' clothes', *Textile History* 34:1 (2003).

21 Phillip Stubbes, *The Anatomie of Abuses*, preface by Arthur Freeman (1583, repr. New York, 1973); spelling modernized by the author.

22 Stubbes, *Anatomie*.

23 See, for example, Richard Brathwait, *The English Gentleman; and The English Gentlewoman* (London, 1641), pp. 10–12, 271–84. The author spends considerably more time

defining the ideal dress for women than that of men.

24 Gregory King's calculations on the national consumption of clothing were initially assessed in N. B. Harte, 'The economics of clothing in the late seventeenth century' in N. B. Harte (ed.), *Fabrics and Fashions: Studies in the Economic and Social History of Dress*, special issue of *Textile History* 22:2 (1991), and their later veracity was proved in Spufford, 'Cost of apparel'.

25 Thirsk, *Economic Policies and Projects*, pp. 106–32; Spufford, *Great Reclothing*, pp. 85–145.

26 Lipovetsky, *Empire of Fashion*, pp. 33–4; and Spufford, 'Adolescents' clothes'.

27 For a full discussion of the linen trade in the early modern period see Philip Olleren-shaw and Brenda Collins (eds), *Linen in Europe* (Oxford, 2003).

28 Carole Shammas, 'The decline of textile prices in England and British America prior to industrialization', *Economic History Review* 47:3 (1994), p. 492. See also table 4, p. 493.

29 Georges Vigarello, *Concepts of Cleanliness: Changing Attitudes in France since the Middle Ages*, translated by Jean Birrell (Cambridge, 1988), p. 62. These transformations in mentality were also evident in England.

30 A. Courtin, *De la civilité qui se pratique en France parmi les honnêtes gens* (Paris, 1671), 100, quoted in Vigarello, *Concepts of Cleanliness*, p. 73.

31 Simon Schama, *The Embarrassment of Riches: An Interpretation of Dutch Culture in the Golden Age* (London, 1987), pp. 375–82.

32 Daniel Roche describes the spreading consumer interest in linens, exploring the cultural and economic significance of this preoccupation in *ancien régime* Paris. Roche, *Culture of clothing*, chapter 6.

33 *Verney Memoirs*, quoted in C. W. Cunnington and Phillis Cunnington, *The History of Underclothes* (London, 1951), p. 56.

34 Spufford, *Great Reclothing*, pp. 187, 203.

35 C 108/34, Public Record Office (hereafter PRO).

36 Quoted in P. J. Thomas, *Mercantilism and the East India Trade* (London, 1926), p. 25. For an examination of protectionist legislation which followed the spread of European linens in England see Harte, 'The rise of protection'.

37 K. N. Chaudhuri, *The Trading World of Asia and the English East India Company* (Cambridge, 1978), pp. 96–7, 282.

38 Among the many pamphlets produced on this question one noted that 'all those who wear Callicoe or Linen now, wou'd not wear Woollen Stuffs if there was no such thing as Printed Callicoe or Linen, but Dutch or Hambro' Strip'd and Chequer'd Linens, and other things of that kind, and for the same Reason that they now wear printed Callicoe or Linen … because nothing else washes near so well'. *A Further Examination of the Weavers Pretences* … (London, 1719), p. 20.

39 There is a vast pamphlet literature surrounding the campaign by landowners, wool merchants and their supporters to ban East Indian textiles from England. The campaign, which began in the 1680s, concluded in England in 1720, when almost all cottons were barred from England. For a fuller examination of the calico campaign see Lemire, *Fashion's Favourite*, chapter 1; Natalie Rothstein, 'The calico campaign of 1719–1721', *East London Papers*, July 1969; and Thomas, *Mercantilism and the East India Trade*.

40 *Mus Rusticus* (London, 1717).

41 *The Just Complaints of the poor Weaver truly Represented*, reprinted in John Smith (ed.), *Chronicon Rusticum-commerciale; or, Memoirs of Wool, etc.* … (1747, repr. New York, 1968) II, p. 195.

42 *Mus Rusticus.*

43 *Old Bailey Records,* July 1719, p. 7.

44 *Weekly Medley,* 8–15 August 1719; *Weekly Journal,* 20 June, 21 July, 8 August 1719; *Weekly Packet,* 21 November 1719.

45 *Thursday's Journal,* 6 August 1719.

46 Alan Hunt, *Governance of the Consuming Passions: A History of Sumptuary Law* (New York, 1996), p. 231.

47 'What signified the riches and the liberty and property which we justly boast of, except that we have the liberty of eating and drinking or wearing these things when we have earned them?' *Weekly Journal or British Gazetteer,* 1719.

48 John Styles's study of the consumer habits of household servants living in rural Yorkshire shows they shared a generally uniform commitment to some elements of fashion, with some of the women going to great expense to create a stylish appearance. Styles, 'Involuntary consumers? Servants and their clothes in eighteenth-century England', *Textile History* 33:1 (2002), pp. 9–21.

49 *The Autobiography of Samuel Bamford* I (London, 1967), p. 5.

50 Acc. 38, York City Archives.

51 J 90/540, PRO.

52 Thorstein Veblen, *The Theory of the Leisure Class* (repr. Boston MA, 1973). For instances of the application of this style of analysis see, for example, Harold Perkin, *The Origins of Modern Society* (London, 1968), and Neil McKendrick, 'The commercialization of fashion' in Neil McKendrick, John Brewer and J. H. Plumb, *The Birth of a Consumer Society* (London, 1983), pp. 34–99. The history of this phenomenon among dress historians is briefly discussed in Burman and Turbin, 'Material strategies', pp. 371–3.

53 Hunt, *Governance of the Consuming Passions,* p. 54.

54 Lipovetsky, *Empire of Fashion,* pp. 46–7.

55 Lemire, *Fashion's Favourite,* pp. 98, 206, 210, 219.

56 Lipovetsky, *Empire of Fashion,* p. 47.

57 There are an increasing number of studies of the dress of working people, adding greater nuance to more aspects of plebeian dress history. See, for example, *Textile History* 33:1 (2002), special issue *The Dress of the Poor,* guest-edited by Steven King and Christiana Payne.

58 John Brewer, *The Pleasures of the Imagination: English Culture in the Eighteenth Century* (London, 1997), pp. 100–4.

59 Erin Mackie, *Market à la mode: Fashion, Commodity and Gender in the* Tatler *and the* Spectator (Baltimore MD, 1997), pp. 7, 148.

60 A heated debate around the moral and economic repercussions of these material changes was unleashed by Bernard Mandeville's *The Fable of the Bees: or, Private Vices, Publick Benefits* (London, 1723). See E. G. Hundert, *The Enlightenment's Fable: Bernard Mandeville and the Discovery of Society* (Cambridge, 1994).

61 *The Gentleman's Magazine* IV (1734), p. 14.

62 Examples of the widening ownership of stylishly utilitarian goods abound. The following illustrate this trend. The owner of an apple stall lost a linen smock and linen shirt, a silk handkerchief and half a yard of lace in the burglary of her family home. A long-time servant working in the Tower was robbed in Well Street of a cloth coat and breeches, a calimanco waistcoat, a linen shirt, a wig and hat, silk stockings, shoes and

a gold ring. A lodger who worked for a sugar refiner had a cloth coat, a satin waistcoat, worsted stockings and leather breeches stolen from his room. A pipe maker was robbed of his muslin cravat, striped handkerchief, leather shoes and iron buckles. A bricklayer lost his silver watch and muslin neckcloth; a coachman working in a livery stable had his blue cloth coat and waistcoat, linen waistcoat, neckcloths, gilt buckle and handkerchiefs stolen; a furrier lost from his lodgings a wool coat and waistcoat with gold lace, two muslin neckcloths, a velvet waistcoat, a silk and cotton waistcoat, stocking breeches and silver knee buckles. *A True Account of the Proceedings on the Crown-side at this Lent Assizes, held for the County of Surrey in the Borough of Southwark* ... March ... 1683; *The Old Bailey Records*, April–May 1742, p. 72; May 1764, pp. 162, 188; August 1700, pp. 28–31; September 1771, pp. 412–13.

63 See David Kuchta, 'The making of the self-made man: class, clothing, and English masculinity, 1688–1832' in Victoria de Grazia (ed.), *The Sex of Things: Gender and Consumption in Historical Perspective* (Berkeley CA, 1996).

64 *The Gentleman's Magazine* IX (1739), p. 28.

65 Later in the eighteenth century, observers attributed the more relaxed elite male dress to the political radicalism of Sir Charles Fox and the spread of Jacobinism that came with the French Revolution. In fact, the impetus had grown with each generation over the century. Anne Buck, *Dress in Eighteenth-Century England* (London, 1979), p. 204.

66 Buck, *Dress in Eighteenth-Century England*, p. 105.

67 C 108/30, PRO.

68 Maria Josepha Holroyd, *The Girlhood of Maria Josepha Holroyd*, ed. J. A. Adeane (1896), p. 331, quoted in Buck, *Dress in Eighteenth-Century England*, p. 109.

69 Lipovetsky, *Empire of Fashion*, p. 47.

70 Phillis Cunnington and Catherine Lucas, *Charity Costumes of Children, Scholars, Almsfolk, Pensioners* (New York, 1978), pp. 66–9, 228–30.

71 Charity Commissioners' Report 7 (1822), p. 503, quoted in Cunnington and Lucas, *Charity Costumes*, p. 57.

72 *Bristol Weekly Intelligencer*, 15 June 1750.

73 Beverly Lemire, *Dress, Culture and Commerce: The English Clothing Trade before the Factory, 1660–1800* (Basingstoke, 1997), pp. 19–41.

74 Mary Thale (ed.), *The Autobiography of Francis Place* (Cambridge, 1972), p. 62.

75 It is worth noting that Place's description bears more than a passing resemblance to the look affected by the young lord, as seen in Plate 5.1.

76 Thale, *Francis Place*, p. 63.

77 Dick Hebdidge, *Subculture: The Meaning of Style* (London, 1979), pp. 16–7.

78 Mary Douglas, 'Bad taste in furnishing' in *Thought Styles: Critical Essays on Good Taste* (London, 1996), pp. 62–3.

79 Riello, *Foot in the Past*. See also J. Merrick, 'Commissioner Faucault, Inspecteur Noël, and the "pederasts" of Paris, 1780–1783', *Journal of Social History* 32:2 (1998).

80 *Fashion: An Epistolary Satire to a Friend* (London, 1742).

81 Christina Fowler, 'Robert Mansbridge: a rural tailor and his customers, 1811–1815', *Textile History* 28:1 (1997), pp. 36–7.

82 Amanda Vickery, *The Gentleman's Daughter: Women's Lives in Georgian England* (London, 1998), p. 180.

83 Negative No. 983.82.1, Department of Textile and Dress, Royal Ontario Museum, Toronto.

84 *The Connoisseur*, October 1754, quoted in C. Willet and Phillis Cunnington, *Handbook of English Costume in the Eighteenth Century* (Boston MA, 1972), p. 300.

85 *Jackson's Oxford Journal*, 20 July 1754.

86 Lemire, *Fashion's Favourite*. See, in particular, chapter 3.

87 My thanks to Linda Baumgarten, Colonial Williamsburg, for information on the Wilkes handkerchief in this collection, Acc. No. G1951-447. Other examples survive in the collection of the Gunnersbury Park Museum, London. My thanks to Sarah Levitt for showing me this item. Also see Frank Lewis, *English Chintz, from Earliest Times to the Present Day* (Benfleet, 1935), plate 2, which includes an image of John Wilkes, and the later political handkerchiefs, plates 21 and 60, depicting the Peterloo Massacre and Lord John Russell of the 1832 Reform Act, respectively.

88 Francis Place noted the greater cleanliness of journeymen and women in the early nineteenth century, a fact he attributed to the flourishing cotton industry. Thale, *Francis Place*, p. 51 n.

89 'I meet milkmaids on the road, with the dress and looks of Strand misses', he repined. C. B. Andrews (ed.), *The Torrington Diaries* (London, 1886), p. 6.

90 *Torrington Diaries*, p. 217.

91 Mary Douglas, 'On not being seen dead: shopping as protest' in *Thought Styles: Critical Essays on Good Taste* (London, 1996), p. 82.

92 John Johnson, Fashion 3. Bodleian Library, Oxford.

93 Douglas, 'Bad taste', p. 67.

94 Through a study of nineteenth-century diaries and letters from Atlantic Canadian women Margaret Conrad has identified this lively and distinctive pattern of socializing largely directed by middle-class women, in my view typical of this time and period in the Atlantic world. Margaret Conrad, 'Home Culture: Evidence from Nineteenth-Century Maritime Women's Diaries and Letters', unpublished paper presented at the University of New Brunswick, November 1996.

95 *London Magazine* 52 (1783), pp. 128–9.

96 Fustian became synonymous with the rising generation of industrial and artisanal workers to such a degree that it became shorthand for their political ambitions in the nineteenth century. Engels was unhappy with working women's choice of 'printed cottons' and working men's preference for 'shirts of bleached or coloured cotton cloth'. He would have preferred that they dress in sturdy woollens, but, as he noted, 'woollen petticoats are seldom seen on the washing-line'. F. Engels, *The Condition of the Working Class in England in 1845*, ed. W. O. Henderson and W. H. Chaloner (Stanford CA, 1968), pp. 78–9.

97 The records from a pawnbroker in the town of Sheffield, in 1816, show this range of goods among a predominantly labouring population. J 90/504, PRO.

6

Savings culture, provident consumerism and the advent of modern consumer society, c. 1780–1900

THE SPIRIT OF SELF-DENIAL and self-help infused the middle class, inspiring commercial and social initiatives.[1] But in this they were not alone, as these sentiments were also vested in prominent sectors of the lower social ranks.[2] The passion for self-help, respectability and material improvement was not class-specific, although different routes were sometimes taken toward the fulfilment of these aims and material expressions often took different forms.[3] This chapter examines the advent of savings banks and the genesis of savings culture, a dramatic innovation of the nineteenth century, which encouraged new forms of fiscal behaviour among a wide segment of society. After 1800, savings banks sprang up in cities, towns and villages across the nation, in communities in every part of the country. The proliferation of these institutions represented an unprecedented initiative which offered more than simply a convenient mechanism for thrift, for the theory of saving spread as well, disseminated in pamphlets and encouraged by mutual benefit societies. Moreover saving was not presented as an end in itself, as, for the first time, the social discipline of saving was linked with what I call provident consumerism.

Saving, as a facet of general economic behaviour, was matched by a theory which approved and even encouraged careful plebeian consumerism – material accumulation was the natural reward of diligent savers. Case studies of family budgets form no part of this work. But in this chapter I examine the conceptual practices of saving and spending, authorized and sanctioned by political and social elites. Consumer spending among the wage-earning classes was no longer decried; on the contrary, careful expenditures were recognized as a stimulus to Britain's industries. Simultaneously, monetized saving flourished as an element of respectable practice in the middle and working classes, applauded as the route to independent self-sufficiency and material respectability. These economic patterns came to define nineteenth-century masculinity, shaping as well the opportunities and expressions of prized female practice. These powerful cultural forms underpinned the gendered social dynamic unleashed by the savings bank movement, complementing the ethos of provident consumerism. Given their significance, savings banks have received relatively little study compared to other nineteenth-century institutions, works today focusing largely on institutional histories.[4] None has addressed the broad effects of the savings bank movement, or the significant cultural implications of this phenomenon as the formalization of saving and the nineteenth-century culture of consumption disciplined and rewarded common people. The pleasures of consumerism followed the exigencies of saving as day followed night and the propaganda heralding this ordered structure may well have figured in the growing acceptance of industrial capitalism by the wage-earning classes as standards of living rose over the nineteenth century.

The rise of saving banks and the doctrine of personal self-sufficiency

Frugality, as an ideal, has always been in vogue, most particularly as applied to the lower social orders, but thrift takes historically contingent forms. Provident practices were encouraged with homilies like those in Aesop's Fables and enforced with innovations such as the introduction of urban workhouses.[5] However, the challenges and responses of the prudent varied across time. The curse of 'interesting times' afflicted those living through the late eighteenth and early nineteenth centuries, with a conjunction of events including a long and costly war, industrial transformations, soaring food prices, rising population, growing poor rates and rapid urban growth. These factors spawned intermittent crises which, in turn, stimulated new political philosophies, including those which advocated greater self-reliance among the wage-earning classes.[6] In addition, the doctrine of self-help took root within a diverse, sometimes radical, artisan culture which sought greater political representation based on the merits of their constituencies.[7] Experimental and innovative thinkers asked: what were the best ways to buffer working people from shifts in personal fortune or from economic crises? The tradition of friendly societies had long been an important avenue for regular investments, as insurance against future want. In 1793, these provident ventures were secured through an Act of Parliament providing registered legal status, and in response the number of registered friendly societies grew to more than 7,200 by the close of the century. But the security of these funds was often in doubt, since embezzlement, fraud and theft were endemic risks. Bankruptcy, as a result of actuarial crises, was another threat,[8] and canny people joined several societies as a rule of thumb, balancing the threat of one society's default by investing in others. Despite these well known structural weaknesses, the concept of collective strength through small individual investments appealed to depositors and patrons.[9]

Ideally, an early personal strategy aimed at self-reliance would avoid later dependence on the poor rate, just as the seasonal industry of Aesop's ant preserved it during winter.[10] In 1786, the Rev. Joseph Townsend fulminated against those who did not take precautions. 'It should be firmly established, made universal and subjected to wholesome Regulation to drive … [working people] into these [friendly] Societies. No man should be entitled to Relief from the Parochial Fund who did not belong to one of them.'[11] However, critiques of these sometimes unstable groups grew as well. Criticisms derived principally from the fact that friendly societies could be disbanded upon a two-thirds vote, contributions were limited even in good times to a standard subscription rate, and embezzlement of funds remained a persistent problem. The unsoundness of the societies seemed all too obvious to some critics,[12] and when a friendly society collapsed the results were disastrous for members, who might then be compelled to seek parochial assistance. Among liberal theorists, these concerns, as well as the soaring rural poor rates, inspired alternative proposals, aimed to encourage long-term personal provision for the future.[13]

An early experimental programme launched by the Quaker Mrs Priscilla Wakefield showed particular promise, as well as sensitivity to the financial exigencies that could face women. By 1796, her husband had squandered his business fortune and Mrs Wakefield was left to support the family, which she did through her writings.[14] Amid these trying events, Wakefield began a Female Benefit Club in 1798, collecting regular contributions from domestics and other working women which became the basis of small pensions after their sixty-fifth birthday. Through additional subscriptions, Wakefield devised a Loans Fund to help reduce the poor's dependence on pawnbrokers, then launched a Children's Bank. She was convinced of the need to train children in thrift, and encouraged regular monthly deposits of their pennies. These were among the most far-sighted of the early fiscal experiments, and the results led her to conclude that secure financial institutions were essential for working people.

> many of the poor, particularly servants, either squandered away their savings or lent them to those less prudent than themselves, from the want of a convenient opportunity of placing them where they would be

secure, [so] it occurred to me that an association might be formed which would afford them complete safety, in their own neighbourhood, by the guarantee of a few respectable persons of property.[15]

Wakefield created a local network of small financial institutions in suburban London to ensure the security of deposits arduously accumulated: for the former she designed the Tottenham Benefit Bank, which opened in 1804, receiving as well deposits from the Children's Bank when the total reached 20s. Accounts accrued interest of 5 per cent, once depositors had £1 to their credit. The whole system was overseen by trustees and supported by charitable individuals who doubtless paid the administrative costs to ensure crucial interest payments.[16] The commitment of patrons was key to this project, and Wakefield admonished other comfortably placed women to involve themselves in similar ventures, insisting that 'In addition to the religious and moral instruction of the poor, advice may be valuable to them ... [to help] to regulate the disposal of their small pittance to the best advantage.'[17]

Jeremy Bentham's advocacy of utilitarian reforms is well known and included what he called 'Frugality Banks' attached either to houses of industry or to local church vestries. In both cases the purpose was the same – to encourage the poor to save and to ensure the safety and profitability of deposits. These were new and ambitious aims. No existing national institutions answered the requirements, as commercial banks, in England,[18] were uninterested in the petty subscriptions of the working poor or in the deposits of friendly societies, and as a consequence neither could secure or augment the monies they set aside. Bentham brought his proposals before a parliamentary committee for consideration in 1811.[19] Supporters enthusiastically championed the benefits of money actively employed, rather than lying dead in friendly society boxes or stuffed into mattresses, prey to every hazard.[20]

Wakefield's experiments and Bentham's advocacy were timely, mirroring a growing interest in such initiatives across the country, encouraging thrift among the working poor through incentives. Safeguarding deposits was essential and in most cases was assured by local authorities. In addition, most of the reformers agreed that poor depositors had to receive interest on deposits. The security of accounts and interest on deposits represented startling innovations for working men and women, the like of which they had not previously enjoyed; indeed, the allure of interest symbolized a beneficent face of capitalism typically unknown to these people. Furthermore, for the early banks, providing interest on deposits whether or not it was economic was an exercise in propaganda encouraging further plebeian participation. Advocates of these schemes, like Patrick Colquhoun, urged support to:

> establish a system that shall not only convince the poor that they have a stake in the country as well as the rich, but that the Government and the legislature will place that stake on so secure and respectable a footing that they may look up to it with certainty as a relief in times of sickness and a prop to old age.[21]

There is a strangely contemporary echo in the words of these reformers. Giving the poor a stake in the country and securing their deposits against theft or waste were among the prime motives of savings bank advocates.[22] In this climate, savings institutions of various sorts were launched in county towns and regional centres between 1808 and 1816,[23] promoted by people with a broad range of political persuasions, from the radicalism of Sir Francis Burdett to the utilitarianism of the Rev. Thomas Malthus. Another of the early savings banks was begun by the Rev. Henry Duncan in the rural parish of Ruthwell, Scotland. Duncan concluded that only innovative institutions, matched by personal frugality and hard work, could address the needs of his parishioners. In contrast, he believed that the receipt of alms undermined the morals and the morale of the poor. Better by far to encourage individual effort, to support industry and assist the poor to provide 'for their own support and comfort'. But he also subscribed to 'judiciously rewarding extraordinary efforts at economy, and extraordinary instances of good conduct',[24] paying 5 per cent interest on money kept with the bank for three years.

In 1814, the Highland Society of Scotland issued its study of friendly societies, menages[25] and savings banks, stating that the latter were preferable, as they 'cannot do harm; which must do good; and which is so extremely simple in its nature, that it may with the greatest ease be established in every town and parish'.[26] In spite of this support, the savings bank movement was intermittently decried from both ends of the political spectrum – *The Times* termed it 'mischief' and William Cobbett characterized savings banks as 'a bubble'.[27] However, the results of experiments were compelling. Between 1814 and 1817, more savings banks were set up across Britain, such as the Pontefract Savings Bank, seen in Plate 6.1, one among many which appealed to 'Apprentices, Domestic Servants, both Male and Female, Journeymen, and Day Labourers'. The *Edinburgh Review* considered the spread of these institutions 'of far more importance, and far more likely to increase the happiness and even the greatness of the nation, than the most brilliant success of its arms, or the most stupendous improvements of its trade or its agriculture'.[28] The problems left

PONTEFRACT
Savings Bank.

The Inhabitants of Pontefract and the surrounding Parishes are informed that a

BANK

FOR THE DEPOSIT OF THE

SAVINGS of the INDUSTRIOUS

Will be immediately established in Pontefract.

A Day for the Nomination of the necessary Officers will shortly be fixed, when the attendance of all Gentlemen willing to Patronize such an Establishment is earnestly requested.

The attention of Apprentices, Domestic Servants, both Male and Female, Journeymen, and Day Labourers, is called to the following Particulars.

They may deposit any sum not less than one shilling, upon which when it amounts to twelve and six pence, they shall receive interest, to be calculated monthly.

The Depositors will not be obliged to continue their payments into this Bank a week longer than they shall choose; they may stop their payments without forfeiture, or withdraw their money without enquiry, whenever they shall have occasion for it.

The money will be invested in Government Securities, under the authority of an Act of Parliament, and in the names, and under the management of the Noblemen and Gentlemen of the Neighbourhood.

Pontefract, September 13th, 1817.

Amount First Year	At 1s. per Week			At 2s. per Week			At 3s. per Week			At 4s. per Week			At 5s. per Week			At 6s. per Week			At 7s. per Week			At 8s. per Week		
	£	s.	d.	£	s.	d.	£	s.	d.	£	s.	d.	£	s.	d.	£	s.	d.	£	s.	d.	£	s.	d.
First Year	2	12	0	5	4	0	7	16	0	10	8	0	13	0	0	15	12	0	18	4	0	20	16	0
Second Year	5	6	0	10	12	2	15	18	3	21	4	3	26	10	5	31	16	6	37	2	6	42	8	8
Third Year	8	2	3	16	4	8	24	7	0	32	9	4	40	11	8	48	14	0	56	16	5	64	18	8
Fourth Year	11	0	10	22	1	7	33	2	5	44	3	2	55	4	0	66	4	10	77	5	7	88	6	5
Fifth Year	14	1	7	28	3	3	42	4	10	56	6	6	70	8	1	84	9	9	98	11	3	112	13	0
Tenth Year	31	4	3	62	8	7	93	8	7	124	17	3	156	1	6	187	5	10	218	10	1	249	14	5

This Table will shew the Produce of Weekly Sums regularly Deposited in this Bank.

PRINTED BY J. FOX, MARKET-PLACE, PONTEFRACT.

Plate 6.1 Advertisement, Pontefract Savings Bank, 1817

to be resolved included a mechanism for securing deposits, a means of earning regular interest on deposits and the continued recruitment of depositors. In 1817, after discussion and debate,[29] the legal basis of trustee savings banks was laid in England and Ireland, with subsequent amendments arising as needed over the century.[30] In order to encourage the poor to deposit their mite, an initial rate of interest of about 4½ per cent was approved; to discourage wealthy depositors from abusing this opportunity, a limit was set on total deposits of £100 the first year and £50 in subsequent years. These limits were reduced several times before mid-century, restricting the upper limit of deposits and moderating interest payments, as all the while savings banks proliferated, each aiming to attract the modest surpluses of hard-working men, women and children.[31]

The practice of saving

The histories of UK savings institutions paint a clear chronology of a dramatic rise, combined with an influence which extended far beyond formal membership.[32] Approximately 3 per cent of the population in Scotland held deposits in savings banks by 1843, and by mid-century in England and Wales the estimated percentage of depositors with institutions designated trustee savings banks amounted to over 6 per cent of the population.[33] Growth continued apace with the launch of penny banks, like the Yorkshire Penny Bank, from the mid-century onwards, while the Post Office Savings Bank was founded in the 1860s, illustrating in broad brush strokes the proliferation of savings institutions of all sorts. The accumulation of modest, hard-won surpluses was not new to labouring men and women; indeed, some might argue that it was this very history of accumulation which distinguished Western European societies typified by late marriages and nuclear families. But previously such surpluses had commonly taken the form of material goods, things to enhance comfort and prestige, but which could be changed into cash as required. As I have shown, through alternative currencies and second-hand markets, the use of mutable, material goods persisted, particularly among the working classes, even as the growing monetization presented new challenges to those dependent on wages.[34] Savings banks offered a new means through which to secure financial security, wrapped up in new philosophies of personal discipline and independence.

Britain's political and social elite reinforced their commitment to savings banks in the first half of the century, with initiatives presented as vital to the nation's security, stability and prosperity, championed by a panoply of eminent figures ennobled by birth or public service. The London Provident Institution had the Duke of Somerset in the president's chair, two royal dukes and a flush of peers as vice-presidents, plus notables including William Wilberforce, David Ricardo, Rev. Thomas Malthus, Patrick Colquhoun and Sir Thomas Baring in the role of managers. The Devon & Exeter Savings Bank, also established in 1816, boasted Lord John Russell at its head, while the Sheffield & Hallamshire Savings Bank, opened in 1819, had the Duke of Norfolk as patron, Earl Fitzwilliam as president and a long list of local luminaries (including the Master Cutler) as trustees and directors.[35] Earl Fitzwilliam was also the patron of the Leeds Savings Bank.[36] The power of position was harnessed to the promotion of these banks, a fact which produced equivocal results. Their patronage appealed to some, reassuring them about the stability and efficacy of the institutions – the financial support of the elites was also timely. But local luminaries had to appeal to the regional sensibilities within the middling and working classes; thus the Sheffield Savings Bank ensured that Dissenting ministers served as trustees and managers, attracting a wider religious cross-section of clients.[37] Nonetheless, the more class-conscious were suspicious of the authorities, fearing intrusion into their personal financial affairs, jeopardizing the very independence that these bodies purported to assist.[38] The autonomy of communally organized friendly societies or co-operative institutions held greater appeal for some precisely because of the mutuality of these groups. On the other hand, for the burgeoning lower middle class the sometimes raucous social rituals of mutual benefit societies were anathema and the more utilitarian character of savings institutions had the greatest appeal;[39] domestic servants and other workers were also drawn to the new provident institutions, not only for the advantages they provided, but also because of the absence of occupational restrictions typical of many friendly societies.[40] Ultimately, however, many mutual benefit societies also came to rely on savings banks to hold the contributions of their members or they established banks of their own as, little by little, savings culture became part of everyday life, extending far beyond the formal membership in trustee savings banks.

Through the account ledger and the pass book, depositors acquiesced to the direct and minute examination of their habits, accepting what Michel Foucault characterized as a new pattern of control, the 'utilitarian rationalization of detail in moral accountability'.[41] Through the aegis of savings banks, moral and fiscal accountability were conflated, tied to monetary accumulation. Bank regulations were the first instruction in this discipline, governing the interaction of banks and their clients (see

Plates 6.1–6.2). Regulation was not itself a new phenomenon; indeed, many friendly societies imposed strict rules on their membership. However, in this case the rules were set and enforced not by their fellows, but by middle-class managers. Account books and 'Depositor's Cards', like the household accounts, domesticated accounting precepts, carrying commercial practice into the homes of plebeian people, constraining and redefining personal goals and habits.

BRANSTON BANK.

WHILST Schools for the Education of the Poor, and Bible Societies, afford a pleasing and well-grounded hope of improving the morals of the rising generation, by teaching the lower Classes of Society their duty towards God and their Neighbours; nothing now seems more likely to complete their comfort in the World than the assistance of the higher Ranks, to enable the Industrious to lay by a part of the earnings of their Youth, in a time of health and strength, before they experience the difficulty of providing for a Family, or encounter the Infirmities attendant on Old Age.

Mr. WHITE has opened a Bank for his poorer Neighbours at BRANSTON; his object is to enable Cottagers, Labourers, or Farmers' Servants, Male or Female, to lay up any Sums as a provision for Rent, future Infirmity, or Sickness.

A regular separate Account will be kept for each Person desirous of profiting by this offer.—Any Sum from *One Shilling* to Twenty Pounds will be received; and legal Interest will be given on all Sums that amount to One Pound, which remain in Mr. WHITE's hands above Six Months.

An Office will be open at the *Hall-Farm-Yard* every Saturday Afternoon, from Four to Six o'Clock, and no Business will be transacted at any other time.

BRANSTON HALL., FEB. 7th, 1814.

Plate 6.2   Advertisement, Branston Bank, 1814

National statistics alone cannot adequately reflect the broad miscellany of people who turned to savings banks as part of a new fiscal rhythm. A large, weighty signature book survives from one of the early savings organizations, the London Provident Institution, which drew clients from Essex, Kent and the surrounding Middlesex villages, plus various parts of London.[42] Table 6.1 summarizes a sample of occupations taken from the first signature book of depositors over two years of entries, which yielded status information on 211 people. While the summary is useful, the details of individual occupations are subsumed under the aggregate headings, masking the miscellany of savers from this great city and its outlying precincts, ranging from porters and watermen to glove maker and printers; the carter, milk-woman, laundress, nurse and bricklayer were convinced of the benefits of this new institution, along with the engineer, warehouseman, millwright, jeweller, druggist, hairdresser, river pilot, shopkeeper, clerk and teacher, all of whom made their way to the Moorfields office during the appointed hours.

The 1842 published report of the London Provident Institution summarizes the shifting occupational ratio of its depositors, and Figures 6.1–6.2 illustrate several important features of these savers. In 1842, one of the largest categories of savers was 'Mechanics, Artisans and Handicraftsmen', numbering nearly 6,000. These depositors averaged about £19 per person in their accounts, suggesting that this group included better-paid skilled workers – although they averaged several pounds less than the average among tradesmen and small shopkeepers or soldiers and

Table 6.1   Occupations of savers with the London Provident Institution, 1816–1818

Occupation	No. of savers
Service	68
Artisan and skilled crafts	49
Minors	44
Retail and wholesale	29
Semi-skilled	22
Single, married and widowed women	20
White-collar	14
Apprentices	2
Military	1

Note: Sample: 478 entries.
Source: TC/75/a/22, Lloyds TSB Group Archives, London.

policemen. However, one of the long-standing charges against the significance of savings banks was that few industrial workers were attracted to these institutions, compared to customers from other sectors of society. This claim was raised first by Neil Smelser and reiterated by Albert Fishlow on the basis of figures from Manchester, where, Neil Smelser calculated, factory workers never made up more than 15 per cent of depositors between 1821 and 1839. In comparison, he noted that domestic servants ranged from 17 per cent to 29 per cent of depositors with the Manchester & Salford Savings Bank.[43] The prominence of domestic servants as savers, it was argued, showed that savings banks were irrelevant to the working class during the industrialization process.[44] Relatively simplistic conclusions such as this could not possibly be sustained today, not least because of the more complex appreciation of industrialization which is not limited to the manufacturing areas of the north-west. Equally important, decades of work on the history of women and the gender politics of this era have reshaped the historiography of the industrial era. Gender dynamics within households, communities and workplaces now receive attention commensurate with their significance.[45] In this context it is worth reiterating that both men and women saved –

Figure 6.1 Occupations of females saving with the London Provident Institution, 1827 and 1842

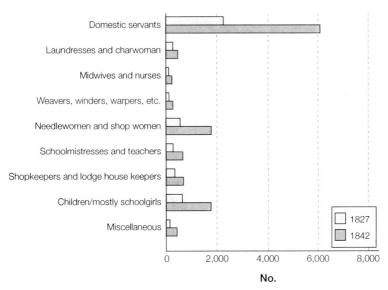

Source: London Provident Institution report (1842)

Figure 6.2 Occupations of males saving with the London Provident Institution, 1827 and 1842

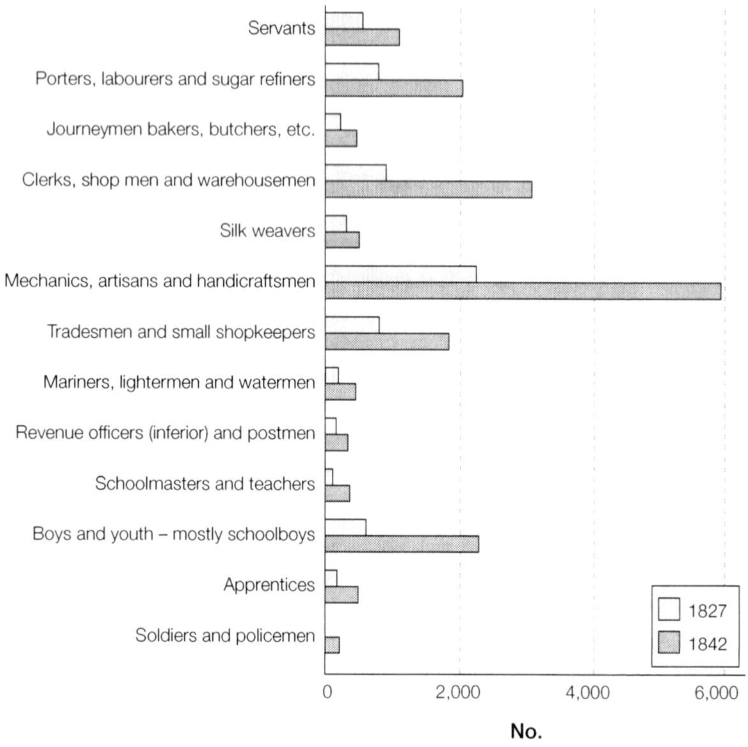

Source: London Provident Institution report (1842)

labourers, artisans and those from the complex middle ranks. The numbers of male and female savers sometimes varied from institution to institution; secondary evidence suggests that motivations may also have varied, and gender tensions between couples were routinely addressed by propagandists for savings banks. Among married couples, there were doubtless pressures regarding the apportioning of resources within the household, including the money saved. What is indisputable, however, is that men and women, boys and girls saved in greater numbers over the course of the nineteenth century, including those affected by industrial trades, incorporating the doctrine of saving and provident consumerism into the public and private settings of which they were part.

There is now little disagreement that what is termed industrialization included widespread and pervasive social, economic and cultural changes affecting various regions of the country.[46] Leonard Schwarz has shown that London was also a major manufacturing centre in this era, and the presence of sugar refiners' men among the depositors with the London Provident Institution reminds us of London's industrial strength and its range of highly capitalized trades.[47] Sugar refinery workers were one group among many in the metropolitan manufacturing sector. Overall, the group defined as mechanics, artisans and handicraft comprised more than 28 per cent of the 21,000 male savers in that one metropolitan bank. And to their numbers could be added the waged workers in production and service industries, some of whom laboured in large industrial settings and others did not. This list includes silk weavers, some apprentices, bakers, butchers and porters; all told, skilled and semi-skilled male workers comprised a significant proportion of this bank's membership. [48] At the same time, the burgeoning white-collar sector and tradesmen – watermen, Revenue officers, clerks and shop men – turned to savings banks, inspired by economic opportunities and dreams of material improvement. Examples from the London Provident Institution come from one of the more than thirty banks that had opened in London and its suburbs by mid-century.[49] The savings banks established from Stoke Newington to Whitechapel, Chelsea to Rotherhithe, attracted a diverse range of working and lower middle-class men and women, and, if Londoners faced particular demands on their resources by virtue of living in the metropolis, by mid-century they also saved in disproportionately higher numbers than those in the rest of the country.[50]

Regional savings bank records reflect local economic features as well as a range of wage-earning patrons. In 1817, the South Shields & District Friendly Bank for Savings opened, with men predominating among the initial depositors, their occupations echoing the manufacturing, mining and maritime trades of the north-east. Glass makers – apprentices, journeymen and masters – signed up in surprising numbers that first year. Joiners and mariners were followed by a scattering of trades arising from the sea and the coal pits: sailmaker, victualler, block maker, pitman, heap keeper and overman.[51] Domestic servants, wives of mariners, spinsters and children also figured as depositors, as in other parts of the country. Nevertheless, it is instructive to uncover the distinctive local variations in trades and occupations hidden in national figures. For example, between 1837and 1838, in Dunfermline, Scotland, 23 per cent (413) of male depositors were weavers, with another 15 per cent described as 'Coal heavers, miners, quarrymen and labourers'; most women savers in that district were categorized in the catch-all occupations of domestic service and farm labourer.[52] In the West Country, the Devon & Exeter Savings Bank drew in over 500 'artificers, mechanics and handicraftsmen' in the first three years of operation, 1815–18. Figure 6.3 illustrates the varied occupational backgrounds of the men, women and children attracted to this regional bank in its first quarter-century. Parents saved for children and children also saved for themselves, facts evident in supporting documents from many banks. Aside from those designated as minors, domestic servants (predominantly female) constituted the largest category of depositors, raising issues of employment opportunities and motivation. Domestic service was often the principal occupation open to women in rural areas, while working men enjoyed access to a wider range of jobs.[53] As I have shown, credit from loan societies and other new financial

Figure 6.3   Occupational distribution, Devon & Exeter Savings Bank, 1815–1839

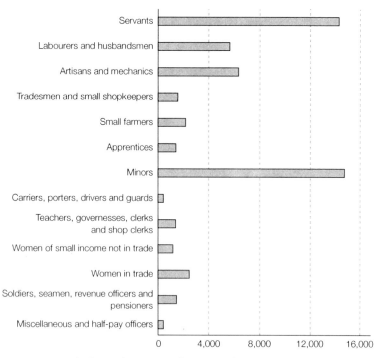

Source: Twenty-third annual statement of the Devon & Exeter Savings Bank (1839), p. 33

institutions was evidently less readily accessible to women than to men by this time, limiting life-cycle and entrepreneurial options. However, women in trade did form a significant number of account holders in this western district, employing their money for productive and consumer ends. At the same time, female domestic servants were collectively among the most prominent category of working women, a feature found in almost every community. The initial motivations behind their first and on-going investments may be a matter for speculation. Authors of a quantitative study of the Philadelphia Saving Fund Society found that female servants followed a particular pattern of saving for life-cycle needs, such as security in old age, although they could also have been saving for marriage.[54] Many female servants were urged to save by their employers for similar ends.[55] Two servants of the Rev. Hanison, in South Shields, opened their accounts on the same day in 1817, depositing £1 2s and £3 15s respectively, and his instruction is almost palpable.[56] The hope of future benefits from present restraint doubtless inspired generations of depositors.

National statistics paint a picture of a steady stepwise increase in deposits and a growing body of regular savers, along with higher total deposits and more savings banks. Yet this outline sketches only a part of the saving process. National figures for the trustee savings banks cannot reflect the motivations of occasional or intermittent savers, and national figures cannot possibly reflect the complex nuances of savings and spending. According to savings doctrine, the ideal depositor practised a routine discipline, setting aside shillings week by week or month by month. Over the years, augmented by compound interest, these turned into tidy nest eggs. But, from the evidence of the South Shields ledger, long-term saving over decades was rare. Cyclical patterns of saving and spending were evident from the outset in the South Shields Savings Bank, a pattern recurring as well in the late nineteenth-century records of the tiny Mere Penny Bank and a commonplace noted in the managers' reports for the Yorkshire Penny Bank.[57] In South Shields, seventy-five accounts were opened in the first year of business, including two from mutual benefit societies, five charitable organizations, forty-three men, twenty-four women and one couple who registered together. Over 52 per cent of the accounts opened with £5 or less, and the largest deposits were those of the local charitable organizations. Account holders included those in the skilled trades, professionals, servants, widows and children, and, of the seventy-five accounts opened in 1817, eight depositors had emptied their accounts by 1820; thirteen more followed suit the following year. From 1817 to 1836 accounts rose and fell, people came and went.[58] Ten years after this bank opened over 66 per cent of the original depositors had withdrawn all of their savings, some taking large amounts, others making piecemeal inroads. In their study of the Philadelphia Saving Fund Society, Alter *et al.* defined three motivational categories of savers in an attempt to tease out the variations found in the account ledgers. The three categories they designated as: precautionary savers, target savers and life-cycle savers. Those in the first group attempted to mitigate the exigencies of illness, unemployment or trade slump, levelling out the vagaries of income and expenditure. The second often had particular consumer expenditures in mind. Finally, the practice of life-cycle saving aimed to maintain long-term regular contributions and was the particular profile of saving found among Philadelphia's female servants, working in low-wage sectors with little prospect of advancement.[59] The patterns I found in various account ledgers and managers' reports suggest similar motivation profiles among English savers.

Jane Reed could have been a poster girl for savings banks. A servant in the South Shields district, she brought £2 to the bank when she opened her account in 1817 and, by 1831, she had saved more than £17, a sum which remained in the bank to the ledger's end. Others showed different priorities. Hannah Walker, a spinster in this community, began with a deposit of £2 in 1820 and the interest she earned added to her total. In December 1824, Walker withdrew it all. Anthony Reed, a mariner, followed exactly this pattern, but showed even less patience, putting in £2 in 1820 and withdrawing £2 0s 4½d in 1821. William Mould, an overman in the local coalfields, made two deposits: the first of £1 in 1817 and the second of £1 5s in 1818. He earned interest on his account and, as the end of the year approached in 1818, he took out the lot. A half-dozen pitmen followed a similar pattern over the next few years, bringing their savings to a secure site, building their small equity and withdrawing the total for clear and evident reasons that are not revealed by bank records.

Account ledgers are mute concerning the designs of depositors, the pressures which precipitated decisions and the needs and desires which motivated fiscal practice. These can be glimpsed only indirectly through this source. Perhaps the sailor's wife, Catherine Harey, was being careful when she salted away £15 in May 1820 and another £5 in July of 1821 – she took out the total with interest in November 1822. In some instances, there is an almost palpable effort in the tempo of small deposits, and such was the case of Thomas Coulson, a glass worker, who paid in almost forty times between December 1817 and 1819, usually 1s at a time. At the end of the second year he felt able to make four withdrawals, taking out £1 and then three smaller sums to spend. Was he buying clothes for a special event, furnishing a home, beginning a marriage, launching a small trade? The ledger is silent on these questions, but expenditures of this sort likely accounted for some of these withdrawals, as later penny bank managers attested. Archer Lee, a ropemaker, made regular contributions of 2s or 3s beginning in 1817, and in the autumn of 1821, with nearly £10 in hand, he too withdrew the whole.[60] Funds trickled slowly into most of these accounts, forming what Duncan Ross describes as a 'short-term liquidity store',[61] only intermittently broached by the account holder as need demanded. Most savings banks set obstacles in the way of easy withdrawals and it was not unusual to require one or two weeks' notice of withdrawal.[62] Nevertheless, these South Shields clients employed the savings bank to suit their interests and meet the self-defined goals consistent with personal aims and local events, balancing consumption and investment strategies evolving over a lifetime.[63]

People saved for many reasons, following various patterns determined by personality in combination with life cycle, economic conditions, gender, class and occupation.[64] However, it was the functional utility of savings banks that was of fundamental importance. Interest payments, once understood, appealed to poor and middling depositors as much as to wealthier investors. The growth of savings through compound interest was explained in detail in most savings propaganda.[65] Modest savers were inspired to try their hand. In the national profiles of savings accounts, in 1830 and 1844, those holding less than £20 made up more than half of all account holders, and this category increased over time, becoming a steadily greater portion of all trustee savings bank accounts. John Tidd Pratt, the barrister responsible for the regulation of savings banks, devised the categories for these data and included in his report the averages within each of the categories. Thus, in 1830, the average amount in the under-£20 category was actually £7; in the next under-£50 category the average account held was £30.[66] Paul Johnson has explored the account profiles of the Post Office Savings Bank at the end of the nineteenth century and the average balance of accounts. Although the poorest of the poor were unlikely to be represented in the statistics, small savers were in the majority, and, in 1899, of the nearly 7 million accounts in operation, fully 83 per cent held less than £25, with the average balance a modest £4.[67] Almost from their inception, banks were quickly accessible in every county, with even the most remote regions provided with the means to save (see Table 6.2). Savings banks, allied to the experience and practice of saving, represented a new culture of capitalist practice diffused through the working and lower middle ranks and, as a partisan of savings

Table 6.2 Trustee savings banks, by county, 1830

County	No. of banks
Bedfordshire	3
Berkshire	10
Buckinghamshire	4
Cambridgeshire	2
Cheshire	10
Cornwall	8
Cumberland	6
Derbyshire	6
Devonshire	4
Dorsetshire	9
Durham	10
Essex	15
Gloucestershire	12
Hampshire	11
Herefordshire	4
Hertfordshire	5
Huntingdonshire	1
Kent	21
Lancashire	24
Leicestershire	5
Lincolnshire	17
London/Middlesex	28
Monmouthshire	4
Norfolk	10
Northamptonshire	3
Northumberland	5
Nottinghamshire	6
Oxfordshire	5
Shropshire	13
Somerset	9
Staffordshire	15
Suffolk	12
Surrey	19
Sussex	12
Warwickshire	6
Westmorland	1
Wiltshire	10
Worcestershire	8
Yorkshire	31

Source: John Tidd, Savings Banks in England .... (London, 1830)

banks wrote in 1850, with a touch of hyperbole, the 'Savings Bank will be to the poor man what the Funds are to the rich'.[68]

The culture of saving

The concept of saving became increasingly normalized over the nineteenth century, at the same time as practical incentives spread the practice itself. For instance, the increasingly cash-based economy encouraged money payments and the growing production of small coins for legal tender became more routine,[69] all of which encouraged money-based transactions. The sometimes painful practice of saving copper and silver coins was balanced by several compelling incentives which blended the possibility of future pleasure with the prevention of calamity. To stave off the threat of penury, men and women were moved to save; they were also inspired by the hope of material acquisitions. Michel Foucault's reflections on the 'gentle way in punishment' explored Enlightenment philosophical developments which balanced misdemeanours with appropriate penalties, such as the abuser of library privileges being deprived of library use. The concept of 'analogical punishment' applies in a somewhat variant form in the case of the diffusion of savings culture. Savings were a prophylactic against want. To avert the shame and infamy of public indigence savers applied variable levels of self-discipline with or without direct experience of poverty. The potential punishments which came with destitution were a real threat in the more punitive climate which produced the New Poor Law. However, by forestalling the threat of pauperism the diligent saver earned a reward, reinforcing a commitment to self-disciplined practice.[70] Paul Johnson's comments on the late nineteenth-century social environment applies equally to the earlier period. He notes that:

> although some saving was undoubtedly determined by economic factors such as income levels and rates of return, much of it took place in response to social pressures. Some distinction can be made between causation and scale. The scale of income had strong bearing on the type and amount of saving or insurance indulged in, but the cause of saving, the individual desire for security and respectability, was independent of income.[71]

A desire for independence, the hope of material comforts and a bulwark against future needs – Samuel Smiles exulted in the spread of this discipline, in the daily drill from which 'men's success as individuals, and ... societies, entirely depends'. Government officials concurred; the organization of savings banks for soldiers and sailors in the mid-nineteenth century bolstered the rational masculine habits so celebrated by Smiles, the expositor of thrift and manly virtues.[72] Similar behaviour was also promoted among the general reading public through fictional as well as factual propaganda. For readers of Charles Dickens's tales, the sums frugally salted away at the bank delivered hero and heroine at crucial junctures. The words 'I've got money in the Savings Bank, dear' signalled a type of hard-won insurance that was also a source of pride.[73] The penalties of dearth were avoided; the relish of tangible attainments anticipated. Table 6.3 summarizes the growth of trustee savings banks between 1830 and 1890, showing the rise and later retrenchment in the number of local banks, but also the notable growth in the number of depositors. By the second half of the century, the trustee savings banks were among many institutions that promoted the savings habit. Through Sunday schools and Mechanics' Institutes, in novels, tracts and cautionary tales, the benefits of money put aside were extolled to children and youth, men and women.[74]

Savings banks mushroomed in the midst of heated public debates about the character of working people, the appropriate collective and personal responses to rising population and new work situations, plus the policies best suited to ensure national stability. One of the best known contributors to this debate, the Rev. Thomas Malthus, characterized plebeian sexual appetites as unbridled, insisting they would bring about inevitable and disastrous population growth, claims which unleashed a firestorm of controversy. On reflection, Malthus accepted his critics' assertions that plebeian sexual appetites could be checked and he accepted 'the possibility of chastity'.[75] Malthus further agreed with the proposition that there existed 'the power of each individual to avoid all the evil consequences to himself and society resulting from the principle

Table 6.3 Growth of trustee savings banks and deposits in the United Kingdom, 1830–1890

Year	No. of savings banks	Total no. of depositors	Total deposits (£)
1830	480	427,830	14,616,936
1850	573	1,112,999	28,930,982
1870	496	1,384,756	38,274,944
1890	324	1,535,782	49,269,114

Note: Includes Scottish savings banks only after 1836, following the Act of 1835 which established trustee savings banks in Scotland.
Source: Horne, History of Savings Banks, appendix II, pp. 386–9.

of population, by the practice of virtue'.[76] In this context, radical libertinism was discarded by working-class theorists in the 1830s and 1840s as politically and practically untenable. Marriage became the idealized template for social harmony, with the breadwinner wage one of the means through which the working-class family could achieve domestic and political harmony.[77] Comfortable domesticity was redefined as the rightful aim of working men, and savings accounts were praised as a tool to take best advantage of male wages. Sexual probity outside marriage was an equivalent facet of masculine self-control encouraged by working-class and middle-class theorists. Combined, they reflected the domesticated fiscal and bodily discipline to which respectable men were called, disciplines which promised material, marital and social rewards.

Expressions of masculinity among the working class varied considerably as a result of social, regional and work-based norms. Anna Clark has charted the complex gender relations in working-class political and domestic practices as these developed in factory and artisan districts around Britain in the first half of the nineteenth century. Clark notes the adoption of the language of the breadwinner wage by radicals and trade unionists, a pivotal shift in male priorities, bringing with it the promise of greater protection for women and a commitment to 'replace the hard-drinking artisan who neglected his family with a respectable patriarch who brought home the bacon'.[78] Thus, the ideal of the working-class man was recreated in light of political expediency, as well as fiscal and social pressures. Samuel Smiles was one among many who extolled this masculine enterprise and celebrated in his writings the energy and self-restraint of male exemplars, many from humble origins.

Children, youth and apprentices were likewise challenged to follow the thrifty path, and the benefits of patience, effort and self-restraint were taught to children and adults in Sunday schools across the country.[79] Thomas Laqueur's insightful inquiry into the Sunday school movement reveals a vigorous range of institutions that were far more than a medium of middle-class indoctrination. Sunday schools were frequently organized and staffed by grateful graduates, and these institutions boasted a large working-class constituency with a deep commitment to self-help and a desire for comfortable respectability. Laqueur argues that 'the Sunday school was a social and recreational centre for a significant part of the working-class community, especially, but not exclusively, in the new industrial towns'.[80] The growth of these schools pre-dated the savings bank movement, but their aims conjoined, with more than 2 million enrolled in Sunday schools by 1850.[81] Literacy and numeracy formed the basic curriculum, with various types of religious instruction according to founding principles. Many schools also prided themselves on the education they offered in commercial conduct. For example, the Bristol Methodist Sunday School Society gave cash rewards for diligent study and amounts from 1d to several shillings were awarded for flawless memorization, as a stimulus to learning.[82] With cash in hand, pupils were then urged to deposit ½d weekly in the school penny bank, and in some schools good behaviour resulted in a 50 per cent or 100 per cent return on deposits at year's end. Savings banks, with or without the yearly bonus, became a staple of Sunday school extra-curricular activities, as halfpennies and pennies, amassed weekly in hundreds of schools, brought the practice of thrift into hundreds of thousands of households. In fact, in 1846, a Sunday school teachers' journal insisted that the school-based banks 'often saved whole families from destitution'.[83]

Following the Education Act in 1870, school banks were quickly set up for elementary students. Examples of school bank programmes in France, Belgium and Hungary were cited to stir public support for these initiatives, with British sponsors insisting that children from the working class would gain 'moral and economical education' through the use of penny banks in primary schools. Some school boards required little convincing. Birmingham inaugurated two penny banks in its board schools in 1876 and by 1885 could claim sixty-eight such branches with 9,000 accounts. The Manchester School Board was also among the earliest to approve the opening of school penny savings banks in three schools in 1877, and their numbers grew, with 136 school penny savings banks holding more than 12,000 accounts by 1885.[84] Here, through the practice of weekly deposits and prudent withdrawals, children could be instructed in thrift with long-term social benefits – 'so that as men and women they may be able to save carefully and spend wisely'.[85]

Pennies were always more easily come by than shillings for working children and poor adults, the most they could spare. Thus, variants on the trustee savings bank were essential to reach the poorest potential clients, and flexible alternatives were initiated not only through Sunday and elementary schools but as free-standing institutions. One such was set up in 1848 by the Rev. Queckett in an 'enclosed railway arch in the East End of London'. Within a year of its launch this penny bank boasted more than 15,000 deposits.[86] Volunteers inspired by religious and social zeal carried the culture of savings into the poorest communities – the Liverpool District Provident Society exemplifies one initiative imbued with such ideals.[87] Its aim was outlined in the frontispiece of the annual report: 'to go into [a man's] … house, and there perform the deed of kindness'.[88] The kindest deed conceived by these evangelists was to introduce the working poor to the concepts of saving: '[to] make them the authors of their own independence and virtue by encouraging them to form prudent and moral habits; but differently from them, it does not confine itself to the mere administration of friendly advice, but supplies in addition a strong stimulus to frugality by the offer of a premium upon savings'.[89] These precepts might have seemed bizarre to the truly destitute, and the goals unattainable. But in each district a team of regular visitors undertook the arduous tasks of fiscal evangelism street by street, house by house, plumbing the roads and alleys of Liverpool's labouring districts. Within the first year of operation visitors had amassed over £700 in savings from local residents converted by the appeal of savings culture. Sums over £2 were quickly transferred to the local savings bank, where, it was hoped, 'they will eventually grow into considerable accumulations, and become a blessing both to those who own, and those whose benevolent offices fostered the frugal habits that amassed them'. Direct, personal interventions were seen as critical in the spread of this doctrine among those who did not attend Sunday school or belong to other provident organizations.[90] Throughout the nineteenth century, similar missionaries trawled poor neighbourhoods in Britain's cities, seeking converts, spreading the message of salvation through saving, a message reiterated in cheap publications aimed at this readership.[91]

In some regions considerable pressure was exerted to enforce the discipline of saving, especially in rural areas, where hierarchical authority was often much in evidence. Where poor rates were especially high, there were added incentives among local elites to try to reform the poor. The Rev. Litchfield supervised just such a project, the Farthinghoe Provident Clothing Society, which aimed 'to encourage the Poor in the habit of small savings, in order that they may thereby supply themselves with Clothing'. Participants from this small Northamptonshire village were divided by age, and each class had rigid stipulations as to the amount and the time their pennies could be submitted. Savings were collected on Sunday after service and failure to comply with the rules resulted in forfeits. Depositors in this scheme could not receive poor relief, nor could members be found guilty of any misdemeanour.[92] In this rural 'theatre of punishment' the vicar sought to instruct the poor and compel a strict set of habits.[93] The severity of these prescriptions attests to the level of discipline that could be imposed in some locales, restrictions which were apparently mitigated by the prospect of new garments. Of course, not every initiative of this sort was so draconian. Surviving regulations from the Hinton Clothing Club, near Bath, St Mary's Provident Institution and Penny Bank and the Chelsworth Shoe Club (see Plates 6.3–6.5) exemplify

HINTON CLOTHING CLUB.

Commenced November, 1833.

Managers } **MRS. H. BROOKE**
MRS. SPENCER

Number of Members .... 147.

Annual Subscribers:

	£	s	d
Mrs. Day	1	1	0
Mrs. Symonds	1	0	0
Miss Humphrys	1	0	0
Mrs. Brooke	1	0	0
Mrs. Browne, *Bath*	1	0	0
Mrs. Marshall, *ditto*	1	0	0
Mrs. Spencer.........................	1	0	0

Rules of the Club.

I.

The Members of this Club shall be Residents in the Parish, or such Parishioners as reside within a short distance.

II.

Any Sum from *one penny* to *one shilling*, may be deposited every Monday Morning.

III.

Each Subscriber shall receive a Ticket, on which the Weekly Payments are to be noted, and which shall be shewn at the end of the Year.

IV.

The Money deposited shall be placed once a month in the Bath Savings' Bank.

V.

The fund raised by Annual Subscriptions, shall be apportioned to the Members of the Club, according to the judgment of the Managers.

VI.

Each Member, towards the end of the Year, shall name the Articles of Clothing to be purchased by the Managers, according to the whole Amount of the Weekly Deposits, together with the portion allotted from the Subscribers' Fund.

Plate 6.3 Rules of Hinton Clothing Club (near Bath), 1833

CHURCH SCHOOLS in ST. MARY'S DISTRICT.

UNDER THE SUPERINTENDENCE OF

THE RECTOR AND THE PAROCHIAL CLERGY.

1. National School, for Boys and Girls, Upper York Street, adjoining St. Mary's Church.—Payment 3d. a week.

Infant School, Upper York Street.—Payment 2d. a week. Entrance in Upper York Street.

2. Evening School for older boys on Mondays, Tuesdays and Wednesdays, from half-past 7 to half-past 9 o'clock — Payment, 3d. weekly. Girls' Evening School on Mondays, Tuesdays and Wednesdays— Payment Half-penny per night.

Infant Schools.

3. At 10, WALMER STREET, and 35, GREAT YORK MEWS—Payment 1d. weekly.

SUNDAY SCHOOLS are held in the above places, and Children who do not attend the week day Schools, can be admitted any Sunday morning on application to the Superintendents.

Applications for entrance to be made on Monday Morning to either of the Day Schools; and to the Night Schools the same evenings they are open.

ST. MARY'S PROVIDENT INSTITUTION AND PENNY BANK.

HELD AT THE BOYS' SCHOOL,

UPPER YORK STREET,

Open every Monday Evening, from half-past 5 till half-past 7.

Manager,—Mr. W. KIMPTON.

Rules.

1. Depositors must be poor labouring persons, residing in St. Mary's District, recommended by the Clergy, or approved of by the Manager.

2. Any sum may be deposited, from One Penny to Five Shillings every Monday Evening between the hours specified above, at the Boys' School Room, in Upper York Street.

3. Depositors may receive the whole or any part of their savings *without interest*, on any Monday Evening, if they have given a week's notice of their intention.

4. Depositors will receive ½d. in the shilling on their deposits, on or after 1st Monday in November. It will not be necessary for them to withdraw all or any part of their deposits at that time.

5. Not less than 40 payments must be made throughout the year, to entitle the Depositor to the full Interest allowed. But less than 40 payments will receive Interest according to the number of payments that have been made in the year.

6. Notice must be given by Depositors not later than the last Monday in October, whether they wish all or any part of their money returned, and if so, whether in Coals, Clothing or Money; and the amount must be reckoned up by themselves and marked in plain figures at the back of the Card.

7. Depositor's Cards in future will cost One Penny, and if damaged or destroyed, will have to be replaced at the cost of sixpence. No person will be allowed to transfer his Card to another under any circumstances, and Depositors giving false residence will be excluded from all benefit in the Club, besides experiencing great difficulty in having their money returned. Notice must also be given if the Depositor removes.

N.B.—Regularity of payment is strongly recommended, whatever may be the money deposited.

Rev. W. H. FREMANTLE.

This Card must be kept clean, and in case it is lost, private memoranda of the number and the amount deposited should be kept by the Depositor, for reference and to prevent mistakes.

Plate 6.4   Depositors' card, St Mary's Provident Institution and Penny Bank (Marylebone, London)

more moderate constraints matched with incentives. Their success was evinced by the fact that clothing banks such as these flourished in poor districts of Britain into the twentieth century.[94]

The unskilled labourer, the small shopkeeper, the skilled artisan, the domestic servant, the teacher and the black-coated clerk lived and worked in communities where there were many choices for formal and informal savings, as Paul Johnson notes. Yet, in spite of the lure of pub clubs and the cultural inducements of burial societies, more and more men and women turned to savings banks, at some time in their lives, as a way to achieve their self-defined goals. The MP and industrialist Edward Akroyd was moved to establish a penny savings bank system in Yorkshire in 1856,

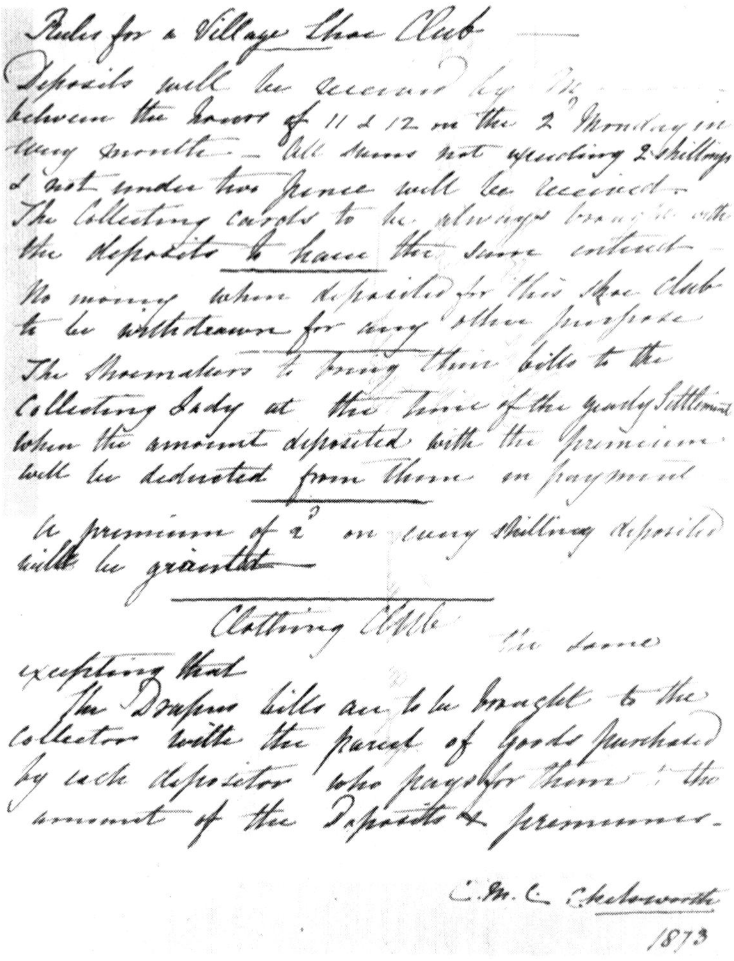
Rules for a Village Shoe Club

Deposits will be received by Mr between the hours of 11 & 12 on the 2d Monday in every month — All sums not exceeding 2 shillings & not under two pence will be received — The Collecting cards to be always brought with the deposits to have the same entered — No money when deposited for this Shoe Club to be withdrawn for any other purpose The Shoemakers to bring their bills to the Collecting Lady at the time of the yearly Settlement when the amount deposited with the premium will be deducted from them on payment

A premium of 2d on every shilling deposited will be granted

Clothing Club the same excepting that The Drapers bills are to be brought to the Collector with the parcel of Goods purchased by each depositor who pays for them the amount of the Deposits & premiums.

C. M. C. Chelsworth
1873

Plate 6.5 Rules for a village shoe club and clothing club, 1873

'to help the poor to help themselves'. By 1874 more than 250 branches of the Yorkshire Penny Bank were spread throughout that county and in the neighbouring towns along its borders, appealing to a clientele largely untouched by the formal savings bank movement[95] (see Figure 6.4). The National Penny Bank movement was initiated in the 1860s at the same time as the Post Office Savings Bank was launched,[96] each with slightly different emphases, each keen to promote the message of saving within the context of its organizational goals.[97] Penny banks, school banks,

Figure 6.4   Growth of the Yorkshire Penny Bank, 1861–1891

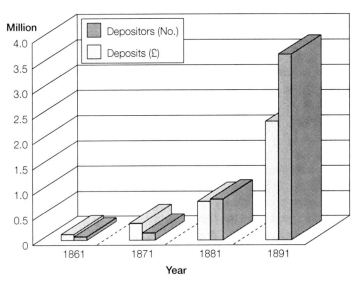

Source: H. B. Sellers, *Memoranda from a Note Book on the Yorkshire Penny Bank* (Leeds, 1901), table 1, appendix.

co-operative banks and church-run provident ventures brought the culture of saving to the poor in ways that trustee savings banks, or even Post Office Savings Banks, could not; collectively, the tenets of thrift were so pervasive that very few escaped contact with savings institutions of some description.

Such small local initiatives are illustrated by the Mere Penny Bank, serving the village of Mere and the surrounding precincts of south-west Wiltshire and north Dorset. Records surviving from 1888 to 1901 illustrate the central role it played in local affairs, holding the accounts of the Men's Adult School, the Women's Adult School, the Mere Football Club (opened in 1898), the Clothing Club and Coal Club, as well as the Liberal Club. The Mere Penny Bank also held the deposits of working men, women and children. A new ledger, begun in 1888, carried forward 167 accounts: 110 men and fifty-seven women. Of these, over 77 per cent of men and 63 per cent of women held 1s or less in their accounts – modest, hard-won savings. Most managed to amass larger totals over the coming years; the ledger frames the ebb and flow of income and expenditures. The entries in this volume also chart a network of relationships, identified by family ties and occupation, hinting at the lives, aspirations and employment patterns of this West Country region. Obvious family influences attracted many of the 167 depositors at the start of the ledger; twenty-eight families had multiple family members at this local penny bank, such as the Norris family, with fifteen individual accounts in play. Children from Mere and neighbouring villages joined in the following years, such as Alice Hooper, 'Daughter of Thomas Hooper Mere Carrier', Llewellyn Farthing, 'Son of James Farthing, Carpenter', and Bessie Coward, 'daughter of George Coward, 3 North St Mere, Porter'. Adults saved more substantial sums, like Emma Cowley, 'wife of Enos Cowley, Well Head, Mere', who moved money in and out of the account from 1891 to 1901, or Maurice Brown, whose designation was simply 'Gas Works, Mere'. The ledger offers a window on this West Country community, where the utility and practicality of this small institution kept loyal customers.[98]

The Mere Penny Bank was humble in size and aspiration. Larger savings ventures trumpeted their benefits in formal advertisements, as well as figuring in popular comic tales. Andrew Halliday's 'My account with Her Majesty' related the exploits of a young married man chronically improvident until he discovers the wonders of the Post Office Savings Bank. First commissioned for Charles Dickens's magazine *All the Year Round,* it was later republished in the *British Workman,* and reprinted again as a penny pamphlet – 'by which means', opined the author, 'I am assured, it has reached the hands of nearly half a million working men'.[99] As with other such tales, it targeted young men; in this instance a new husband confesses his failure to save until the Post Office Savings Bank removes temptation. The moral trials, tribulations and ultimate benefits of saving figured as prominent themes in nineteenth-century literature for adults and children, with the test of character neatly tied to monetary rewards. Here, too, many of these cautionary stories have the reform of boys' and men's behaviour as their focus. These authors recognized that the man's spending decisions had profound effects on family life; thus the reformation of boyish indulgence and manly improvidence was greatly to be desired. The hero of Halliday's tale concludes, 'It's my belief that saving is a habit, like smoking … If you begin it and go on with it for a little time, you come to have a sort of passion for it.'[100] The addiction to saving promised healthier consequences.

Saving rewarded: provident consumerism and gender politics

Saving was never simply an end in itself. It was as well a means to enable provident consumerism. Proponents hoped that cumulative purchases and an improved material standard of life among the working population would cement their acceptance of industrial capitalism. Savings, in the words of a Liverpool partisan, 'would enable the lower orders to acquire a taste for the comforts of civilized life, and thus promote industry, contentment, and tranquillity'.[101] The whole formed a sequential process, with discipline at the core, but occasional indulgence as a counterpoint – first save, then spend. Plebeian spending had been a fraught topic for generations, and until the second half of the eighteenth century there was general unanimity among elites that the labouring classes should buy only bare necessities. But 'necessities' by their nature changed with time and what had once seemed superfluous was ultimately accepted as essential.[102] An increasing number of writers also argued for careful plebeian spending as a means to ensure the security and prosperity of the nation. In 1816, Charles Taylor prophesied that the working class would accept the political and economic structure of the country 'in proportion as the possessor ... has a stake in his country, which makes his country's tranquillity his own prosperity – his country's good, his own benefit – his country's security, his own safety'.[103] The creation of a general savings culture, as a precursor to material improvement, was judged the best prescription for a peaceful and thriving nation.[104] The tumultuous decades of the early nineteenth century brought even more reason to encourage domestic consumers, and, far from denouncing consumerism by labouring men and women, provident consumer spending was hailed as a blessing to British industry. As savings were encouraged, so consumerism was approved.

Respectability required relative comfort and the capacity to avoid both the need for poor relief or the humiliation of crippling debt or pauperism. Other material and social markers took different forms in various sectors of society, as I have shown in the discussion on dress.[105] Although there have been many studies of nineteenth-century respectability, in most cases these focused exclusively on the work culture of elite male workers.[106] Brian Harrison concludes that an exclusively 'work-centred approach to respectability ignores the crucial importance of both housewife and cultural context'.[107] The husband's wages and his engagement with respectable aspirations were essential; but the drive toward respectability also required the active intervention of the housewife, as it was typically through her mediation that the husband's wage was stretched to best advantage. The high proportion of domestic servants with savings accounts, many of whom went on to marry, carried the tenets of diligent saving and careful spending into new family settings. The significant number of savers among female servants suggest that many domestics recognized the potential benefits from setting something aside prior to married life. Although their relative prominence declined over the nineteenth century, the records for 1830 suggest that domestic servants were among the most prominent groups of savers.[108] If marriage followed, the domestic politics of savings, along with consumer priorities, would then be theirs to balance in a new milieu. This scenario defined the lives of many working couples, as Ian Levitt and Christopher Smout note in their discussion of savings banks in Scotland. These, they contend:

> had a unique importance for working-class women who learnt their thrift as young domestic servants saving for their wedding day and maintained the good tradition as housewives. The Edinburgh savings bank treasurer described the category of 'married women' in his returns as 'generally the wives of operatives'. Without savings banks such women would not have enjoyed even the small degree of financial independence and security that was theirs in early Victorian Britain.[109]

The managers of the Yorkshire Penny Bank were very mindful of the priorities of their clients and used a commemorative volume to recount the savings and spending patterns observed over many years. From branch No. 2 we learn that 'the Penny Bank has been very useful in this village to young people about to get married. I have often noticed both young men and young women open accounts, and when they have got a few pounds in the Bank withdraw the amount and get married.' Similar reports were posted from other branches where, in the words of one official, 'a great many young men who have deposited their savings with us for several years, whose balances have reached from £10 to £30 ... have ... withdrawn [their money] at marriage for furnishing their cottages'. Children were also involved in the annual cycles of saving and spending. At branch No. 4 the manager recounted that the: 'Bank has also been very useful for children; a great number save annually from 5s. to 20s., which is withdrawn for the purpose of purchasing articles of clothing at different seasons of the year; and I may add that the above sums, had they not found their way into the Bank, would have been spent in sweets'. Saving was practised by young and old, and, in addition to putting money aside for 'useful and necessary articles of furniture', older married men also used their savings to buy pigs for fattening over the season for sale or to augment the owner's own larder. Others began small enterprises with the money saved, such as a collier who escaped the coal face after saving £20 which he used to buy a horse and cart.[110]

Good husbands followed Smiles's injunctions to prudence and manly restraint. But tensions between the breadwinner's social habits or desires and the dependent wife's budgetary needs doubtless led to strife in many homes. Wifely skills were doubly challenged; as housewives women recognized that their careful administration helped determine the fashion in which their families lived. But their husbands' decisions were ultimately crucial to family fortunes. Savings bank evangelists hinted that wives should adopt diplomatic tactics to win their spouses over, ensuring domestic peace and the patriarchal hierarchy. One tale of wifely guile was reproduced a number of times over the nineteenth century – illustrative of the diplomatic form guidance should take. In the 1868 edition, a newly wed Manchester couple negotiate the household budget (as a calico printer he earns a comfortable wage)[111] and along with the household mite the young wife asks for a few more pence to pay for her daily ale. The smitten young husband accedes to the request and then continues to follow his pattern of regular bibulous evenings with his workmates, habits long established as a single man. But as their first anniversary approaches he becomes concerned that nothing has been set aside, confessing to her on the day that, though he loves her, he cannot offer a treat to celebrate their anniversary. At this the clever young wife pulls a brick from the chimney where she has secreted over £4 saved from her weekly ale money. The value of thrift is made manifest and she convinces her spouse to follow new habits, without nagging.[112] This was one of many stories aimed at transforming would-be respectable working men. Ideally, income should be carefully parcelled to meet immediate needs and longer-term saving, and, with luck, this strategy secured material gains and the accoutrements of respectability.

Instruction in provident practices could be entertaining as well as instructive. Few authors were as eloquent in their espousal of thrift as Charles Dickens, but many took up their pen to provide provident tales. *The Savings Bank: A Dialogue between Ralph Ragged and Will Wise* typifies nineteenth-century themes of careful saving and provident consumerism at the heart of new working-class respectability. One of several instructional narratives composed by George Davys, Bishop of Peterborough, this story will have circulated in Sunday school libraries, various editions being published throughout the country.[113] The plot combines social drama and savings bank propaganda with clear explanations of the mathematics of thrift. At the same time, the gender responsibilities shouldered within the household are made explicit for men and women.

As the story opens Ralph Ragged spies the hero, Will Wise, behind a garden fence and stands amazed at the 'fine' state of his erstwhile drinking companion. Will Wise proudly shows off his garden, 'a few young fruit trees I've planted' and the other amenities of family life: 'everything to make us comfortable, in our small way. We've a snug fireside, we've good warm clothing, we've enough to eat and drink ... what I call clean and wholesome; and what can a man want more?' Davys outlines an exemplary labouring household where man and wife fulfil their designated duties. Wise advises his friend to turn from belief in luck to the power of saving. 'A young man should save all he can, a good many years before he marries; and then he'll have something to marry with and to keep a family.' Mrs Wise offers more explicit examples, contrasting the order in her home with the 'crazy, tumble-down things' found in less orderly homes. The household wares proudly displayed by Wise and his wife are not ostentatious, nor are their furnishings outside the legitimate aspirations of hard-working folk: teapot, cups and matching saucers, tables and chairs, coal for the fire, and bread and butter for the plate. Temperance is credited with some of their comfort; but the rest comes directly as a benefit of allegiance to the local savings bank.[114]

Will Wise has not come easily to provident conduct, but when his sweetheart refuses him he sheds his spendthrift ways after a type of epiphany where, like Aesop, he considers the ant. Walking out one Sunday, Wise observes the busy industry and careful labours of a hill of ants, precipitating a sort of crisis of masculinity. 'Here are they', confides Wise, 'moiling and toiling all summer, to lay by something against the winter; and I, like a fool, never think of saving a penny against a rainy day ... And so with that, Ralph, I made a resolution in my own mind.'[115] Wise reforms, thereby winning himself a wife, epitomizing the ideals of the age. The man's role outlined in this tale is the archetypal ideal of savings propagandists. 'Young men want it [savings] most of all', trumpeted an Oxford Penny Bank tract, for to marry without savings 'means too often a poor, dirty, ill-furnished home, ill-clad wife, hungry children, debts, misery, and the beer-house for relief. *What a difference a few pounds would make.*'[116]

Mary Wise epitomizes providential behaviour appropriate to her sex. Like thousands of her real-life contemporaries, she puts money aside while a young servant, increasing her deposits as her wages increase until after eight or nine years she has 'Fifty or Sixty Pounds of her own'.[117] This sum may have seemed unattainable to many readers, but was explained by a routine fiscal discipline combined with compound interest.[118]

Housewifely duties typically included portioning out ready money for daily and weekly needs,[119] a task Francis Place describes as his wife's province as they struggle to rise in the world. 'My wife had always been the cash keeper, and when I wanted sixpence which was very seldom I asked her for it, neither of us spent any money or ever tasted any liquor stronger than small beer.' Place remarked on the dire results where these housewifely charges were not carefully administered by the wife, recalling a neighbouring family that: 'might have saved money but there was sad want of economy on the part of the wife, ultimately he died very poor and she with two or three children went to the workhouse'.[120] A mid-century booklet on 'Cottage Housekeeping' advised its female readers 'to persevere in putting away only 1s. [regularly] ... which would be most useful in case of sickness ... [or] to purchase some articles of clothing or household goods to add to your comfort'. Ellen Ross charts similar economical traits within the gendered 'internal wage' system customary in the homes of late nineteenth-century London working families; and Robert Roberts noted the economical skills of his mother, who kept the family afloat in Edwardian Salford.[121] Security and comfort were the ultimate responsibility of the housewife – her duty – but she relied on her husband to provide the means through which to practice her craft. The roles cultivated by the fictional Will and Mary Wise epitomized the domestic paradigm for generations of working men and women, who sought each material element of their household from

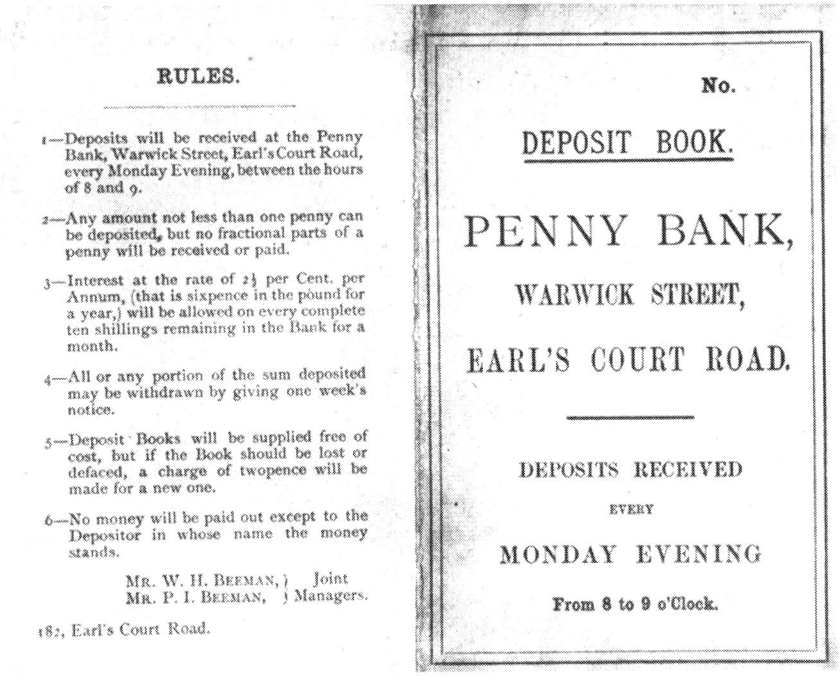

RULES.

1—Deposits will be received at the Penny Bank, Warwick Street, Earl's Court Road, every Monday Evening, between the hours of 8 and 9.

2—Any amount not less than one penny can be deposited, but no fractional parts of a penny will be received or paid.

3—Interest at the rate of 2½ per Cent. per Annum, (that is sixpence in the pound for a year,) will be allowed on every complete ten shillings remaining in the Bank for a month.

4—All or any portion of the sum deposited may be withdrawn by giving one week's notice.

5—Deposit Books will be supplied free of cost, but if the Book should be lost or defaced, a charge of twopence will be made for a new one.

6—No money will be paid out except to the Depositor in whose name the money stands.

Mr. W. H. BEEMAN,   } Joint
Mr. P. I. BEEMAN,   } Managers.

182, Earl's Court Road.

No.

DEPOSIT BOOK.

PENNY BANK,

WARWICK STREET,

EARL'S COURT ROAD.

DEPOSITS RECEIVED

EVERY

MONDAY EVENING

From 8 to 9 o'Clock.

Plate 6.6   Deposit book, Penny Bank, Warwick Street, Earl's Court Road (London)

British manufacturing and retail sectors, respectable niceties that were more than a fictional ideal. The ostensibly simple tale of Will Wise and Mary Wise captures the intersecting expectations of public and private probity. Domestic comfort was celebrated as the righteous aim of all right-thinking people, the ideal to which working men and women *should* aspire – self-discipline and the agency of the savings bank helped realize this objective. Paternal assistants, like the savings bank administrators and penny bank managers, are presented as allies, not adversaries, in this dynamic.[122]

Conclusion

In a 1901 volume, *Spending and Saving: A Primer of Thrift,* Alfred Pinhorn addressed himself specifically to young men, confiding that 'We were created to be happy. If we are not, the fault, in most cases, is our own. ... I am not writing this book to induce you to sacrifice comfort or happiness; but rather to show you how you can easily obtain more of both.'[123] This was one of many guides to habits of thrift, presented as the passport to a good life. Thomas Lipton considered that young men had no better friend 'so steadfast, so constant ... so capable of pushing him ahead, as a little leather-covered book with the name of a bank on its cover'.[124] The broad participation in this endeavour is suggested in the combined total of over nine and a half million accounts held in the Post Office Savings Bank and trustee savings banks by 1899.[125]

Savings banks offered the means for social advancement and material amelioration 'of every class'.[126] That was the intent of their founders. Moreover, each step taken toward this goal was a step toward respectability, an advancement that was incremental for most. As Brian Harrison observes: 'Respectability was always a process, a dialogue with oneself and one's fellows, never a fixed position.'[127] Respectability was also a relative category, a goal secured piecemeal, redefined over a lifetime. Of course, buying goods on credit did not disappear as a practice and, if anything, hire-purchase and other credit mechanisms became a more organized means of selling to the wage-earning classes.[128] But cash purchases had a higher social cachet which enhanced the experience of consumerism. The multiplication of savings banks in various forms reflected the general commitment to savings culture as a cornerstone of common provident behaviour.[129] As Paul Johnson confirms, 'The most respectable members of the working class were those who did not have to turn to the pawnbroker, local charity or the Poor Law Guardians in times of low transitory income or high transitory consumption ... . Financial security was demonstrated by the behaviour that established respectability.'[130] As the nineteenth century closed and the twentieth century opened, authors exhorted their readers to renewed vigilance in the management of personal resources in order to ensure comfort; 'every hard-working careful man or woman can save something – however small' cheered a partisan in 1901. In the same year a published address to the Mothers' Union offered a further reminder that 'it is our duty as Christian women, as well as our profit as reasonable beings, to learn to spend well and to spare well'.[131] Thus, savings culture and provident consumerism became the benchmark of respectability, unrivalled as normative behaviour until the introduction of new consumer credit practices in the second half of the twentieth century.

The discipline of saving was a unique phenomenon. The slow accretion of shillings and pence depended on immense self-restraint, a measure of good fortune and the voluntary imposition of limits. Discipline was internalized, the results were measured and monitored in personal account books and the process of self-control was interspersed with material and physical gratification in a delicate balancing act. The mantel clock, new suit, window curtains and china objects marked the provident consumers within the community, reinforcing their commitment to the process which brought recognition and rewards.[132] Smiles opined that 'There is no reason why the condition of the average workman should not be a useful, honourable, respectable, and happy one.' His advice on how to reach this goal was not given naively or blithely, recognizing that luck was a factor. But frugality was within an individual's control, and economy could be learned and practised. Of course, many did not or could not save; however, those unable or unwilling to follow such measured steps could not reach the acme of respectable manhood, the 'comfort in worldly circumstance' to which everyman aspired.[133] Equally important in this progress was his partner in life, as it fell to her to collect and then administer the resources, keeping careful account, discerning needs from wants, essentials from luxuries, advising her husband without challenging the domestic hierarchy, raising a new generation of children wise in the ways of economy. Children, in turn, learned the system of discipline and pleasure from family, school and children's books, all of which celebrated the careful saver,[134] while cast iron money boxes and ceramic banks brought the practice into the home as part of childhood training.[135] Men, women and children exercised thrift in many forms: children inserted pennies into earthenware pigs; adults walked up to bank counters to have their accounts inspected and the masculine and feminine ideals were formed in the process.[136] The intersection of steady restraint with intermittent indulgence defined the ideal of Victorian fiscal discipline, enabling the respectability of the aspiring classes. And, over the nineteenth century, savings culture and provident consumerism became pre-eminent discourses of the Modern Age.

Notes

1 Historians who have addressed this subject include, for example, Leonore Davidoff and Catherine Hall, *Family Fortunes: Men and Women of the English Middle Class, 1780–1850* (Cambridge, 1987), especially chapter 5, and Theodore Koditschek, *Class Formation and Urban Industrial Society: Bradford, 1750–1850* (Cambridge, 1990). Margaret Hunt proposes a different chronology in the development of the middle-class ethos, as does Peter Earle. See *The Middling Sort: Commerce, Gender and the Family in England, 1680–1780* (Berkeley CA, 1996) and *The Making of the English Middle Class: Business, Society and Family Life in London, 1660–1730* (London, 1989).

2 The deep-rooted commitment to respectability is explored by Thomas Laqueur, *Religion and Respectability: Sunday Schools and Working Class Culture, 1780–1850* (New Haven CT, 1976), and Brian Harrison, *Peaceable Kingdom: Stability and Change in Modern Britain* (Oxford, 1982), especially chapter 4. See also Paul Johnson, 'Credit and thrift and the British working class, 1870–1937' in Jay Winter (ed.), *The Working Class in Modern British History: Essays in Honour of Henry Pelling* (Cambridge, 1983); Geoffrey Crossick (ed.), *The Lower Middle Class in Britain* (London, 1977); Geoffrey Crossick and Heinz-Gerhard Haupt (eds), *The Petite Bourgeoisie in Europe, 1780–1914* (New York, 1995); John Tosh, *A Man's Place: Masculinity and the Middle-Class Home in Victorian England* (New Haven CT, 1999).

3 Harrison, *Peaceable Kingdom*, pp. 158–9.

4 For example, *Commemoration of the Centenary of the Death of the Rev. Henry Duncan, Founder of Savings Banks* (1910, repr. 1946); Robert Eadon Leader, *A Century of Thrift: An Historical Sketch of the Sheffield Savings Bank, 1819–1919* (Sheffield, 1920); Charles Eason, *The Trustee Savings Banks of Great Britain and Ireland from 1817 to 1928* (Dublin, 1929); Oliver Horne, *A History of Savings Banks* (Oxford, 1947); C. Donald Hebden, *The Trustee Savings Bank of Yorkshire and Lincoln* (Hull, 1981); M. Moss and A. Slaven, *From Ledger Book to Laser Beam: A History of the TSB in Scotland from 1810 to 1990* (Glasgow, 1992); M. Moss and I. Russell, *An Invaluable Treasure: A History of the TSB* (London, 1994). The significant exception being Paul Johnson, *Spending and Saving: the Working-Class Economy in Britain, 1870–1939* (Cambridge, 1985).

5 See, for example, Mary Fissell, 'Charity universal? Institutions and moral reform in eighteenth-century Bristol' in L. Davidson, T. Hitchcock, T. Keirn and R. B. Shoemaker (eds), *Stilling the Grumbling Hive: The Response to Social and Economic Problems in England, 1689–1750* (New York, 1992).

6 John Rule provides a very effective summary of the changing attitudes towards the Old Poor Law among the political elites in *Albion's People: English Society, 1714–1815* (London, 1992). See also Anne Digby, *The Poor Law in Nineteenth-Century England and Wales* (London, 1982).

7   Brian Harrison contends that 'although the term "respectability", with its connotations of political and economic "independence", had only recently come to be applied to working people, some of its essential cultural constituents go back at least to the seventeenth century and in some respects as far back as the division of function between craftsman and labourer, with its associated concept of apprenticeship.' Harrison, *Peaceful Kingdom*, p. 158.

8   1793, 33 Geo. III, cap. 54. Moss and Russell, *Invaluable Treasure*, p. 13; Neil Smelser, *Social Change in the Industrial Revolution* (London, 1959), pp. 352–6.

9   In 1789 one author enthused that those working people 'by subscribing small sums as they could afford weekly or monthly, alleviated the distress of each other'. *Laws and Articles for the Government of all the Members of the Provident Brotherhood, first founded by William Hill … and William Cook, September the 7th 1789* (Hull, 1789), p. iv.

10 Friendly societies were created with rules on their size, the trades to which members could belong, as well as the sex and marital status of members. For example, the United Briton Friendly Society had relatively high weekly fees and aimed to pay out a benefit to widows of members, while the Society of Women, at the School House, Battersea, was organized by a patroness, had low fees and aimed to provide benefits during lying-in and illness. *Rules and Orders to be observed by a Friendly Society, called the United Britons, held at the House of Mr Thomas Mead, the Crooked Billet, King David Lane, Shadwell – instituted 1783* (1793); *Rules to be observed by a Society of Women, at the School-House, Battersea; begun 1st January 1798* (1798).

11 Quoted in Margaret D. Fuller, *West Country Friendly Societies* (Lingfield, 1964), p. 8.

12 Barber Beaumont, *An Essay on Provident or Parish Banks, for the Security and Improvement of the Savings of Tradesmen, Artificers, Servants, etc …* (1816), pp. 28–9.

13 In 1816, George Rose, a long-time champion of friendly societies, now took up savings banks and insisted that the 'benefits derived to every part of the community from the system of Banks for Savings have been proved so incontrovertibly … as to render it unnecessary to dwell much on them'. George Rose, *Observations on Banks for Savings* (1816), p. 3.

14 Bridget Hill, 'Priscilla Wakefield as a writer of children's educational books', *Women Writers* 4:1 (1997).

15 Quoted in Horne, *History of Savings Banks*, pp. 25–6.

16 Horne, *History of Savings Banks*, pp. 25–7.

17 Priscilla Wakefield, *Reflections on the Present Condition of the Female Sex* (1798, repr. New York, 1974), p. 111.

18 Scottish commercial banks accepted small deposits and paid interest on such accounts, an important difference between the Scottish and English banking systems. Horne, *History of Savings Banks*, pp. 39–58.

19 Horne, *History of Savings Banks*, pp. 27–9.

20 Other critics included J. Acland, *A Plan for rendering the Poor independent of Public Contribution …* (1786); George Rose, *Observations on the Act for the Relief and Encouragement of Friendly Societies* (1794) and *Observations on the Poor Laws …* (1805). See also, Smelser, *Social Change*, pp. 358–60.

21 Patrick Calquhoun, *A Treatise on Indigence …* (1806), quoted in Horne, *History of Savings Banks*, p. 32.

22 For a discussion of the benefits accruing to poor Indian women members of SEWA Bank, see Jayshree Vyas, 'Banking with poor self-employed women' in B. Lemire,

R. Pearson and G. Campbell (eds), *Women and Credit: Researching the Past, Refiguring the Future* (Oxford, 2002).

23 Horne, *History of Savings Banks*, p. 27; John Tidd Pratt, *An Account of the Number of Depositors and of the Sums deposited in Savings Banks in Great Britain and Ireland … 1829 to 1844 … .*(1845); Rose, *Banks for Savings*, pp. 6–8.

24 Duncan, quoted in Beaumont, *Essay on Provident or Parish Banks*, p. 37; *Commemoration of the Centenary of the Death of the Rev. Henry Duncan*.

25 A regional term used to describe types of rotating savings and credit circles.

26 Horne, *History of Savings Banks*, pp. 48–9. Duncan's system did not garner universal support, however. Joseph Hume believed that 'The plan of Mr Duncan of Ruthwell is so complicated, and involves so many inquisitorial acts towards the Depositor and his family, unless conducted on such purely patriarchal principles as can be exercised only in a limited sphere, that I cannot consider it applicable to general use'. Hume, *An Account of the Provident Institution for Savings, Established in the Western Part of the Metropolis …* (1816), p. 37.

27 William Lewins, *A History of Banks for Savings* (1866), pp. 81, 84.

28 *Edinburgh Review*, June 1815, quoted in Hume, *Provident Institution*, p. 53.

29 Lewins, *History of Banks for Savings*, pp. 85–9.

30 Deposits in savings banks were ultimately invested in government debentures tied to the national debt, yielding interest on deposits. At several times in the 1820s the rate paid on these deposits was adjusted to reflect the commercial value of the deposits. Paul Johnson notes that, by 1858, the government was being criticized for 'manipulating trustee savings bank funds in the interest of the national exchequer'. However, in the early years, depositors enjoyed returns that were occasionally higher than regular consol yields and costly to the government. Paul Johnson, 'Class law in Victorian society', *Past and Present* 141 (1993), p. 153; Horne, *History of Savings Banks*, p. 100.

31 Horne, *History of Savings Banks*, pp. 74–7; Smelser, *Social Change*, p. 370.

32 Lewins, *History of Banks for Savings*; Horne, *History of Savings Banks*; *Commemoration of the Centenary of the Death of the Rev. Henry Duncan*; S. Hall, *Dr Duncan of Ruthwell, Founder of Savings Banks* (1910); Leader, *A Century of Thrift*; Eason, *Trustee Savings Banks of Great Britain and Ireland*; Smelser, *Social Change*; Albert Fishlow, 'The trustee savings banks, 1817–1861', *Journal of Economic History*, 2nd series 21 (1961); Hebden, *Trustee Savings Bank of Yorkshire and Lincoln*; Moss and Slaven, *From Ledger Book to Laser Beam*; Moss and Russell, *Invaluable Treasure*. The conference 'Savings Banks as Financial Institutions: Role, Performance and Impact' at the Centre for Business History in Scotland, University of Glasgow, September 2001, illustrates the current more intense focus on this question.

33 Ian Levitt and Christopher Smout, *State of the Scottish Working Class in 1843* (Edinburgh, 1979), p. 144, table 6C; Horne, *History of Savings Banks*, p. 387, appendix II. The figure for England and Wales is an estimate only. Unfortunately, it is not clear from Horne's figure whether he included Scottish TSBs after that style of bank was introduced in the late 1840s. However, the typical savings bank in Scotland continued to invest its deposits in commercial banks, as had been the norm.

34 Paul Johnson, along with Melanie Tebbutt, charts the persistence of pawning among working-class communities, even as this becomes a less respectable avenue to secure credit. Paul Johnson, *Savings and Spending: The Working-Class Economy in Britain,*

1870–1939 (Cambridge, 1985); Johnson, 'Credit and thrift'; Melanie Tebbutt, *Making Ends Meet: Pawnbroking and Working-Class Credit* (Leicester, 1983).

35 Hume, *Provident Institution*, pp. 7–8; TC/113/a/18.1, *Rules and Regulations of the Sheffield and Hallamshire Savings-Bank, for the Safe Custody and Increase of Small Savings belonging to the Labouring and Industrious …* (1821), p. 2; *The Twenty-third Annual Statement of the Devon and Exeter Savings Bank* (Exeter, 1839).

36 TC/65/a/21, *Rules and Regulations of the Leeds Skyrack and Morley Savings Bank …* (1818).

37 TC/113/a1, Sheffield Savings Bank Minute Book, pp. 1–2, Lloyds TSB Group Archives, London.

38 Levitt and Smout, *State of the Scottish Working Class*, pp. 133–4; I. J. Prothero, *Artisans and Politics in early Nineteenth-Century London: John Gast and his Times* (Folkestone, 1979), pp. 232–3. When the Post Office Savings Bank was established, in 1861, over one million accounts were opened within the first decade, reflecting the broad acceptance of savings banks among the working class, a preference for institutions not directly overseen by local elites.

39 Johnson, 'Credit and thrift'.

40 For a discussion on this issue see Duncan Ross, '"Penny banks" in Glasgow, 1850–1914', *Financial History Review* 9:1 (2002).

41 Michel Foucault, *Discipline and Punish: The Birth of the Prison* (Harmondsworth, 1979), p. 139.

42 TC/75/a/22, Signature Book, London Provident Society, Lloyds TSB Group Archives, London.

43 Smelser, *Social Change*, p. 374, table 14.

44 Fishlow confirmed Smelser's assessment, concluding that there was a disappointing level of involvement by industrial labourers. 'The trustee savings banks', pp. 36–8.

45 Among the works which examine the interaction of gender and the industrialization process with household, community and workplace are Anna Clark, *Struggle for the Breeches: Gender and the Making of the British Working Class* (Berkeley CA, 1995); Maxine Berg, *The Age of Manufactures*, 2nd edn (London, 1994) and 'Women's work, mechanisation and the early phases of industrialisation' in Patrick Joyce (ed.), *The Historical Meaning of Work* (Cambridge, 1987); Pat Hudson, *The Industrial Revolution* (Cambridge, 1992); Pamela Sharpe, *Adapting to Capitalism: Working Women in the English Economy, 1700–1850* (Basingstoke, 1996) and Pamela Sharpe (ed.), *Women's Work: The English Experience, 1650–1914* (London, 1998); Sonya Rose, *Limited Livelihoods: Gender and Class in Nineteenth-Century England* (Berkeley CA, 1992); Beverly Lemire, *Dress, Culture and Commerce: The English Clothing Trade before the Factory* (Basingstoke, 1997); Katrina Honeyman, *Well Suited: A History of the Leeds Clothing Industry, 1850–1990* (Oxford, 2000).

46 David Levine and Keith Wrightson, *The Making of an Industrial Society: Wickham, 1560–1765* (Oxford, 1991), and Pat Hudson, *The Genesis of Industrial Capital: A Study of the West Riding Wool Textile Industry, c. 1750–1850* (Cambridge, 1986), reflect the varied chronologies of industrial change.

47 L. D. Schwarz, *London in the Age of Industrialisation: Entrepreneurs, Labour Force, and Living Conditions, 1700–1850* (Cambridge, 1992).

48 The statistics from a savings bank opened in Welbeck Street, London, in 1835 show that over 15 per cent of the accounts were opened by labourers, mechanics and artisans.

Saturday Magazine, 21 May 1836, p. 199.

49 Horne, *History of Savings Banks*, appendix I.

50 This finding was based on returns for 1835. *Penny Magazine*, 15 October 1836, p. 406.

51 An overman was a 'miner with responsibility for the working of an individual pit ... Later they became salaried middle-management employees of coal-owners.' Pitman and heap keeper were below-ground and above-ground occupations in the coal industry. Levine and Wrightson, *Wickham*, pp. 158–63, 447–8.

52 Horne, *History of Savings Banks*, p. 98. See also Ross, 'Penny banks in Glasgow'.

53 The average amount saved by male servants in the London-based Marylebone Savings Bank was about £21 and that saved by female servants nearly £16. *Penny Magazine*, 15 October 1836, p. 407. Similar patterns are in evidence in the Devon & Exeter Savings Bank.

54 George Alter, Claudia Goldin and Elyce Rotella, 'The savings of ordinary Americans: the Philadelphia Saving Fund Society in the mid-nineteenth century', *Journal of Economic History* 54:4 (1994), pp. 735–8, 750–67.

55 Priscilla Wakefield contended that it was the responsibility of genteel and middle-ranking mistresses to train their servants in habits of economy. Wakefield, *Reflections*, pp. 111–12, 159–63.

56 TC/78/a/1, South Shields & District Friendly Bank for Savings, Ledger 1, Lloyds TSB Group Archives, London.

57 Discussed below. For another example of common short-term savings see Rohit Daniel Wadhwani, 'Banking from the bottom up: the case of migrant savers at the Philadelphia Saving Fund Society during the late nineteenth century', *Financial History Review* 9:1 (2002).

58 TC/78/a/1, South Shields & District Friendly Bank for Savings, Ledger 1, Lloyds TSB Group Archives, London.

59 Alter *et al.*, 'Savings of ordinary Americans', pp. 735–67; Wadhwani, 'Banking from the bottom up'.

60 TC/78/a/1, South Shields & District Friendly Bank for Savings, Ledger 1, Lloyds TSB Group Archives, London.

61 Ross, 'Penny savings banks in Glasgow'.

62 *The London Provident Bank for Savings* ... (1833), p. 6; *Rules and Regulations of the Sheffield and Hallamshire Savings-Bank* ... (1821), pp. 8, 10–11.

63 Paul Johnson points out that short-term savings remained a common feature in savings bank use, as, for example, in 1870, when nearly a quarter-million Post Office Savings accounts were closed, a pattern that continued into the twentieth century, reflecting perhaps the short-term goals achieved by depositors, as well as the absence of any cost associated with the opening and closing of accounts. Johnson, *Saving and Spending*, pp. 98–100.

64 Consumption was a political process, Peter Gurney observes in his introduction to *Co-operative Culture and the Politics of Consumption in England, 1870–1930* (Manchester, 1996), p. 7. Indeed, consumption has significant social, cultural, gender and political dimensions, many of which are alluded to in memoirs of the time. What is not in doubt, however, is that the consumer momentum accelerated over this period, engaging both men and women, working and middle classes.

65 Hume, *Provident Institution*, pp. 10–11.

66 John Tidd Pratt was appointed the Savings Bank Barrister, in 1828, certifying the

regulations of savings banks. He also compiled most of the early statistics. John Tidd Pratt, *Savings Banks in England* ... (1830), p. 42.

67 Johnson, *Saving and Spending*, pp. 100–1.

68 Rev. S. Best, *Thoughts on Prudence; or, The Means of Improving the Condition of a Family* ... (1850), p. 2.

69 See Christine Wiskin, 'The "People's Money" Reconsidered', unpublished paper presented at the Association of Business Historians conference, Portsmouth, June 2001. She re-examined the broad significance of the minting of copper coins in 1797–1807.

70 Foucault, *Discipline and Punish*, pp. 104–7.

71 Johnson, 'Credit and thrift', p. 168. For similar contemporary comments see Nassau W. Senior, 'Two lectures on population' (1829) in Philip Appleman (ed.), *An Essay on the Principles of Population: Text, Sources and Background Criticism* (New York, 1976), pp. 146–7.

72 Samuel Smiles, *Thrift* (London, 1875), pp. 130–5; Judith Walkowitz, *Prostitution and Victorian Society* (Cambridge, 1980), p. 73.

73 Quoted in Horne, *History of Savings Banks*, pp. 111–12.

74 Smiles, *Thrift*, pp. 123–58. Smiles observed that in 1874, in Preston, one in five people had money in savings accounts.

75 Robert Southey, *Annual Review*, January 1804, reprinted in Andrew Pyle (ed.), *Population: Contemporary Responses to Thomas Malthus* (Bristol, 1994), p. 125.

76 Southey, *Annual Review*, p. 130. His revised views may account for his support of savings bank initiatives.

77 Clark, *Struggle for the Breeches*, chapters 10–11. The search for political recognition and authority by working-class men, who defined their political status in domestic terms as heads of households, is examined by Keith McClelland in Catherine Hall, Keith McClelland and Jane Rendall, *Defining the Victorian Nation: Class, Race, Gender and the Reform Act of 1867* (Cambridge, 2000).

78 Clark, *Struggle for the Breeches*, p. 218.

79 This author commented about depositors in the Marylebone Savings Bank that 'it is pleasing to learn that about a tenth proportion consists of children and youth of both sexes; viz., 284 females and 342 males. ... There are eighty-two apprentices who have each put by about 4l.' *Penny Magazine*, 15 October 1836, p. 407.

80 Laqueur, *Religion and Respectability*, p. 175.

81 Laqueur, *Religion and Respectability*, pp. 2–62. See especially table 5, p. 44.

82 Laqueur, *Religion and Respectability*, pp. 224–5.

83 *Sunday School Teachers' Magazine* (1846), p. 219, quoted in Laqueur, *Religion and Respectability*, p. 175. The jump in children's membership in the London Provident Institution, between 1827 and 1842, may perhaps be explained by school training of this sort. Mechanics' Institutes also extended the benefits of education to working men. Francis Place championed this body against critics, asserting that 'Increase of knowledge produced increase of self-respect', and challenged his readers to 'get all the knowledge you can'. Francis Place, *New Times*, 23 July 1826, quoted in Prothero, *Artisans and Politics*, p. 196. Horne, *History of Savings Banks*, p. 186.

84 Agnes Lambert, *A School Bank Manual for the Use of Managers, Masters and Mistresses, and Teachers of Public Elementary Schools* (1886), pp. 2–14. See also Ross, 'Penny savings banks in Glasgow'.

85 Lambert, *School Bank Manual*, pp. 21–2. The Yorkshire Penny Bank celebrated the

establishment of the School Transfer Department in 1873, leading to the steady spread of branch activity in local elementary schools; 1,902,856 transactions took place in 1898, with a net balance of £15,256 15s through the accumulation of students' pennies. H. B. Sellers, *Memoranda from a Note Book on the Yorkshire Penny Bank* (Leeds, 1901), pp. 58–64.

86 Horne, *History of Savings Banks*, pp. 183–7.

87 In 1839 the Devon & Exeter annual report listed over twelve pages of contact names in the villages and towns of Devon to whom deposits could be given. Clergy comprised the majority of these contacts, from Rev. Richard Keats Walter in Abbotsham to Rev. John Hole in Woolfardisworthy. *Devon and Exeter Savings Bank*, pp. 42–55.

88 *The First Annual Report of the Liverpool District Provident Society for the Year 1830, with the Rules of the Society, and a List of Subscribers* (Liverpool, 1831).

89 *Liverpool District Provident Society*, p. 7.

90 *Liverpool District Provident Society*, p. 10.

91 Similar initiatives using 'District Visitors' to encourage saving are described in *St Giles's Saving Fund, Established in Connection with the District Visiting Society, for the Purpose of enabling the Labouring Classes to provide themselves with … Necessaries of Life …* (London, 1830) and R. Henry Killick, *The Rector's Address … with an Account of the District Visiting Society, Bible Women Missions, the Mission House, and other Institutions of the Parish* [St Clement Dane, The Strand] (London, 1864), p. 18. 'The incalculable benefits which the industrious classes derive from these institutions, cannot be too frequently or impressively brought before the notice of the public.' *Saturday Magazine*, 21 May 1836, p. 199; 22 March 1834. Produced by the Society for Promoting Christian Knowledge, this magazine, which sold for 1d, was a firm friend of the savings bank movement.

92 Litchfield, *Farthinghoe Clothing Society*, pp. 4–5.

93 Foucault, *Discipline and Punish*, p. 113.

94 John Johnson Collection, Charity, Bodleian Library, Oxford. For an early example of such a venture see *An Account of a Plan, which has been successfully pursued for Three Years, in the conducting of a Penny Savings Bank for Children, with the addition of a Working Fund for Females; including Directions and Patterns for Cutting Out every Sort of Wearing Apparel for Girls, Shirts and Pinafores for Boys, and Linen usually lent to the Poor …* (London, 1822). Examples from the late nineteenth and early twentieth centuries show that church and school clothing clubs continued to reward diligent savers with a bonus that enabled them to buy boots or clothing. But, as Paul Johnson notes, the members of these savings clubs had to accept the regulations underpinning the organizations. Johnson, *Saving and Spending*, pp. 150–1.

95 'In praise of the Yorkshire Penny Bank', *Our Era* 2 (Darlington, 1895); Sellers, *Note Book on the Yorkshire Penny Bank*, pp. 5–7, 13–17. The most recent and wide-ranging study of the Yorkshire Penny Bank is being undertaken by John F. Wilson and Karen Ward, for example their paper 'From penny bank to multinational partner: strategy and structure of the Yorkshire Bank, 1895–2001', presented at the conference 'Savings Banks as Financial Institutions', University of Glasgow, September 2001.

96 *Penny Banks for Villages and Small Towns: Guide for their Formation and Management both as Branches of larger Penny Banks, and under the new Post Office Savings Bank Act … by the Honorary Secretary of the Gloucester Penny Bank* (London, 1861). See also *The Oxford Penny Bank* (Oxford, 1859). Penny banks spread from north to south, east to

west, from mid-century onwards. See, for example, the Balls Pond Penny Bank, Islington, with records surviving from 1858 to 1952, or the Rufford Penny Bank, Lancashire, with documentation from 1859 to 1883, or the Mere Penny Bank, Wiltshire, with records form 1888 to 1902. P83/PAU/50–58, London Metropolitan Archives; DDX 129, Lancashire Record Office; MS Johnson b2, Bodleian Library, Oxford.

97 An author from the Central Co-operative Board emphasized that their penny banks should be seen as the children's arm of the institution, and he encouraged the establishment of penny savings banks 'in every society throughout the movement', a first step to later enrolment in the Co-op savings banks. Amos Scotton, *Penny Banks: Lessons of Thrift for the Young Ones. A Paper … to be read at Members' Meetings or Social Gatherings. Issued by the Central Co-operative Board … Manchester* (Manchester, 1889?), p. 3.

98 Ms Johnson b2, Bodleian Library, Oxford.

99 Andrew Halliday, 'My account with Her Majesty' (1863), reprinted in *Every Day Papers* I (London, 1864), p. x.

100 Halliday, 'My account with Her Majesty', p. 13. Halliday recounts in a later collection of his works, which included 'My account', that this story was 'printed in slips and distributed among the Post-office Savings Banks throughout the country, for the information and encouragement of depositors'. *Every Day Papers* I, p. x. There were also broadsheets, like *The Penny Bank News*, which promoted a provident manner of living, as well as self-help through 'Provident Knowledge Papers' and 'Intellectual Recreation'. *Penny Bank News*, 15 September 1877. This four-page broadsheet was priced at ½*d.*

101 *Liverpool District Provident Society*, p. 8.

102 Necessities were redefined from the sixteenth century to the nineteenth, with demand for goods from cooking pots to shoe buckles firing many small trades. This redefinition affected the common people as well as the middle classes and has been the focus of considerable scholarship: Joan Thirsk, *Economic Policies and Projects: The Development of a Consumer Society in Early Modern England* (Oxford, 1978); Neil McKendrick, John Brewer and J. H. Plumb, *The Birth of a Consumer Society: The Commercialization of Eighteenth-Century England* (London, 1983); Margaret Spufford, *The Great Reclothing of Rural England: Petty Chapmen and their Wares in the Seventeenth Century* (London, 1984); Lorna Weatherill, *Consumer Behaviour and Material Culture in Britain, 1660–1760* (London, 1988); Beverly Lemire, *Fashion's Favourite: The Cotton Trade and the Consumer in Britain, 1660–1800* (Oxford, 1991) and *Dress, Culture and Commerce: the English Clothing Trade before the Factory* (Basingstoke, 1997); Lori Loeb, *Consuming Angels: Advertising and Victorian Women* (Oxford, 1994); Maxine Berg and Helen Clifford (eds), *Consumers and Luxury: Consumer Culture in Europe, 1650–1850* (Manchester, 1999); Bill Lancaster, *The Department Store: A Social History* (London, 1995); Erica Rappaport, '"The halls of temptation": gender, politics, and the construction of the department store in late Victorian London', *Journal of British Studies* 35:1 (1996); Steven King, 'Reclothing the English poor', *Textile History* 33:1 (2002).

103 Charles Taylor, *A Summary Account of the London Savings Bank, including its Formation, Progress, and Present State … *(1816), p. 6.

104 Jonathan White has traced a shift in elite policy toward popular consumerism to the second half of the eighteenth century, discerning clear changes over this period as commentators recognized the boost to British industry from the collective consumer

demand. Jonathan White, 'From Unruly Appetites to Rational Wants: Changing Ideas of Labouring-Class Consumption in Eighteenth-Century England', unpublished paper presented at the New Researchers' Session II, Economic History Conference, Bristol, 2000. A fuller elaboration of these points can be found in 'Luxury and Labour: Ideas of Labouring-Class Consumption in Eighteenth-Century England', unpublished PhD thesis, University of Warwick, 2001.

105 Mary Douglas, *Thought Styles: Critical Essays on Good Taste* (London, 1996).

106 The concept of the aristocracy of labour captured the attention of historians in the 1960s and 1970s. Thereafter, respectability was assessed from a broader class and gender perspective. Examples of these historiographies include: E. J. Hobsbawm, 'The labour aristocracy in nineteenth-century Britain' in *Labouring Men* (London, 1964), and A. E. Musson, 'Class struggle and the labour aristocracy, 1830–1960', *Social History* 3 (1976); Davidoff and Hall, *Family Fortunes*; Koditschek, *Class Formation*.

107 Harrison, *Peaceable Kingdom*, p. 157.

108 Fishlow, 'Trustee savings banks', pp. 28–30; Horne, *History of Savings Banks*, p. 97. Horne notes that the relative proportion of domestic servants declined over the nineteenth century. In London, for example, domestic servants initially made up 24 per cent of savings bank depositors in 1816 and only 12 per cent of savers by 1850. Horne, *History of Savings Banks*, p. 97.

109 Levitt and Smout, *State of the Scottish Working Class*, p. 135.

110 One manager revealed the assistance he gave wives of drunkards to keep the wives' small savings out of reach of their husbands, the moral failure of the male householders offered as justification. *The Yorkshire Penny Bank: A Narrative, with an Introduction by Edward Akroyd, MP* (London, 1872), pp. 30, 32, 34–5, 38–9, 50, 56. What R. W. Connell terms 'calculative, rational and regulated' masculinity was expressed in many contexts. R. W. Connell, 'The big picture: masculinities in recent world history', *Theory and Society* 22:5 (1993), p. 609.

111 Anna Clark notes the workplace strategies employed by male calico printers in the 1830s, designed to reinforce their status as a masculine elite. The strategy they found most effective was one Clark terms 'patriarchal co-operation', with male calico printers' positions defended by subordinate female workers. Clark, *Struggle for the Breeches*, pp. 204–6.

112 George Matthews, *Little by Little; or, The Penny Bank. With Rules and Method of Working* (London, 1868), pp. 4–7. Page 3 of this volume shows in chart form the results of saving 3*d* per day. The story is reproduced in a number of other guides to domestic thrift, including H. M. Poynter, *Thrift: An Address to the Mothers' Union at Aspley Guise* (Oxford, 1901). Samuel Smiles retells the tale in *Thrift* (London, 1875), pp. 164–5.

113 For example, the surviving British Library edition was published in Saffron Walden about 1820 (?), while the edition in the Bodleian Library, Oxford, was published in Louth, 1824. Volumes with similar messages appeared regularly throughout the nineteenth and early twentieth centuries: Rev. F. Wrangham, *The Savings-Bank, in Two Dialogues* (Scarborough, 1800); Thomas Walker, *Observations on the Utility of Savings' Banks* (Newcastle, 1841); *Thrift; or Hints for Cottage Housekeeping* (London, 1855); *What shall I Do with my Money? By Old Chatty Cheerful* (London, 1860?); Matthews, *Little by Little*; Andrew Halliday, *Every Day Papers* I; *A Few Words from Lady Mildred's Housekeeper* (London, 1874); *Willie Smith's Money-box* (London, 1873); R. André,

Georgie's Money-box (London and New York, 1882).

114 George Davys, *The Savings Bank: A Dialogue between Ralph Ragged and Will Wise* (1820?), pp. 1–9.

115 *The Savings Bank, Part Second: Ralph Ragged and Will Wise*, pp. 3–4. The metaphor of the industrious ant recurs in more than Aesop's fables. A similar scenario is repeated in Wrangham, *The Savings-Bank*, p. 3.

116 *The Oxford Penny Bank* (Oxford, 1859). See also 'The value of a penny', *The Youth's Monitor* 1:1 (1836), pp. 8–10. See also Alter *et al.*, 'Savings of ordinary Americans', p. 752.

117 *The Savings Bank, Part Second: Ralph Ragged and Will Wise*, p. 10.

118 In fact, in 1842, the average sum in the accounts of domestic servants at one bank was more than £23. *London Provident Institution … 1842*.

119 Samuel Smiles describes the ideal practices of the provident husband, who takes care of the pennies, 'putting some weekly into a benefit society or insurance fund, others into a savings bank, and confiding the rest to his wife to be carefully laid out, with a view to the comfortable maintenance and education of his family'. *Self-help*, p. 295.

120 Mary Thale (ed.), *The Autobiography of Francis Place* (Cambridge, 1972), pp. 127, 174. For an example of the practice of thrift in the late nineteenth century see Margaret Llewelyn Davies (ed.), *Life as We have Known it: by Co-operative Working Women* (1931, repr. New York, 1975), pp. 34–8.

121 Ellen Ross, 'Survival networks: women's neighbourhood sharing in London before World War I', *History Workshop Journal* 15 (1983); Robert Roberts, *A Ragged Schooling* (Manchester, 1976), pp. 2–18. See also Maud Pember Reeves, *Round about a Pound a Week* (1913, repr. London, 1988), pp. 11–13.

122 George Davys wrote another short volume on the subject of benefit clubs, which, like the original tale of Ragged Ralph and Will Wise, was reproduced in the *Cottager's Monthly Visitor*. George Davys, *The Benefit Club: a Dialogue, with a Statement of the Sums to be Paid and Received by the Different Classes according to the Rev. I. T. Becher's Tables …* (London, 1828).

123 Alfred Pinhorn, *Spending and Saving: A Primer of Thrift* (London, 1901), pp. 23, 25.

124 Arthur W. Brown, *Economy: The Self-denying Depositor and Prudent Paymaster at the Bank of Thrift* (London, 1915), pp. 57–8.

125 Johnson, *Saving and Spending*, table 4.1, pp. 91–2, 95.

126 *The Penny Magazine*, 15 October 1836, p. 407.

127 Harrison, *Peaceable Kingdom*, p. 161.

128 The cultural characteristics of late nineteenth to mid-twentieth-century credit are being considered by Sean O'Connell. See, for example, 'Credit, Debt and Guilt: Cultural and Moral Obstacles to the Development of Consumer Society', unpublished paper presented at the European Business History Conference, Barcelona, 2004, www.econ.upf.edu/ebha2004/programme2.html#session1.

129 Illustrated in the occupational distribution in the Aberdeen Savings Bank in 1880 and the even broader social make-up of the Post Office Savings Bank depositors in 1896. Johnson, *Saving and Spending*, pp. 95–6.

130 Johnson, 'Credit and thrift', p. 169.

131 Pinhorn, *Spending and Saving*. Pinhorn also taught evening classes on this subject. Poynter, *Thrift*, p. 11.

132 Robert Roberts opens his chapter on 'Possessions' with the statement that 'The social

standing of every person within the community was constantly affected by material possessions, some of the slightest ... '. Roberts, *The Classic Slum* (Manchester, 1973), p. 32. See also Johnson, 'Credit and thrift', pp. 169–70.

133 Smiles, *Self-help*, p. 280.

134 See, for example, Walker, *Observations on the Utility of Savings' Banks*; Scotton, *Penny Banks: Lessons of Thrift for the Young Ones*; and Lambert, *A School Bank Manual*; *Willie Smith's Money-box*; André, *Georgie's Money-box*.

135 For examples of these inventions and other styles of money banks see Savi Arbola and Marco Onesti, *Piggy Banks* (San Francisco, 1992), pp. 50–1, 72, 81, 85, 115. In Hans Andersen's tale *The Money-box* (1855), the pottery piggy bank is such a standard feature of a middle-class child's room that it needs no explanation or discussion.

136 Of course, the ultimate bodily form of savings was that widely practised by poor wives who, in times of dearth, almost starved themselves to ensure that their husband, the principal breadwinner, had sufficient to eat. See Davies, *Life as We have Known it*, pp. 35–7.

7

Accounting for the household:
gender and the culture of household
management, c. 1600–1900

THINKING IN NUMBERED FORMS was initially an elite and esoteric practice, a Renaissance innovation that took hold among the common people only after many centuries. This new practise refashioned Western thinking, propelling new applications in technical, scientific and commercial spheres, producing what Alfred Crosby calls 'a new model of reality' wherein a 'quantitative model ... [began] to displace the ancient qualitative model'.[1] The disciplines which emerged reframed perceptions of the world, changing in the first instance the priorities of kings, generals and merchant princes, providing the mechanisms for the imperial and industrial advances of later centuries. By the sixteenth century, as Crosby notes, 'The West was making up its mind (most of its mind, at least) to treat the universe in terms of quanta uniform in one or more characteristics ... music staffs, platoons, ledger columns'.[2] The 'most' in his parentheses is an important and essential modifier. For if the sixteenth-century male elites of Europe's government, military and commerce were buoyed by their allegiance to quantitative disciplines, launching imperial adventures around the globe and building large commercial enterprises, much of Western society remained relatively untouched by these developments. Traditions of qualitative valuation were slow to accede to quantitative thinking. The history of numeracy has been examined from many perspectives, from the impact of time keeping to the spread of accounting in business, but, for all the accumulated insights, these studies privilege the public arenas where predominantly masculine cultures were reconceived from the fifteenth century to the nineteenth.[3] In his brief survey of numeracy in England Keith Thomas acknowledges that 'we are still largely ignorant about the numerical skills of the population at large'.[4] In that context, I will examine the impact of quantitative culture on the household, where predominantly female and customary practices intersected with the acquisition and use of goods, with the intimacy and practicality of family life. Over several centuries, the slow spread of applied numeracy changed the practices of husbands and housewives in the most personal of settings, introducing numerate discipline into the home, including at its core the precepts of debit and credit.

There are few more ubiquitous institutions than the family. Households were the centres of human interaction, the sites of reproduction, the building blocks of communities, and the source of the strongest human ties.[5] Households, like nations, have histories; but, unlike the nation, most individual households never receive the minute attention devoted to even the smallest state. However, in their aggregate, families and households have been scrutinized intensely over the last several decades in an effort to historicize their collective experience, to chart gender politics and to explain the nature of family life.[6] In this chapter I will explore the evolving practices of numerate household management which varied with the time, place, class, sex and predisposition of the practitioners. The balance between the new reckoning and customary social relations ebbed in the direction of the former. What I think of as the new reckoning can be described as the application of numerate costing analyses, designed to track income and expenses and ensure profitability or solvency through objective, skilled record-keeping. Reciprocity and hospitality, on the other hand, are terms that reflect traditional concerns guided by injunctions of benevolence, deference or obligation to kin, neighbours, servants or superiors whether or not the money value of exchanges balanced in each encounter. Numerate reckoning did not extinguish all traditional claims; however, there was a long, complex evolution in favour of the former. In the site of the most concentrated female culture of reproduction, child-rearing, co-operation, customary and productive practices – what Mendelson and Crawford call the 'female-dominated milieu'[7] – there were increasing demands for rational calculation. The victory of quantification in the household took generations, and the experience of men and women, bourgeois and plebeian, varied in the face of the persistent advances of numeric calculation from the treasury and the counting house to the heart of family affairs. Between 1600 and 1900, household cultures were transfigured by powerful concepts and, as the consolidation of industrial capitalism took place in the market, there was a normalization of derivative economic theories within the home. By the nineteenth century, the middle-class domestic world, long celebrated in the Victorian era as a haven from commerce, reflected all the numerate priorities of that utilitarian age. Nineteenth-century middle-class households, purportedly the most private and intimate spheres, were minutely chronicled according to accounting precepts. Surviving records from England, as well as suggestive North American examples, point to differential gender and class responses as the discipline of household management worked its way through homes and families.

Numbering and accounting

The practice of numerate accounting is so deeply ingrained in our culture that we respond unquestioningly to its imperatives, but this has been a gradual indoctrination. From the late Middle Ages onward, the fiscal surveillance at the heart of this system gradually gained ascendancy, as, in our own age, have the disciplining constraints of balanced cheque books and tax forms, which set out rewards or penalties, successes or failures. The history of everyday quantification includes as well the transformation in human interactions associated with number-based, monetized relations and communication, whereby applied numeracy assumed an ever greater authority. Bookkeeping or accounting is the most important conceptual model of applied numeracy for my purposes, incorporating the skills of arithmetic, currency and commercial forms, to chart the fiscal health of a person or company. There is some debate about the origins of double-entry bookkeeping in Europe. Some suggest that it flourished first among the great merchant companies of northern Italy; others contend that it was devised as a means to map personal wealth. In both cases, control lay in the hands of merchants determined to systematize risks and rewards in what Mary Poovey calls a new '*system of writing* ... that exceeded transcription and calculation'.[8] First published in 1494, the double-entry accounting system spread throughout Europe,[9] offering a new mastery over commercial records – the capacity to chart profits and costs. Schematically, it also reflected a compelling analytical duality, with income and outflow neatly summarized on facing pages, apparently offering the ultimate clarity of thought, and the power of double-entry bookkeeping entranced adherents.[10] The dicta spread through the commercial and trading classes and beyond, moving from their original base in the cities of Italy, north and west along the commercial highways of Europe. By 1551, an English text advocated that arithmetic be taught in all grammar schools as a precursor to learning to cast accounts, and instruction manuals appeared aimed at the English reader, such as James Peele's 1566 volume *The Pathewaye to Perfectnes, in the Accomptes of Debitour, and Creditour*. Scattered records from the early sixteenth century onwards confirm the application of this system among the propertied class in at least a rudimentary form. Numerous English grammar schools followed suit by the seventeenth century and, in 1653, a school established by Oliver Cromwell for Essex children included accounts in the basic syllabus, even as Cromwell acknowledged that he had 'as little skill in Arithmetic as … in the Law'.[11]

Numeracy was becoming one of the most desirable skills of the Mercantile Age, the mastery of which could lead to commercial preferment or help secure a personal fortune. Margaret Hunt describes the techniques of bookkeeping as a 'democratic mystery in the best Baconian tradition … [which] promised its initiates an unprecedented sense of control over the intimidating universe of credit, debt, and cash-flow'.[12] Rebecca Conner terms the fashion for figures 'quantification fever', noting that by 1700 'there was a vigorous movement afoot to make numbers pre-eminent'.[13] These rituals of writing, of distilling minutiae from daily ledgers to weekly or monthly volumes, removed narrative detail and preserved a version of transactions in numeric form. As Mary Poovey notes, numbered entries in themselves took on the appearance of objective reality.[14] The skills could be acquired with moderate diligence, and they laid out a new world of order, filling merchants' ledgers. Enthusiasm for this system was unbounded among the mercantile elite, who esteemed the accountant's capacity to sift through coded transactions, to assign value to all exchanges.[15] Generation by generation, the children of merchant and middling families, as well as a few from the poorer classes, became steeped in the new numerate discipline, through schools and apprentice-ships. In national debates and personal affairs, the new reckoning intrigued the literate elites or would-be elites. A rising bureaucrat in the navy, Samuel Pepys, swore an oath before God in 1662, promising to make up his private accounts regularly 'to give a good account of my time and to grow rich'. Ultimately, he taught his wife some of the precepts of arithmetic as well.[16] Years later, Daniel Defoe derided old fashioned tradesmen who prided themselves on keeping all their business in their heads,[17] at a time when expanding overseas and domestic traffic demanded books which accurately traced the twists and turns of goods and money.

Michel Foucault named the 'calculable man' the quintessential modern figure on whom the 'new technology of power and a new political anatomy of the body were implemented', depicting a burgeoning modern era with authorities tasked to oversee citizens and constrain behaviour through 'scientific-disciplinary mechanisms'. Accounting was a metaphoric and growing professional Panopticon with the capacity to anatomize and judge according to seemingly objective criteria. Within the evolving capitalist society, accounting brought with it the power of a fresh perspective, with 'domains of objects and rituals of truth'.[18] The disciplinary philosophy, emblematic of modern experience, forms a core element in the culture of accounting, and the practices and perspectives typically employed with debit and credit accounts set the terms for one of the pre-eminent human measures. Ultimately, keeping, or failing to keep, good accounts came to determine how a man – gentleman or trading man – would be esteemed by his fellows.[19]

In late seventeenth-century England, the fashion for quantification preoccupied lords as well as merchants, and in 1714 a gentleman, Roger North, described his encounter with the accounting system as a type of love affair. North had no commercial aspirations, so he felt the need to justify pedagogic aims well outside the scope of a man of his standing:

> It may be demanded, How it comes to pass, that an Alien in Merchandise … assumes the Doctorate, and in a tutoring way, pretends to recommend and instruct others in Merchants Accompts. To this I have Authority to give for Answer, That by Accident the Author fell in love, and ever since has been enamoured with them; and out of the abundance of the Heart, the Pen Uttereth.[20]

North was one of many partisans who felt that the world was viewed more clearly and logically through the eyes of the accountant. And, to describe this most masculine of enterprises, North employed the language of love, an arresting juxtaposition of concepts. Love, in this instance, he argued, was based on a clear-sighted logic, not the sort of infatuation that blurs the senses. The object of his affection was figured in female form – double-entry accounting.[21] Intense satisfaction was felt by those who learned the rules and procedures and, like North, applied them to the management of affairs. North's romantic metaphor led next to pen and ledger:

> then by a Course of Practice, he became capable … which is a Consummation of Pleasure, this Art affords. And [he adds] That Lovers of Art have that to say for themselves, which no other Species of Lovers can pretend to, which is to be Kind and Communicative. And on that Account, thinking other Persons may possibly … be as Amorous as himself, has ventured to express in writing … the best of his Skills.[22]

North enticed others of his rank to careful record keeping, employing the classic language of love to express his devotion to the venture. His rapture was not a unique response to this discipline, and the intoxicating epistemological power of this system gained disciples. The basis of this passion perhaps lay in the fact that, as Mary Poovey observes, 'bookkeeping constituted one of the earliest systems to privilege both things in themselves (the objects and money the merchants traded) and a formal system of writing numbers that transformed representations of these things into usable facts'.[23]

Accounting precepts diffused throughout Europe, resting in no single centre, achieving pre-eminence wherever trade and industry were most advanced, extending their influence with the rise of political arithmetic.[24] This system of written reckoning preceded large factories, assisting first in the growing international commercial hegemony of Europe, where, with a sharp pencil and a sharper eye, the accountant fixed order on complex records, weeded out the bankrupt and confirmed the profitable. Accounting, with its techniques of training and surveillance, became an everyday practice. Moreover, Foucault's characterization of factory production is equally apt with regard to the spread and application of accounting. 'Surveillance thus becomes a decisive economic operator', he noted, 'both as an internal part of the production machinery and as a specific mechanism in the disciplinary power.'[25] Furthermore, while a powerful means of assessing monetary value, this system wielded its authority across a wider terrain than merchants' ledgers, becoming one of the dominant cultural tropes of the age.

Accounting and the household may perhaps seem an odd conjunction. However, the transforming power of capitalism has long been recognized for its effects on community, individual and family life.[26] Bookkeeping techniques were another mechanism, another philosophical discipline, which integrated the supervision of wealth and family. Prescriptive writing on household arrangements, physical and personal, emphasized the desirability of a male space at the seat of patriarchal control in which the most confidential domestic accounts could be constructed.[27] This new form of reckoning was carried well beyond the community of elite merchants, travelling through the more democratic channels of commerce and thereafter into the domestic environs more generally.[28] By the seventeenth century, concepts of fiscal regulation were becoming so commonplace among the propertied ranks that these precepts began to order genteel, middling and, ultimately, even plebeian households. Adherents believed that if rational commerce should be guided by the casting of accounts, so too should other individuals and institutions, including the family.

Valuing the household

Society rested on the foundation of the family, with kinship and community ties that held unique significance. Through marriage came the daily and age-old rites of passage which helped define social standing and personal experience, celebrated with timely gifts and customary exchanges, knitting together the network of relations, friends, dependants and superiors.[29] Church ceremonies delineated the milestones of life: marriage, baptisms, churching and funerals. All the blessings and vagaries of a lifetime were played out within that sometimes equivocal but ubiquitous forum.[30] Husbands and wives assumed different areas of responsibility, to the end of sustaining and promoting the family. The good wife was expected to conserve resources, nurture and educate children, and care for the sick, while fostering ties with extended kin and community. Above all, the good wife held her family together, employing thrift to stave off disaster, sustaining charitable and reciprocal obligations within their community. During periodic travails, the ideal housewife employed a combination of godly commitment, plus a large dose of family effort and housewifely care. Tied by affection and fate, the currency of these unions superseded market specie, however buffeted by commercial fluctuations. The sentiments sustaining these complementary qualities are intangible, yet the power of these customary values cannot be doubted.

Nevertheless, households at virtually every level of society were gradually becoming more monetized. In the first instance, these changes were experienced among the propertied classes, where numbered accounts offered a different measure of life, distinct from written religious observances or narrative diaries. A growing chorus of writers pressed genteel women to learn these numerate skills.[31] In 1714, Richard Steele urged ladies to try their hand at accounts, for the 'Pleasure of reducing things from Confusion to Order by the Power of Numbers, wou'd be the greater for the Advantage which wou'd accrue to [the women] by their Exactness.'[32] Naturally, the power of bookkeeping was wielded first by men of substance, and, unlike literacy, it is virtually impossible to track with precision the spread of this applied numeracy even among the literate women who learned its techniques.[33] It is apparent that by the late seventeenth century enthusiasts began advising more women to learn this art and to apply it in the home. These authors were precursors to the later flood of writers after 1750 who espoused a similar message, agents in a profound social transformation as numerate valuation became an increasingly common feature of domestic discourse. In an important late seventeenth-century text, Stephan Monteage affected the voice of a woman to describe the purpose and process of double-entry bookkeeping. Monteage's *Advice to the Women and Maidens of London* was published first in 1678 and reprinted in at least one later edition, addressed to urban commercial families. The full title provides an indication of the author's argument: 'Shewing, that

Instead of their Usual Pastime; and education in Needlework, Lace and Point-making, it were Far more Necessary and Profitable to Apply Themselves to the Right Understanding and Practice of the Method of Keeping Books of Accounts.'[34] Monteage intended these skills for business purposes as well as domestic tasks, noting that 'I have heard it affirmed by those who have lived in forraign parts, that Merchants and other tradesmen have no other Book-keepers then their Wives.' He further contended that 'I never found this Masculine Art harder or more difficult than the effeminate achievements of Lace-making.' The hearthside was deemed a forum as suitable for numerate skills as for bobbin and thread, and the fictionalized female accountant described her progress, which began first by keeping 'an exact account of the expence of House-keeping, and other petty Charges'.[35] Once the basics of bookkeeping were ingrained, the next step was to master the double-entry system, where 'each Action or Contract is to be Entered in your Leiger [sic] … twice, viz. Debtor and Creditor.' The introduction of the formal categories of debtor and creditor carry immense cultural weight, recognized by the author. He emphasizes that:

> you must consider, that every Receipt or Payment, every Buying and Selling or other Contract is a transferring of Property from one to another; so that the Person, or thing, who is the Receiver or Borrower, is intended here for the Debtor; and the Person who pays, or the thing delivered or lent, is the Creditor.[36]

With these instructions, commercial and domestic practices began to be conflated into a single epistemology. The process itself was gradual, with visible gender and class differences in the application and introduction of accounting precepts. But the ideal was clearly expressed during the seventeenth century, lessons being put in practice with greater frequency by 1800.[37] Now, as the middling sort struggled to sustain trades and to rise in professions, the discipline which promised so great a clarity in the shop and counting house was proposed as an effective technique for their sitting rooms and kitchens, even as the middle ranks increasingly applauded the separation of home and work. The intellectual conflation of commercial categories with household practice marks a profound transformation. Profit and loss were becoming domestic as well as commercial concerns and, at the same time, numeric records took on greater significance, intruding into personal diaries, creating a hybrid form of numeric narrative. Along with the formal discipline of accounting, a visible material discipline entered the home with a new type of book, the account ledger. Like a biblical text, the authority of the ledger began to shape the values and

priorities of disciples. Its authority was very real, vested in objective principles, and few questioned the wholesale transition of these techniques
from the market place to the family.

Keeping books and the bookkeeping family

The rationality of numbers was expressed in a seemingly objective, value-
free manner which, like ledger entries, seemed to express reality. But, as
Gareth Morgan remarks, accounting is a process of 'reality construction'
offering a partial, imperfect synthesis of events, 'exactly as an artist is
obliged to produce a partial view of the reality he or she wishes to represent'.[38] The costs of goods and the wages of servants were indeed objective,
in one sense. However, constraining and summarizing interactions into a
tabulated form invariably removed many other dimensions of social
interplay; subsumed within this system of accounts were the ingrained
social and gender inequities excluded from the bookkeeper's systematic
reckoning. Overlooked as well were the continuing traditional exchanges
in goods, services and time, which found no category in accounts, since
the activities were typically outside the money exchange, inspired by
custom, principle or sentiment. The motivation for some of these activities also sprang from what could be called caring. Reciprocal relationships, charitable actions, exchanges of gifts, hospitality and favours,
continued to bind together networks of kin and neighbours.[39] Furthermore, women's disproportionate involvement in reproductive activities,
family and community duties, rooted in the community and the household, may well have created a particular tension between these functions
and the newly developing economic theories which assigned value and
defined normative behaviour in very different utilitarian terms.[40]

Numeric records of various sorts proliferated among England's genteel and even middling families, taking disparate shapes from the seventeenth century to the nineteenth – most business records took the form
of single-entry accounts, some attempted the more complex double-
entry form with multiple ledgers; hybrid narrative and numeric styles
were also evident.[41] Archives and record offices hold untold numbers of
personal and business accounts, a sampling of which have been discussed
elsewhere in this volume, all of which reflect the evolution of literate
communication. The power of this mode of writing, of this transcendent
method of expression, deserves our closest attention, marking a qualitative change in Western culture. Jack Goody observes that 'Culture,
after all, is a series of communicative acts, and differences in the mode
of communication are often as important as differences in the mode of

production, for they involve developments in the storing, analysis, and creation of human knowledge, as well as the relationships between the individuals involved.'[42]

The first instance I examine comes from the later seventeenth century and is of interest not least because of the relative rarity of documents of this sort, at this date, among men distinguished by their undistinguished lives. Unlike the accounts of John Pope, constructed over approximately the same period (1661–71) and explored in earlier chapters, this author named his record a 'diary', a common terminology for what was often a blending of diary and account ledger. Although William Smart was undoubtedly an adherent of accounting, no ledgers of that type survive. But a powerful numeric imperative compelled him to make his diary a modified statement of accounts. By no means the earliest of domestic accountants, nor the most forthcoming in his notations, this document marks a further stage in the application of numeric categories, in the 'representation of … things' and construction of reality. The surviving volume begins on 20 December 1666 and runs for twelve years; as the author recounts, it was 'A continuation of my Diary books'.[43] William Smart was sixty-three years old when he began this volume, living in Westminster, though he later moved north to Durham, married, with one son. He earned his living as a moneylender and almost certainly kept a full set of business ledgers – given the complexity of the number of borrowers, rates of interest and patterns of repayment, it would be surprising if he did not. Numerate monitoring of income and outflow was a passion, a routine integrated into his life and thoughts, maintained until the final months before his death. Over the twelve years of entries only two events occasioned significant gaps – the move from London to the north-east and a later severe illness. Smart recommenced as soon as he was able.

Smart also followed the dictates of hospitality and custom. Favoured clients routinely received refreshment during the course of business, the costs of hospitality noted; 'Sp[en]t with him 6d.' was inscribed beside many of the memoranda of meetings held or borrowers met, when beer or food was shared. Domestic expenditures, whether at the market, entertaining friends or clients, or purchasing scurvy physic, were duly entered in a fashion that bespoke a deep-seated commitment.[44] The diary offers only oblique hints at the relationships among his wide circle of acquaintances, mediated according to still powerful dictates of custom. Friendship can, perhaps, be assumed in some instances, as with the 1669 entry for 18 January: ' Robb. Plumpton dined with me, spt with him att Atk'son [a local hostelry] 8d.' Gifts, such as the goose sent by a relative in the winter of 1669, circulated between kin much as they had for centuries, tokens of esteem and obligation. Natalie Davis's reflections on gift-giving in sixteenth-century France have resonance for this time and place, when 'many presents changed hands irrespective of the rhythm of season and rite of passage. They were part of the complicated history of obligations and expectations between persons and households of roughly the same status, including those of kin.'[45] In Smart's diary, customary events imbued with an unspecified emotional quotient march beside numerate chronicles of cost. Both expressed his rank, gender, occupation and the time in which he wrote. Then, at seventy-eight, widowed, ill and facing death, he could no longer keep up his daily reports. His entries scrawled, his hand failing, Smart's strength was on the ebb and he wrote only once a week, choosing at the last to record weekly expenses for February and March of 1678. Smart gave precedence to the numeric notations at the disciplinary core of his life. Over the course of the diary William Smart also routinely noted religious observances, saints' days, prayers said, psalms sung, sermons read and services attended forming a quotidian refrain.[46] Smart ended all reference to religious matters in the second-to-last month of his diary and, if faith persisted, religious enumeration did not. However, for five more weeks he persevered, counting weekly expenditures in the face of failing strength. In his last entry Smart recounts the fair that had returned once again to Durham – a fitting confirmation of the commercial life which defined him. William Smart died in the winter of the following year and his property was inventoried in January of 1679, with personal and domestic goods valued at £40 and money lent out in secure or desperate debts amounting to more than £400.[47] In Smart we see how meditations on commerce were usurping the monopoly of self-examination once exclusive to religion.

A quarter-century later, an exemplar of the next generation of male accountants was equally immersed in the minutiae of record-keeping. Thomas Mort, a wealthy country gentleman and landowner in southwest Lancashire, began his domestic account book well schooled in the objectives of the quantitative narrative. His opening notations, in March 1703, were probably a continuation from an earlier volume and proceeded in a vein with which he was comfortable:

March 26th 1703, pd to Sam: Stockton ye 4 lb quarterly
       assessmt for Ashley   – 03: 06: 06
       27th pd to my Br[other] 6d wch he had to
       Mr Martin for mending my watch   – 00: 00: 06
       29th given att Michl Wards to ye maid dining
       there ye Thursday   – 00: 01: 00

31st given to Will: Co: Maidsley's boy bringing
piggy home; & then having a dogg from Hiskin   – 00: 01: 00
upon ye 30th pd for 5 doz:n of white cuffs att
4/.d the dozen bought att Ormskirk   – 00: 01: 10$\frac{1}{2}$/48

This became a twenty-two-year chronicle, from 1703 to 1725, detailing his familial, business and neighbourly ties from the position of the authoritative accountant. Vails to servants and charitable impulses were listed routinely, as were items which caught his fancy or expenses from his properties. Syllabub glasses, claret, cinnamon and a new edition of Aesop's Fables were priced precisely, along with physic for a cow, Christmas gifts for servants and twill cloth for flour sacks. Mort made none of the overt religious observances found among Smart's sparse entries; he was, however, more forthcoming in itemizing the activities filling his days. Whatever their differences, both Smart and Mort exemplify men of property who subscribed to a belief pre-eminent in their circles that the principal duty of sound men was to keep clear numeric records as a testament to their standing. Life in his brother's house, years with his serving man, visits with friends and family, his passion for books and his common acts of charity took a numbered form; customary practices were still respected by the author, but reduced to costs in shillings and pence.[49]

The volume produced by Joshua Wharton, a Bristol mercer, is another male-authored chronology of home life filtered through the accountant's lens. Wharton's self-described domestic account book runs from 1733 to 1736, charting his later adult life at a time when at least one of his children was married. Accounting precepts infused this work but, in this case, neither his training nor the structure of the ledger could enforce uniformity. One of the most telling features of this volume is the tension between the two cursive forms (rational numeric or discursive narrative) and between the two priorities and two contending mentalities mirrored in these mediums. Wharton was trained in monetized reckoning, an essential ingredient in his business. As with so many men, as well as educated elite women, he transferred these teachings to a private domestic domain, affirming the value of this concept through the careful listing of homely expenditures, noting as well the routine and special indulgences afforded his wife, daughters, family and friends. Mrs Wharton's clothing outlays were meticulously detailed: 'for a paire Blew Stockins … 3s 6d', 'for making 2 Gouns & Dying them'. As with the earlier Italian patriarch, the reins of domestic finances passed through his hands. Gifts were also marked, such as the 'Barell oisters' sent to 'Cozen Hicks … as token', the 'Pint Brandy & 3 lb Tobacco' sent to family in Cromhall as a 'token', signs of affection and esteem. These entries represented debits for which there was no formal expectation of repayment, beyond the unstated consolation of kinship. In the autumn, cider was dispatched in copious quantities to cousins and friends and, in turn, Wharton noted with satisfaction the receipt of a 'chese'.[50] What Davis terms 'the chain of food-giving'[51] were exercises in shared consumption and had a more subtly productive end than could be tracked in formal liberal economics. The balance of normative cultural accounts could not tot up these exchanges as bookkeeping techniques demanded. Wharton commemorated momentous events with material expressions of sentiment like 'a halfe a lb Chocolett' sent to his future son-in-law – an emotional economy interlaced these notations, even as the price was inscribed on the page.[52]

Smart, Mort and Wharton represent generations of men who absorbed and adopted the manly precepts of numerate record-keeping, making this their practical and moral compass.[53] Personal records took many forms and some chroniclers put greater emphasis on letters and discursive diaries, while others subscribed to purely numerate notation.[54] To some, private life demanded no less systematic a reckoning than business affairs. Wharton, however, could not confine himself to neat ledger entries, occasionally breaking through the fetters of numerate regulation in the face of overwhelming emotions. Among the many pages of systematic, measured entries are unexpected bursts of narrative, recounting events that, to Wharton, could not be abstracted into itemized costings. Wrenching tales of the illness of one daughter and the lingering decline and funeral of another form two of the longest narratives. In 1735 he wrote of a dramatic exchange of letters with his new son-in-law as his oldest daughter fell to a sudden terrible illness; Wharton was consumed by the frantic search for a doctor to attend her and the passionate hope of her recovery.

> 27 Dec 1735 Saterday my son Stephens sent a man and his horse with a Letter to acquaint me his Wife was very ill and so Desire Dr Hardwick to goe to Cirencester to her which he promised me if he could possible goe he would, butt, the badnes of ye wether etc prevented him from going ... Thursday night I had a Letter which gave an acct, the ffever was sum thing abated and had sum hopes of my Daughters Recovery: Friday: 2 Janu^y we sent by the Cirencester Carrier 6 mins Pies and 2 Cheny orenges.[55]

His description jumps from the page, scrawled in paragraph form above a list of additional gifts intended to speed her recovery: 'sent my Daughter Stephens 2 l. Chocolett'.[56] Even as an experienced businessman,

Wharton's expressions of family life could not be embodied in numbers alone and followed a hybrid form where the numerate and discursive forms intertwined.[57]

Domestic financial records were intensely personal exercises representing hours of careful labour over years or over a lifetime, a commitment to a quantitative representation of the domestic. Richard Latham's account book covers almost the whole of the adult life of a yeoman farmer from 1727 to 1767, a compendium of family and farming fiscal activities not easily disentangled. Although Latham was of lower social standing than Thomas Mort, gentleman and scholar, both records arise from rural south Lancashire and it is interesting to observe how widely this 'formal system of writing'[58] had spread throughout male ranks. This is an exceptional document in several respects, both in the duration covered and in the social rank of the record keeper. Without servants, virtually all the work was done by the family, and yet Latham carved out the hours to create this chronicle week by week and year by year, measuring the passage of time and the growing prosperity hard won, inscribed in this small leather-covered ledger. Latham's account is mute on many questions, however, such as the visits and voluntary labour of kin, when, as Lorna Weatherill notes, 'many favours and informal help would not have been recorded', help on which all relied. Like the majority of bookkeepers, Latham was largely silent on emotional questions, less forthcoming than Wharton, accepting the premiss behind the structure of the accounts. Only the uniquely detailed description of his mother's gravestone hints at the unstated emotions.[59] In contrast, Joshua Wharton exemplifies the accountant for whom, on some occasions, the mechanics of numeric notation were too limiting an articulation. These telling lapses speak to the growing pre-eminence of reckoning among literate propertied men across a range of occupations, as well as to the circumstances in which at least one man found this form wanting. Wharton's intent was to construct a financial catalogue of domestic life; the emotional force of that life, however, demanded another kind of expression.

Nevertheless, the impetus behind this numerate transformation was powerful and inexorable, though the applications took heterogeneous forms among men and women, richer and poorer, city and country dwellers. Household costs were listed by and for aristocratic and wealthy women long before the start of this study.[60] Well known examples from the seventeenth century illustrate the spread of this discipline. The spinster Joyce Jefferies is probably best known as a moneylender;[61] however, aside from the 'diaries', in which she accounted for monies lent and repaid, Jefferies also kept detailed books relating her annual 'disbursements'. With a yearly income of about £360 to £650, between 1637 and 1646[62] Jefferies carefully listed costs, from the 'new russet hat, felt, from London' for 15s to the 6d given to the maid who found her spectacles. But her entries was more than stark lists of debits, revealing the emotional circuit of her life as well as the financial – her joy at the safe birth of her cousin's new son and her status as gossip at the birth of another child – blending throughout the nuances of her economic and social life.[63] In Jefferies's diaries, as well as in the extensive record of household expenses kept by Lady Grisell Baillie from 1692 to 1733, and in the more modest accounts of Sarah Fell, from 1673 to 1678, the chatelaine's duties are recalled. Neither Jefferies's, Baillie's nor Fell's numeracy, nor their engagement with accounting, was remarkable considering the status of these women. Indeed, as literate women were encouraged to think about their domestic roles in a more rationale way, records of this agenda among their sex become increasingly common.[64]

Property-holding families produced a growing flow of domestic ledgers, more of which were composed by women and more of which trickled into archives to survive to the present day. From the Littleton family of Staffordshire comes a small volume inscribed 'Ann Whitehall her book', in which personal, household and charitable expenses were inscribed, an activity deemed so commonplace to a later ancestor that 'Nothing in the Book of any Consequence' was scrawled across the cover.[65] Mrs Elizabeth Dummer was another lady of the period, in touch with metropolitan events though resident in a Hampshire village except during the London season. Her personal accounts span the mid years of the eighteenth century, from 1736 to 1765, and reflect an education in numeric principles consistent with her standing and her sex. In one small section Dummer lists monies received, initially from an agent or her father. Her mother's periodic generosity is also noted, while in 1742 she is explicit in her notation of £40 income 'My own', subsequently citing income from annuities, investments and legacies.[66] If household costs were included in this account then they were hidden in the anonymous listing of bills from suppliers. Clothing, accoutrements and servants' fees comprise the bulk of the entries, with notes for charitable gifts and payments for the schooling of nurse's children among the steady stream of payments. Mrs Dummer managed her annual personal budget of £125 to just under £300, with an average expenditure of about £250, from the 1740s onward. Only occasionally does she report the 'Money I can't account for' or the sum of £35 'Taken for Card money' in 1751.[67] Propertied women, such as Dummer, were more commonly schooled in commercial precepts as the eighteenth century continued, active participants in the commercial nexus. Dummer may have been one of the numerous female investors whose income through their adult years rested in sound, conservative investments at 4 per cent.[68] She was also immersed in a complex network of kin and neighbourly ties, but the allusions are brief and oblique. The sorts of favours and obligations she dispensed had been common for countless generations: buying goods for those more distant from shops, like 'Tea for my Aunt B' or 'Mrs Ports Wigg'; offering charity for 'poor people' at Winton; giving perquisites for 'Aunts Maid Hooper' and for the 'Servants at Christmas'.[69]

Women's shift to numeric record-keeping was a gradual process, at a slower pace than men's, just as literacy rates varied between the sexes. Among literate plebeian women, more traditional discursive forms were often preferred as a means to articulate their relationships and codify the facets of their lives. Neither their conception of the world, their education nor their place within the community fitted comfortably within a purely quantitative measure.[70] Mary Abbott epitomizes this perspective. She began life at Wapping Wall, the daughter of a mariner, born in 1713, a contemporary of Dummer. In common with other literate women Abbott recorded her periodic thoughts and fears in a type of intermittent memoir. While young she inscribed salutary quotations and stories in a soft-covered 'Commonplace Book'. A later notebook captures events from 1738 to 1791 and is entitled by Mary Abbott 'Things to be Remembered 1738'. She married in that year, and in those to follow Mary Abbott recorded her experiences as a mother, marking the birth of her children and their periodic illnesses, as well as deaths. Events such as these formed the fabric of women's lives, the very ubiquity of which in no way extinguishes the emotions embodied in these records.[71] Her first child was born dead, in 1739; she survived the ordeal with difficulty – 'I was Lad [laid] By The Docter of a Son Born Dead had a very bad Time', reads her short entry. Abbott's mingled pain and relief are palpable with the safe birth of her beloved Tommy in 1740. His inexplicable illness eight years later was a life-altering experience, and her lengthy account of his suffering and death stand as a centrepiece to her young adult life. Abbott recounted happier occasions as well, recording trials survived and fears overcome. In that regard it is one of the rare surviving documents prior to 1750 illuminating a female life and perspective from the plebeian ranks, albeit from a family that slowly rose in status. This diary exemplifies facets of the 'culture of women' that Mendelson and Crawford describe as 'closely connected to the forces of life and death, to sexuality, and to the communal life of society'.[72] Money, when it is discussed at all, appears in the form of gifts and charitable bequests. Doctors may have been paid, along with school fees and local tithes, but such costings did not concern this chronicler; they were simply a background to the main facets of life. Abbot's 'Things to Remember' reflected nothing of the counting house.[73] It would be in her granddaughter's generation that these procedures predominated among middle-class women; it was they who commonly turned to numerate forms as the paradigm of family discourse. Abbott's granddaughter clearly and unequivocally embraced the priorities of quantitative calculation as the sole and ideal form for chronicling domestic life. For Mary Abbott, however, episodes of the everyday held an emotional force and took a storied form which defied reckoning.

The spread of quantitative culture through England, as with much of Western society, was irregular and uneven, reflecting the particularities of regions, sex and rank.[74] In many circles, the heterodoxies of custom persisted and ancient reciprocities prevailed. with only a gradual or intermittent addition of the calculative practices consistent with liberal and utilitarian theories. Yet, even as traditional community practices persisted within an evolving moral economy, formal economic markers assumed greater and greater importance. In tracking the spread of the accounting mentality I have relied from time to time on pertinent North American examples which illustrate persistent traditional practices, or adaptations to new quantitative thinking. In the first instance, Laurel Ulrich uncovered very suggestive material in the diary of a Maine midwife. Ulrich's work on Maine diaries, and Nancy Osterud's work on New York diaries, suggest important gender difference in the mentality and priorities of many male and female diarists in the eighteenth and early nineteenth centuries, echoes of the English examples, in spite of the geographic interval. Ulrich confirmed Osterud's observation that male diarists, on the whole, perceived their relations within a clear pattern of credit and debit accounting. Tutored in this discipline formally or informally, they accepted and adopted this numerate schedule as a tool, theorizing their personal interactions accordingly.[75] The moneylender William Smart was deeply sensitive to the oscillations in his clients' fortunes and to their capacity to repay, writing with satisfaction when 'Welsh dischargd his bond' and with gloom that 'W: Stevenson fayleth'.[76] In England, those who kept detailed domestic accounts were part of the same Western movement of quantification culture that travelled to the North American colonies. However, in concert with women such as Mary Abbott, Ulrich contends that exclusively monetized relationships were *not* the norm among the women diarists she uncovered in eighteenth and early nineteenth-century America. This is one of her most important findings for this study, suggesting the persistent customary values among even middle-ranked women diarists of this generation. Despite the spread and normalization of accounting precepts, these women did not yet perceive their world according to the credo of accounting manuals. Ulrich explains that 'Martha Ballard's accounts are indirect and vague. ... While it is quite clear from other entries in the diary that Martha Ballard had [for example] a long-standing economic relation with Mrs. Edson only with great effort can the credits and debits in that account be extracted and arranged.'[77]

Now, it might be said that Ulrich's findings have little significance for the English scene. Distance from large urban centres, it might be argued, limited general access to accounting training for women in America. But Ulrich concludes that gender differences, rather than geography, account for this phenomenon, a phenomenon which may well have been heightened by the influences of social rank and locale. The time period in which these examples were gleaned was also a telling factor, as later examples make clear. In this period, all the male and female American diarists were engaged in similar sorts of interactions within their communities; they exchanged labour, sold services and shared some resources, helping in times of need. Martha Ballard was a midwife and apothecary for her community, with a husband who followed a skilled trade as well as working his property. Nonetheless, there were striking distinctions in men's and women's perceptions of their relations with neighbours and community. Ulrich notes that 'men tended to assign ... transactions a monetary value even when no money was exchanged, while women "generally recorded their cooperative work as a direct, personal relationship, unmediated by market value"'.[78] This difference may well have been heightened further by women's involvement in reciprocal productive and customary activities of the family and community that defined their adult years. Moreover, in both England and America, even middle-class women did not yet receive routine instruction in numerate skills beyond the basics, and certainly not in the first half of the eighteenth century when Abbott and Ballard were both being educated.[79] Where women like Martha Ballard or Mary Abbott did write, they constructed a form at odds with rational numerate ideals, suggesting different priorities and different rates of acceptance of quantitative precepts. Training in accounts was certainly prescribed for some women by some authors. However, a continuing lag in training for plebeian women doubtless contributed to a persistently gender-based moral economy which valued interpersonal and customary practices in ways different from the increasingly utilitarian credo of the age. Quite simply, family, friend and neighbourly relations posed a complex set of priorities that resisted formal numerate valuations.

In all parts of the West, men and women of different social ranks, in a variety of circumstances, were being challenged by the combined visions of economic liberalism and an increasingly numerate and quantitative culture. Commercial and political elites most quickly allied with these concepts, although even within these circles family heads did not immediately place enlightened financial self-interest ahead of kin and community. For example, Laurence Fontaine demonstrates that eighteenth-century French traditional elites regularly lent money to relatives when there was little chance that the loans would be repaid. This generosity was seen as one of the obligations of more affluent relatives, at least for a time.[80] Craig Muldrew's extensive study of the social context of English credit relations affirms that early modern sensibilities required the lending or guaranteeing of loans to family and neighbours. However, even within the family, the strains of competing allegiances became more visible throughout the eighteenth century, with growing tensions between customary obligations and the commercial imperatives of profit and probity. Should the minimization of risk take priority over traditional neighbourly and family duties? Over the eighteenth and nineteenth centuries the most intimate relations were being scrutinized by the calculus of potential profit and loss by a growing sector of the middle classes.[81]

There were many more accounts kept routinely over the eighteenth and nineteenth centuries, recording the most basic household information. The authors of these chronicles responded to the numeric imperative, even if they did not meet the standards enshrined in manuals of accounting. Muldrew concludes that, even among tradesmen, double-entry books were rare before 1700, even as the growing number of instructional guides commanded attention.[82] These texts were part of a expanding literature addressing the requirements of the numerate life and, as the second half of eighteenth century progressed, there was more frequent instruction for women.[83] Annual pocketbooks, diaries and almanacs included tables of weights, costs and other valuations to encourage their readers, male and female, to think in standard numeric terms and to dispense with customary forms. By the end of the century, printed diaries 'for Ladies' included space for the keeping of accounts.[84] Overall, the culture of accounting was set in place during this era, however imperfectly applied by new acolytes. Yet, as the seat of sentiment,[85] as the site of most emotional ties, the household itself offered a particular challenge to the tenets of quantification. Capturing a vision of the household within the medium of accounts required that categories be identified and assigned value that had no easy measure, or that practices be omitted from domestic account books if their properties proved too intractable.

Gender categories and accounting for the household

With each generation, more middling and genteel families endeavoured to keep better and more accurate records that would capture household activities and the conduct of its inmates. By the late eighteenth and early nineteenth centuries, a further conjunction of factors affected perceptions of female enterprise, arising from the formalization of economic categories in the wider society and the codification of women's domestic labour. One of the peculiarities of women's many activities, in and out of the home, was their almost complete invisibility in the formulation of liberalism and liberal economics. The economic philosophy, theorized by John Locke, Adam Smith, Jeremy Bentham, John Stuart Mill and others, was founded on concepts of individualism. These authors, with the exception of Mill, accepted existing gender structures and ignored inconvenient gender differences in definitions of fundamental economic activities.[86] Adam Smith was not alone in doubting women's capacity to engage in rational economic judgement, and he felt justified, therefore, in excluding their endeavours from serious consideration, whether in the household or in the community.[87]

Leonora Davidoff and Catherine Hall have shown eloquently how the domestic resort was reshaped by the early nineteenth century as a refuge from the world of commerce for industrious husbands, even as wives' and sisters' financial capital and labour made important (sometimes hidden) contributions to men's business lives. Paradoxes abounded within the evolving Victorian home, as most middle-class women were discouraged from taking paid employment; but the angels of the house were strongly encouraged to apply management techniques to their household tasks in order to cope more efficiently. In addition to other homely duties, modern management demanded that the wife assume the mantle of auditor, with many called to account for their budgets by their husbands. Not surprisingly, the wives and daughters of the middle class were called first to these duties. Priscilla Wakefield, active in the early savings bank movement, was an exponent of female training in domestic economy. The arts of careful economy were not needed by titled or wealthy genteel women, she opined; however, the 'art of œconomising' should be a prudent woman's constant guide. Early tutelage in basic mathematics was essential to prepare a young woman for the keeping of accounts, ready for whatever her future held in store.[88] Husband and wife had always taken different roles in family life; what was distinct during this era was the growing insistence that housewifely skill was epitomized through the creation of numerate records.

By 1800, one author insisted that no servant should be hired 'that could not read, write and keep a common account',[89] attempting to bring the domestic sphere in line with utilitarian business practice, discouraging customary perquisites among servants, introducing a higher rationality to households.[90] To this end, management skills were essential, proclaimed an anonymous author, for the comfort of the husband and family, 'which is better understood and more valued in England, than in any other country in the world'.[91] Reform of the household was now the pervasive aim of many domestic activists. Little wonder that, by the early nineteenth century, committed disciples made such efforts to achieve the objectives outlined for the bookkeeping family. Nevertheless, the husband's role as the domestic accountant did not immediately change, nor did every male householder cheerfully divest himself of this authority, even as the fashion for female accounting grew. Certainly, expectations mounted over the late eighteenth century that wives should grapple with accountancy, but some husbands were apparently happy to maintain the *status quo* and hold the reins of domestic finance. For some, the power which came with this task was sufficient; for others, the technical deficiencies of their wives made the job unavoidable; while for still other men the intermingling of business costs with the household budget made their continued bookkeeping efforts a logical decision.[92] Prescriptive texts increasingly assigned the whole of such tasks to the wife, even if superintended by her husband, and for those needing guideposts to marital bliss and domestic solvency there was a great deal of advice to be had.[93]

One noteworthy guide is the *Home Book; or, Young Housekeeper's Assistant*, a sophisticated manual couched in the form of letters from a fictive grandmother to her granddaughter. Accounting literature employed an extraordinary malleability of gender: North feminised the discipline itself, as did Defoe, who followed him, as something to be embraced by men,[94] while Monteage and this later fictional grandmother made accounting more palatable to literate women through the reversal of gender roles. Here the grandmotherly author offered a cautionary tale of two young lovers, well suited and newly married, who barely skirted bankruptcy because of incautious expenditures and profound ignorance of accounts. She advised that domestic bliss on a budget could be achieved only through the assiduous employment of a series of five cross-referenced ledgers and memoranda: the kitchen, weekly account, cash account, commonplace and annual account books, a 'system of books' first used centuries before to order commercial ventures.[95] Readers were called to 'unremitting attention to the duties of family economy' and, to give added weight to her instructions, she insisted that 'regularity ... has been justly called "the soul of business".[96] Thus, the new bulwarks of the family were cross-referenced ledgers, the content traced by the housewife's careful pen in a ceaseless struggle for thrift and solvency.

Studies of nineteenth-century women's diaries have tended to focus on accessible forms that 'speak to us without the need of a mediator',[97] privileging the narrative, leading some to suppose that there were few other surviving types of personal or domestic chronicles. In fact, what have been called account-book diaries survive in numbers from the nineteenth century, both in North America and in England, reflecting the period's more intense preoccupation with domestic management.[98] Mary Young was one of the most thoroughgoing exemplars of the new ideals. The granddaughter of Mary Abbott, Young's expression of family life epitomized the rational, numerate calculus typical of the time and her social rank. Mary Young's husband made his mark as a Thames-based shipbuilder and later Member of Parliament, and Mrs Young applied her passion for household accounting after her marriage in 1813. The surviving products of her labours summarize from 1817 to 1844 with exceptional detail and precision, charting as well her evolution as a bookkeeper and her wholehearted commitment to this calling. Mary Young began with basic record-keeping, lists of money spent at the butcher, baker, fishmonger, greengrocer or poulterer, followed by monthly totals.[99] These rudimentary memoranda were soon superseded by registers both more detailed and more inclusive.

Mary Young next devised an 'Abstract of Housekeeping Expenses for the Years' 1817 to 1825, neatly summarizing her family's fortunes, distillations of the minutiae of daily purchases.[100] In the 1830s, large, gold-leafed ledgers were filled with itemized columns of accounts divided by categories – household linen and furniture, children's clothes, books, Mr. Young's accounts, wages, medicine and fees, charity and 'My own Clothes'. The size and quality of the weighty leather-bound volumes, the gold lettering on their spines and the quality of the paper bespeak the importance awarded these quotidian observances. The repetitive ceremonies of account-taking delineated her days and the enduring task itself reinforced its significance, reflecting what Foucault saw as a new pattern of control.[101] In this instance, however, institutional change was rooted in the most private of bodies, the family. Invoices, pen and ledgers were assembled in a space over which she presided. The looping script is never blurred, the entries are never aborted, her timetable is everywhere apparent. In this day-to-day adherence, Catherine Bell observes: 'ritual is more complex than the mere communication of meanings and values; it is a set of activities that construct particular types of meanings and values in specific ways. Hence, rather than ritual as the vehicle for the *expression* of authority, practice theorists tend to explore how ritual is a vehicle for the *construction* of relationships of authority and submission.'[102] Young accepted the rightness of her meticulous reckoning, committing her time, energy and intelligence.

Whatever emotional turmoil paralleled some notations, it left no overt trace. A son's departure to boarding school, a child's illness and doctor's visit, these received only the most perfunctory entries as itemized costs to be inscribed. If her concern over such events took a narrative form they were nowhere in these ledgers. For Mary Young and her ilk, the emotional entanglements of family life were smoothed out and reduced in size to single entries in assigned categories. Annual purchases and expenditures of all sorts were enumerated, from shoe ribbons to the cost of a church pew. Hospitality and social interactions were similarly itemized in a manner entirely distinct from the notions of previous centuries. Outings were costed from the 'Exhibition of fleas 4/-' to 'seeing House of Commons 7/6'. Under the 'Miscellaneous' heading was mention of ginger beer, 'Lunch in Town 5/-', bird glasses, pink dye, rabbits, doll's clothes and the hundreds of other small consignments that formed the fabric of Victorian family life. Expenses in each category were then summarized and could be charted across the years, cross-referenced with total yearly accounts, the whole offered as a model of a rational family memorialized.[103]

Mary Young, like her grandmother, Mary Abbott, felt impelled to chronicle her home life: both women lost several children in childhood; others survived and flourished. Yet, despite these common experiences, their written representations were strikingly different. The mental lenses through which they interpreted their roles and their lives, their duties as wives and mothers, were moulded by different elucidatory forms. The intervening years witnessed an intensification of numerate capitalist culture and an emphasis on quantitative measurement previously unmatched, all of which shaped Young's ambitions and accomplishments. Young exceeded many, but not all, middle-class women in her diligent application of accounting precepts, but she was far from unique in subscribing to this domestic regime.[104]

By 1845, housewifery was described in terms of pure commercial management, with the 'profit' in the home arising from the wife's frugality. Charts, tables and accounting forms, published annually, enabled the provident housewife to plot her course whether with £1 a week or £40,000 per year, and publishers throughout the country offered every variety of assistance as part of the now pre-eminent numeric discourse of family life.[105] While 'comfort' and order were the purported end products of household management, the housewife was also advised to make her struggles to this end all but invisible. Hester Chapone opined that economy was central to womanly virtue, but insisted that her readers 'avoid all parade and bustle' in the management of their homes. 'The best sign of a house being well governed is that nobody's attention is called to any of the little affairs of it, but all goes so well … that one is not led to make remarks upon any thing, nor to observe any extraordinary effort that produces the general result of ease and elegance.'[106] The running of a respectable home demanded no overt sign of exertion, for, in the looking-glass world of the Victorian household, domestic labour did not constitute toil, household management was an ephemeral act never brought to public notice, while family life sounded more and more like the fodder of utilitarian commerce.

The middle-class family took on a different form over the nineteenth century, replete with ambiguities, as Victorian culture sentimentalized women's family lives, yet sought to regulate this sanctuary like a counting house.[107] In an era of expanding material choice, rationality was enforced on the female consumer through the discipline of tables, punctually made up, furnishing concrete evidence of probity, offered up to her husband's scrutiny. John Tosh describes the careful supervision the head of Wellington College afforded his young wife's accounts. Tosh considered that the 'wife's effective management of the household under the overall control of her husband was a practical application of the principle of separate spheres'.[108] Given the origins of this numerate discipline, and the retail expenditures which went into each line of accounts, its separateness is open to conjecture. Though Tosh overlooks the ambiguities inherent in applied commercial skills in the home, he rightly observes that the formalization of domestic accounts presented another arena for the play of gender power dynamics. But how 'separate' these spheres were remains a contested question. Husbands trained in commercial skills could, if they wished, audit domestic records, comparing their efficacy with those of the market place. Tosh notes that 'Domesticity supposedly allowed workhorses and calculating machines to become men again, by exposing them to human rhythms and human affections.'[109] In fact, the 'calculating machines' were not transposed at the doorstep, as Charles Dickens's Clara Copperfield found to her dismay.

> 'I kept my housekeeping-book regularly, and balanced it with Mr Copperfield every night,' cried my mother in another burst of distress … 'And I am sure we never had a word of difference respecting it, except when Mr Copperfield objected to my threes and fives being too much like each other, or to my putting tails to my sevens and nines,' resumed my mother in another burst.[110]

In 1871, the letter pages of *The English-Woman's Domestic Magazine* were filled with questions from neophyte housewives on matters of budgeting and domestic politics. How to make up for money overspent in previous months? How to follow a budget appropriate to family income? Respondents offered advice and testimonials aplenty. Similar exchanges had been published by the *Daily Telegraph* in the summer of 1868, where the question of provident marriage practices occasioned intense debate for weeks. Cautionary tales of trials overcome, or economies observed, were offered up to a fascinated readership, who replied in kind with narratives of their private battles to marry and budget well. One bruised young swain recounted being spurned by his sweetheart after she estimated the income needed for a comfortable marriage. 'Her reply, enclosing a budget, suggested without subtlety that delay was necessary, as her estimate was that at least £217 16s [annually] would be needed.'[111] The consensus among correspondents was that newly married wives should study their accounts, above all else, as the basis of a happy marriage, and on that subject published authors were in general agreement.[112]

Gail Campbell's extensive work with New Brunswick family papers led to the identification of a short journal written between November 1878 and April 1879.[113] The creator of this document was Mary Hill, eldest daughter of a member of the New Brunswick Legislative Assembly, in Atlantic Canada. During the winter and spring of 1878–79, Mary Hill rented a house in the small port town of St Andrews, New Brunswick, on the border with Maine. In this second North American example, from a region in close proximity to that of Martha Ballard, there is every evidence of numerate calculation among the generation of women, of the same social class, who succeeded Ballard. Mary Hill came from loyalist stock, but with continuing strong family ties to New England, where she attended school. She was raised in a prosperous middle-class family, absorbed in the social, political and religious life of the region and beyond, living independently as a single woman, now in her late forties. The record Hill constructed reflects the training she received and the preoccupations of the period; but it is in many ways an amalgam of reckoning and traditional neighbourly activities. The diary resonates with the culture of reciprocity, at the same time as Hill kept a careful and consistent reckoning of all her debits and credits, employing the vocabulary of accounting:

Wednesday Nov 13th [1878] Debit
      1 p[in]t milk from Mrs Craig
      2 lbs lard, 1 gal Ker[osine?], Mrs Campbell

Thursday 14th 1 lb raisins, F. Campbell
           1 oz Clove
           2 oz Nutmeg
                            Paid Nov 22nd

Income and expenditure are prudently recorded. Nonetheless, for all its punctilious accounting, the diary was not a simple listing of debits and credits and it bears little resemblance to the rigid formulaic chronicles produced by Mary Young. Hill's neighbourly ties are fully in evidence, forming the substance of her day and the material of her journal: trips to the shops and post office, visiting and receiving visits – 'Maria Sutherland, Anne Porter and Mrs Campbell called. Lizzie took lesson on Piano', reads the 5 March entry. 'Ida, George, Albert, Anne, Mary and G Johnson in the evening, they made candy in Kitchen', she wrote for 8 March 1879. Friendships and favours within her circle were a signal part of Hill's life, a feature of equal weight to the meticulous budgeting. Hill, like Emma Chadwick Stretch, a British emigrant to neighbouring Prince Edward Island, followed the now fully articulated middle-class female expression of numerate costing, interspersed with other personal and domestic notations, a pattern that survives in the dozens of extant account diaries from that era.[114]

By 1900, all literate young women were expected to master domestic accounts. Mrs Valentine, the editor of the 1895 *Girl's Home Companion*, included a clear exposition of the household duties a young person might shoulder, including accounting, a fact so self-evident that no space was expended on details, since 'so many good housekeeper's-books are now published that much need not be said'.[115] Of course, not all women, even middle-class women, practised accountancy with equal diligence – prescription and practice did not always match. But this task might be picked up in times of crisis. About 100 years after Mary Young began her accounts, she inspired a descendant. At the back of one of Young's ledgers is a telling addition, the work of a palpably unhappy woman during the Great War. Mrs Dallas Young had read and perhaps been inspired by the meticulous entries constructed by her forebear, promising regularity in chaotic times. The writer identified herself and defiantly stated her purpose: 'Mrs Dallas Young begun Aug. 16th 1918, during these hard times of WAR whereby the bare necessities of LIFE do cost more than double that which beforetimes they did. And that was money enough, God wot!' Her resolution lasted two weeks, during which time she listed the expenses of chemist, grocer, baker, wages, washing, fares, eggs, dairy, bread, writing paper and, on one occasion, 'soldiers (Peter)'. She did not persist, but instead resorted to verse, lamenting her straitened middle-class condition and the burden of accounting that Mary Young had mastered so well in different times.

> What is the food?
> Where is the use?
>
> Five Pounds a week –
> no less – no more
> Keep within – thats all.
> Who cares?
>
> Maybe it will be better
> When the war is over.[116]

The trials of wartime, an absent husband and soaring prices prompted these two expositions: one numerate, the other poetic. Mrs Dallas Young found no solace in the numbered categories treasured by her predecessor, throwing off their mediating structures with relative abandon. If their authority proved inadequate to the travails of this Mrs (Dallas) Young, accounts were widely accepted as a sensible resort for modern housewives from the middle class and beyond. But here, too, there was both resistance and variation in expression.[117] In the later nineteenth century, strong neighbourhood and kinship ties continued in many working-class districts through acts of sharing and community events, organized to a large degree by working-class women. The cultural practices in these communities were sometimes antithetical to middle-class norms.[118] However, numerate discipline spread even into poor districts with the promotion of savings banks and penny savings banks among youth and children, combined with the weekly family contributions to burial, clothing or crockery clubs, fixing a pattern of monetary calculation that delineated even very modest incomes.[119] Yet, in these precincts, the doctrines of domestic accounting were still slow to claim ascendancy. An initiative by the Fabian Women's Group, between 1909 and 1913, confirms the continuing cultural divide between the dominant numerate middle-class culture and that of the working poor, especially in matters related to household management. As the century opened, reforming Fabian women determined to uncover the hardships endured by south London wives struggling to balance their husbands' earnings with family needs. The Fabian women hoped that a study of these desperate domestic economies could result in social reforms. Subjects were selected carefully, families with 'respectable men in full work', the wives 'quiet, decent' and their neighbourhood 'drearily decent'. Next, the female reformers sought to quantify the patterns of domestic budgeting, the habits of making-do that characterized these families. But to uncover the data they deemed most essential, the facts with the greatest political and cultural weight, the south London housewives were asked to keep accounts; only numeric tabulations would satisfy government bureaucrats, social agencies and social reformers. The exchanges between the reforming Fabians, steeped in the tenets of statistical evaluation, and the women of south London attest to the continuing divide between the now normative quantitative culture and the different sort of reckoning that endured among the working poor. The Fabian observer noted: 'The women were with one consent appalled at the idea of keeping accounts. Not that they did not "know it in their heads," as they anxiously explained; but the clumsy writing and the difficult spelling, and the huge figures which refused to keep within any appointed bounds, and wandered at will about the page, thoroughly daunted them.'[120] Illiteracy was a bar for a number of women, several of whose husbands offered themselves as scribes. But while the husbands' writing was 'excellent', the men's knowledge of domestic affairs was partial and incomplete, with little detailed knowledge of the shifts employed to get by. The housewives practised a 'kind of mental arithmetic' which enabled them to make ends meet; but the calculations absorbing these working-class women took a more traditional discursive form, what the Fabian women described as 'a prolix style, founded, doubtless, on the maternal manner of recollecting'.[121] The south London housewives still conceived of their interactions in terms of relational narratives, explaining the context of decisions, valuing the adjudication of each purchase, frustrating reformers steeped in the rationale of stark numeric tabulations. This social disjuncture vividly illuminates the fractured and fragmentary progress of the 'quantitative model' in the early twentieth century, long after most women accepted the numbered duties of housewifery.

Conclusion

Mary Poovey's richly theorized analysis of the rise of the modern (numeric) fact begins with a review of new systems of numeracy, like double-entry accounting, and continues with detailed analyses of the offshoots which evolved and their accompanying philosophical applications, such as political economy. Poovey emphasizes the immense significance of the epistemological forms which developed with the spread of quantification. But she points out the difficulty in tracking this process, as 'few scholars have tackled subjects related to the history of numerical representation in eighteenth-century Britain, and even those who have done so have found it almost impossible to assemble evidence. Moreover, any answer we give must remain partial because the determinants of this semantic revolution are so numerous and diverse.'[122] This chapter is a contribution to the broader history of popular numeracy, in particular the impact of accounting on the household, when non-elite men and women began to apply a calculative discipline to their everyday lives. The impetus to quantify was unevenly and intermittently expressed by the majority of people who lived their lives in the subsequent centuries. Their reticence was not seen to be a problem for many years, since, as Poovey notes, even in the eighteenth century 'many Britons did not consider counting particularly relevant to knowledge or see costing as essential to value'.[123] However, by the eighteenth century, changes in thinking were well under way, as is illustrated by the growing number of enumerators at work, even within the home. Not satisfied with a basic exercise in personal costing, such as was provided after death through a probate inventory,[124] elite and middling men, followed by their wives, sisters and servants, began constructing daily domestic chronicles centred on the valuation of goods and services circulating through their homes. Haltingly at first, the application of this new reckoning took hold among great merchants, gentlemen and ladies, followed by esquires, tradesmen and yeomen, travelling with colonists to the other side of the Atlantic, moving bit by bit through the aegis of schoolrooms and instructional guides to shape the habits of shopkeepers and manufacturers and mediate the lives of middle-class and working daughters of the Victorian Age. Priorities changed, as private matters were tabulated in a manner suitable for public audits. Ultimately, all respectable households were called upon to monitor their savings books and domestic duties through the neat columns of figures. Success (in accounting terms) may not have followed all attempts at this form, but there is little doubt that by 1900 numbered expressions were the pre-eminent measure of reality inside and outside the home.

For middle and working-class families, the prosperity which followed industrialization brought rising material affluence, although it was unequally distributed. Shops were filled with a tantalizing array of practical and decorative housewares, and more enticing goods were available on credit. Housekeeping included the organization of more things. In a very real sense, the sustained promotion of household accounting was a means of reforming personal comportment and fostering the thoughtful management of resources in ways modified from the warehouse. Increasingly, women were urged to measure their attainments as wives and mothers in the context of the household 'manager', with balanced account books and meticulous measurement as visible evidence of their achievements.[125] Tensions between this new management system and traditional neighbourly and customary forms were never explicitly addressed in household accounting manuals. But gender tensions within the family based on husbandly expectations and wifely reservations were evident in the letters to Britain's nineteenth-century newspapers and even in the marginalia of some prescriptive guides.[126] Domestic strains were acknowledged in one publication directed at the respectable working-class wife where the author admits the 'difficulty of the past … to get the housekeeper to … make up her accounts', promising that his system will be 'a pleasure'. Pleasure or not, at the dawn of the twentieth century, women were urged to gauge their attainments as wives, mothers and household 'managers' with balanced account books and meticulous measurement. This sort of reckoning was now one of the principal facets of human conceptualization; indeed, the new discipline of home economics developed as an academic specialism imbued with these precepts. Some women economists in the early twentieth-century academy proclaimed the importance of women's role in the family, bolstering their claims for the significance of the household by emphasizing the paradigm of the female domestic manager. Others recognized the deficiencies in existing household analysis which needed to be addressed. Margaret G. Reid, an early home economist, considered the general neglect of the household by economists to be a serious fault. She offered an explanation for this neglect, noting that 'perhaps it is due even more to the fact that the household is not a money-making institution. The more we have concentrated on money values the more we have overlooked that part of our economic system which is not organized on a profit basis.'[127]

The triumph of quantitative thought was all but complete by 1900, having swept through business and intellectual circles, applied first in the interests of precision and profit, directed next at ordering public and then family life. Men and women, rich and poor, from city and hinterland, followed a different chronology in this process and carried from these encounters different priorities. Many familial and traditional practices did not easily fit formal numeric and economic categories. Neither accounting practices nor liberal economics were designed to capture the complex aspiration, inspiration and perseverance which comprised family dynamics and caring interactions. Tabulated accounts created in the household arena are necessarily partial, though subsequent generations give thanks for surviving records. We must examine these documents with a critical eye, recognizing they mirror a partial representation of past experience, for these numeric observations conceal gender and social practices that are only now receiving a full accounting.

Notes

1 Alfred W. Crosby, *The Measure of Reality: Quantification and Western Society, 1250–1600* (Cambridge, 1997), p. xi.

2 Crosby, *The Measure of Reality*, pp. 10–11.

3 Lewis Mumford, *Technics and Civilization* (New York, 1934); Charles Singer *et al.* (eds), *A History of Technology* (Oxford, 1956); Neil McKendrick, 'Josiah Wedgwood and factory discipline', *Historical Journal* 4 (1961); Carlo M. Cipolla, *Clocks and Culture, 1300–1700* (London, 1967); Carlo M. Cipolla (ed.), *The Fontana Economic History of Europe* (New York, 1976–77) II, especially chapter 3, and III, especially chapters 3, 4 and 6; Kenneth F. Welch, *Time Measurement: An Introductory History* (Newton Abbot, 1972); E. P. Thompson, 'Time, work-discipline and industrial capitalism' (1963) in *Customs in Common* (New York, 1993); Richard W. Hadden, *On the Shoulders of Merchants: Exchange and the Mathematical Conception of Nature in Early Modern Europe* (Albany NY, 1994); Derek Matthews, Malcolm Anderson and John Richard Edwards, *The Priesthood of Industry : The Rise of the Professional Accountant in British Management* (Oxford, 1998).

4 Thomas also notes that 'There is no systematic study of the role of numbers and numerical thinking in England at a popular level, comparable to the many works on literacy and the written word.' Keith Thomas, 'Numeracy in early modern England', *Transactions of the Royal Historical Society* 37 (1987), p. 104.

5 Keith Wrightson, *English Society, 1580–1680* (New Brunswick NJ, 1982), pp. 66–118; Amy Louise Erickson, *Women and Property in Early Modern England* (London, 1993); Ilana Krausman Ben-Amos, *Adolescence and Youth in Early Modern England* (New Haven CT, 1994), pp. 48–68. However, no one would dispute that violent and inequitable social relations were also facets of family life, even as it was the principal site of nurturing.

6 Examples of these studies include Laurence Stone, *The Family, Sex, and Marriage in England, 1500–1800* (Oxford, 1977); Leonore Davidoff and Catherine Hall, *Family Fortunes: Men and Women of the English Middle Class, 1780–1850* (Chicago, 1987); Margaret Hunt, *The Middling Sort: Commerce, Gender, and the Family in England, 1680–1780* (Berkeley CA, 1996); Julie Hardwick, *The Practice of Patriarchy: Gender and the Politics of Household Authority in Early Modern France* (University Park PA, 1998); John Tosh, *A Man's Place: Masculinity and the Middle-Class Home in Victorian England* (London, 1999); significant parts of Sara Mendelson and Patricia Crawford, *Women in Early Modern England* (Oxford, 1998); Leonore Davidoff, Megan Doolittle, Janet Fink and Katherine Holden (eds), *The Family Story: Blood, Contract and Intimacy, 1830–1960* (London, 1999). Studies of individuals and their households include Amanda Vickery, *The Gentleman's Daughter: Women's Lives in Georgian England* (New Haven CT, 1998), and Laurel Thatcher Ulrich, *A Midwife's Tale: The Life of Martha Ballard, based on her Diary, 1785–1812* (New York, 1990). For a recent historiographic overview of the family see Ellen Ross, 'Long live the family', *Journal of British Studies* 41:4 (2002).

7 Mendelson and Crawford, *Women in Early Modern England*, p. 205.

8 Mary Poovey, *A History of the Modern Fact: Problems of Knowledge in the Sciences of Wealth and Society* (Chicago, 1998), p. 30; author's emphasis. Accounting history as a disciplinary specialization is largely confined to business schools, though practitioners are working to bring it into the mainstream of historical study. See, for example,

Stephen P. Walker, review of Richard K. Fleichman, Vaughn S. Radcliffe and Paul A. Shoemaker (eds), *Doing Accounting History*, in *Accounting and Business Research* 34:1 (2004), pp. 77–8.

9   For a good general summary of the conditions which led to the rise and spread of information on double-entry accounting see Geoffrey T. Mills, 'Early accounting in northern Italy: the role of commercial development and the printing press in the expansion of double-entry from Genoa, Florence and Venice', *Accounting Historians' Journal* 21:1 (1994). Accounting systems also developed independently in China. See R. Gardella, 'Squaring accounts: commercial bookkeeping methods and capitalist rationalism in late Qing China', *Journal of Asian Studies* 51:2 (1992), and Wei Lu and Max Aiken, 'Accounting history: Chinese contributions and challenges', *Accounting, Business and Financial History* 13:1 (2003).

10   The significance of the double-entry system of accounting was recognized by theorists such as Max Weber and Joseph Schumpeter. For a discussion of its rational and rhetorical authority see Bruce G. Carruthers and Wendy Nelson Espeland, 'Accounting for rationality: double-entry bookkeeping and the rhetoric of economic rationality', *American Journal of Sociology* 97:1 (1991), and for a more popular assessment see James Buchan, *Frozen Desire: An Inquiry into the Meaning of Money* (London, 1997), pp. 66–7.

11   Rosemary O'Day, *Education and Society, 1500–1800: The Social Foundations of Education in Early Modern Britain* (London, 1982), pp. 60–2; Matthews *et al.*, *Priesthood of Industry*, p. 16, quoted in Thomas, 'Numeracy', p. 116. For examples of early household accounting see CR 895/45, 1513, 1518, 1533, Sir Edward Don's household accounts, Warwickshire County Record Office; DR/3/731a, household accounts of the Ferrers family, of Baddesley Clinton, 1533–34, Shakespeare Birthplace Trust Records Office; CR 1998/Box 63/Folder 1/4, household accounts of the Throckmorton family of Coughton, 1585–86, Warwickshire County Record Office; FEL 888, 556 x6, household accounts of Robert Bransby, 1608–1620, Norfolk Record Office; D661/21/1/1, household accounts of the Dyott family, Lichfield (this book first used in 1631/32 and then again from 1734 onwards), Staffordshire Record Office.

12   Hunt, *The Middling Sort*, p. 58.

13   Rebecca E. Connor, '"Can you apply arithmetick to everythink?" *Moll Flanders*, William Petty, and social accounting' *Studies in Eighteenth-Century Culture* 27 (1998).

14   Poovey, *Modern Fact*, p. 30.

15   Poovey, *Modern Fact*, pp. 32, 66–91.

16   Hunt, *The Middling Sort*, p. 61.

17   Hunt, *The Middling Sort*, pp. 58–62. Keith Thomas describes strategies employed by innumerate shopkeepers and traders to keep track of their affairs. 'Numeracy', pp. 119–23.

18   Michel Foucault, *Discipline and Punish: The Birth of the Prison*, translated by Alan Sheridan (New York, 1979), pp. 193–4. A further exploration of accounting and surveillance can be found in S. Burchell, C. Clubb, A. Hopwood, S. Hughes and J. Nahapiet, 'The roles of accounting in organizations and society', *Accounting, Organizations and Society* (1980). And for issues of accounting and power see P. Miller and T. O'Leary, 'Accounting and the construction of the governable person', *Accounting, Organizations and Society* 12:3 (1987).

19   Joseph Addison defined this pattern of social adjudication in a 1711 issue of *The Spectator*: 'This phrase ['he has not kept true Accoumpts'] … bears the highest Reproach;

for a Man to be mistaken in the Calculation of his Expence, in his Ability to answer future Demands, or to be impertinently sanguine in putting his Credit to too great Adventure, are all Instances of as much Infamy, as with gayer Nations to be failing in Courage or common Honesty.' Quoted in Carruthers and Espeland, 'Accounting for rationality', p. 42.

20 Roger North, *The Gentleman Accomptant: or, An Essay to unfold the Mystery of Accompts by Way of Debtor and Creditor, Commonly called Merchants Accompts … .* (London, 1714), p. i. John Locke also believed young gentlemen should be instructed in 'merchants' accounts' as an essential preparation for their adult responsibilities. John W. Yolton and Jean S. Yolton (eds), *Some Thoughts Concerning Education* (Oxford, 1989), pp 261–3. My thanks to Sara Mendelson for this reference.

21 North, *Gentleman Accomptant*, pp. i and ii.

22 North, *Gentleman Accomptant*, pp. iii–vi.

23 Poovey, *Modern Fact*, p. 29.

24 Poovey, *Modern Fact*, chapters 2–3.

25 Foucault, *Discipline and Punish*, p. 175; also see Miller and O'Leary, 'Accounting and the governable person'.

26 E. P. Thompson's classic articles reflect the tensions arising as new capitalist systems collided with customary practices. 'Time, work-discipline and industrial capitalism', 'Custom, law and common right' and 'The moral economy of the English crowd in the eighteenth century' in *Customs in Common*; and for the clash of customary with new capitalist interests see K. D. M. Snell, *Annals of the Labouring Poor: Social Change and Agrarian England, 1660–1900* (Cambridge, 1985); J. M. Neeson, *Commoners: Common Right, Enclosure and Social Change in England, 1700–1820* (Cambridge, 1993); Peter Linebaugh, *The London Hanged: Crime and Civil Society in the Eighteenth Century* (Harmondsworth, 1991).

27 Mark Wrigley, 'Untitled: the housing of gender' in Beatriz Colomina (ed.), *Sexuality and Space* (Princeton NJ, 1992), pp. 329, 348.

28 Xenophon appeared first in English translation in 1532 and the ancient Greek principles, extolled by Alberti in the fifteenth century, became part of English discourse in succeeding centuries. See Craig Muldrew, *The Economy of Obligation: The Culture of Credit and Social Relations in Early Modern England* (Basingstoke, 1998).

29 Natalie Zemon Davis, *The Gift in Sixteenth-Century France* (London, 2000), pp. 28–9.

30 Wrightson, *English Society*, pp. 66–7. Patricia Crawford and Laura Gowing conclude that 'For most early modern people, marriage necessarily involved both partnership and hierarchy, love and mastery.' Patricia Crawford and Laura Gowing (eds), *Women's Worlds in Seventeenth-Century England: A Source Book* (London, 2000), p. 164.

31 Among the wealthiest households accounts of some description survive from the thirteenth century onwards. Christopher Dyer, *Everyday Life in Medieval England* (London, 1994), p. 258.

32 Quoted in Connor, 'Can you apply arithmetick', p. 183.

33 Hunt, *The Middling Sort*, p. 89. Archival evidence suggests the earlier involvement of men and the later appearance of female household accountants. See, for example, Egerton Ms 3054, Joyce Jeffreys Disbursement Accounts, British Library. I am grateful to Judith Spickley for allowing me access to her transcription of this document prior to publication. Dame Philippa Gore, of Barrow Gurney, Somerset, began her household account ledger in 1666, though she soon passed the task on to servants.

DD/GB/113, Somerset Archive and Record Office. Also, Gertrude Drake's household accounts, 1699–1703, 346M/F497–499, Devon Record Office; Elizabeth Bridger's household accounts 1702–29, SHR/1364, East Sussex Record Office.

34 Stephan Monteage, *Advice to the Women and Maidens of London. … by One of that Sex* (London, 1682). This edition survives in a volume of collected works by this author, including *Debtor and Creditor made Easie: or, A Short Instruction for the Attaining the Right Use of Accounts* … and *A Maiden Scholars Advice* … (London, 1682).

35 Monteage, *Advice to the Women*, pp. 1, 3.

36 Monteage, *Advice to the Women*, p. 19.

37 Amy Louise Erickson notes that both Bathsua Makin's school for ladies in Tottenham and Hannah Wolley's for servants included accounting in the curricula. Erickson, *Women and Property*, pp. 56–9 n. 34, p. 253. See also Crawford and Gowing, *Women's Worlds*, pp. 124–6, and Thomas, 'Numeracy', p. 113.

38 Gareth Morgan, 'Accounting as reality construction: towards a new epistemology for accounting practice', *Accounting, Organizations and Society* 13:5 (1988).

39 For example, see Davis, *The Gift*, especially chapters 1–3. The classic study on this subject is Marcel Mauss, *The Gift: The Form and Reason for Exchange in Archaic Societies*, translated by W. D. Halls (repr. London, 1990). See also Margot Finn, *The Character of Credit: Personal Debt in English Culture, 1740–1914* (Cambridge, 2003), pp. 34–45; Avner Offer, 'Between the gift and the market: the economy of regard', *Economic History Review*, 2nd series 50:3 (1997).

40 For examples of women formalizing these activities into occupations see Crawford and Gowing, *Women's Worlds*, pp. 95–100; for examples of women's culture based in the household see Mendelson and Crawford, *Women in Early Modern England*, pp. 202–12. Carol Stack identified the essential roles of poor African-American women in sharing and redistributing resources in their urban community. Time, money and goods were circulated in a reciprocal system of exchange which enabled the family networks to survive. Carol B. Stack, *All our Kin: Strategies for Survival in a Black Community* (New York, 1974), pp. 22–44. I thank Margaret Hunt for bringing this source to my attention.

41 Alan MacFarlane, *The Family Life of Ralph Josselin, a Seventeenth-Century Clergyman* (Cambridge, 1970), pp. 33–67. See also William Cunningham's 'Diary and Household Book' for another example of such hybrids, in James Dodd (ed.), *The Diary and General Expenditure Book of William Cunningham of Craigsend, 1673–1680* (Edinburgh, 1887). An illustration of the spread of this practice can be found in G. E. Fussell, *Robert Loder's Farm Accounts, 1610–1620*, Camden Society, 3rd series, vol. 53 (1936). The Barbara Johnson Sample Book is another example of a modified account book, recording the clothing she purchased, from her teenage years in the mid-eighteenth century until her death early in the next century. Natalie Rothstein (ed.), *Barbara Johnson's Album of Fashions and Fabrics* (London, 1987); also, T219-1973, Department of Textile and Dress, Victoria and Albert Museum.

42 Jack Goody, *The Domestication of the Savage Mind* (Cambridge, 1977), p. 37.

43 Ms Rawlinson A 299/1, Diary of William Smart of Westminster and Durham, 1666–1678, Bodleian Library.

44 Ms Rawlinson A 299/1. For example, the entries for 27 February 1667, 7 August, 3, 12, 19 September, 12 December 1670, 3 February, 28 March, 13 May 1671, 3–4 April 1674.

45 Davis, *The Gift*, p. 34.

46 Ms Rawlinson A 299/1. For example, 12 May 1670, 28 May, 11 June 1671; 20, 27 April, 2, 18, 25 May, 8, 15 June 1673.

47 1678/S11/1, Durham University Library Archives and Special Collections.

48 Ms L3 A1, Huntington Library, San Marino CA. Thomas Mort lived in the vicinity of the villages of Bedford, Ashley and Tyldesley, where he held property, between the town of Leigh on the west and Manchester approximately twelve miles to the east.

49 Accounting and the spread of capitalist modes of thinking and practice are explored in Rob Byer, 'The roots of modern capitalism: a Marxist accounting history of the origins and consequences of capitalist landlords in England', *Accounting Historians' Journal* 31:1 (2004).

50 6783, Bristol Record Office. Keith Wrightson notes the fundamental value of these links as a hedge against the vagaries of early modern life, although risks were also evident. Wrightson, *English Society*, pp. 44–57; Hunt, *The Middling Sort*, pp. 28–49.

51 Davis, *The Gift*, p. 35.

52 I would like to thank Margaret Hunt for her discussion of these issues.

53 Examples of such records include N. W. Alcock (ed.), *Warwickshire Grazier and London Skinner, 1532–1555. The Account Book of Peter Temple and Thomas Heritage* (Oxford, 1981); Donald Woodward (ed.), *The Farming and Memorandum Books of Henry Best of Elmswell, 1642* (Oxford, 1984); Lorna Weatherill (ed.), *The Account Book of Richard Latham, 1724–1767* (Oxford, 1990) and, much earlier, Dodd, *Diary and General Expenditure Book of William Cunningham*. Less fully elaborated domestic accounts survive in many archives, for example the domestic papers from the Ledbury household of bookseller Jacob Tonson, Add. Mss 28,276, British Library.

54 It is hardly surprising that the well known eighteenth-century diaries of the shopkeeper Thomas Turner and Parson James Woodforde reflect an equivalent instruction in the theory of accounts and a similar commitment to this project, even while the bulk of their writings take a narrative form. Both show habits of numeracy in routine notation of costs expended and monies received. David Vaisey (ed.), *The Diary of Thomas Turner, 1754–1765* (Oxford, 1984); John Beresford (ed.), *The Diary of a Country Parson, 1758–1802, by James Woodforde* (Oxford, 1978). See also Paul V. Thompson and Dorothy Jay Thompson (eds), *The Account Book of Jonathan Swift* (London, 1984), which reveals Swift's careful record of expenses throughout his adult life.

55 6783, Bristol Record Office.

56 6783, Bristol Record Office.

57 B. S. Yamey, 'Functional development of double-entry bookkeeping', *Accountant*, November 1940, quoted in Poovey, *Modern Fact*, p. 338 n. 16. See also these examples which combined accounts on one side of the sheet of paper with philosophic verses and memoranda on the other: CR 895/106, household accounts of Sir Edward Don, 1510, Warwickshire County Record Office; 189M-3/F5/5–7, household accounts of William Bidlake, 1685–1711, interspersed with Latin, Greek and English proverbs, Devon Record Office. In this regard, Wharton's account ledger was more similar to another male-authored memorandum book: 'An Account of my Children in this Book and the Deaths of my Cozen Miss Ann Grewold and my ever dear Wife by me Da: Lewis', intermixed within were nearly ten years of domestic accounts. CR 1291/451, Warwickshire County Record Office.

58 Poovey, *Modern Fact*, p. 29.

59 Weatherill, *Account Book of Richard Latham*, p. xv.

60 For example, the extracts of accounts kept by a steward for Lady Marie Stewart in the early seventeenth century. C. K. Sharpe, *Extracts from the Household Book of Lady Marie Stewart, Daughter of Esme, Duke of Lennox, and Countess of Mar* (Edinburgh, 1815). See also Cynthia Huff, *British Women's Diaries* (New York, 1985), pp. xiv, xx–xxi, xxxiii, 2, 11, 14, 21, 124.

61 See, for example, Robert Tittler, 'Moneylending in the West Midlands: the activities of Joyce Jefferies, 1638–1649', *Historical Research* 67 (1994).

62 Tittler, 'Moneylending', p. 255.

63 Egerton Ms 3054, British Library.

64 N. Penney (ed.), *The Household Account Book of Sarah Fell of Swarthmoor Hall* (Cambridge, 1920). In 1670, Sarah Fell bought 'a booke called the younge clarkes tutor' to help her keep good accounts. Quoted in Amy Louise Erickson, *Women and Property in Early Modern England* (London, 1993), p. 56. R. Scott-Moncrieff (ed.), *The Household Book of Lady Grisell Baillie, 1692–1733* (Edinburgh, 1911). Examples of female accountants from the propertied classes include Dame Philippa Gore, of Barrow Gurney, Somerset, who began to keep a ledger in 1666 and then passed the task along to her servants, DD/GB/113, Somerset Archive and Record Office. Gertrude Drake, of Buckland Abbey, Devon, likewise kept household accounts in 1703, 346M/F497–499, Devon Record Office; as did Elizabeth Bridger, of Coombe Place, Hamsey, East Sussex, from 1702 to 1729, SHR/1364, East Sussex Record Office.

65 D260/M/E/429/25 and 26, Staffordshire Record Office, and personal correspondence. For other examples see 5M52/F33, Dorothy Portal's household accounts, 1715–19, Hampshire Record Office; Mrs Gibson's household accounts, 1723–47, ACC/1045/148, London Metropolitan Archives; Susanna Frederick's personal and household accounts, 1747–62, 183/33/18, Surrey History Centre; Elizabeth Gould's household accounts, 1746–50, DD/HLM/12, Somerset Archive and Record Centre; Jane Riggall's household accounts, 1748–1755, FRE/8056, East Sussex Record Office.

66 BRU ASR 103, Northampton Record Office. Little is known of this accountant, aside from what can be gleaned from the internal evidence of the document.

67 BRU ASR 103, Northampton Record Office.

68 Amy Froide, 'The Silent Partner of Britain's Financial Revolution: Single Women and their Public Investments', unpublished paper presented at the Association of Business Historians' conference, Portsmouth, 2001; Barbara Todd, 'Small Sums to Risk: London Women's Investments in the Age of the Financial Revolution', unpublished paper presented at the North American Conference of British Studies, Boston MA, 1999.

69 BRU ASR 103, Northampton Record Office.

70 Amanda Vickery's extensive study of the letters, diaries and accounts of the Lancashire gentlewoman Elizabeth Shackleton (1726–81) make clear the complexity of Shackleton's preoccupation with goods bought for herself and her household, which in no way reflected the purely quantitative. 'Women and the world of goods: a Lancashire consumer and her possessions, 1751–1781' in John Brewer and Roy Porter (eds), *Consumption and the World of Goods* (London, 1993), and *The Gentleman's Daughter: Women's Lives in Georgian England* (London, 1998). See also, Thomas, 'Numeracy', p. 113.

71 Similar preoccupations are noted in other women's diaries, for this period and later. Huff, *British Women's Diaries*, p. xx.

72 Mendelson and Crawford, *Women in Early Modern England*, p. 255.

73 48.107/1, Young Mss, Museum of London. The preoccupations of this author appear to be very similar to those expressed by Sarah Savage, whose diary survives for the years 1714–23. Mendelson and Crawford, *Women in Early Modern England*, pp. 235–6.

74 John Money, 'Teaching in the market place, or "Caesar adsum jam forte: Pompey aderat": the retailing of knowledge in provincial England during the eighteenth century' in Brewer and Porter (eds), *Consumption and the World of Goods*, p. 336.

75 Laurel Thatcher Ulrich, 'Martha Ballard and her girls: women's work in eighteenth-century Maine' in S. Innes (ed.), *Work and Labor in early America* (Chapel Hill NC, 1988), pp. 80–1.

76 Ms Rawlinson A 299/1, 3, 21 May, 23 September 1673.

77 Ulrich, 'Martha Ballard', p. 80.

78 Nancy Grey Osterud, 'Strategies of Mutuality: Relations among Women and Men in an Agricultural Community', PhD dissertation, Brown University, 1984, quoted in Ulrich, 'Martha Ballard', p. 81.

79 Hunt, *The Middling Sort*, pp. 73– 100; Erickson, *Women and Property*, pp. 58–9.

80 Laurence Fontaine, 'Antonio and Shylock: credit and trust in France, *c.* 1680–1780', *Economic History Review*, 2nd series 54:1 (2001), pp. 45–7.

81 Muldrew, *Economy of Obligation*, p. 160; Hunt, *The Middling Sort*, chapter 1; Theodore Koditschek notes the combination of family, social and financial pressures in industrializing Bradford. *Class Formation and Urban Industrial Society: Bradford, 1750–1850* (Cambridge, 1990).

82 Muldrew, *Economy of Obligation*, pp. 62–5. Stephen Monteage, *Debtor and Creditor made Easie: or, A Short Instruction for the attaining the Right Use of Accounts. To which is added a Maiden Scholars Advice*, 2nd edn (London, 1682); Alexander Malcolm, *A New Treatise of Arithmetick and Book-keeping* (Edinburgh, 1718); Hustcraft Stephens, *Italian Book-keeping Reduced into an Art* (1735); Daniel Defoe, *The Complete English Tradesman* (London, 1745); Wardaugh Thompson, *The Accomptant's Oracle; or, Key to Science, a Treatise of Common Arithmetic* (Whitehaven, 1771); James Morrison, *The Elements of Book keeping, by Single and Double Entry, to which is annexed an Introduction on Merchants Accounts*, new edn (London, 1825).

83 Mrs Johnson, *Madam Johnson's Present: or, The Best Instructions for Young Women, in Useful Knowledge, with a Summary of the late Marriage Act, and Instructions how to marry pursuant thereto* (London, 1754), p. 102. Published in at least five editions, at more than 1s in price, this volume was intended for middle-ranked readers. A handbill from about the mid-eighteenth century also offered to teach 'Gentlemen and Ladies' 'the True System of Italian Book-keeping' in 'Theory and Practice in 18 hours'. Guildhall Library, London.

84 Tables of weights, measures, currency and the like were included in most of these printed volumes, along with space for keeping accounts. However, standardized measurement was accepted only reluctantly by common folk, and regional variations continued well into modern times. Thomas, 'Numeracy', pp. 122–4; Huff, *British Women's Diaries*, p. 2.

85 I am not suggesting a pre-capitalist domestic idyll. Pragmatic decisions were routine in families; coercion and violence were also routine. However, the behaviours which defined families also arose from complex personal and cultural conjunctures which had clearly defined emotional cores.

86 The one activity which received attention was women's role as consumers, particularly

as this involved organizing purchases for the household. However, here too early economists usually suggested that women were 'irrational' in their choices. See Ronald G. Bodkin, 'Economic thought: Adam Smith, Harriet Taylor Mill, and J. S. Mill', *Feminist Economics* 5:1 (1999), pp. 55–6. These issues are also discussed in Davidoff and Hall, *Family Fortunes*, pp. 185–6.

87 Bodkin, 'Economic thought', pp. 45–60.

88 Wakefield, *Reflections*, pp. 100–2, 118. Bridget Hill, 'Priscilla Wakefield as a writer of children's educational books', *Women's Writing* 4:1 (1997).

89 *Domestic Management, or, The Art of Conducting a Family; with Instructions to Servants in General* (London, 1800?), p. 10.

90 *Domestic Management …* , p. 30.

91 *The Home Book; or, Young Housekeeper's Assistant: forming a Complete System of Domestic Economy, and Household Accounts … by a Lady* (London, 1829), p. 1.

92 For an example of the persistence of male domestic accounting see Eng. Ms 989, John Rylands Library, Manchester.

93 For example, *The Female Instructor; or Young Woman's Companion and Guide to Domestic Happiness; being an Epitome of all the Acquirements necessary to form the Female Character in every Class of Life, with Examples of Illustrious Women* (London, 1824) – several editions may have been published, as the preface is dated 1818. John Armstrong, *The Young Woman's Guide to Virtue, Economy, and Happiness; Being an improved and pleasant Directory for Cultivating the Heart and Understanding; with a Complete and Elegant System of Domestic Cookery …* , 6th edn (Newcastle upon Tyne, 1825?). Both included instructions in arithmetic and an 'Easy Mode of Keeping A Family Account' with printed tables.

94 Connor, 'Can you apply arithmetick', p. 193 n. 40.

95 *The Home Book*, p. 24. See also Poovey, *Modern Fact*, pp. 42–3.

96 *The Home Book*, p. 27.

97 Cynthia Huff, '"That profoundly female and feminist genre": the diary as feminist practice', *Women's Studies Quarterly* 3–4 (1989), p. 6.

98 Kathryn Carter, 'An economy of words: Emma Chadwick Stretch's account book diary', *Acadiensis* 29:1 (1999). For other British examples see Huff, *British Women's Diaries*, pp. 1–2, 10–11, 14–15, 26–7, 31, 46–8, 55–7, 65–6, 72–3, 97–9, 104–5.

99 49.15 Young Mss, Museum of London.

100 48.85/1 Young Mss, Museum of London.

101 Foucault, *Discipline and Punish*, p. 139.

102 Catherine Bell, *Ritual: Perspectives and Dimensions* (New York, 1997), p. 82; author's emphasis.

103 48.85/4 Young Mss, Museum of London.

104 For example, Mariabella Howard, the wife of a chemist, kept detailed household accounts: ACC/1071/ 1394–1396, London Metropolitan Archives. And the Ladies Caroline, Amelia and Laetitia Knollis kept a volume entitled 'A General Account of every Article whatever & in short all cash expended' between 1803 and 1813. 1M44/2, Hampshire Record Office. Henrietta Jex-Blake likewise kept household accounts at Rugby, 1858–1912. MC 233/58, 681x1, Norfolk Record Office. The influence of these precepts continued well into the twentieth century. Mrs Patricia Woods (b. 1912, d. 2001), a long-time Montreal resident, kept daily records of every personal and household expenditure for over fifty years, until her sight failed. Personal communication.

105　The term 'profit' is specifically employed in an 1845 volume. *Economy for the Single and Married: or, The Young Wife and Bachelor's Guide to Income and Expenditure on £50 Per Annum, £100 Per Annum ... by One who 'Makes ends Meet'*, 2nd edn (London, 1845), p. 10. Another example is *The Original Housekeeper's Accompt-Book, for the Year 1833, Improved ...* , published in London, Bath, Edinburgh, Glasgow, 'etc', which includes a table to calculate interest, tables of expenses and 'Marketing Tables'. In addition see *The Domestic Account Book, for 1848* (London, 1848), price 2s; *A Model Wife* (London, 1859); and G. W. Johnson, *The Domestic Economist and Adviser in every Branch of the Family Establishment* (London, 1850). A further example of these ubiquitous guides is *The Working Man's Diary, and Family Record of Receipts and Expenditures, for 1862 by the editor of Poor Richard's Almanac*, price 1d. *How to Live on £1 a Week* ('Published at the Office of *Wit and Wisdom*', London, 1888). The contents of this document are divided into the following sections which offer advice, guidance, examples and model budgets: Lodgings; Food and drink; Clothing; Recreation; Thrift; Summary of total expenditure; Co-operation; Valedictory remarks. And later in the century see *Cassell's Household Guide: Being a Complete Encyclopædia of Domestic and Social Economy, and forming a Guide to every Department of Practical Life*, 4 vols (London and New York, 1869–71); *D. H. Evans & Co. Ltd Diary and Housekeeper's Book for 1914. Contains a mass of useful information to all Housekeepers, a Diary, a system of Household Accounts whereby the entire expenditure of the Household may be kept under control, and an Insurance against Accidents for £1,000* (London, 1914), price 1d; and on a more academic note a book produced by the former Dean of the New York School of Commerce, C. W. Haskins, *How to Keep Household Accounts: A Manual of Family Finance* (New York, 1903).

106　Hester Chapone, *Letters on the Improvement of the Mind addressed to a Lady* (London, 1786), pp. 146–7. This book was published in multiple editions to the mid-nineteenth century.

107　For examples of this gendered sentimentality see Lynda Nead, *Myths of Sexuality: Representations of Women in Victorian Britain* (Oxford, 1988), especially chapter 1, and Davidoff and Hall, *Family Fortunes*, especially chapter 8.

108　John Tosh, *A Man's Place: Masculinity and the Middle-Class Home in Victorian England* (London, 1999) pp. 62–3.

109　Tosh, *A Man's Place*, p. 6.

110　Charles Dickens, *David Copperfield* (1849–50), quoted in John M. Robson, *Marriage or Celibacy? The* Daily Telegraph *on a Victorian Dilemma* (Toronto, 1995), p. 81.

111　Robson, *Marriage or Celibacy*, p. 122.

112　Guides include: *The Economy for the Single and Married* (London, 1845) or *A Manual of Domestic Economy* (London, 1857, 1873); *The Girl's Own Annual* 2:40 (1880); J. Mather, *Common Sense for Housewives: A Course of Lectures given at the Manchester School of Domestic Economy, South Parade, Deansgate* (Manchester, 1896).

113　MC 1001 MS3E4, New Brunswick Archives. I am grateful to Gail Campbell for bringing this diary to my attention and allowing me to use her transcription of the document.

114　Carter, 'Economy of words'. See also Marilyn Ferris Motz, 'Folk expressions of time and place: nineteenth-century Midwestern rural diaries', *Journal of American Folklore* 100 (April–June 1987). Carter also lists the many similar nineteenth-century account book diaries which survive in Canadian archives: pp. 49–50.

115   Mrs Valentine (ed.), *The Girl's Home Companion: A Book of Pastimes in Work and Play* (London and New York, 1895), pp. 715, 721. Frederick Warne & Co. published a range of useful domestic guides.

116   49.15 Young Mss, Museum of London.

117   'So, men and women, encourage and help each other! Do not throw this book aside as useless, but keep it and use it to your mutual advantage.' Iles, *Complete Housekeeper's Book*, p. 5.

118   Ellen Ross describes the various interventions which were seen by poor working-class women as their responsibility. Ross, 'Survival networks', pp. 4–11. See also Judith Walkowitz, *City of Dreadful Delight: Narratives of Sexual Danger in Late Victorian London* (London, 1994), pp. 56–8.

119   For a discussion of budgets among London's poor see Maud Pember Reeves, *Round about a Pound a Week* (1913, repr. 1988), pp. 75–93; Ellen Ross, *Love and Toil: Motherhood in Outcast London, 1870–1914* (Oxford, 1993), pp. 40–55.

120   Pember Reeves, *Round about a Pound*, p. 12.

121   Pember Reeves, *Round about a Pound*, pp. 13–15.

122   Poovey, *Modern Fact*, p. 280.

123   Poovey, *Modern Fact*, p. 282.

124   For a discussion of probate inventories see Weatherill, *Consumer Behaviour*, pp. 1–22, 201–14; David Vaisey, *Probate Inventories of Lichfield and District, 1580–1680*, Staffordshire Record Society, 4th series, V (1969); Philip Riden (ed.), *Probate Records and the Local Community* (Gloucester, 1985); J. A. Johnston (ed.), *Probate Inventories of Lincoln Citizens, 1661–1714* (Woodbridge, 1991).

125   Davidoff and Hall, *Family Fortunes*, p. 384. Working-class mothers also measured their success by their skill at getting by, as Ross shows in *Love and Toil*, pp. 40–55.

126   Mather, *Common Sense for Housewives*, p. 16, reader's scoring.

127   Margaret G. Reid, *Economics of Household Production* (New York, 1934), p. 3.

Conclusion

The route to a monetized, industrialized, numerate society was long and circuitous, and many who travelled along that road clung to long-held, proven customs while others adopted new practices; needs, aspirations and expectations were made manifest in a variety of ways. Those who continued their allegiance to older forms of budgeting believed them a rational way to balance resources with the exigencies of their lives. The longevity of alternative currencies, of substitute mediums of exchange, persisted through the nineteenth century and into the twentieth, a pattern of economic and cultural expression unremarked in liberal economics, but essential to life nonetheless. This old style became progressively invisible as the nineteenth-century discourse on the industrial economy evolved. But, though increasingly marginalized, these elements were also startlingly persistent and represent a notable complexity in an advanced Western society. Rosemary Ommer and Nancy Turner observe of the late twentieth century that:

> The restructuring of economic life that ensued appeared to render the old ways increasingly obsolete and certainly put them outside the boundaries of formal economic behaviour, even in the countryside. We contend, however, that the old system did not disappear. Rather, it evolved over time into what we now call 'the rural informal economy': sets of economic activities that operate outside the formal legalised structures of a nation's capitalist economy. ... based in community or family reciprocities ... as occupational pluralism ... which involved the utilisation of a range of ecological niches to provide year-round sustenance.[1]

Acknowledging the variations in form and function of economic and social practices, including those seemingly archaic, brings into strong relief the transformations which engaged generations. It gives a fuller representation of lives lived. It highlights as well the full measure of change that accompanied capitalist commerce and industry, where thrift was exercised in monied ways, the household was numbered and gender practices of credit were reconceived.

How unique was the English experience? Were the cultural and economic variants expressed in this nation distinct from those found in other (Western) regions? These are important but difficult questions for which I have only provisional observations. From a global perspective the claims of English exceptionalism, as the industrial forerunner of a superior

West have historically been overdrawn. The elements in this equation that precipitated the first industrial nation did not arise from a pre-eminent rationalism, or a unique cast of mind. As Jack Goody shows, the rationality of numbers and accounting was not an exclusively Western achievement, however useful to the industrial project.[2] The timing and regional expressions of economic change certainly favoured Europe for the centuries considered here – the nineteenth century in particular. But, again, as Goody observes, 'the superior achievements of the West can no longer be seen as permanent or even long-standing features of those cultures but as the result of one of the swings of the pendulum that have affected these societies over the millennia'.[3] Moreover, if formalized financial institutions, long-distance insurance and other mechanisms of capitalism surged ahead in England and Europe in this era, these developments did not erase older, persistent patterns that had a wide currency chronologically and geographically. In this broader context, some forms of barter, some alternative currencies, showed surprising resilience; the use of textiles as a credit medium, for example, was common practice in the medieval Mediterranean world – as common as in the early modern Indonesian archipelago or as common as in medieval Paris.[4] Contexts clearly varied, but the value and uses assigned these materials continued to be accepted facets of life. With regard to credit practices, women's roles as the organizers of small-scale credit were also consistent throughout the Western world and beyond. Rather than being exceptional, English experiences reflect all the elements of a dynamic society, where consumer needs and aspirations worked in tandem with productive forces. As the birthplace of industrial manufacturing, explanations abound about the timeliness and conjunction of events supporting England's great leap forward. The experience of subsequent generations shows that England was not uniquely placed to make this move, but enjoyed a temporary advantage. However, questions about comparative advantage continue to preoccupy scholars,[5] as do questions concerning societal features which some claim as unique cultural stimuli.

Prasannan Parthasarathi identifies state discipline and control of labour in England as having no counterpart in Asia, and possibly uniquely important in this nation's development.[6] If the regulation and disciplining of labour figure in the equation explaining English achievement, then the cultural and economic features of consumerism – the reordering of family life to facilitate material acquisition, for example – also play a role. But key facets remain equivocal. Fashion is one of the central but most ambiguous motivational factors in the change of personal and societal patterns, defiant of government injunction, a driving force behind the redefinition of societal norms. The genesis and function of fashion have raised compelling questions about the exceptionalism of the West. Western scholars have unequivocally laid claim to fashion as a European social 'invention', a Western phenomenon that underpinned consumer desires and the transformation of societies and economies. Fashion itself is described by the French theorist Gilles Lipovetsky as 'an exceptional process inseparable from the origin and development of the modern West'.[7] Typically, treatments of this phenomenon are framed as part of a Western tradition, its chronology conceived in conjunction with milestones like the Renaissance, the commercial revolution or industrial capitalism. Fernand Braudel was satisfied that for much of history 'society stood still' with regard to material culture and that dress was unchanging for the very poor of East and West, equally static for the mandarins and merchants of Asia and the Middle East. A French resident in Persia in the late seventeenth century insisted that 'the East is not subject to fashion', a claim which Braudel and many others accepted uncritically – a further manifestation of the trope of the unchanging East and the dynamic West.[8] Recent research confirms that the fashion dynamic was very much at work in Asian societies.[9] The fashion/consumer nexus remains to be explored in a comparative, worldwide context, to explain what forms fashion took in the transformation of societies. Research is still to be done, though local or regional particularities were most probably the norm. In the Western context, significant revisions are remodelling the way the fashion impetus is understood, once a phenomenon exclusively identified with elite practice, with emulation as sole driving force among non-elites. But historians now recognize fashion's multiple expressions among a range of social groups and the contending means of communication it engendered. Fashion, as an adjunct of consumerism, as an impetus for the acquisition of goods, as a stimulus to the ordering of budgets and family priorities, surely had multiple forms in societies at various levels of material advancement, then as now. The motivations of generations remain to be unearthed.

The economic and cultural nexus

The plastic cards in our wallets and the cash in our pockets are testament to our economic lives, enabling transactions, reflecting the formal fiscal structures distinctive of the late twentieth and early twenty-first centuries. These financial mediums mirror some, but not all, of the ways by which women and men arrange their material possessions, their ownership and use of goods. Access to formal financial tools, such as bank loans and credit cards, is general in most of the developed world and nominally governed by ideals of equity, objective bias-free appraisal and fair access to such facilities. In fact, the struggle to achieve equity is on-going, developed in the last decades of the twentieth century as part of a broader critique of legal and financial structures. In this context, it is easy to see how apparently neutral artefacts, like cash and credit cards, reflect the societal contexts in which they are employed. Looking at the long evolution toward a modern industrial society, I show the profound divergences that accompanied new financial and cultural forms. This volume is part of a wider qualitative reappraisal of the social and cultural context of economic practice. My work joins that of others enquiring into the economic/cultural nexus: Craig Muldrew's work, for example, along with Margot Finn's, frames the cultural context of credit relations, exploring the social dynamic and moral economy of daily lending and borrowing in early modern England. Finn offers important correctives in the gendered legal and social history of credit in the nineteenth century. Among the creative studies of informal credit and the second-hand trade Karen Tranberg Hansen illuminates contemporary issues of regional development.[10] In concert with these and others, I traced the antecedents of our routine fiscal lives, the ways in which men and women ordered their resources to meet the demands of daily life. Changes in this dynamic brought significant outcomes, such as those which came with the formalization of lending. The old practices of the second-hand trade and gender patterns of small-scale borrowing were deeply embedded in early modern society and had complex histories. Their different shapes in the late nineteenth century produced new expectations, changing the context of age-old patterns. Moreover, the formalization of credit and the standardization of lending took place with contiguous changes in gender expectations. Traced across centuries, the culture of credit and the history of daily transactions formed part of the long shift to modernity concurrent with industrialization.[11]

Buying, lending, saving and domestic management were gradually transformed as the household was reconceived, new institutions were launched and others reordered, bringing new expectations for both women and men. In the preceding chapters I traced evolving patterns of plebeian daily life, beginning with the use of small-scale credit. Answers to some issues were elusive. The absence of credit alternatives, such as the *mont de piété*, cannot be gauged and there is no way to measure how the lack of cheaper credit touched ordinary Londoners. It is evident, however, that the failure of charitable lending institutions in England, such as throve in other parts of Europe, burdened working families and petty traders.[12] Withal, fiscal practices continued to evolve, and the use of alternative currencies is a case in point. Once a practice found in almost all social classes, it withered to the bounds of the working poor. And, gradually, what had been a fixture in daily transactions took on purely decorative or utilitarian functions for more and more householders. Respectability now required that credit be secured through formal institutions and that the materials remain only as functional or decorative accoutrements. Feelings toward material goods – clothing, furnishings and accessories – were always complex, with nuances which repay close investigation. These chapters retraced changing attitudes and practices, the interaction of everyday things with common lives. Over three centuries, such homely events followed new customs.

Over time, the habits revealed in domestic ledgers and savings passbooks became commonplace, part of a standard societal curriculum, the subtext of novels. These accumulated changes marked extraordinary alterations in thought, practice and social politics. By uncovering these elements, a broader social landscape is revealed, set within a wider gendered economy, transcending the public/private dichotomy, extending beyond the study of work or formal economic institutions – in sum, redefining the balance of historical structures. The shift to money wages, to an increasingly monetized society, brought along with it a host of other outcomes which shaped personal and family agendas among the middle and working classes. Domestic accounting and the spread of savings culture coincided with an era of heightened consumerism and ultimately with rising standards of living. Personal oversight and prudent husbandry brought more possibilities of enhanced material comfort even as some sectors of the working poor continued to employ alternative strategies to get by. Societal uniformity was never entirely achieved, nor were the new fiscal norms ever fully absorbed in all segments of society – bank accounts and money transactions were never as all-encompassing as they might appear. Even in developed societies, in marginal communities, and more generally in times of crisis, alternative strategies reminiscent of early modern forms reappear as a means of survival, 'reinvented' as needed by each new generation.[13] Thus, for a comparative perspective on current structures, and for a cogent assessment of changing practices and priorities from centuries past, it is essential to consider the quotidian traffic of generations. Their long history of everyday transactions offers a unique vantage point from which to gauge the first industrial society.

Notes

1 Rosemary E. Ommer and Nancy J. Turner, 'Informal rural economies in history', *Labour/Le Travail* 53:1 (2004), p. 127. My thanks for being allowed to read an advance copy of this work.

2 Jack Goody, *The East in the West* (Cambridge, 1996), pp. 6–7, 72–5.

3 Goody, *The East in the West*, p. 7.

4 S. D. Goitein, *A Mediterranean Society: The Jewish Communities of the Arab World as Portrayed in the Documents of the Cairo Geniza* IV, *Daily Life* (Berkeley CA, 1983), pp. 170, 332–3; Bronislaw Geremek, *The Margins of Society in Late Medieval Paris* (Cambridge, 1987), pp. 264–8; John Guy, *Woven Cargo: Indian Textiles in the East* (London, 1998), pp. 9–11.

5 Prasannan Parthasarathi, 'The great divergence', *Past and Present* 176 (2002).

6 Parthasarathi, 'Great divergence', p. 292.

7 Gilles Lipovetsky, *The Empire of Fashion: Dressing Modern Democracy* (Princeton NJ, 1994), p. 15.

8 Quoted in Fernand Braudel, *Civilization and Capitalism, Fifteenth–Eighteenth Century* I, *The Structures of Everyday Life*, translation from the French revised by Siân Reynolds (New York, 1985), p. 323. See also Goody, *The East in the West*, pp. 1–10.

9 These issues are addressed in Craig Clunas, 'Modernity global and local: consumption and the rise of the West', *American Historical Review* 104:5 (1999), and Craig Clunas, *Superfluous Things: Material Culture and Social Status in Early Modern China* (Cambridge, 1991). See also Peter Burke, '*Res et verba*: conspicuous consumption in the early modern world' in John Brewer and Roy Porter (eds), *Consumption and the World of Goods* (London, 1993).

10 C. Muldrew, *The Economy of Obligation: The Culture of Credit and Social Relations in Early Modern England* (New York, 1988); Karen Tranberg Hansen, 'Budgeting against uncertainty: cross-class and transethnic redistribution mechanisms in urban Zambia', *African Urban Studies* 21 (1985) and *Salaula: The World of Secondhand Clothing and Zambia* (Chicago, 2000); Margot Finn, 'Men's things: masculine possession in the consumer revolution', *Social History* 25:2 (2000); see also 'Men's Markets: Male Consumers in Nineteenth-century England', unpublished paper presented at the Economic History Society conference, Birmingham, 2002, and *The Character of Credit: Personal Debt in English Culture, 1740–1914* (Cambridge, 2003).

11 See B. Lemire, R. Pearson and G. Campbell (eds), *Women and Credit: Researching the Past, Refiguring the Future* (Oxford, 2002).

12 Laurence Fontaine has explored the importance of *mont de piété* throughout Europe. See 'The Institutionalization of Pawnbroking: The Comparative European Experience', unpublished paper presented at session 71, International Economic History Congress, Buenos Aires, 2002, and 'Women's economic spheres and credit in pre-industrial Europe' in Lemire *et al.*, *Women and Credit*, pp. 15–32.

13 See, for example, Ruth Pearson, 'Argentina's Barter Network: New Currency for New Times?', Susan Porter Benson, 'What Goes Round Comes Round: Second-hand Clothing, Furniture and Tools in Working-class Lives in the Interwar USA', and Lynne Milgram, '(Re)Dressing Identity and Modernity through Secondhand Clothing in the Philippine Cordillera', unpublished papers presented at the conference 'Les Circulations des objects d'occasion', Florence, 2002.

Select bibliography

Allerston, Patricia, 'Reconstructing the second-hand clothes trade in sixteenth- and seventeenth-century Venice', *Costume* 33 (1999).

Alter, George, Claudia Goldin and Elyce Rotella, 'The savings of ordinary Americans: the Philadelphia Saving Fund Society in the mid-nineteenth century', *Journal of Economic History* 54:4 (1994).

Anderson, B. L., 'Money and the structure of credit in the eighteenth century', *Business History*, 12 (1970).

Andrew, Donna T., *Philanthropy and Police: London Charity in the Eighteenth Century* (Princeton NJ: Princeton University Press, 1989).

Andrews, Kenneth R., *Trade, Plunder and Settlement: Maritime Enterprise and the Genesis of the British Empire, 1480–1630* (Cambridge: Cambridge University Press, 1984).

Ardener, Shirley, and Sandra Burman, *Money-go-Rounds: The Importance of Rotating Savings and Credit Associations for Women* (Oxford: Berg, 1995).

Ashton, T. S., *Iron and Steel in the Industrial Revolution* (Manchester: Manchester University Press, 1924).

Baldwin, Francis E., *Sumptuary Legislation and Personal Regulation in England* (Baltimore MD: Johns Hopkins University Press, 1926).

Bateson, Mary (ed.), *Records of the Borough of Leicester, 1509–1603* (Cambridge: Cambridge University Press, 1905).

Baulant, M., A. J. Shuurman and P. Servais (eds), *Inventaires après-décès et ventes de meubles : apports à une histoire de la vie économique et quotidienne, XIVe–XIXe siècle* (Louvain-la-Neuve, 1988).

Beattie, John M., *Crime and the Courts in England, 1660–1800* (Princeton NJ: Princeton University Press, 1986).

Beattie, John M., 'The criminality of women in eighteenth-century England', *Journal of Social History* 8 (1975).

Bell, Catherine, *Ritual: Perspectives and Dimensions* (New York: Oxford University Press, 1997).

Ben-Amos, Ilana Krausman, *Adolescence and Youth in Early Modern England* (New Haven CT: Yale University Press, 1994).

Benson, John, 'Working-class consumption, saving and investment in England and Wales, 1851–1911', *Journal of Design History* 9:2 (1996).

Benson, Susan Porter, 'Living on the margin: working-class marriages and family survival strategies in the United States, 1919–1941' in Victoria de Grazia (ed.), *The Sex of Things: Gender and Consumption in Historical Perspective* (Berkeley CA: University of California Press, 1996).

Berg, Maxine, 'Women's work, mechanization and the early phases of industrialization' in Patrick Joyce (ed.), *The Historical Meaning of Work* (Cambridge: Cambridge University Press, 1987).

Berg, Maxine, 'The first women economic historians', *Economic History Review*,

2nd series 45:2 (1992).

Berg, Maxine, 'Women's property and the industrial revolution', *Journal of Interdisciplinary History*, 34:2 (1993).

Berg, Maxine, *The Age of Manufactures, 1700–1820: Industry, Innovation and Work in Britain*, 2nd edn (London: Routledge, 1994).

Berg, Maxine, *A Woman in History: Eileen Power, 1889–1940* (Cambridge: Cambridge University Press, 1996).

Berg, Maxine, and Helen Clifford (eds), *Consumers and Luxury: Consumer Culture in Europe, 1650–1850* (Manchester: Manchester University Press, 1999).

Blondé, Bruno, 'Tableware and changing consumer patterns: dynamics of material culture in Antwerp, seventeenth to eighteenth centuries', in J. Veeckman (ed.), *Majolica and Glass from Italy to Antwerp and Beyond: The Transfer of Technology in the Sixteenth to early Seventeenth Century* (Antwerp: Stadt Antwerpen, 2002).

Bodkin, Ronald G., 'Economic thought: Adam Smith, Harriet Taylor Mill and J. S. Mill', *Feminist Economics* 5:1 (1999).

Bohstedt, John, 'Gender, household and community politics: women in English riots, 1790–1810', *Past and Present* 120 (1988).

Boserup, Ester, *Women's Role in Economic Development*, 2nd edn (Aldershot: Gower, 1986).

Boulton, Jeremy, *Neighbourhood and Society: A London Suburb in the Seventeenth Century* (Cambridge: Cambridge University Press, 1987).

Bowden, Sue, and Avner Offer, 'The technological revolution that never was: gender, class and the diffusion of household appliances in interwar England', in Victoria de Grazia (ed.), *The Sex of Things: Gender and Consumption in Historical Perspective* (Berkeley CA: University of California Press, 1996).

Bowen, H. V., '"The pests of human society": stockbrokers, jobbers and speculators in mid-eighteenth-century Britain', *History* 78:1 (1993).

Braudel, Fernand, *Civilization and Capitalism, Fifteenth–Eighteenth Century: The Structures of Everyday Live*, I, translated by Siân Reynolds (New York: Harper & Row, 1981; rev. edn 1985).

Breward, Christopher, *The Culture of Fashion: A New History of Fashionable Dress* (Manchester: Manchester University Press, 1995).

Breward, Christopher, *The Hidden Consumer: Masculinities, Fashion and City Life, 1860–1914* (Manchester: Manchester University Press, 1999).

Brewer, John, *The Sinews of Power: War, Money and the English State* (London: Unwin Hyman, 1989).

Brewer, John, *The Pleasures of the Imagination: English Culture in the Eighteenth Century* (London: HarperCollins, 1997).

Brewer, John, and John Styles (eds), *An Ungovernable People: The English and their Law in the Seventeenth and Eighteenth Centuries* (London: Hutchinson, 1980).

Bryer, Rob, 'The roots of modern capitalism: a Marxist accounting history of the origins and consequences of capitalist landlords in England', *Accounting Historians Journal* 31:1 (2004).

Buchan, James, *Frozen Desire: An Inquiry into the Meaning of Money* (London, 1997).

Buck, Anne, *Dress in Eighteenth-Century England* (London: Batsford, 1979).

Bulloch, J. M., *Notes and Queries*, 4 April 1931.

Burchell, S., C. Clubb, A. Hopwood, S. Hughes and J. Nahapiet, 'The roles of accounting in organizations and society', *Accounting, Organizations and Society* (1980).

Burman, Barbara, and Carole Turbin, 'Material strategies engendered', *Gender and History* 14:3 (2002).

Carruthers, Bruce G., and Wendy Nelson Espeland, 'Accounting for rationality: double-entry bookkeeping and the rhetoric of economic rationality', *American Journal of Sociology* 91: (1991).

Carter, Kathryn, 'An economy of words: Emma Chadwick Stretch's account book diary', *Acadiensis* 29:1 (1999).

Cavallo, Sandro, *Charity and Power in Early Modern Italy: Benefactors and their Motives in Turin, 1541–1789* (Cambridge: Cambridge University Press, 1996).

Chaudhuri, K. N., *The Trading World of Asia and the English East India Company* (Cambridge: Cambridge University Press, 1978).

Cipolla, Carlo M., *Clocks and Culture, 1300–1700* (London: Collins, 1967).

Cipolla, Carlo M. (ed.), *The Fontana Economic History of Europe*, II (New York: Barnes & Noble, 1976–77).

Clapham, J. H., *The Bank of England: A History*, 2 vols (Cambridge: Cambridge University Press, 1944).

Clark, Alice, *The Working Life of Women in the Seventeenth Century* (1919, repr. New York: Kelley, 1968).

Clark, Anna, *The Struggle for the Breeches: Gender and the Making of the British Working Class* (Berkeley CA: University of California Press, 1995).

Coffin, Judith, *The Politics of Women's Work: The Paris Garment Trades, 1750–1914* (Princeton NJ: Princeton University Press, 1996).

Connell, R. W. 'The big picture: masculinities in recent world history', *Theory and Society* 22:5 (1993).

Connor, Rebecca E., '"Can you apply arithmetick to everythink?" *Moll Flanders*, William Petty and social accounting', *Studies in Eighteenth-Century Culture* 27 (1998).

Cowan, Ruth Schwartz, *More Work for the Mother: The Ironies of Household Technology fromthe Open Hearth to the Microwave* (London: Free Association, 1983).

Craig, Béatrice, 'Women and credit in nineteenth-century northern France', in Beverly Lemire, Ruth Pearson and Gail Campbell (eds), *Women and Credit: Researching the Past, Refiguring the Future* (Oxford: Berg, 2001).

Crawford, Patricia, and Laura Gowing (eds), *Women's Worlds in Seventeenth-Century England: A Sourcebook* (London: Routledge, 2000).

Crosby, Alfred W., *The Measure of Reality: Quantification and Western Society, 1250–1600* (Cambridge: Cambridge University Press, 1997).

Crossick, Geoffrey (ed.), *The Lower Middle Class in Britain* (London: Croom Helm, 1977).

Crossick, Geoffrey and Heinz-Gerhard Haupt (eds), *The Petite Bourgeoisie in Europe, 1780–1914* (New York: Routledge, 1995).

Crouzet, François (ed.), *Capital Formation in the Industrial Revolution* (London: Methuen, 1972).

Crouzet, François, 'French economic growth in the nineteenth century reconsidered', *History* 59 (1974).

Cummings, A. J. G., 'The York Buildings Company: a Case Study in Eighteenth Century Corporation Mismanagement', unpublished PhD thesis (University of Strathclyde, 1980).

Cunnington, C. W., and Phillis Cunnington, *The History of Underclothes* (London: Michael Joseph, 1951).

Cunnington, Phillis, and Catherine Lucas, *Charity Costumes of Children, Scholars, Almsfolk, Pensioners* (New York: Barnes & Noble, 1978).

Daunton, M. J., *Progress and Poverty: An Economic and Social History of Britain, 1700–1850* (Oxford: Oxford University Press, 1995).

Davidoff, Leonore, and Catherine Hall, *Family Fortunes: Men and Women of the English Middle Class, 1780–1850* (Chicago: University of Chicago Press, 1987).

Davidoff, Leonore, Megan Doolittle, Janet Fink and Katherine Holden (eds), *The Family Story: Blood, Contract and Intimacy, 1830–1960* (London: Longman, 1999).

Davidson, Lee, Tim Hitchcock, Tim Keirn and Robert B. Shoemaker (eds), *Stilling the Grumbling Hive: The Response to Social and Economic Problems in England, 1689–1750* (New York: St Martin's Press, 1992).

Davies, Margaret Llewelyn (ed.), *Life as we Have Known it: by Co-operative Working Women* (1931, repr. New York: Norton, 1975).

Davis, Natalie Zemon, 'History's two bodies', *American Historical Review* 93 (1988).

Davis, Natalie Zemon, 'Women and the world of the *Annales*', *History Workshop* 33 (1992).

Davis, Natalie Zemon, *The Gift in Sixteenth-Century France* (Madison WI: University of Wisconsin Press, 2000).

Davis, Natalie Zemon, and Arlette Farge (eds), *A History of Women: Renaissance and Enlightenment Paradoxes* (Cambridge: Cambridge University Press, 1993).

Deane, Phyllis, *The First Industrial Revolution* (Cambridge: Cambridge University Press, 1965).

Deceulaer, Harald, 'Urban artisans and their countryside customers', in B. Blondé, E. Vanhaute and M. Garland (eds), *Labour and Labour Markets between Town and Countryside, Middle Ages–Ninteenth Century* (Turnhout: Brepols, 2001).

De Grazia, Victoria (ed.), *The Sex of Things: Gender and Consumption in Historical Perspective* (Berkeley CA: University of California Press, 1996).

DeMeulenaere, Stephen, 'Reinventing the market: alternative currencies and community development in Argentina', *International Journal of Community Currency Research* 4, http://www.geog.le.ac.uk/ijccr/, February 2002.

De Roover, Raymond, *Money, Banking and Credit in Mediaeval Bruges: Italian Merchant Bankers , Lombards and Money-changers: A Study in the Origins of Banking* (Cambridge MA: Medieval Academy of America, 1948).

De Vries, Jan, 'Peasant demand patterns and economic development: Friesland, 1550–1750' in William N. Parker and Eric L. Jones (eds), *European Peasants and their Markets: Essays in Agrarian Economic History* (Princeton NJ: Princeton University Press, 1975).

De Vries, Jan, *European Urbanization, 1500–1800* (London: Methuen, 1984).

De Vries, Jan, 'The population and economy of the preindustrial Netherlands', *Journal of Interdisciplinary History* 25 (1985).

De Vries, Jan, 'The industrial revolution and the industrious revolution', *Journal of Economic History* 54:2 (1994).

De Vries, Jan, 'Between purchasing power and the world of goods: understanding the household economy in early modern Europe' in Pamela Sharpe (ed.), *Women's Work: The English Experience, 1650–1914* (London: Arnold, 1998).

Dickson, P. G. M., *The Financial Revolution in England: A Study in the Development of Public Credit, 1688–1756* (London: Macmillan, 1967).

Digby, Anne, *The Poor Law in Nineteenth-Century England and Wales* (London: Historical Association, 1982).

Douglas, Mary, *Thought Styles: Critical Essays on Good Taste* (London: Sage, 1996).

Douglas, Mary, and Baron Isherwood, *The World of Goods: Towards an Anthropology of Consumption.* (New York: Basic Books, 1979).

Dyer, Christopher, *Everyday Life in Medieval England* (London: Hambledon Press, 1994).

Earle, Peter, 'The female labour market in London in the late seventeenth and early eighteenth centuries', *Economic History Review*, 2nd series 42:3 (1989).

Earle, Peter, *The Making of the English Middle Class: Business, Society and Family Life in London, 1660–1730* (London: Methuen, 1989).

Eason, Charles, *The Trustee Savings Banks of Great Britain and Ireland from 1817 to 1928* (Dublin: Eason, 1929).

Egeberg, Olaf, *Non-money: That 'Other Money' you Didn't Know you Had* (Washington DC, 1995).

Erickson, Amy Louise, *Women and Property in Early Modern England* (London: Routledge, 1993).

Ernst, Joseph A., '"The labourers have been the greatest sufferers": the truck system in early eighteenth-century Massachusetts', in Rosemary Ommer (ed.), *Merchant Credit and Labour Strategies in Historical Perspective* (Fredericton NB: Acadiensis Press, 1990).

Fairchilds, Cissie C., *Poverty and Charity in Aix-en-Provence, 1640–1789* (Baltimore MD: Johns Hopkins University Press, 1976).

Fairchilds, Cissie C., 'The production and marketing of populuxe goods in eighteenth-century Paris' in John Brewer and Roy Porter (eds), *Consumption and the World of Goods*. (London: Routledge, 1993).

Fairchilds, Cissie C., 'Fashion and freedom in the French revolution', *Continuity and Change* 15:3 (2000).

Finn, Margot, 'Men's things: masculine possession in the consumer revolution', *Social History* 25:2 (2000).

Finn, Margot, *The Character of Credit: Personal Debt in English Culture, 1740–1914* (Cambridge: Cambridge University Press, 2003).

Fishlow, Albert, 'The trustee savings banks, 1817–1861', *Journal of Economic History* 21 (1961).

Fissell, Mary, 'Charity universal? Institutions and moral reform in eighteenth-century Bristol' in L. Davidson, T. Hitchcock, T. Kelm and R. B. Shoemaker (eds), *Stilling the Grumbling Hive: The Response to Social and Economic Problems in England, 1689–1750* (New York: St Martin's Press, 1992).

Fontaine, Laurence, 'Antonio and Shylock: credit and trust in France, *c.* 1680–1780', *Economic History Review*, 2nd series 54:1 (2001).

Fontaine, Laurence, 'Women's economic spheres and credit in pre-industrial Europe' in Beverly Lemire, Ruth Pearson and Gail Campbell (eds), *Women and Credit: Researching the Past, Refiguring the Future* (Oxford: Berg, 2001).

Foucault, Michel, *Discipline and Punish: The Birth of the Prison* (Harmondsworth: Penguin Books, 1979).

Fowler, Christina, 'Robert Mansbridge: a rural tailor and his customers, 1811–1815', *Textile History* 28:1 (1997).

Fox, Richard W., and T. J. Jackson Lears (eds), *The Culture of Consumption: Critical Essays in American History, 1880–1980* (New York: Pantheon Books, 1983).

Fraser, W. Hamish, *The Coming of the Mass Market, 1850–1914* (London: Macmillan, 1981).

Fuller, Margaret D., *West Country Friendly Societies* (Lingfield: Oakwood Press for the University of Reading, 1964).

Fussell, G. E., *Robert Loder's Farm Accounts, 1610–1620*, Camden Society, 3rd series, vol. 53 (1936).

Gardella, R., 'Squaring accounts: commercial bookkeeping methods and capitalist rationalism in late Qing China', *Journal of Asian Studies* 51:2 (1992).

George, M. Dorothy, *London Life in the Eighteenth Century*, 2nd edn (1925, repr. Harmondsworth: Penguin Books, 1965).

Goody, Jack, *The Domestication of the Savage Mind* (Cambridge: Cambridge University Press, 1977).

Goody, Jack, *The East in the West* (Cambridge: Cambridge University Press, 1996).

Gurney, Peter, *Co-operative Culture and the Politics of Consumption in England, 1870–1930* (Manchester: Manchester University Press, 1996).

Hadden, Richard W., *On the Shoulders of Merchants: Exchange and the Mathematical Conception of Nature in Early Modern Europe* (Albany NY, 1994).

Hall, Catherine, Keith McClelland and Jane Rendall, *Defining the Victorian Nation: Class, Race, Gender and the Reform Act of 1867* (Cambridge: Cambridge University Press, 2000).

Hanham, Andrew Arthur, 'Whig Opposition to Sir Robert Walpole in the House of Commons, 1727–1734', unpublished PhD thesis (University of Leicester, 1992).

Hansen, Karen Tranberg, 'Budgeting against uncertainty: cross-class and transethnic redistribution mechanisms in urban Zambia', *African Urban Studies* 21 (spring 1985).

Hansen, Karen Tranberg, *Salaula: The World of Secondhand Clothing and Zambia* (Chicago: University of Chicago Press, 2000).

Hardwick, Julie, *The Practice of Patriarchy: Gender and the Politics of Household Authority in Early Modern France* (University Park PA: Pennsylvania State University Press, 1998).

Harrison, Brian Howard, *Peaceable Kingdom: Stability and Change in Modern Britain* (Oxford: Clarendon Press, 1982).

Harrison, John, 'The political economy of housework', *Bulletin of the Conference of Socialist Economists* (winter 1973).

Harte, N. B., 'State control of dress and social change in pre-industrial England' in D. C. Coleman and A. H. John (eds), *Trade, Government and Economy in Pre-industrial England: Essays presented to F. J. Fisher* (London: Weidenfeld & Nicolson, 1976).

Harte, N. B., 'The economics of clothing in the late seventeenth century' in N. B. Harte (ed.), *Fabrics and Fashions: Studies in the Economic and Social History of Dress*, special issue of *Textile History* 22:2 (1991).

Hartmann, Heidi, 'The family as the locus of gender, class and political struggle: the example of housework', *Signs: Journal of Women in Culture and Society* 6:3 (1991).

Hebden, C. Donald, *The Trustee Savings Bank of Yorkshire and Lincoln: The Story of its Formation and of the Six Savings Banks from which it was Constituted* (Hull: Trustee Savings Bank of Yorkshire and Lincoln, 1981).

Hebdige, Dick, *Subculture: The Meaning of Style* (London: Methuen, 1979).

Hill, Bridget, *Women, Work and Sexual Politics in Eighteenth-Century England* (Oxford: Blackwell, 1989).

Hill, Bridget, 'Priscilla Wakefield as a writer of children's educational books', *Women Writers* 4:1 (1997).

Hilton, George, *The Truck System, including a History of the British Truck Acts, 1465–1960* (Cambridge: Heffer, 1960).

Himmelweit, Susan, 'The discovery of "unpaid work": the social consequences of the expansion of "work"', *Feminist Economics* 1:2 (1995).

Hobsbawm, E. J., 'The labour aristocracy in nineteenth-century Britain', *Labouring Men: Studies in the History of Labour* (London: Weidenfeld & Nicolson, 1964).

Hoehl, R., 'French industrialization: a reconsideration', *Explorations in Economic History* 13:2 (1976).

Hogendom, Jan, 'Slaves as money in the Sokoto Caliphate' in Endre Stiansen and Jane I. Guyer (eds), *Credit, Currencies and Culture: African Financial Institutions in Historical Perspective* (Uppsala: Nordiska Afrikainstitutet, 1999).

Holderness, B. A., 'The clergy as moneylenders in England, 1550–1700' in Rosemary O'Day and Felicity Heal (eds), *Princes and Paupers in the English Church, 1500–1800* (Leicester: Leicester University Press, 1981).

Holderness, B. A., 'Credit in English rural society before the nineteenth century', *Agricultural History Review* 24 (1984).

Holderness, B. A., 'Widows in pre-industrial society: an essay upon their economic functions' in Richard M. Smith (ed.), *Land, Kinship and Life-cycle* (Cambridge: Cambridge University Press, 1984).

Hollis, Aidan, 'Women and microcredit in history: gender in the Irish loan funds' in Beverly Lemire, Ruth Pearson and Gail Campbell (eds), *Women and Credit: Researching the Past, Refiguring the Future* (Oxford: Berg, 2001).

Hollis, Aidan, and Arthur Sweetman, 'Microcredit: what can we learn from the past?' *World Development* 26:10 (1998).

Hollis, Aidan, and Arthur Sweetman, 'Microcredit in prefamine Ireland', *Explorations in Economic History* (October 1998).

Honeyman, Katrina, *Well Suited: A History of the Leeds Clothing Industry, 1850–1990* (Oxford: Oxford University Press, 2000).

Honeyman, Katrina, *Women, Gender and Industrialization in England, 1700–1870* (Basingstoke: Macmillan, 2000).

Hoppit, Julian, 'Financial crisis in eighteenth-century England', *Economic History Review*, 2nd series 39:1 (1986).

Hoppit, Julian, 'The use and abuse of credit in eighteenth-century England' in N. McKendrick and R. B. Outhwaite (eds), *Business Life and Public Policy: Essays in Honour of D. C. Coleman* (Cambridge: Cambridge University Press, 1986).

Hoppit, Julian, *Risk and Failure in English Business, 1700–1800* (Cambridge: Cambridge University Press, 1987).

Hoppit, Julian, 'Attitudes to credit in Britain, 1680–1790', *Historical Journal* 33:2 (1990).

Horne, Oliver, *A History of Savings Banks* (Oxford: Oxford University Press, 1947).

Horowitz, Daniel, *The Morality of Spending: Attitudes toward the Consumer Society in America, 1875–1940* (Baltimore MD: Johns Hopkins University Press, 1985).

Hostetler, John A., *Amish Society*, 3rd edn (Baltimore MD: Johns Hopkins University Press, 1980).

Hudson, Kenneth, *Pawnbroking: An Aspect of British Social History* (London: Bodley Head, 1982).

Hudson, Pat, *The Genesis of Industrial Capital: A Study of the West Riding Wool Textile Industry, c. 1750–1850* (Cambridge: Cambridge University Press, 1986).

Hudson, Pat, *The Industrial Revolution* (London: Edward Arnold, 1992).

Huff, Cynthia, *British Women's Diaries: A Descriptive Bibliography of Selected Nineteenth Century Women's Manuscript Diaries* (New York: AMS Press, 1985).

Huff, Cynthia, "'That profoundly female and feminist genre": the diary as feminist practice', *Women's Studies Quarterly* 3–4 (1989).

Hufton, Olwen, 'Women, work and family' in Natalie Zemon Davis and Arlette Farge (eds), *A History of Women: Renaissance and Enlightenment Paradoxes* (Cambridge: Cambridge University Press, 1993).

Hufton, Olwen, *The Prospect before Her: A History of Women in Western Europe, 1500–1800* (London: HarperCollins, 1995).

Humphries, Jane, "'Lurking in the wings": women in the historiography of the industrial revolution', *Business and Economic History*, 2nd series 20 (1991).

Humphries, Jane, 'Introduction' in Jane Humphries (ed.), *Gender and Economics* (1995).

Hundert, E. G., *The Enlightenment's Fable: Bernard Mandeville and the Discovery of Society* (Cambridge: Cambridge University Press, 1994).

Hunt, Alan, 'Moralizing luxury: the discourses of the governance of consumption', *Journal of Historical Sociology* 8:4 (1995).

Hunt, Alan, *Governance of the Consuming Passions: A History of Sumptuary Law* (New York: St Martin's Press, 1996).

Hunt, Margaret R., *The Middling Sort: Commerce, Gender and the Family in England, 1680–1780* (Berkeley CA: University of California Press, 1996).

Hunt, Margaret R., 'Women and the fiscal-imperial state in the late seventeenth and early eighteenth centuries' in Kathleen Wilson (ed.), *A New Imperial History: Culture, Identity and Modernity in Britain and the Empire, 1660–1840* (Cambridge: Cambridge University Press, 2004).

James, Francis Godwin, 'Charity endowments as sources of local credit in seventeenth- and eighteenth-century England', *Journal of Economic History* 8 (1948).

Johnson, Paul, 'Credit and thrift in the British working class, 1870–1939' in Jay Winter (ed.), *The Working Class in Modern British History: Essays in Honour of Henry Pelling* (Cambridge: Cambridge University Press, 1983).

Johnson, Paul, *Saving and Spending: The Working-class Economy in Britain, 1870–1939* (Oxford: Clarendon Press, 1985).

Johnson, Paul, 'Class law in Victorian society', *Past and Present* 141 (1993).

Johnson, Susan, and Ben Rogaly, *Microfinance and Poverty Reduction* (Oxford: Oxfam, 1997).

Johnston, J. A. (ed.), *Probate Inventories of Lincoln Citizens, 1661–1714* (Woodbridge: Boydell Press, 1991).

Jones, Ann Rosalind, and Peter Stallybrass, *Renaissance Clothing and the Materials of Memory* (Cambridge: Cambridge University Press, 2000).

Jones, J. R., *Britain and the World, 1649–1815* (London: Fontana, 1980).

Jones, N., *God and the Moneylenders: Usury and Law in Early Modern England* (Oxford: Blackwell, 1989).

Jordan, W. C., *Women and Credit in Pre-industrial and Developing Societies* (Philadelphia: University of Pennsylvania Press, 1993).

Joslin, D. M., 'London private bankers, 1720–1785', *Economic History Review*, 2nd series 7:2 (1954).

Joyce, Patrick, 'The historical meanings of work: an introduction' in Patrick Joyce (ed.), *The Historical Meanings of Work* (Cambridge: Cambridge University Press, 1987).

Kane, Abdoulaye, 'Financial arrangements across borders: women's predominant participation in popular finance, from Thilogne and Dakar to Paris: a Senegalese case study' in Beverly Lemire, Ruth Pearson and Gail Campbell (eds), *Women and Credit: Researching the Past, Refiguring the Future* (Oxford: Berg, 2001).

Kessler-Harris, Alice, *In Pursuit of Equality: Women, Men and the Quest for Economic Citizenship in Twentieth-Century America* (New York: Oxford University Press, 2001).

Khandker, Shahidur R., *Fighting Poverty with Microcredit: Experience in Bangladesh* (Oxford: Oxford University Press, 1998).

King, Steven, 'Reclothing the English poor', *Textile History* 33:1 (2002).

Koditschek, Theodore, *Class Formation and Urban–Industrial Society: Bradford, 1750–1850* (Cambridge: Cambridge University Press, 1990).

Korda, Natasha, 'Household property/stage property: Henslowe as pawnbroker', *Theatre Journal* 48 (1996).

Kuchta, David, 'The making of the self-made man: class, clothing and English masculinity, 1688–1832' in Victoria de Grazia (ed.), *The Sex of Things: Gender and Consumption in Historical Perspective* (Berkeley CA: University of California Press, 1996).

Lambert, Miles, '"Cast-off wearing apparell": the consumption and distribution of second-hand clothing in northern England during the long eighteenth century', *Textile History* 35:1 (2004).

Lancaster, Bill, *The Department Store: A Social History* (London: Leicester University Press, 1995).

Laqueur, Thomas, *Religion and Respectability: Sunday Schools and Working Class Culture, 1780–1850* (New Haven CT: Yale University Press, 1976).

Lemire, Beverly, 'Consumerism in preindustrial and early industrial England: the trade in secondhand clothes', *Journal of British Studies* 27:1 (1988).

Lemire, Beverly, *Fashion's Favourite: The Cotton Trade and the Consumer in Britain, 1660–1800* (Oxford: Oxford University Press, 1991).

Lemire, Beverly, 'Peddling fashion: salesmen, pawnbrokers, tailors, thieves and the secondhand clothes trade in England, c. 1700–1800', *Textile History* 22:1 (1991).

Lemire, Beverly, *Dress, Culture and Commerce: The English Clothing Trade before the Factory* (Basingstoke: Macmillan, 1997).

Lemire, Beverly, Ruth Pearson and Gail Campbell (eds), *Women and Credit: Researching the Past, Refiguring the Future* (Oxford: Berg, 2001).

Levine, David, and Keith Wrightson, *The Making of an Industrial Society: Wickham, 1560–1765* (Oxford: Oxford University Press, 1991).

Levitt, Ian, and Christopher Smout, *State of the Scottish Working Class in 1843* (Edinburgh: Scottish Academic Press, 1979).

Lewis, Frank, *English Chintz; A History of Printed Fabrics from Earliest Times until the Present Day* (Benfleet: Lewis, 1935).

Liesch, P., and D. Birch, 'Community-based LET systems in Australia: localised barter in a sophisticated Western economy', *International Journal of Community and Currency Research*, vol. 4, http://www.geog.le.ac.uk/ijccr/, February 2002.

Linebaugh, Peter, *The London Hanged: Crime and Civil Society in the Eighteenth Century* (Harmondsworth: Penguin Press, 1991).

Lipovetsky, Gilles, *The Empire of Fashion: Dressing Modern Democracy* (Princeton NJ: Princeton University Press, 1994).

Lockyer, Roger, *Tudor and Stuart Britain, 1471–1714*, 2nd edn (New York: Longman, 1985).

Loeb, Lori, *Consuming Angels: Advertising and Victorian Women* (New York: Oxford University Press, 1994).

MacFarlane, Alan, *The Family Life of Ralph Josselin, a Seventeenth-Century Clergyman: An Essay in Historical Anthropology* (Cambridge: Cambridge University Press, 1970).

Mackie, Erin, *Market à la mode: Fashion, Commodity and Gender in the* Tatler *and the* Spectator (Baltimore MD: Johns Hopkins University Press, 1997).

Mancke, Elizabeth, 'At the counter of the general store: women and the economy in eighteenth-century Horton, Nova Scotia' in Margaret Conrad (ed.), *Intimate Relations: Family and Community in Planter Nova Scotia, 1759–1800* (Fredericton NB: Acadiensis Press, 1995).

Marshall, Dorothy, *The English Poor in the Eighteenth Century: A Study in Social and Administrative History* (London: Routledge, 1926).

Mathias, Peter, *The First Industrial Nation: An Economic History of Britain, 1700–1914* (London: Methuen, 1969; 2nd edn 1983).

Mathias, Peter, *The Transformation of England: Essays in the Economic and Social History of England in the Eighteenth Century* (London: Methuen, 1979).

Matthews, Derek, Malcolm Anderson and John Richard Edwards, *The Priesthood of Industry: The Rise of the Professional Accountant in British Management* (Oxford: Oxford University Press, 1998).

Mauss, Marcel, *The Gift: The Form and Reason for Exchange in Archaic Societies*, translated by W. D. Halls (London: Routledge, 1990).

McCants, Anne, 'Petty debts and family networks: the credit market of widows and wives in eighteenth-century Amsterdam' in Beverly Lemire, Ruth Pearson and Gail Campbell (eds), *Women and Credit: Researching the Past, Refiguring the Future* (Oxford: Berg, 2001).

McCracken, Grant, *Culture and Consumption: New Approaches to the Symbolic Character of Consumer Goods and Activities* (Bloomington IN: Indiana University Press, 1987).

McIntosh, M., 'Moneylending on the periphery of London, 1300–1600', *Albion* 20:4 (1988).

McIntosh, Marjorie K., 'The diversity of social capital in English communities,

1300–1640 (with a glance at modern Nigeria)', *Journal of Interdisciplinary History* 29:3 (1999).

McKendrick, Neil, 'The commercialization of fashion' in Neil McKendrick, John Brewer and J. H. Plumb, *The Birth of a Consumer Society: The Commercialization of Eighteenth-Century England* (London: Hutchinson, 1983).

McKendrick, Neil, John Brewer and J. H. Plumb, *The Birth of a Consumer Society: The Commercialization of Eighteenth-Century England*. (London: Hutchinson, 1983).

Mendelson, Sara, and Patricia Crawford, *Women in Early Modern England* (Oxford: Clarendon Press, 1998).

Merrick, J., 'Commissioner Faucault, Inspecteur Noël, and the "pederasts" of Paris, 1780–1783', *Journal of Social History* 32:2 (1998).

Miller, Michael, *The Bon Marché: Bourgeois Culture and the Department Store, 1869–1920* (Princeton NJ: Princeton University Press, 1981).

Miller, P., and T. O'Leary, 'Accounting and the construction of the governable person', *Accounting, Organizations and Society* 12:3 (1987).

Mills, Geoffrey T., 'Early accounting in northern Italy: the role of commercial development and the printing press in the expansion of double-entry from Genoa, Florence and Venice', *Accounting Historians' Journal* 21:1 (1994).

Money, John, 'Teaching in the market-place, or "Caesar adsum jam forte: Pompey aderat": the retailing of knowledge in provincial England during the eighteenth century' in John Brewer and Roy Porter (eds), *Consumption and the World of Goods* (London: Routledge, 1993).

Morgan, Gareth, 'Accounting as reality construction: towards a new epistemology for accounting practice', *Accounting, Organizations and Society* 13:5 (1988).

Moss, Michael, and Iain Russell, *Invaluable Treasure: A History of TSB* (London: Weidenfeld & Nicolson, 1994).

Moss, Michael, and Anthony Slaven, *'From Ledger Book to Laser Beam': A History of the TSB in Scotland from 1810 to 1990* (Glasgow: TSB Scotland, 1992).

Motz, Marilyn Ferris, 'Folk expressions of time and place: nineteenth-century Midwestern rural diaries', *Journal of American Folklore* 100 (April–June 1987).

Muldrew, Craig, 'Interpreting the market: the ethics of credit and community relations in early modern England', *Social History* 18:2 (1993).

Muldrew, Craig, *The Economy of Obligation: The Culture of Credit and Social Relations in Early Modern England* (Basingstoke: Macmillan, 1998).

Mumford, Lewis, *Technics and Civilization* (1934, repr. New York: Harcourt Brace, 1963).

Musson, A. E., 'Class struggle and the labour aristocracy, 1830–1860', *Social History* (1976).

Nead, Lynda, *Myths of Sexuality: Representations of Women in Victorian Britain* (Oxford: Blackwell, 1988).

Neale, Walter C., *Monies in Societies* (San Francisco: Chandler & Sharp, 1976).

Neeson, J. M., *Commoners: Common Right, Enclosure and Social Change in England, 1700–1820* (Cambridge: Cambridge University Press, 1993).

Nef, John U., *Industry and Government in France and England, 1540–1640* (Ithaca NY: Great Seal Books, 1957).

Oakley, Anne, *Housewife* (London: Allen Lane, 1974).

O'Day, Rosemary, *Education and Society, 1500–1800: The Social Foundations of Education in Early Modern Britain* (London: Longman, 1982).

Ollerenshaw, Philip, and Brenda Collins (eds), *The European Linen Industry in Historical Perspective* (Oxford: Oxford University Press, 2003).

Ommer, Rosemary, 'One hundred years of fishery crisis in Newfoundland', *Acadiensis* 23:2 (1994).

Ommer, Rosemary, and Nancy Turner, 'Informal rural economies in history', *Labour/Le Travail* 53:1 (2004).

Parr, Joy, *The Gender of Breadwinners: Women and Change in two Industrial Towns, 1880–1990* (Toronto: University of Toronto Press, 1990).

Parr, Joy, 'Gender history and historical practice' in Joy Parr and Mark Rosenfeld (eds), *Gender and History in Canada.* (Toronto: Copp Clark, 1996)

Parr, Joy, *Domestic Goods: The Material, the Moral and the Economic in the Postwar Years* (Toronto: University of Toronto Press, 1999).

Pearson, Ruth, 'Micro-credit as a path from welfare to work: the experience of the Full Circle Project, UK' in Beverly Lemire, Ruth Pearson and Gail Campbell (eds), *Women and Credit: Researching the Past, Refiguring the Future* (Oxford: Berg, 2001).

Pearson, Ruth, and Erika Watson, 'Giving women the credit: the Norwich Full Circle Project', *Gender and Development* 5:3 (1997).

Peiss, Kathy Lee, *Hope in a Jar: The Making of America's Beauty Culture* (New York: Metropolitan Books, 1998).

Perkin, Harold James, *The Origins of Modern English Society, 1700–1880* (London: Routledge, 1968).

Phillips, Ruth B., *Trading Identities: The Souvenir in Native North American Art from the Northeast, 1700–1900* (Seattle: University of Washington Press, 1998).

Pinchbeck, Ivy, *Women Workers and the Industrial Revolution* (London: Routledge, 1930).

Poovey, Mary, *A History of the Modern Fact: Problems of Knowledge in the Sciences of Wealth and Society* (Chicago: University of Chicago Press, 1998).

Pressnell, L. S., 'Public monies and the development of English banking', *Economic History Review*, 2nd series 5:3 (1953).

Pressnell, L. S., *Country Banking in the Industrial Revolution* (Oxford: Clarendon Press, 1956).

Price, Jacob M., *Capital and Credit in British Overseas Trade: The View from the Chesapeake, 1700–1776* (Cambridge MA: Harvard University Press, 1980).

Prothero, I. J., *Artisans and Politics in Early Nineteenth-Century London: John Gast and his Times* (Folkestone: Dawson, 1979).

Pujol, Michele, *Feminism and Anti-feminism in Early Economic Thought* (Aldershot: Elgar, 1992).

Pullan, Brian, *Rich and Poor in Renaissance Venice: The Social Institutions of a Catholic State, to 1620* (Cambridge MA: Harvard University Press, 1971).

Pyle, Andrew (ed.), *Population: Contemporary Responses to Thomas Malthus* (Bristol: Thoemmes, 1994).

Rappaport, Erica. '"The halls of temptation": gender, politics and the construction of the department store in late Victorian London', *Journal of British Studies* 35:1 (1996).

Ratcliff, B., 'Manufacturing in the metropolis: the dynamism and dynamics of Parisian industry at the mid-nineteenth century', *Journal of European Economic History* 23:2 (1993).

Richards, Sarah, *Eighteenth-Century Ceramics: Products for a Civilized Society* (Manchester: Manchester University Press, 1999).

Richards, Thomas, *The Commodity Culture of Victorian England* (Stanford CA: Stanford University Press, 1990).

Riden, Philip (ed.), *Probate Records and the Local Community* (Gloucester: Sutton, 1985).

Riello, Giorgio, 'The Boot and Shoe Trades in London and Paris in the Long Eighteenth Century', unpublished PhD thesis (University College London, 2002).

Roberts, Robert, *The Classic Slum* (Manchester: Manchester University Press, 1973).

Roberts, Robert, *A Ragged Schooling* (Manchester: Manchester University Press, 1976).

Robson, John M., *Marriage or Celibacy? The Daily Telegraph on a Victorian Dilemma* (Toronto: University of Toronto Press, 1995).

Roche, Daniel, *The Culture of Clothing: Dress and Fashion in the Ancien Régime* (Cambridge: Cambridge University Press, 1989).

Roche, Daniel, *A History of Everyday Things: The Birth of Consumption in France, 1600–1800* (Cambridge: Cambridge University Press, 2000).

Rogaly, Ben, 'Micro-finance evangelism, "destitute women" and the hard selling of a new anti-poverty formula', *Development in Practice* 6:2 (1996).

Rogers, Nicholas, 'Popular protest in early Hanoverian London', *Past and Present* 79 (1978).

Rose, Sonya, *Limited Livelihoods: Gender and Class in Nineteenth-Century England* (Berkeley CA: University of California Press, 1992).

Ross, Duncan, '"Penny banks" in Glasgow, 1850–1914', *Financial History Review* 9:1 (2002).

Ross, Ellen, 'Survival networks: women's neighbourhood sharing in London before World War I', *History Workshop Journal* 15 (1983).

Ross, Ellen, *Love and Toil: Motherhood in Outcast London, 1870–1918* (Oxford: Oxford University Press, 1993).

Ross, Ellen, 'Long live the family', *Journal of British Studies* 41:4 (2002).

Rothstein, Natalie, 'The calico campaign of 1719–1721', *East London Papers* (July 1969).

Rothstein, Natalie (ed.), *Barbara Johnson's Album of Fashions and Fabrics* (London: Thames & Hudson, 1987).

Rule, John, *Albion's People: English Society, 1714–1815* (London: Longman, 1992).

Sanderson, Elizabeth, *Women and Work in Eighteenth-Century Edinburgh* (Basingstoke: Macmillan, 1996).

Sanderson, Elizabeth, 'Nearly new: the second-hand clothing trade in eighteenth-century Edinburgh', *Costume* 31 (1997).

Schama, Simon, *The Embarrassment of Riches: An Interpretation of Dutch Culture in the Golden Age* (London: Collins, 1987).

Schraven, Jorim, 'The economics of local exchange and trading systems: a theoretical perspective', *International Journal of Community Currency Research*, vol. 4, http://www.geog.le.ac.uk/ijccr/, February 2002.

Schwarz, L. D., *London in the Age of Industrialisation: Entrepreneurs, Labour Force and Living Conditions, 1700–1850* (Cambridge: Cambridge University Press, 1992).

Sen, Amartya Kumar, *Development as Freedom* (New York: Knopf, 1999).

Sen, Amartya Kumar, *Social Exclusion: Concept, Application and Scrutiny* (Manila: Asian Development Bank, 2000).

Shammas, Carole, *The Pre-industrial Consumer in England and America* (Oxford: Clarendon Press, 1990).

Shammas, Carole, 'The decline of textile prices in England and British America prior to industrialization', *Economic History Review*, 2nd series 47:3 (1994).

Sharpe, Pamela, *Adapting to Capitalism: Working Women in the English Economy, 1700–1850* (Basingstoke: Macmillan, 1996).

Sharpe, Pamela (ed.), *Women's Work: The English Experience, 1650–1914* (London: Arnold, 1998).

Silverstein-Willmott, Cory, 'An Ojibway artifact unraveled: the case of the bag with the snake skin strap', *Textile History* 34:1 (2003).

Sim, Alison, *The Tudor Housewife* (Montreal: McGill–Queen's University Press, 1996).

Simpson, I. J., 'Sir Archibald Grant and the Charitable Corporation', *Scottish Historical Review* 44 (1965).

Singer, Charles, *et al.* (eds), *A History of Technology* (Oxford: Clarendon Press, 1956).

Slack, Paul (ed.), *Rebellion, Popular Protest and the Social Order in Early Modern England* (Cambridge: Cambridge University Press, 1984).

Smail, John, *The Origins of Middle-Class Culture: Halifax, Yorkshire, 1660–1780* (Ithaca NY: Cornell University Press, 1994).

Smelser, Neil, *Social Change in the Industrial Revolution: An Application of Theory to the Lancashire Cotton Industry, 1770–1840* (London: Routledge, 1959).

Snell, K. D. M., *Annals of the Labouring Poor: Social Change and Agrarian England, 1660–1900* (Cambridge: Cambridge University Press, 1985).

Spufford, Margaret, *The Great Reclothing of Rural England: Petty Chapmen and their Wares in the Seventeenth Century* (London: Hambledon Press, 1984).

Spufford, Margaret, 'The cost of apparel in seventeenth-century England and the accuracy of Gregory King', *Economic History Review*, 2nd series 53:4 (2000).

Spufford, Peter, *Money and its Use in Medieval Europe* (Cambridge: Cambridge University Press, 1988).

Stack, Carol, *All our Kin: Strategies for Survival in a Black Community* (New York: Harper & Row, 1974).

Styles, John, 'Clothing the north: the supply of non-élite clothing in the eighteenth-century north of England', *Textile History* 25 (1994).

Styles, John, 'Involuntary consumers? Servants and their clothes in eighteenth-century England', *Textile History* 33:1 (2002).

Tebbutt, Melanie, *Making Ends Meet: Pawnbroking and Working-Class Credit* (London: Methuen, 1983).

Tebbutt, Melanie, *Women's Talk? A Social History of "Gossip" in Working-Class Neighbourhoods, 1880–1960* (Aldershot: Scolar Press, 1995).

Thirsk, Joan, 'The fantastical folly of fashion: the English stocking knitting industry, 1500–1700' in N. B. Harte and K. G. Ponting (eds), *Textile History and Economic History: Essays in Honour of Miss Julia de Lacy Mann* (Manchester: Manchester University Press, 1973).

Thirsk, Joan, *Economic Policy and Projects: the Development of a Consumer Society in Early Modern England* (Oxford: Clarendon Press, 1978).

Thomas, Keith, 'Numeracy in early modern England', *Transactions of the Royal Historical Society* 37 (1987).

Thomas, P. J., *Mercantilism and the East India Trade: An Early Phase of the Protection v. Free Trade Controversy* (London: King, 1926).

Thompson, E. P., *The Making of the English Working Class* (London: Gollancz, 1963).

Thompson, E. P., 'Custom, law and common right', in *Customs in Common: Studies in Traditional Popular Culture* (New York: New Press, 1993).

Thompson, E. P., 'The moral economy of the English crown in the eighteenth century' in *Customs in Common: Studies in Traditional Popular culture* (New York: New Press, 1993).

Thompson, E. P., 'Time, work-discipline and industrial capitalism' in *Customs in Common: Studies in Traditional Popular Culture* (New York: New Press, 1993).

Tinker, Irene, 'The making of a field: advocates, practitioners and scholars' in *Persistent Inequalities: Women and World Development* (New York: Oxford University Press, 1990).

Tinker, Irene (ed.), *Persistent Inequalities: Women and World Development* (Oxford: Oxford University Press, 1990).

Tittler, Richard, 'Moneylending in the West Midlands: the activities of Joyce Jefferies, 1638– 1649', *Historical Journal* 67 (1994).

Todd, Barbara, 'Freebench and free enterprise: widows and their property in two Berkshire villages' in John Chartres and David Hey (eds), *English Rural Society, 1500–1800: Essays in Honour of Joan Thirsk* (Cambridge: Cambridge University Press, 1990)

Tosh, John, *A Man's Place: Masculinity and the Middle-Class Home in Victorian England* (New Haven CT: Yale University Press, 1999).

Tracy, James D., *The Rise of Merchant Empires: Long-distance Trade in the Early Modern World, 1350–1750* (Cambridge: Cambridge University Press, 1990).

Ulrich, Laurel Thatcher, 'Martha Ballard and her girls: women's work in eighteenth-century Maine' in Stephen Innes (ed.), *Work and Labor in Early America* (Chapel Hill NC: University of North Carolina Press, 1988).

Ulrich, Laurel Thatcher, *A Midwife's Tale: The Life of Martha Ballard, based on her Diary, 1785–1812* (New York: Knopf, 1990).

Ulrich, Laurel Thatcher, *The Age of Homespun: Objects and Stories in the Creation of an American Myth* (New York: Knopf, 2001).

Verhoef, Grietjie, '*Stokvels* and economic empowerment: the case of African women in South Africa, *c.* 1930–1998' in Beverly Lemire, Ruth Pearson and Gail Campbell (eds), *Women and Credit: Researching the Past, Refiguring the Future* (Oxford: Berg, 2001).

Vickery, Amanda, 'Golden Age to separate spheres: a review of the categories and chronology of English women's history', *Historical Journal* 36:2 (1993).

Vickery, Amanda, 'Women and the world of goods: a Lancashire consumer and her possessions' in John Brewer and Roy Porter (eds), *Consumption and the World of Goods* (London: Routledge, 1993).

Vickery, Amanda, *The Gentleman's Daughter: Women's Lives in Georgian England* (London: Yale University Press, 1998).

Vigarello, Georges, *Concepts of Cleanliness: Changing Attitudes in France since the Middle Ages*, translated by Jean Birrell (Cambridge: Cambridge University Press, 1988).

Vyas, Jayshree, 'Banking with poor self-employed women' in Beverly Lemire, Ruth Pearson and Gail Campbell (eds), *Women and Credit: Researching the Past, Refiguring the Future* (Oxford: Berg, 2001).

Wadhwani, Rohit Daniel, 'Banking from the bottom up: the case of migrant savers at the Philadelphia Saving Fund Society during the late nineteenth century', *Financial History Review* 9:1 (2002).

Walker, Garthine, 'Women, theft and the world of stolen goods' in Jenny Kermode and Garthine Walker (eds), *Women, Crime and the Courts in Early Modern England* (London: UCL Press, 1994).

Walkowitz, Judith, *Prostitution and Victorian Society* (Cambridge: Cambridge University Press, 1980).

Walkowitz, Judith, *City of Dreadful Delight: Narratives of Sexual Danger in late Victorian London* (London: Virago, 1994).

Waring, Marilyn, *If Women Counted: A New Feminist Economics*, introduction by Gloria Steinem (San Francisco: Harper & Row, 1988).

Weatherill, Lorna, *Consumer Behaviour and Material Culture in Britain, 1660–1760* (London: Routledge, 1988).

Weiner, Annette, *Inalienable Possessions: The Paradox of Keeping-while-Giving* (Berkeley CA: University of California Press, 1992).

Welch, Kenneth F., *Time Measurement: An Introductory History* (Newton Abbot: David & Charles, 1972).

White, Jonathan, 'Luxury and Labour: Ideas of Labouring-class Consumption in Eighteenth- century England', unpublished PhD thesis (University of Warwick, 2001).

Wiesner, Merry E., 'Women's work in the changing city economy, 1500–1650' in Marilyn J. Boxer and Jean H. Quartaert (eds), *Connecting Spheres: Women in the Western World, 1500 to the Present* (New York: Oxford University Press, 1987).

Wiesner, Merry E., *Women and Gender in Early Modern Europe* (Cambridge: Cambridge University Press, 1993).

Williams, Rosalind, *Dream Worlds: Mass Consumption in late Nineteenth-Century France* (Berkeley CA: University of California Press, 1982).

Willet, C., and Phillis Cunnington, *Handbook of English Costume in the Eighteenth Century* (Boston MA: Plays, 1972).

Wilson, Charles, *England's Apprenticeship, 1603–1763*, 2nd edn (London: Longman, 1984).

Wrightson, Keith, *English Society, 1580–1680* (New Brunswick NJ: Rutgers University Press, 1982).

Wrightson, Keith, *Earthly Necessities: Economic Lives in Early Modern Britain* (New Haven CT: Yale University Press, 2000).

Wrigley, E. A., *Continuity, Chance and Change: The Character of the Industrial Revolution* (Cambridge: Cambridge University Press, 1988).

Wrigley, Mark, 'Untitled: the housing of gender' in Beatriz Colomina (ed.), *Sexuality and Space* (Princeton NJ: Princeton University Press, 1992).

Yamey, B. S., 'Functional development of double-entry bookkeeping', *Accountant* (November 1940).

Yolton, John W., and Jean S. Yolton (eds), *Some Thoughts concerning Education* (Oxford: Clarendon Press, 1989).

Yunus, Muhammad, 'The Grameen bank', *Scientific American* (November 1999).

Index

Note: 'n.' after a page number indicates the number of a note on that page.

Lightning Source UK Ltd.
Milton Keynes UK
UKOW040915220312

189404UK00001B/6/P